Processes of Constitutional Decisionmaking

2012 Supplement

2012 Supplement
Processes of Constitutional Decisionmaking
Cases and Materials

Fifth Edition

Prepared by Jack M. Balkin

Paul Brest
Professor, Stanford Law School
and President, William and Flora Hewlett Foundation

Sanford Levinson
W. St. John Garwood & W. St. John Garwood, Jr.
Regents Chair in Law
University of Texas

Jack M. Balkin
Knight Professor of Constitutional Law
and the First Amendment
Yale Law School

Akhil Reed Amar
Sterling Professor of Law
Yale Law School

Reva B. Siegel
Nicholas deB. Katzenbach Professor of Law
Yale Law School

Wolters Kluwer
Law & Business

Library of Congress Cataloging-in-Publication Data

Processes of constitutional decisionmaking : cases and materials / Paul Brest . . . [et al.]. — 5th ed.
    p. cm.
  Includes bibliographical references and index.
  ISBN 0-7355-5062-9 (casebook)
  ISBN 978-1-4548-1816-8 (supplement)
   1. Constitutional law — United States — Cases. 2. Judicial review — United States — Cases. 3. Separation of powers — United States — Cases. I. Brest, Paul.

KF4549.B74 2006
342.73 — dc22

                                                              2006003927

About Wolters Kluwer Law & Business

Wolters Kluwer Law & Business is a leading global provider of intelligent information and digital solutions for legal and business professionals in key specialty areas, and respected educational resources for professors and law students. Wolters Kluwer Law & Business connects legal and business professionals as well as those in the education market with timely, specialized authoritative content and information-enabled solutions to support success through productivity, accuracy and mobility.

Serving customers worldwide, Wolters Kluwer Law & Business products include those under the Aspen Publishers, CCH, Kluwer Law International, Loislaw, Best Case, ftwilliam.com and MediRegs family of products.

CCH products have been a trusted resource since 1913, and are highly regarded resources for legal, securities, antitrust and trade regulation, government contracting, banking, pension, payroll, employment and labor, and healthcare reimbursement and compliance professionals.

Aspen Publishers products provide essential information to attorneys, business professionals and law students. Written by preeminent authorities, the product line offers analytical and practical information in a range of specialty practice areas from securities law and intellectual property to mergers and acquisitions and pension/benefits. Aspen's trusted legal education resources provide professors and students with high-quality, up-to-date and effective resources for successful instruction and study in all areas of the law.

Kluwer Law International products provide the global business community with reliable international legal information in English. Legal practitioners, corporate counsel and business executives around the world rely on Kluwer Law journals, looseleafs, books, and electronic products for comprehensive information in many areas of international legal practice.

Loislaw is a comprehensive online legal research product providing legal content to law firm practitioners of various specializations. Loislaw provides attorneys with the ability to quickly and efficiently find the necessary legal information they need, when and where they need it, by facilitating access to primary law as well as state-specific law, records, forms and treatises.

Best Case Solutions is the leading bankruptcy software product to the bankruptcy industry. It provides software and workflow tools to flawlessly streamline petition preparation and the electronic filing process, while timely incorporating ever-changing court requirements.

ftwilliam.com offers employee benefits professionals the highest quality plan documents (retirement, welfare and non-qualified) and government forms (5500/PBGC, 1099 and IRS) software at highly competitive prices.

MediRegs products provide integrated health care compliance content and software solutions for professionals in healthcare, higher education and life sciences, including professionals in accounting, law and consulting.

Wolters Kluwer Law & Business, a division of Wolters Kluwer, is headquartered in New York. Wolters Kluwer is a market-leading global information services company focused on professionals.

Contents

Processes of Constitutional Decisionmaking

2012 Supplement

Chapter 4

From Reconstruction to the
New Deal: 1866-1934

Insert the following before the Note on p. 309:

SENATOR JACOB HOWARD, SPEECH INTRODUCING
THE FOURTEENTH AMENDMENT
Speech delivered in the U.S. Senate, May 23, 1866
Congressional Globe, 39th Cong., 1st Sess. 2764-68

[Senator Jacob Howard of Michigan was a member of the Joint Committee on Reconstruction that drafted the Fourteenth Amendment. He was the floor manager for the Amendment in the Senate. In this speech, he introduces the Amendment on the floor of the Senate and explains its purposes.]

Mr. HOWARD. . . . I can only promise to present to the Senate, in a very succinct way, the views and the motives which influenced th[e] committee, so far as I understand those views and motives, in presenting the report which is now before us for consideration, and the ends it aims to accomplish. . . .

The first section . . . relates to the privileges and immunities of citizens of the several States, and to the rights and privileges of all persons, whether citizens or others, under the laws of the United States. It declares that—

> No State shall make or enforce any law which shall abridge the privileges or immunities of citizens of the United States; nor shall any State deprive any person of life, liberty, or property without due process of law; nor deny to any person within its jurisdiction the equal protection of the laws.

It will be observed that this is a general prohibition upon all the States, as such, from abridging the privileges and immunities of the citizens of the United States. That is its first clause, and I regard it as very important. . . . [It] relates to the privileges and immunities of citizens of the United States as such, and as distinguished from all other persons not citizens of the United States. It is not, perhaps, very easy to define with accuracy what is meant by the expression, "citizen of the United States,"[1] although that expression occurs twice in the

---

1. Senator Howard delivered this speech before the first sentence, the Citizenship Clause, which defined citizenship, was added to the proposed amendment.

1

Constitution, once in reference to the President of the United States, in which instance it is declared that none but a citizen of the United States shall be President, and again in reference to Senators, who are likewise to be citizens of the United States. Undoubtedly the expression is used in both those instances in the same sense in which it is employed in the amendment now before us. A citizen of the United States is held by the courts to be a person who was born within the limits of the United States and subject to their laws. Before the adoption of the Constitution of the United States, the citizens of each State were, in a qualified sense at least, aliens to one another, for the reason that the several States before that event were regarded by each other as independent Governments, each one possessing a sufficiency of sovereign power to enable it to claim the right of naturalization; and, undoubtedly, each one of them possessed for itself the right of naturalizing foreigners, and each one, also, if it had seen fit so to exercise its sovereign power, might have declared the citizens of every other State to be aliens in reference to itself. With a view to prevent such confusion and disorder, and to put the citizens of the several States on an equality with each other as to all fundamental rights, a clause was introduced in the Constitution declaring that "the citizens of each State shall be entitled to all privileges and immunities of citizens in the several States."

The effect of this clause was to constitute *ipso facto* the citizens of each one of the original States citizens of the United States. And how did they antecedently become citizens of the several States? By birth or by naturalization. They became such in virtue of national law, or rather of natural law which recognizes persons born within the jurisdiction of every country as being subjects or citizens of that country. Such persons were, therefore, citizens of the United States as were born in the country or were made such by naturalization; and the Constitution declares that they are entitled, as citizens, to all the privileges and immunities of citizens in the several States. They are, by constitutional right, entitled to these privileges and immunities, and may assert this right and these privileges and immunities, and ask for their enforcement whenever they go within the limits of the several states of the Union.

I am not aware that the Supreme Court have ever undertaken to define either the nature or extent of the privileges and immunities thus guarantied. . . . But we may gather some intimation of what probably will be the opinion of the judiciary by referring to a case adjudged many years ago in one of the circuit courts of the United States by Judge Washington. . . . It is the case of Corfield vs. Coryell. . . . Judge Washington says:

"The next question is whether this act infringes that section of the Constitution which declares that 'the citizens of each State shall be entitled to all privileges and immunities of citizens in the several states?'

"The inquiry is, what are the privileges and immunities of citizens in the several States? We feel no hesitation in confining these expressions to those privileges and immunities which are in their nature fundamental, which belong of right to the citizens of all free Governments, and which have at all times been enjoyed by the citizens of the several States which compose this Union from the time of their becoming free, independent, and sovereign. What these fundamental principles are it would, perhaps, be more tedious than difficult to enumerate. They may, however, be all comprehended under the following general heads: protection by the Government, the enjoyment of life and liberty, with the right to acquire and possess property of every kind, and to pursue and obtain happiness and safety, subject nevertheless to such restraints as the Government may justly prescribe for the general good of the whole. The right of a citizen of one State to pass through or to reside in any other State, for purposes of trade, agriculture, professional pursuits, or otherwise; to claim the benefit of the writ of *habeas corpus*; to institute and maintain actions of any kind in the courts of the State; to take, hold, and dispose of property, either real personal, and an exemption from higher taxes or impositions than are paid by the other citizens of the State, may be mentioned as some of the particular privileges and immunities of citizens which are clearly embraced by the general description of privileges deemed to be fundamental, to which may be added the elective franchise, as regulated and established by the laws or constitution of the State in which it is to be exercised. These, and many others which might be mentioned, are, strictly speaking, privileges and immunities, and the enjoyment of them by the citizens of each State in every other State was manifestly calculated (to use the expressions of the preamble of the corresponding provision in the old Articles of Confederation) 'the better to secure and perpetuate mutual friendship and intercourse among the people of the different States of the Union.'"

Such is the character of the privileges and immunities spoken of in the second section of the fourth article of the Constitution. To these privileges and immunities, whatever they may be—for they are not and cannot be fully defined in their entire extent and precise nature—to these should be added the personal rights guarantied and secured by the first eight amendments of the Constitution; such as the freedom of speech and of the press; the right of the people peaceably to assemble and petition the Government for a redress of grievances, a right appertaining to each and all the people; the right to keep and to bear arms; the right to be exempted from the quartering of soldiers in a house without the consent of the owner; the right to be exempt from unreasonable searches and seizures, and from any search or seizure except by virtue of a warrant issued upon a formal oath or affidavit; the right of an accused person to be informed of the nature of the accusation against him, and his right to be tried by an impartial jury of the vicinage; and also the right to be secure against excessive bail and against cruel and unusual punishments.

Now, sir, here is a mass of privileges, immunities, and rights, some of them secured by the second section of the fourth article of the Constitution, which I have recited, some by the first eight amendments of the Constitution; and it is a fact well worthy of attention that the course of decision of our courts and the present settled doctrine is, that all these immunities, privileges, rights, thus guarantied by the Constitution or recognized by it, are secured to the citizen solely as a citizen of the United States and as a party in their courts. They do not operate in the slightest degree as a restraint or prohibition upon State legislation.

States are not affected by them, and it has been repeatedly held[2] that the restriction contained in the Constitution against the taking of private property for public use without just compensation is not a restriction upon State legislation, but applies only to the legislation of Congress.

Now, sir, there is no power given in the Constitution to enforce and to carry out any of these guarantees. They are not powers granted by the Constitution to Congress, and of course do not come within the sweeping clause of the Constitution authorizing Congress to pass all laws necessary and proper for carrying out the foregoing or granted powers, but they stand simply as a bill of rights in the Constitution, without power on the part of Congress to give them full effect; while at the same time the States are not restrained from violating the principles embraced in them except by their own local constitutions, which may be altered from year to year. The great object of the first section of this amendment is, therefore, to restrain the power of the States and compel them at all times to respect these great fundamental guarantees. . . . This is done by the fifth section of this amendment, which declares that "the Congress shall have power to enforce by appropriate legislation the provisions of this article." Here is a direct affirmative delegation of power to Congress to carry out all the principles of all these guarantees, a power not found in the Constitution.

The last two clauses of the first section of the amendment disable a State from depriving not merely a citizen of the United States, but any person, whoever he may be, of life, liberty, or property without due process of law, or from denying to him the equal protection of the laws of the State. This abolishes all class legislation in the States and does away with the injustice of subjecting one caste of persons to a code not applicable to another. It prohibits the hanging of a black man for a crime for which the white man is not to be hanged. It protects the black man in his fundamental rights as a citizen with the same shield which it throws over the white man. Is it not time, Mr. President, that we extend to the black man, I had almost called it the poor privilege of the equal protection of the law? Ought not the time to be now passed when one measure of justice is to be meted out to a member of one caste while another and a different measure is meted out to the member of another caste, both castes being alike citizens of the United States, both bound to obey the same laws, to sustain the burdens of the same Government, and both equally responsible to justice and to God for the deeds done in the body?

But, sir, the first section of the proposed amendment does not give to either of these classes the right of voting. The right of suffrage is not, in law, one of the privileges or immunities thus secured by the Constitution. It is merely the creature of law. It has always been regarded in this country as the result of positive local law, not regarded as one of those fundamental rights lying at the basis of all society and without which a people cannot exist except as slaves, subject to a despotism.

---

2. This is probably a reference to Barron v. City of Baltimore, 32 U.S. 243 (1833).

As I have already remarked, section one is a restriction upon the States, and does not, of itself, confer any power upon Congress. The power which Congress has, under this amendment, is derived, not from that section, but from the fifth section, which gives it authority to pass laws which are appropriate to the attainment of the great object of the amendment. Look upon the first section, taken in connection with the fifth, as very important. It will, if adopted by the States, forever disable every one of them from passing laws trenching upon those fundamental rights and privileges which pertain to citizens of the United States, and to all persons who may happen to be within their jurisdiction. It establishes equality before the law, and it gives to the humblest, the poorest, the most despised of the race the same rights and the same protection before the law as it gives to the most powerful, the most wealthy, or the most haughty. That, sir, is republican government, as I understand it, and the only one which can claim the praise of a just Government. Without this principle of equal justice to all men and equal protection under the shield of the law, there is no republican government and none that is really worth maintaining.

. . .

[Section five] gives to Congress power to enforce by appropriate legislation all the provisions of this article of amendment. Without this clause, no power is granted to Congress by the amendment or any one of its sections. It casts upon congress the responsibility of seeing to it, for the future, that all the sections of the amendment are carried out in good faith, and that no State infringes the rights of persons or property. I look upon this clause as indispensable for the reason that it thus imposes upon Congress this power and this duty. It enables Congress, in case the States shall enact laws in conflict with the principles of the amendment, to correct that legislation by a formal congressional enactment.

Discussion

1. *The Privileges or Immunities Clause and the Privileges and Immunities Clause.* Senator Howard begins his explanation of the Fourteenth Amendment by pointing to the Privileges and Immunities Clause of Article IV, section 2. Like many Republican thinkers of the time, Howard argued that the Privileges and Immunities Clause in Article IV already bound the states to protect fundamental rights of national citizenship. See Michael Kent Curtis, No State Shall Abridge: The Fourteenth Amendment and the Bill of Rights 47-48, 62-91 (1986). In other words, Howard and other Republicans read "of the several states" to mean "of the United States." Nevertheless, the Republican argument went, there was no method in the 1787 Constitution to enforce these guarantees. Hence the Privileges or Immunities Clause of the new Fourteenth Amendment would establish a clear legal obligation enforceable by the courts; moreover Congress could also pass enforcing legislation under its section 5 powers. Thus, it was no accident that what Howard believed to be the central clause

in section one of the Fourteenth Amendment uses the same language as Article IV, section 2.

The new Privileges or Immunities clause had another important effect. Just as states had to treat outsiders equally with their own citizens with respect to certain fundamental rights, so too they would now have to treat their own citizens equally with respect to these rights. Thus, the privileges and immunities clause was not only a guarantee of liberty; it was also a guarantee of equality with respect to the basic rights of national citizenship.

As we shall soon see, the Supreme Court quickly robbed the Privileges or Immunities Clause of any importance in the Slaughter-House Cases. As described in Chapter Nine, a century later the Warren Court once again raised the idea that the Fourteenth Amendment protects equal fundamental rights, this time through the Equal Protection Clause.

2. *Incorporation.* According to Senator Howard, the Privileges or Immunities Clause protects the "the personal rights guarantied and secured by the first eight amendments of the Constitution." Thus, Howard believed—and represented to the Senate when he introduced the Amendment—that the Fourteenth Amendment incorporated the personal rights guarantees of the Bill of Rights. As we will see later on in the casebook (pp. 487-89), the Supreme Court did not take up this invitation, and the Bill of Rights (or most of it, at any rate) did not become incorporated until the 20th century. Moreover, incorporation, when it occurred, came through a creative reading of the Due Process Clause, and not the Privileges or Immunities Clause.

3. *Unenumerated rights.* Note Senator Howard's reliance on *Corfield v. Coryell* and his remark that the privileges and immunities of citizens of the United States "are not and cannot be fully defined in their entire extent and precise nature." Howard offers a declaratory theory of privileges or immunities. That is, he assumes that these rights are natural rights that preexist the state, and that the Constitution merely declares their existence and makes them enforceable in positive law. How can courts and legislatures determine what those rights are? We will return to this question in Chapter Eight. (Recall the debate between Justices Chase and Iredell in Calder v. Bull concerning whether courts could protect natural rights against infringements by state governments. How would the inclusion of the Privileges or Immunities clause change the terms of that debate?)

4. *Class and caste legislation.* When Howard turns to the equal protection and due process clauses he argues that they serve a different function: "This abolishes all class legislation in the States and does away with the injustice of subjecting one caste of persons to a code not applicable to another." What does the principle against "caste" legislation mean? One possibility suggested by Howard's speech is simple colorblindness. Another is that "caste" legislation is legislation that subordinates one social group to another.

The related notion of "class legislation" involved singling out a particular group for special burdens or special benefits. Indeed, the expression "equal protection" famously appeared in Andrew Jackson's July 10, 1832 veto message, where he stated

> It is to be regretted that the rich and powerful too often bend the acts of government to their selfish purposes. Distinctions in society will always exist under every just government. Equality of talents, of education, or of wealth can not be produced by human institutions. In the full enjoyment of the gifts of Heaven and the fruits of superior industry, economy, and virtue, every man is equally entitled to protection by law; but when the laws undertake to add to these natural and just advantages artificial distinctions, to grant titles, gratuities, and exclusive privileges, to make the rich richer and the potent more powerful, the humble members of society—the farmers, mechanics, and laborers—who have neither the time nor the means of securing like favors to themselves, have a right to complain of the injustice of their Government. There are no necessary evils in government. Its evils exist only in its abuses. If it would confine itself to equal protection, and, as Heaven does its rains, shower its favors alike on the high and the low, the rich and the poor, it would be an unqualified blessing.

4. *Voting.* Note that Justice Washington included "the elective franchise, as regulated and established by the laws or constitution of the State in which it is to be exercised" in his list of privileges and immunities. Senator Howard, however, takes pains to insist that voting is not one of the rights guaranteed by the new Fourteenth Amendment. In part that was because he and other supporters of the Amendment did not believe it could pass if blacks were given the right to vote. Hence they settled for the compromise measure of section 2, which sought to penalize states that denied black men the vote. As Howard explained in his discussion of section 2

> Let me not be misunderstood. I do not intend to say, nor do I say, that the proposed amendment, section two, proscribes the colored race. It has nothing to do with that question, as I shall show before I take my seat. I could wish that the elective franchise should be extended equally to the white man and to the black man; and if it were necessary, after full consideration, to restrict what is known as universal suffrage for the purpose of securing this equality, I would go for a restriction; but I deem that impracticable at the present time, and so did the committee.

> The colored race are destined to remain among us. They have been in our midst for more than two hundred years; and the idea of the people of the United States ever being able by any measure or measures to which they may resort to expel or expatriate that race from their limits and to settle them in a foreign country, is to me the wildest of all chimeras. The thing can never be done; it is impracticable. For weal or for woe, the destiny of the colored race in this country is wrapped up with our own; they are to remain in our midst, and here spend their years and here bury their fathers and finally repose themselves. We may regret it. It may not be entirely compatible with our taste that they should live in our midst. We cannot help it. Our forefathers introduced them, and their destiny is to continue among us; and the practical question which now presents itself to us is as to the best mode of getting along with them.

The committee were of opinion that the States are not yet prepared to sanction so fundamental a change as would be the concession of the right of suffrage to the colored race. We may as well state it plainly and fairly, so that there shall be no misunderstanding on the subject. It was our opinion that three-fourths of the states of this Union could not be induced to vote to grant the right of suffrage, even in any degree or under any restriction, to the colored race. We may be right in this apprehension or we may be in error. Time will develop the truth; and for one I shall wait with patience the movements of public opinion upon this great and absorbing question. The time may come, I trust it will come, indeed I feel a profound conviction that it is not far distant, when even the people of the States themselves where the colored population is most dense will consent to admit them to the right of suffrage. Sir, the safety and prosperity of those States depend upon it; it is especially for their interest that they should not retain in their midst a race of pariahs, so circumstanced as to be obliged to bear the burdens of Government and to obey its laws without any participation in the enactment of the laws.

The second section leaves the right to regulate the elective franchise still with the States, and does not meddle with that right. . . .

As it turned out, the Fifteenth Amendment was ratified four years later in 1870. Does this history mean that the Fourteenth Amendment has no application with respect to voting or the right to hold public office?

5. *The status of women.* Women's rights arose during Howard's discussion of black suffrage, since section 2 imposed a penalty only for denying the right to vote to males. In defending his position that blacks should have been given the right to vote, Senator Howard quoted Madison for the "vital principle of free government, that those who are to be bound by the laws ought to have a voice in making them." Howard asserted that this principle, was "the vital principle of republican government; it is not representation because of taxation." Responding to a question by Senator Sumner, Howard argued that the principle applied to all persons irrespective of color, and "whether they can read or write or not." When asked by Senator Johnson whether this included women, Howard answered

Mr. Madison does not say anything about females. . . . I believe Mr. Madison was old enough and wise enough to take it for granted there was such a thing as the law of nature which has a certain influence even in political affairs, and that by that law women and children were not regarded as the equals of men. Mr. Madison would not have quibbled about the question of women's voting or of an infant's voting. He lays down a broad democratic principle, that those who are to be bound by the laws ought to have a voice in making them; and everywhere mature manhood is the representative type of the human race.

In the debates over the Fourteenth Amendment, the proponents of the new Amendment were careful to avoid claiming that it would invalidate any laws regarding women. Although the framers of the Fourteenth Amendment asserted that women and men were civilly equal, they assumed that existing laws and practices—including coverture—did not deny women equal citizenship. See Cong. Globe, 39th Cong. 1st session, at 1089 (February 28th, 1866) (remarks of Rep. Bingham) (noting that states would retain ability to regulate married women's ownership of property because property rights were governed by local law while "[t]he rights of life and liberty are theirs [i.e., women's'] whatever States may enact"); Cong. Globe, 39th Cong., 1st Sess. 1064 (1866) (February 27th, 1866)(remarks of Rep. Stevens) ("When a distinction is made between two married people or two femmes sole, then it is unequal legislation; but where all of the same class are dealt with in the same way then there is no pretense of inequality."). Responding to Stevens, Representative Hale remarked: "[the] argument seems to me to be more specious than sound. The language of the section gives to *all persons* equal protection. Now if that means you shall extend to one married women the same protection you extend to another, and not the same you extend to unmarried women or men, then by parity of reasoning it will be sufficient if you extend to one negro the same rights you do to another, but not those you extend to a white man. . . . The line of distinction is, I take it, quite as broadly marked between negroes and white men as between married and unmarried women."

What weight should we give these remarks in deciding how the Fourteenth Amendment should apply to questions of sex equality today?

Part Two

Constitutional Adjudication in the Modern World

Insert at the end of p. 497:

DISTRICT OF COLUMBIA v. HELLER
554 U.S. 570 (2008)

Justice SCALIA delivered the opinion of the Court.

We consider whether a District of Columbia prohibition on the possession of *Q* usable handguns in the home violates the Second Amendment to the Constitution.

I

The District of Columbia generally prohibits the possession of handguns. It is a *st.* crime to carry an unregistered firearm, and the registration of handguns is prohibited. See D.C. Code §§7-2501.01(12), 7-2502.01(a), 7-2502.02(a)(4) (2001). Wholly apart from that prohibition, no person may carry a handgun without a license, but the chief of police may issue licenses for 1-year periods. See §§22-4504(a), 22-4506. District of Columbia law also requires residents to keep their lawfully owned firearms, such as registered long guns, unloaded and dissembled or bound by a trigger lock or similar device unless they are located in a place of business or are being used for lawful recreational activities. See §7-2507.02.

Respondent Dick Heller is a D.C. special police officer authorized to carry a handgun while on duty at the Federal Judicial Center. He applied for a registration certificate for a handgun that he wished to keep at home, but the District refused. He thereafter filed a lawsuit in the Federal District Court for the District of Columbia seeking, on Second Amendment grounds, to enjoin the city from enforcing the bar on the registration of handguns, the licensing requirement insofar as it prohibits the carrying of a firearm in the home without a license, and the trigger-lock requirement insofar as it prohibits the use of functional firearms within the home. . . .

II

. . .

11

A

The Second Amendment provides: "A well regulated Militia, being necessary to the security of a free State, the right of the people to keep and bear Arms, shall not be infringed." In interpreting this text, we are guided by the principle that "[t]he Constitution was written to be understood by the voters; its words and phrases were used in their normal and ordinary as distinguished from technical meaning. Normal meaning may of course include an idiomatic meaning, but it excludes secret or technical meanings that would not have been known to ordinary citizens in the founding generation." . . .

The Second Amendment is naturally divided into two parts: its prefatory clause and its operative clause. . . . The former does not limit the latter grammatically, but rather announces a purpose. The Amendment could be rephrased, "Because a well regulated Militia is necessary to the security of a free State, the right of the people to keep and bear Arms shall not be infringed." . . .

Logic demands that there be a link between the stated purpose and the command. . . . But apart from [its] clarifying function, a prefatory clause does not limit or expand the scope of the operative clause. Therefore, while we will begin our textual analysis with the operative clause, we will return to the prefatory clause to ensure that our reading of the operative clause is consistent with the announced purpose.

1.   Operative Clause.

a. "Right of the People."   The first salient feature of the operative clause is that it codifies a "right of the people." The unamended Constitution and the Bill of Rights use the phrase "right of the people" two other times, in the First Amendment's Assembly-and-Petition Clause and in the Fourth Amendment's Search-and-Seizure Clause. The Ninth Amendment uses very similar terminology ("The enumeration in the Constitution, of certain rights, shall not be construed to deny or disparage others retained by the people"). All three of these instances unambiguously refer to individual rights, not "collective" rights, or rights that may be exercised only through participation in some corporate body. Three provisions of the Constitution refer to "the people" in a context other than "rights"—the famous preamble ("We the people"), §2 of Article I (providing that "the people" will choose members of the House), and the Tenth Amendment (providing that those powers not given the Federal Government remain with "the States" or "the people"). Those provisions arguably refer to "the people" acting collectively—but they deal with the exercise or reservation of powers, not rights. Nowhere else in the Constitution does a "right" attributed to "the people" refer to anything other than an individual right. What is more, in all six other provisions of the Constitution that mention "the people," the term unambiguously refers to all members of the political community, not an unspecified subset. . . . This contrasts markedly with the phrase "the militia" in the prefatory clause. As we will describe below, the "militia" in colonial America consisted of a subset of "the people"—those who were male, able bodied, and within a certain age range. Reading the Second Amendment as protecting only the right to "keep and bear Arms" in an organized militia therefore fits poorly with the operative clause's description of the holder of that right as "the people."

We start therefore with a strong presumption that the Second Amendment right is exercised individually and belongs to all Americans.

b. "Keep and bear Arms."   . . . The 18th-century meaning [of "Arms"] is no different from the meaning today. The 1773 edition of Samuel Johnson's dictionary defined "arms" as "weapons of offence, or armour of defence" . . . The term was applied, then as now, to weapons that were not specifically designed for military use and were not employed in a military capacity. . . . Although one founding-era thesaurus limited "arms" (as opposed to "weapons") to "instruments of offence *generally* made use of in war," even that source stated that all firearms constituted "arms." . . .

Some have made the argument, bordering on the frivolous, that only those arms in existence in the 18th century are protected by the Second Amendment. We do not interpret constitutional rights that way. Just as the First Amendment protects modern forms of communications, and the Fourth Amendment applies to modern forms of search, the Second Amendment extends, prima facie, to all instruments that constitute bearable arms, even those that were not in existence at the time of the founding.

We turn to the phrases "keep arms" and "bear arms." . . . No party has apprised us of an idiomatic meaning of "keep Arms." Thus, the most natural reading of "keep Arms" in the Second Amendment is to "have weapons." . . . Petitioners point to militia laws of the founding period that required militia members to "keep" arms in connection with militia service, and they conclude from this that the phrase "keep Arms" has a militia-related connotation. This is rather like saying that, since there are many statutes that authorize aggrieved employees to "file complaints" with federal agencies, the phrase "file complaints" has an employment-related connotation. "Keep arms" was simply a common way of referring to possessing arms, for militiamen *and everyone else.*

At the time of the founding, as now, to "bear" meant to "carry." When used with "arms," however, the term has a meaning that refers to carrying for a particular purpose—confrontation. . . . Although the phrase implies that the carrying of the weapon is for the purpose of "offensive or defensive action," it in no way connotes participation in a structured military organization.

From our review of founding-era sources, we conclude that this natural meaning was also the meaning that "bear arms" had in the 18th century. In numerous instances, "bear arms" was unambiguously used to refer to the carrying of weapons outside of an organized militia. The most prominent examples are those most relevant to the Second Amendment: Nine state constitutional provisions written in the 18th century or the first two decades of the

19th, which enshrined a right of citizens to "bear arms in defense of themselves and the state" or "bear arms in defense of himself and the state." It is clear from those formulations that "bear arms" did not refer only to carrying a weapon in an organized military unit. . . .

The phrase "bear Arms" also had at the time of the founding an idiomatic meaning that was significantly different from its natural meaning: "to serve as a soldier, do military service, fight" or "to wage war." But it *unequivocally* bore that idiomatic meaning only when followed by the preposition "against," which was in turn followed by the target of the hostilities. (That is how, for example, our Declaration of Independence §28, used the phrase: "He has constrained our fellow Citizens taken Captive on the high Seas to bear Arms against their Country. . . . ") . . .

Petitioners justify their limitation of "bear arms" to the military context by pointing out the unremarkable fact that it was often used in that context—the same mistake they made with respect to "keep arms." It is especially unremarkable that the phrase was often used in a military context in the federal legal sources (such as records of congressional debate) that have been the focus of petitioners' inquiry. Those sources would have had little occasion to use it *except* in discussions about the standing army and the militia. And the phrases used primarily in those military discussions include not only "bear arms" but also "carry arms," "possess arms," and "have arms"—though no one thinks that those *other* phrases also had special military meanings. . . .

Justice Stevens places great weight on James Madison' inclusion of a conscientious-objector clause in his original draft of the Second Amendment: "but no person religiously scrupulous of bearing arms, shall be compelled to render military service in person." He argues that this clause establishes that the drafters of the Second Amendment intended "bear Arms" to refer only to military service. It is always perilous to derive the meaning of an adopted provision from another provision deleted in the drafting process. In any case, what Justice Stevens would conclude from the deleted provision does not follow. It was not meant to exempt from military service those who objected to going to war but had no scruples about personal gunfights. Quakers opposed the use of arms not just for militia service, but for any violent purpose whatsoever . . . Thus, the most natural interpretation of Madison's deleted text is that those opposed to carrying weapons for potential violent confrontation would not be "compelled to render military service," in which such carrying would be required. . . .

c. Meaning of the Operative Clause.   Putting all of these textual elements together, we find that they guarantee the individual right to possess and carry weapons in case of confrontation. This meaning is strongly confirmed by the historical background of the Second Amendment. We look to this because it has always been widely understood that the Second Amendment, like the First and Fourth Amendments, codified a *pre-existing* right. The very text of the Second Amendment implicitly recognizes the pre-existence of the right and declares only that it "shall not be infringed." . . .

Between the Restoration and the Glorious Revolution, the Stuart Kings Charles II and James II succeeded in using select militias loyal to them to suppress political dissidents, in part by disarming their opponents. Under the auspices of the 1671 Game Act, for example, the Catholic James II had ordered general disarmaments of regions home to his Protestant enemies. These experiences caused Englishmen to be extremely wary of concentrated military forces run by the state and to be jealous of their arms. They accordingly obtained an — assurance from William and Mary, in the Declaration of Right (which was codified as the English Bill of Rights), that Protestants would never be disarmed: "That the subjects which are Protestants may have arms for their defense suitable to their conditions and as allowed by law." 1 W. & M., c. 2, §7, in 3 Eng. Stat. at Large 441 (1689). This right has long been understood to be the predecessor to our Second Amendment. It was clearly an individual right, having nothing whatever to do with service in a militia. To be sure, it was an individual right not available to the whole population, given that it was restricted to Protestants, and like all written English rights it was held only against the Crown, not Parliament. But it was secured to them as individuals, according to "libertarian political principles," not as members of a fighting force.

By the time of the founding, the right to have arms had become fundamental for English subjects. Blackstone, whose works, we have said, "constituted the preeminent authority on English law for the founding generation," cited the arms provision of the Bill of Rights as one of the fundamental rights of Englishmen. His description of it cannot possibly be thought to tie it to militia or military service. It was, he said, "the natural right of resistance and self-preservation," and "the right of having and using arms for self-preservation and defence." . . . Thus, the right secured in 1689 as a result of the Stuarts' abuses was by the time of the founding understood to be an individual right protecting against both public and private violence.

And, of course, what the Stuarts had tried to do to their political enemies, George III had tried to do to the colonists. In the tumultuous decades of the 1760's and 1770's, the Crown began to disarm the inhabitants of the most rebellious areas. That provoked polemical reactions by Americans invoking their rights as Englishmen to keep arms. A New York article of April 1769 said that "[i]t is a natural right which the people have reserved to themselves, confirmed by the Bill of Rights, to keep arms for their own defence." They understood the right to enable individuals to defend themselves. As the most important early American edition of Blackstone's Commentaries (by the law professor and former Antifederalist St. George Tucker) made clear in the notes to the description of the arms right, Americans understood the "right of self-preservation" as permitting a citizen to "repe[l] force by force" when "the intervention of society in his behalf, may be too late to prevent an injury."

There seems to us no doubt, on the basis of both text and history, that the Second Amendment conferred an individual right to keep and bear arms. Of course the right was not unlimited, just as the First Amendment's right of free speech was not. Thus, we do not read the Second Amendment to protect the right of citizens to carry arms for *any sort* of confrontation, just as we do not read the First Amendment to protect the right of citizens to speak for *any purpose*. Before turning to limitations upon the individual right, however, we must determine whether the prefatory clause of the Second Amendment comports with our interpretation of the operative clause.

2.   Prefatory Clause.

The prefatory clause reads: "A well regulated Militia, being necessary to the security of a free State. . . . "

   a. "Well-Regulated Militia."   In *United States v. Miller,* 307 U.S. 174 (1939), we explained that the Militia comprised all males physically capable of acting in concert for the common defense." . . . Petitioners take a seemingly narrower view of the militia, stating that "[m]ilitias are the state- and congressionally-regulated military forces described in the Militia Clauses (art. I, §8, cls.15-16)." Although we agree with petitioners' interpretive assumption that "militia" means the same thing in Article I and the Second Amendment, we believe that petitioners identify the wrong thing, namely, the organized militia. Unlike armies and navies, which Congress is given the power to create ("to raise . . . Armies"; "to provide . . . a Navy," Art. I, §8, cls. 12-13), the militia is assumed by Article I already to be *in existence*. Congress is given the power to "provide for calling forth the militia," §8, cl. 15; and the power not to create, but to "organiz[e]" it . . . connoting a body already in existence, *ibid.,* cl. 16. This is fully consistent with the ordinary definition of the militia as all able-bodied men. From that pool, Congress has plenary power to organize the units that will make up an effective fighting force. That is what Congress did in the first militia Act, which specified that "each and every free able-bodied white male citizen of the respective states, resident therein, who is or shall be of the age of eighteen years, and under the age of forty-five years (except as is herein after excepted) shall severally and respectively be enrolled in the militia." Act of May 8, 1792, 1 Stat. 271. To be sure, Congress need not conscript every able-bodied man into the militia, because nothing in Article I suggests that in exercising its power to organize, discipline, and arm the militia, Congress must focus upon the entire body. Although the militia consists of all able-bodied men, the federally organized militia may consist of a subset of them.
   Finally, the adjective "well-regulated" implies nothing more than the imposition of proper discipline and training.

   b. Security of a Free State.   The phrase "security of a free state" meant "security of a free polity," not security of each of the several States . . . [t]he presence of the term "foreign state" in Article I and Article III shows that the word "state" did not have a single meaning in the Constitution.

There are many reasons why the militia was thought to be "necessary to the security of a free state." First, of course, it is useful in repelling invasions and suppressing insurrections. Second, it renders large standing armies unnecessary—an argument that Alexander Hamilton made in favor of federal control over the militia. The Federalist No. 29 (A. Hamilton). Third, when the able-bodied men of a nation are trained in arms and organized, they are better able to resist tyranny.

3.   Relationship between Prefatory Clause and Operative Clause

We reach the question, then: Does the preface fit with an operative clause that creates an individual right to keep and bear arms? It fits perfectly, once one knows the history that the founding generation knew and that we have described above. That history showed that the way tyrants had eliminated a militia consisting of all the able-bodied men was not by banning the militia but simply by taking away the people's arms, enabling a select militia or standing army to suppress political opponents. This is what had occurred in England that prompted codification of the right to have arms in the English Bill of Rights.

The debate with respect to the right to keep and bear arms, as with other guarantees in the Bill of Rights, was not over whether it was desirable (all agreed that it was) but over whether it needed to be codified in the Constitution. During the 1788 ratification debates, the fear that the federal government would disarm the people in order to impose rule through a standing army or select militia was pervasive in Antifederalist rhetoric. Federalists responded that because Congress was given no power to abridge the ancient right of individuals to keep and bear arms, such a force could never oppress the people. It was understood across the political spectrum that the right helped to secure the ideal of a citizen militia, which might be necessary to oppose an oppressive military force if the constitutional order broke down.

It is therefore entirely sensible that the Second Amendment's prefatory clause announces the purpose for which the right was codified: <u>to prevent elimination of the militia</u>. The prefatory clause does not suggest that preserving the militia was the only reason Americans valued the ancient right; most undoubtedly thought it even more important for <u>self-defense</u> and <u>hunting</u>. But the threat that the new Federal Government would destroy the citizens' militia by taking away their arms was the reason that right—unlike some other English rights—was codified in a written Constitution. Justice Breyer's assertion that individual self-defense is merely a "subsidiary interest" of the right to keep and bear arms, is profoundly mistaken. He bases that assertion solely upon the prologue—but that can only show that self-defense had little to do with the right's *codification;* it was the *central component* of the right itself.

Besides ignoring the historical reality that the Second Amendment was not intended to lay down a "novel principl[e]" but rather codified a right "inherited from our English ancestors," petitioners' interpretation does not even achieve the narrower purpose that prompted codification of the right. If, as they believe, the Second Amendment right is no more than the right to keep and use weapons as a member of an organized militia—if, that is, the *organized* militia is the sole institutional beneficiary of the Second Amendment's guarantee—it does not assure the existence of a "citizens' militia" as a safeguard against tyranny. For Congress retains plenary authority to organize the militia, which must include the authority to say who will belong to the organized force. That is why the first Militia Act's requirement that only whites enroll caused States to amend their militia laws to exclude free blacks. Thus, if petitioners are correct, the Second Amendment protects citizens' right to use a gun in an organization from which Congress has plenary authority to exclude them. It guarantees a select militia of the sort the Stuart kings found useful, but not the people's militia that was the concern of the founding generation.

B

Our interpretation is confirmed by analogous arms-bearing rights in state constitutions that preceded and immediately followed adoption of the Second Amendment. Four States adopted analogues to the Federal Second Amendment in the period between independence and the ratification of the Bill of Rights. Two of them—Pennsylvania and Vermont—clearly adopted individual rights unconnected to militia service. Pennsylvania's Declaration of Rights of 1776 said: "That the people have a right to bear arms *for the defence of themselves, and the state. . . .*" In 1777, Vermont adopted the identical provision, except for inconsequential differences in punctuation and capitalization.

North Carolina also codified a right to bear arms in 1776: "That the people have a right to bear arms, for the defence of the State. . . ." This could plausibly be read to support only a right to bear arms in a militia—but that is a peculiar way to make the point in a constitution that elsewhere repeatedly mentions the militia explicitly. Many colonial statutes required individual arms-bearing for public-safety reasons—such as the 1770 Georgia law that "for the security and *defence of this province* from internal dangers and insurrections" required those men who qualified for militia duty individually "to carry fire arms" to places of public worship. That broad public-safety understanding was the connotation given to the North Carolina right by that State's Supreme Court in 1843.

The 1780 Massachusetts Constitution presented another variation on the theme: "The people have a right to keep and to bear arms for the common defence. . . ." Once again, if one gives narrow meaning to the phrase "common defence" this can be thought to limit the right to the bearing of arms in a state-organized military force. But once again the State's highest court thought otherwise [in 1825].

We therefore believe that the most likely reading of all four of these pre-Second Amendment state constitutional provisions is that they secured an individual right to bear arms for defensive purposes. . . .

Between 1789 and 1820, nine States adopted Second Amendment analogues. Four of them—Kentucky, Ohio, Indiana, and Missouri—referred to the right of the people to "bear arms in defence of themselves and the State." Another three States—Mississippi, Connecticut, and Alabama—used the even more individualistic phrasing that each citizen has the "right to bear arms in defence of himself and the State." Finally, two States—Tennessee and Maine—used the "common defence" language of Massachusetts. That of the nine state constitutional— protections for the right to bear arms enacted immediately after 1789 at least seven unequivocally protected an individual citizen's right to self-defense is strong evidence that that is how the founding generation conceived of the right. And with one possible exception . . . 19th-century courts and commentators interpreted these state constitutional provisions to protect an individual right to use arms for self-defense.

The historical narrative that petitioners must endorse would thus treat the Federal Second Amendment as an odd outlier, protecting a right unknown in state constitutions or at English common law, based on little more than an overreading of the prefatory clause.

C

Justice Stevens relies on the drafting history of the Second Amendment—the various proposals in the state conventions and the debates in Congress. It is dubious to rely on such history to interpret a text that was widely understood to codify a pre-existing right, rather than to fashion a new one. But even assuming that this legislative history is relevant, Justice Stevens flatly misreads the historical record.

It is true, as Justice Stevens says, that there was concern that the Federal Government would abolish the institution of the state militia. That concern found expression, however, *not* in the various Second Amendment precursors proposed in the State conventions, but in separate structural provisions that would have given the States concurrent and seemingly nonpre-emptible authority to organize, discipline, and arm the militia when the Federal Government failed to do so. The Second Amendment precursors, by contrast, referred to the individual English right already codified in two (and probably four) State constitutions. The Federalist-dominated first Congress chose to reject virtually all major structural revisions favored by the Antifederalists, including the proposed militia amendments. Rather, it adopted primarily the popular and uncontroversial (though, in the Federalists' view, unnecessary) individual-rights amendments. The Second Amendment right, protecting only individuals' liberty to keep and carry arms, did nothing to assuage Antifederalists' concerns about federal control of the militia. . . .

Justice Stevens' view . . . relies on the proposition, unsupported by any evidence, that different people of the founding period had vastly different conceptions of the right to keep and bear arms. That simply does not comport with our longstanding view that the Bill of Rights codified venerable, widely understood liberties.

D

We now address how the Second Amendment was interpreted from immediately after its ratification through the end of the 19th century. Before proceeding, however, we take issue with Justice Stevens' equating of these sources with postenactment legislative history, a comparison that betrays a fundamental misunderstanding of a court's interpretive task. "Legislative history," of course, refers to the pre-enactment statements of those who drafted or voted for a law; it is considered persuasive by some, not because they reflect the general understanding of the disputed terms, but because the legislators who heard or read those statements presumably voted with that understanding. "Postenactment legislative history," a deprecatory contradiction in terms, refers to statements of those who drafted or voted for the law that are made after its enactment and hence could have had no effect on the congressional vote. It most certainly does not refer to the examination of a variety of legal and other sources to determine *the public understanding* of a legal text in the period after its enactment or ratification. That sort of inquiry is a critical tool of constitutional interpretation.

[V]irtually all interpreters of the Second Amendment in the century after its enactment interpreted the amendment as we do. . . . Antislavery advocates routinely invoked the right to bear arms for self-defense. . . . In his famous Senate speech about the 1856 "Bleeding Kansas" conflict, Charles Sumner proclaimed:

> "The rifle has ever been the companion of the pioneer and, under God, his tutelary protector against the red man and the beast of the forest. Never was this efficient weapon more needed in just self-defence, than now in Kansas, and at least one article in our National Constitution must be blotted out, before the complete right to it can in any way be impeached. And yet such is the madness of the hour, that, in defiance of the solemn guarantee, embodied in the Amendments to the Constitution, that "the right of the people to keep and bear arms shall not be infringed," the people of Kansas have been arraigned for keeping and bearing them, and the Senator from South Carolina has had the face to say openly, on this floor, that they should be disarmed—of course, that the fanatics of Slavery, his allies and constituents, may meet no impediment." The Crime Against Kansas, May 19-20, 1856, in American Speeches: Political Oratory from the Revolution to the Civil War 553, 606-607 (2006).

[T]he 19th-century cases that interpreted the Second Amendment universally support an individual right unconnected to militia service. . . . Many early 19th-century state cases indicated that the Second Amendment right to bear arms was an individual right unconnected to militia service, though subject to certain restrictions. . . . In the aftermath of the Civil War, there was an outpouring of discussion of the Second Amendment in Congress and in public discourse, as people debated whether and how to secure constitutional rights for newly free slaves. Since those discussions took place 75 years after the ratification of the Second Amendment, they do not provide as much insight into its original meaning as earlier sources. Yet those born and educated in the early 19th century faced a widespread effort to limit arms ownership by a large number of citizens; their understanding of the origins and continuing significance of the Amendment is instructive.

Blacks were routinely disarmed by Southern States after the Civil War. Those who opposed these injustices frequently stated that they infringed blacks' constitutional right to keep and bear arms. Needless to say, the claim was not that blacks were being prohibited from carrying arms in an organized state militia. . . . Congress enacted the Freedmen's Bureau Act on July 16, 1866. Section 14 stated: "[T]he right . . . to have full and equal benefit of all laws and proceedings concerning personal liberty, personal security, and the acquisition, enjoyment, and disposition of estate, real and personal, including the constitutional right to bear arms, shall be secured to and enjoyed by all the citizens . . . without respect to race or color, or previous condition of slavery. . . ." 14 Stat. 176-177. The understanding that the Second Amendment gave freed blacks the right to keep and bear arms was reflected in congressional discussion of the bill. . . . Similar discussion attended the passage of the Civil Rights Act of 1871 and the Fourteenth Amendment. . . . It was plainly the understanding in the post-Civil War Congress that the Second Amendment protected an individual right to use arms for self-defense. . . .

Every late-19th-century legal scholar that we have read interpreted the Second Amendment to secure an individual right unconnected with militia service. The most famous was the judge and professor Thomas Cooley, who wrote a massively popular 1868 Treatise on Constitutional Limitations. . . . Cooley understood the right not as connected to militia service, but as securing the militia by ensuring a populace familiar with arms. . . . All other post-Civil War 19th-century sources we have found concurred with Cooley. . . .

E

We now ask whether any of our precedents forecloses the conclusions we have reached about the meaning of the Second Amendment. . . . Justice Stevens places overwhelming reliance upon this Court's decision in *United States v. Miller*, 307 U.S. 174 (1939). . . . *Miller* . . . upheld against a Second Amendment challenge two men's federal convictions for transporting an unregistered short-barreled shotgun in interstate commerce, in violation of the National Firearms Act. It is entirely clear that the Court's basis for saying that the Second Amendment did not apply was *not* that the defendants were "bear[ing] arms" not "for . . . military purposes" but for "nonmilitary use." Rather, it was that the *type of weapon at issue* was not eligible for Second Amendment protection: "In the absence of any evidence tending to show that the possession or use of a [short-barreled shotgun] at this time has some reasonable relationship to the preservation or efficiency of a well regulated militia, we cannot say that the Second Amendment guarantees the right to keep and bear *such an instrument*" (emphasis added). "Certainly," the Court continued, "it is not within judicial notice that this weapon is any part of the ordinary military equipment or that its use could contribute to the common defense." . . . This holding is not only consistent with, but positively suggests, that the Second Amendment confers an individual right to keep and bear arms (though only arms that "have some reasonable relationship to the preservation or efficiency of a well regulated militia"). Had the Court believed that the Second Amendment protects only those serving in the militia, it would have been odd to examine the character of the weapon rather than simply note that the two crooks were not militiamen. . . . It is particularly wrongheaded to read *Miller* for more than what it said, because the case did not even purport to be a thorough examination of the Second Amendment. . . . The respondent made no appearance in the case, neither filing a brief nor appearing at oral argument; the Court heard from no one but the Government (reason enough, one would think, not to make that case the beginning and the end of this Court's consideration of the Second Amendment). . . .

We may as well consider at this point (for we will have to consider eventually) *what* types of weapons *Miller* permits. Read in isolation, *Miller'* s phrase "part of ordinary military equipment" could mean that only those weapons useful in warfare are protected. That would be a startling reading of the opinion, since it would mean that the National Firearms Act's restrictions on machineguns (not challenged in *Miller*) might be unconstitutional, machineguns being useful in warfare in 1939. We think that *Miller*'s "ordinary military equipment" language must be read in tandem with what comes after: "[O]rdinarily when called for [militia] service [able-bodied] men were expected to appear bearing arms supplied by themselves and of the kind in common use at the time." The traditional militia was formed from a pool of men bringing arms "in common use at the time" for lawful purposes like self-defense. In the colonial and revolutionary war era, [small-arms] weapons used by militiamen and weapons used in defense of person and home were one and the same. Indeed, that is precisely the way in which the Second Amendment's operative clause furthers the purpose announced in its preface. We therefore read *Miller* to say only that the Second Amendment does not protect those weapons not typically possessed by law-abiding citizens for lawful purposes, such as short-barreled shotguns. That accords with the historical understanding of the scope of the right. . . .

We conclude that nothing in our precedents forecloses our adoption of the original understanding of the Second Amendment. It should be unsurprising that such a significant matter has been for so long judicially unresolved. For most of our history, the Bill of Rights was not thought applicable to the States, and the Federal Government did not significantly regulate the possession of firearms by law-abiding citizens. Other provisions of the Bill of Rights have similarly remained unilluminated for lengthy periods. This Court first held a law to violate the First Amendment's guarantee of freedom of speech in 1931, almost 150 years after the Amendment was ratified, and it was not until after World War II that we held a law invalid under the Establishment Clause. Even a question as basic as the scope of proscribable libel was not addressed by this

Court until 1964, nearly two centuries after the founding. See *New York Times Co. v. Sullivan,* 376 U.S. 254 (1964). It is demonstrably not true that, as Justice Stevens claims, "for most of our history, the invalidity of Second-Amendment-based objections to firearms regulations has been well settled and uncontroversial." For most of our history the question did not present itself.

III

Like most rights, the right secured by the Second Amendment is not unlimited. From Blackstone through the 19th-century cases, commentators and courts routinely explained that the right was not a right to keep and carry any weapon whatsoever in any manner whatsoever and for whatever purpose. For example, the majority of the 19th-century courts to consider the question held that prohibitions on carrying concealed weapons were lawful under the Second Amendment or state analogues. Although we do not undertake an exhaustive historical analysis today of the full scope of the Second Amendment, nothing in our opinion should be taken to cast doubt on longstanding prohibitions on the possession of firearms by felons and the mentally ill, or laws forbidding the carrying of firearms in sensitive places such as schools and government buildings, or laws imposing conditions and qualifications on the commercial sale of arms.

We also recognize another important limitation on the right to keep and carry arms. *Miller* said, as we have explained, that the sorts of weapons protected were those "in common use at the time." We think that limitation is fairly supported by the historical tradition of prohibiting the carrying of "dangerous and unusual weapons."

It may be objected that if weapons that are most useful in military service—M-16 rifles and the like—may be banned, then the Second Amendment right is completely detached from the prefatory clause. But as we have said, the conception of the militia at the time of the Second Amendment's ratification was the body of all citizens capable of military service, who would bring the sorts of lawful weapons that they possessed at home to militia duty. It may well be true today that a militia, to be as effective as militias in the 18th century, would require sophisticated arms that are highly unusual in society at large. Indeed, it may be true that no amount of small arms could be useful against modern-day bombers and tanks. But the fact that modern developments have — limited the degree of fit between the prefatory clause and the protected right cannot change our interpretation of the right.

IV

We turn finally to the law at issue here. As we have said, the law totally bans handgun possession in the home. It also requires that any lawful firearm in the home be disassembled or bound by a trigger lock at all times, rendering it inoperable.

[T]he inherent right of self-defense has been central to the Second Amendment right. The handgun ban amounts to a prohibition of an entire class of "arms" that is overwhelmingly chosen by American society for that lawful purpose. The prohibition extends, moreover, to the home, where the need for defense of self, family, and property is most acute. Under any of the standards of scrutiny that we have applied to enumerated constitutional rights, banning from the home "the most preferred firearm in the nation to 'keep' and use for protection of one's home and family," would fail constitutional muster.

Few laws in the history of our Nation have come close to the severe restriction of the District's handgun ban. . . . It is no answer to say, as petitioners do, that it is permissible to ban the possession of handguns so long as the possession of other firearms (*i.e.,* long guns) is allowed. It is enough to note, as we have observed, that the American people have considered the handgun to be the quintessential self-defense weapon. There are many reasons that a citizen may prefer a handgun for home defense: It is easier to store in a location that is readily accessible in an emergency; it cannot easily be redirected or wrestled away by an attacker; it is easier to use for those without the upper-body strength to lift and aim a long gun; it can be pointed at a burglar with one hand while the other hand dials the police. Whatever the reason, handguns are the most popular weapon chosen by Americans for self-defense in the home, and a complete prohibition of their use is invalid.

We must also address the District's requirement (as applied to respondent's handgun) that firearms in the home be rendered and kept inoperable at all times. This makes it impossible for citizens to use them for the core lawful purpose of self-defense and is hence unconstitutional. The District argues that we should interpret this element of the statute to contain an exception for self-defense. But we think that is precluded by the unequivocal text, and by the presence of certain other enumerated exceptions: "Except for law enforcement personnel . . . , each registrant shall keep any firearm in his possession unloaded and disassembled or bound by a trigger lock or similar device unless such firearm is kept at his place of business, or while being used for lawful recreational purposes within the District of Columbia." D.C.Code §7-2507.02. The nonexistence of a self-defense exception is also suggested by the D.C. Court of Appeals' statement that the statute forbids residents to use firearms to stop intruders, see *McIntosh v. Washington,* 395 A.2d 744, 755-756 (1978).

Apart from his challenge to the handgun ban and the trigger-lock requirement respondent asked the District Court to enjoin petitioners from enforcing the separate licensing requirement "in such a manner as to forbid the carrying of a firearm within one's home or possessed land without a license." The Court of Appeals did not invalidate the licensing requirement, but held only that the District "may not prevent [a handgun] from being moved throughout one's house." It then ordered the District Court to enter summary judgment "consistent with [respondent's] prayer for relief." Before this Court petitioners have stated that "if the handgun ban is struck down and respondent registers a handgun, he could obtain a license, assuming he is not otherwise disqualified," by which they apparently mean if he is not a felon and is not insane. Respondent conceded at oral argument that he does not "have a problem with . . . licensing" and that the District's law is permissible so long as it is "not enforced in an arbitrary and capricious manner." We therefore assume that petitioners' issuance of a license will satisfy respondent's prayer for relief and do not address the licensing requirement.

Justice Breyer has devoted most of his separate dissent to the handgun ban. He says that, even assuming the Second Amendment is a personal guarantee of the right to bear arms, the District's prohibition is valid. He first tries to establish this by founding-era historical precedent, pointing to various restrictive laws in the colonial period. . . . [These laws did not burden the right of self defense.] All of them punished the discharge (or loading) of guns with a small fine and forfeiture of the weapon (or in a few cases a very brief stay in the local jail), not with significant criminal penalties. They are akin to modern penalties for minor public-safety infractions like speeding or jaywalking. And although such public-safety laws may not contain exceptions for self-defense, it is inconceivable that the threat of a jaywalking ticket would deter someone from disregarding a "Do Not Walk" sign in order to flee an attacker, or that the Government would enforce those laws under such circumstances. Likewise, we do not think that a law imposing a 5-shilling fine and forfeiture of the gun would have prevented a person in the founding era from using a gun to protect himself or his family from violence, or that if he did so the law would be enforced against him. The District law, by contrast, far from imposing a minor fine, threatens citizens with a year in prison (five years for a second violation) for even obtaining a gun in the first place.

Justice Breyer . . . criticizes us for declining to establish a level of scrutiny for evaluating Second Amendment restrictions. He proposes, explicitly at least, none of the traditionally expressed levels (strict scrutiny, intermediate scrutiny, rational basis), but rather a judge-empowering "interest-balancing inquiry" that "asks whether the statute burdens a protected interest in a way or to an extent that is out of proportion to the statute's salutary effects upon other important governmental interests." After an exhaustive discussion of the arguments for and against gun control, Justice Breyer arrives at his interest-balanced answer: because handgun violence is a problem, because the law is limited to an urban area, and because there were somewhat similar restrictions in the founding period (a false proposition that we have already discussed), the interest-balancing inquiry results in the constitutionality of the handgun ban. QED.

We know of no other enumerated constitutional right whose core protection has been subjected to a freestanding "interest-balancing" approach. The very enumeration of the right takes out of the hands of government—even the Third Branch of Government—the power to decide on a case-by-case basis whether the right is *really worth* insisting upon. A constitutional guarantee subject to future judges' assessments of its usefulness is no constitutional guarantee at all. Constitutional rights are enshrined with the scope they were understood to have when the people adopted them, whether or not future legislatures or (yes) even

future judges think that scope too broad. We would not apply an "interest-balancing" approach to the prohibition of a peaceful neo-Nazi march through Skokie. The First Amendment contains the freedom-of-speech guarantee that the people ratified, which included exceptions for obscenity, libel, and disclosure of state secrets, but not for the expression of extremely unpopular and
— wrong-headed views. The Second Amendment is no different. Like the First, it is the very *product* of an interest-balancing by the people—which Justice Breyer would now conduct for them anew. And whatever else it leaves to future evaluation, it surely elevates above all other interests the right of law-abiding, responsible citizens to use arms in defense of hearth and home.

Justice Breyer chides us for leaving so many applications of the right to keep and bear arms in doubt, and for not providing extensive historical justification for those regulations of the right that we describe as permissible. But since this case represents this Court's first in-depth examination of the Second Amendment, one should not expect it to clarify the entire field . . . And there will be time enough to expound upon the historical justifications for the exceptions we have mentioned if and when those exceptions come before us.

H   In sum, we hold that the District's ban on handgun possession in the home violates the Second Amendment, as does its prohibition against rendering any lawful firearm in the home operable for the purpose of immediate self-defense. Assuming that Heller is not disqualified from the exercise of Second Amendment rights, the District must permit him to register his handgun and must issue him a license to carry it in the home.

* * *

We are aware of the problem of handgun violence in this country, and we take seriously the concerns raised by the many *amici* who believe that prohibition of handgun ownership is a solution. The Constitution leaves the District of Columbia a variety of tools for combating that problem, including some measures regulating handguns. But the enshrinement of constitutional rights necessarily takes certain policy choices off the table. These include the absolute prohibition of handguns held and used for self-defense in the home. Undoubtedly some think that the Second Amendment is outmoded in a society where our standing army is the pride of our Nation, where well-trained police forces provide personal security, and where gun violence is a serious problem. That is perhaps debatable, but what is not debatable is that it is not the role of this Court to pronounce the Second Amendment extinct.

. . .

Justice STEVENS, with whom Justice SOUTER, Justice GINSBURG, and Justice BREYER join, dissenting.

The question presented by this case is not whether the Second Amendment protects a "collective right" or an "individual right." Surely it protects a right that can be enforced by individuals. But a conclusion that the Second

Amendment protects an individual right does not tell us anything about the scope of that right.

Guns are used to hunt, for self-defense, to commit crimes, for sporting activities, and to perform military duties. The Second Amendment plainly does not protect the right to use a gun to rob a bank; it is equally clear that it *does* encompass the right to use weapons for certain military purposes. Whether it also protects the right to possess and use guns for nonmilitary purposes like hunting and personal self-defense is the question presented by this case. The text of the Amendment, its history, and our decision in *United States v. Miller,* 307 U.S. 174 (1939), provide a clear answer to that question.

The Second Amendment was adopted to protect the right of the people of each of the several States to maintain a well-regulated militia. It was a response to concerns raised during the ratification of the Constitution that the power of Congress to disarm the state militias and create a national standing army posed an intolerable threat to the sovereignty of the several States. Neither the text of the Amendment nor the arguments advanced by its proponents evidenced the slightest interest in limiting any legislature's authority to regulate private civilian uses of firearms. Specifically, there is no indication that the Framers of the Amendment intended to enshrine the common-law right of self-defense in the Constitution.

In 1934, Congress enacted the National Firearms Act, the first major federal firearms law. Upholding a conviction under that Act, this Court held that, "[i]n the absence of any evidence tending to show that possession or use of a 'shotgun having a barrel of less than eighteen inches in length' at this time has some reasonable relationship to the preservation or efficiency of a well regulated militia, we cannot say that the Second Amendment guarantees the right to keep and bear such an instrument." *Miller.* The view of the Amendment we took in *Miller*—that it protects the right to keep and bear arms for certain military purposes, but that it does not curtail the Legislature's power to regulate the nonmilitary use and ownership of weapons—is both the most natural reading of the Amendment's text and the interpretation most faithful to the history of its adoption.

Since our decision in *Miller,* hundreds of judges have relied on the view of the Amendment we endorsed there; we ourselves affirmed it in 1980. See *Lewis v. United States,* 445 U.S. 55, 65-66, n. 8 (1980). No new evidence has surfaced since 1980 supporting the view that the Amendment was intended to curtail the power of Congress to regulate civilian use or misuse of weapons. Indeed, a review of the drafting history of the Amendment demonstrates that its Framers *rejected* proposals that would have broadened its coverage to include such uses.

The opinion the Court announces today fails to identify any new evidence supporting the view that the Amendment was intended to limit the power of Congress to regulate civilian uses of weapons. . . .

Even if the textual and historical arguments on both sides of the issue were evenly balanced, respect for the well-settled views of all of our predecessors on this Court, and for the rule of law itself would prevent most jurists from endorsing such a dramatic upheaval in the law. . . .

I

[T]he preamble to the Second Amendment ["A well regulated Militia, being necessary to the security of a free State"] makes three important points. It identifies the preservation of the militia as the Amendment's purpose; it explains that the militia is necessary to the security of a free State; and it recognizes that the militia must be "well regulated." In all three respects it is comparable to provisions in several State Declarations of Rights that were adopted roughly contemporaneously with the Declaration of Independence. Those state provisions highlight the importance members of the founding generation attached to the maintenance of state militias; they also underscore the profound fear shared by many in that era of the dangers posed by standing armies. While the need for state militias has not been a matter of significant public interest for almost two centuries, that fact should not obscure the contemporary concerns that animated the Framers.

The parallels between the Second Amendment and these state declarations, and the Second Amendment's omission of any statement of purpose related to the right to use firearms for hunting or personal self-defense, is especially striking in light of the fact that the Declarations of Rights of Pennsylvania and Vermont *did* expressly protect such civilian uses at the time. Article XIII of Pennsylvania's 1776 Declaration of Rights announced that "the people have a right to bear arms for the defence *of themselves* and the state," (emphasis added); §43 of the Declaration assured that "the inhabitants of this state shall have the liberty to fowl and hunt in seasonable times on the lands they hold, and on all other lands therein not inclosed," *id.,* at 274. And Article XV of the 1777 Vermont Declaration of Rights guaranteed "[t]hat the people have a right to bear arms for the defence *of themselves* and the State" (emphasis added). The contrast between those two declarations and the Second Amendment reinforces the clear statement of purpose announced in the Amendment's preamble. It confirms that the Framers' single-minded focus in crafting the constitutional guarantee "to keep and bear arms" was on military uses of firearms, which they viewed in the context of service in state militias.

The preamble thus both sets forth the object of the Amendment and informs the meaning of the remainder of its text. Such text should not be treated as mere surplusage, for "[i]t cannot be presumed that any clause in the constitution is intended to be without effect." *Marbury v. Madison,* 1 Cranch 137, 174 (1803).

[W]hile the Court makes the novel suggestion that it need only find some "logical connection" between the preamble and the operative provision, it does acknowledge that a prefatory clause may resolve an ambiguity in the text. Without identifying any language in the text that even mentions civilian uses of firearms, the Court proceeds to "find" its preferred reading in what is at best an ambiguous text, and then concludes that its reading is not foreclosed by the preamble. Perhaps the Court's approach to the text is acceptable advocacy, but it is surely an unusual approach for judges to follow. . . .

The centerpiece of the Court's textual argument is its insistence that the words "the people" as used in the Second Amendment must have the same meaning, and protect the same class of individuals, as when they are used in the First and Fourth Amendments. According to the Court, in all three provisions— as well as the Constitution's preamble, section 2 of Article I, and the Tenth Amendment—the term unambiguously refers to all members of the political community, not an unspecified subset. But the Court *itself* reads the Second Amendment to protect a "subset" significantly narrower than the class of persons protected by the First and Fourth Amendments; when it finally drills down on the substantive meaning of the Second Amendment, the Court limits the protected class to "law-abiding, responsible citizens" But the class of persons protected by the First and Fourth Amendments is *not* so limited; for even felons (and presumably irresponsible citizens as well) may invoke the protections of those constitutional provisions. The Court offers no way to harmonize its conflicting pronouncements.

The Court also overlooks the significance of the way the Framers used the phrase "the people" in these constitutional provisions. In the First Amendment, no words define the class of individuals entitled to speak, to publish, or to worship; in that Amendment it is only the right peaceably to assemble, and to petition the Government for a redress of grievances, that is described as a right of "the people" These rights contemplate collective action. While the right peaceably to assemble protects the individual rights of those persons participating in the assembly, its concern is with action engaged in by members of a group, rather than any single individual. Likewise, although the act of petitioning the Government is a right that can be exercised by individuals, it is primarily collective in nature. For if they are to be effective, petitions must involve groups of individuals acting in concert.

Similarly, the words "the people" in the Second Amendment refer back to the object announced in the Amendment's preamble. They remind us that it is the collective action of individuals having a duty to serve in the militia that the text directly protects and, perhaps more importantly, that the ultimate purpose of the Amendment was to protect the States' share of the divided sovereignty created by the Constitution.

As used in the Fourth Amendment, "the people" describes the class of persons protected from unreasonable searches and seizures by Government officials. It is true that the Fourth Amendment describes a right that need not be exercised in any collective sense. But that observation does not settle the meaning of the phrase "the people" when used in the Second Amendment. For, as we have seen, the phrase means something quite different in the Petition and Assembly Clauses of the First Amendment. Although the abstract definition of the phrase "the people" could carry the same meaning in the Second Amendment as in the Fourth Amendment, the preamble of the Second Amendment suggests that the uses of the phrase in the First and Second Amendments are the same in referring to a collective activity. By way of contrast, the Fourth Amendment describes a right *against* governmental interference rather than an affirmative right *to* engage in protected conduct, and so refers to a right to protect a purely individual interest. As used in the Second Amendment, the words "the people" do not enlarge the right to keep and bear arms to encompass use or ownership of weapons outside the context of service in a well-regulated militia.

[The words "To keep and bear Arms"] describe a unitary right: to possess arms if needed for military purposes and to use them in conjunction with military activities. [T]he Court does not read that phrase to create a right to possess arms for "lawful, private purposes." Instead, the Court limits the Amendment's protection to the right "to possess and carry weapons in case of confrontation." No party or *amicus* urged this interpretation; the Court appears to have fashioned it out of whole cloth. But . . . the Amendment's text *does* justify a different limitation: the "right to keep and bear arms" protects only a right to possess and use firearms in connection with service in a state-organized militia.

The term "bear arms" is a familiar idiom; when used unadorned by any additional words, its meaning is "to serve as a soldier, do military service, fight." It is derived from the Latin *arma ferre,* which, translated literally, means "to bear *[ferre]* war equipment *[arma]*." . . . Had the Framers wished to expand the meaning of the phrase "bear arms" to encompass civilian possession and use, they could have done so by the addition of phrases such as "for the defense of themselves," as was done in the Pennsylvania and Vermont Declarations of Rights. The *unmodified* use of "bear arms," by contrast, refers most naturally to a military purpose, as evidenced by its use in literally dozens of contemporary texts. The absence of any reference to civilian uses of weapons tailors the text of the Amendment to the purpose identified in its preamble. But when discussing these words, the Court simply ignores the preamble.

[T]he Amendment's use of the term "keep" in no way contradicts the military meaning conveyed by the phrase "bear arms" and the Amendment's preamble. To the contrary, a number of state militia laws in effect at the time of the Second Amendment's drafting used the term "keep" to describe the requirement that militia members store their arms at their homes, ready to be used for service when necessary. The Virginia military law, for example, ordered that "every one of the said officers, non-commissioned officers, and privates, shall constantly *keep* the aforesaid arms, accoutrements, and ammunition, ready to be produced whenever called for by his commanding officer." Act for Regulating and Disciplining the Militia, 1785 Va. Acts ch. 1, §3, p. 2 (emphasis added). "[K]eep and bear arms" thus perfectly describes the responsibilities of a framing-era militia member.

This reading is confirmed by the fact that the clause protects only one right, rather than two. It does not describe a right "to keep arms" and a separate right "to bear arms." Rather, the single right that it does describe is both a duty and a right to have arms available and ready for military service, and to use them for military purposes when necessary. Different language surely would have been used to protect nonmilitary use and possession of weapons from regulation if such an intent had played any role in the drafting of the Amendment.

* * *

When each word in the text is given full effect, the Amendment is most naturally read to secure to the people a right to use and possess arms <u>in conjunction with service in a well-regulated militia</u>. So far as appears, no more than that was contemplated by its drafters or is encompassed within its terms. Even if the meaning of the text were genuinely susceptible to more than one interpretation, the burden would remain on those advocating a departure from the purpose identified in the preamble and from settled law to come forward with persuasive new arguments or evidence. The textual analysis offered by respondent and embraced by the Court falls far short of sustaining that heavy burden. . . . Indeed, not a word in the constitutional text even arguably supports the Court's overwrought and novel description of the Second Amendment as "elevat[ing] above all other interests" the right of law-abiding, responsible citizens to use arms in defense of hearth and home.

II

The proper allocation of military power in the new Nation was an issue of central concern for the Framers. The compromises they ultimately reached, reflected in Article I's Militia Clauses and the Second Amendment, represent quintessential examples of the Framers' "splitting the atom of sovereignty."

Two themes relevant to our current interpretive task ran through the debates on the original Constitution. On the one hand, there was a widespread fear that a national standing Army posed an intolerable threat to individual liberty and to the sovereignty of the separate States. . . . On the other hand, the Framers recognized the dangers inherent in relying on inadequately trained militia members "as the primary means of providing for the common defense"; during the Revolutionary War, "[t]his force, though armed, was largely untrained, and its deficiencies were the subject of bitter complaint." In order to respond to those twin concerns, a compromise was reached: Congress would be authorized to raise and support a national Army and Navy, and also to organize, arm, discipline, and provide for the calling forth of "the Militia." U.S. Const., Art. I, §8, cls. 12-16. The President, at the same time, was empowered as the "Commander in Chief of the Army and Navy of the United States, and of the Militia of the several States, when called into the actual Service of the United States." Art. II, §2. But, with respect to the militia, a significant reservation was made to the States: Although Congress would have the power to call forth, organize, arm, and discipline the militia, as well as to govern "such Part of them as may be employed in the Service of the United States," the States respectively would retain the right to appoint the officers and to train the militia in accordance with the discipline prescribed by Congress. Art. I, §8, cl. 16.

But the original Constitution's retention of the militia and its creation of divided authority over that body did not prove sufficient to allay fears about the dangers posed by a standing army. For it was perceived by some that Article I contained a significant gap: While it empowered Congress to organize, arm, and discipline the militia, it did not prevent Congress from providing for the militia's *dis*armament. As George Mason argued during the debates in Virginia on the ratification of the original Constitution:

> "The militia may be here destroyed by that method which has been practiced in other parts of the world before; that is, by rendering them useless—by disarming them. Under various pretences, Congress may neglect to provide for arming and disciplining the militia; and the state governments cannot do it, for Congress has the exclusive right to arm them."

This sentiment was echoed at a number of state ratification conventions; indeed, it was one of the primary objections to the original Constitution voiced by its opponents. The Anti-Federalists were ultimately unsuccessful in persuading state ratification conventions to condition their approval of the Constitution upon the eventual inclusion of any particular amendment. But a number of States did propose to the first Federal Congress amendments reflecting a desire to ensure that the institution of the militia would remain protected under the new Government. The proposed amendments sent by the States of Virginia, North Carolina, and New York focused on the importance of preserving the state militias and reiterated the dangers posed by standing armies. New Hampshire sent a proposal that differed significantly from the others; while also invoking the dangers of a standing army, it suggested that the Constitution should more broadly protect the use and possession of weapons, without tying such a guarantee expressly to the maintenance of the militia. The States of Maryland, Pennsylvania, and Massachusetts sent no relevant proposed amendments to Congress, but in each of those States a minority of the delegates advocated related amendments. While the Maryland minority proposals were exclusively concerned with standing armies and conscientious objectors, the unsuccessful proposals in both Massachusetts and Pennsylvania would have protected a more broadly worded right, less clearly tied to service in a state militia. Faced with all of these options, it is telling that James Madison chose to craft the Second Amendment as he did. . . .

Madison, charged with the task of assembling the proposals for amendments sent by the ratifying States, was the principal draftsman of the Second Amendment. He had before him, or at the very least would have been aware of, all of these proposed formulations. In addition, Madison had been a member, some years earlier, of the committee tasked with drafting the Virginia Declaration of Rights. That committee considered a proposal by Thomas Jefferson that would have included within the Virginia Declaration the following language: "No freeman shall ever be debarred the use of arms [within his own lands or tenements]." But the committee rejected that language, adopting instead the provision drafted by George Mason[, which focused on defense of the state, civilian control of the military and avoidance of standing armies in time of peace].

With all of these sources upon which to draw, it is strikingly significant that Madison's first draft omitted any mention of nonmilitary use or possession of weapons. Rather, his original draft repeated the essence of the two proposed amendments sent by Virginia, combining the substance of the two provisions succinctly into one, which read: "The right of the people to keep and bear arms shall not be infringed; a well armed, and well regulated militia being the best security of a free country; but no person religiously scrupulous of bearing arms, shall be compelled to render military service in person."

Madison's decision to model the Second Amendment on the distinctly military Virginia proposal is therefore revealing, since it is clear that he considered and rejected formulations that would have unambiguously protected civilian uses of firearms. When Madison prepared his first draft, and when that draft was debated and modified, it is reasonable to assume that all participants in the drafting process were fully aware of the other formulations that would have protected civilian use and possession of weapons and that their choice to craft the Amendment as they did represented a rejection of those alternative formulations.

Madison's initial inclusion of an exemption for conscientious objectors sheds revelatory light on the purpose of the Amendment. It confirms an intent to describe a duty as well as a right, and it unequivocally identifies the military character of both. The objections voiced to the conscientious-objector clause only confirm the central meaning of the text. Although records of the debate in the Senate, which is where the conscientious-objector clause was removed, do not survive, the arguments raised in the House illuminate the perceived problems with the clause: Specifically, there was concern that Congress "can declare who are those religiously scrupulous, and prevent them from bearing arms." The ultimate removal of the clause, therefore, only serves to confirm the purpose of the Amendment—to protect against congressional disarmament, by whatever means, of the States' militias.

The Court also contends that because "Quakers opposed the use of arms not just for militia service, but for any violent purpose whatsoever," the inclusion of a conscientious-objector clause in the original draft of the Amendment does not support the conclusion that the phrase "bear arms" was military in meaning. But that claim cannot be squared with the record. [B]oth Virginia and North Carolina included the following language: "That any person religiously scrupulous of bearing arms ought to be exempted, upon payment of an equivalent *to employ another to bear arms in his stead*" (emphasis added). There is no plausible argument that the use of "bear arms" in those provisions was not unequivocally and exclusively military: The State simply does not compel its citizens to carry arms for the purpose of private "confrontation," or for self-defense.

The history of the adoption of the Amendment thus describes an overriding concern about the potential threat to state sovereignty that a federal standing army would pose, and a desire to protect the States' militias as the means by which to guard against that danger. But state militias could not effectively check the prospect of a federal standing army so long as Congress retained the power to disarm them, and so a guarantee against such disarmament was needed. As we explained in *Miller:* "With obvious purpose to assure the continuation and render possible the effectiveness of such forces the declaration and guarantee of the Second Amendment were made. It must be interpreted and applied with that end in view." The evidence plainly refutes the claim that the Amendment was motivated by the Framers' fears that Congress might act to regulate any civilian uses of weapons. And even if the historical record were genuinely ambiguous, the burden would remain on the parties advocating a change in the law to introduce facts or arguments "'newly ascertained'"; the Court is unable to identify any such facts or arguments.

III

Although it gives short shrift to the drafting history of the Second Amendment, the Court dwells at length on four other sources: the 17th-century English Bill of Rights; Blackstone's Commentaries on the Laws of England; postenactment commentary on the Second Amendment; and post-Civil War legislative history. All of these sources shed only indirect light on the question before us, and in any event offer little support for the Court's conclusion. . . .

The Court suggests that by the post-Civil War period, the Second Amendment was understood to secure a right to firearm use and ownership for purely private purposes like personal self-defense. While it is true that some of the legislative history on which the Court relies supports that contention, such sources are entitled to limited, if any, weight. All of the statements the Court cites were made long after the framing of the Amendment and cannot possibly supply any insight into the intent of the Framers; and all were made during pitched political debates, so that they are better characterized as advocacy than good-faith attempts at constitutional interpretation. . . .

IV

The brilliance of the debates that resulted in the Second Amendment faded into oblivion during the ensuing years, for the concerns about Article I's Militia Clauses that generated such pitched debate during the ratification process and led to the adoption of the Second Amendment were short lived.

In 1792, the year after the Amendment was ratified, Congress passed a statute that purported to establish "an Uniform Militia throughout the United States." 1 Stat. 271. The statute commanded every able-bodied white male citizen between the ages of 18 and 45 to be enrolled therein and to "provide himself with a good musket or firelock" and other specified weaponry. The statute is significant, for it confirmed the way those in the founding generation viewed firearm ownership: as a duty linked to military service. The statute they enacted, however, "was virtually ignored for more than a century," and was finally repealed in 1901. . . . In 1901 the President revitalized the militia by creating "'the National Guard of the several States'"; meanwhile, the dominant understanding of the Second Amendment's inapplicability to private gun ownership continued well into the 20th century. The first two federal laws directly restricting civilian use and possession of firearms—the 1927 Act prohibiting mail delivery of "pistols, revolvers, and other firearms capable of being concealed on the person," and the 1934 Act prohibiting the possession of sawed-off shotguns and machine guns—were enacted over minor Second Amendment objections dismissed by the vast majority of the legislators who participated in the debates. Members of Congress clashed over the wisdom and efficacy of such laws as crime-control measures. But since the statutes did not infringe upon the military use or possession of weapons, for most legislators they did not even raise the specter of possible conflict with the Second Amendment.

Thus, for most of our history, the invalidity of Second-Amendment-based objections to firearms regulations has been well settled and uncontroversial. Indeed, the Second Amendment was not even mentioned in either full House of Congress during the legislative proceedings that led to the passage of the 1934 Act. Yet enforcement of that law produced the judicial decision that confirmed the status of the Amendment as limited in reach to military usage. After reviewing many of the same sources that are discussed at greater length by the Court today, the *Miller* Court unanimously concluded that the Second Amendment did not apply to the possession of a firearm that did not have "some reasonable relationship to the preservation or efficiency of a well regulated militia."

The key to that decision did not, as the Court belatedly suggests, turn on the difference between muskets and sawed-off shotguns; it turned, rather, on the basic difference between the military and nonmilitary use and possession of guns. Indeed, if the Second Amendment were not limited in its coverage to military uses of weapons, why should the Court in *Miller* have suggested that some weapons but not others were eligible for Second Amendment protection? If use for self-defense were the relevant standard, why did the Court not inquire into the suitability of a particular weapon for self-defense purposes?. . . .

V

The Court concludes its opinion by declaring that it is not the proper role of this Court to change the meaning of rights "enshrine[d]" in the Constitution. But the right the Court announces was not "enshrined" in the Second Amendment by the Framers; it is the product of today's law-changing decision. The majority's exegesis has utterly failed to establish that as a matter of text or history, "the right of law-abiding, responsible citizens to use arms in defense of hearth and home" is "elevate[d] above all other interests" by the Second Amendment.

Until today, it has been understood that legislatures may regulate the civilian use and misuse of firearms so long as they do not interfere with the preservation of a well-regulated militia. The Court's announcement of a new constitutional right to own and use firearms for private purposes upsets that settled understanding, but leaves for future cases the formidable task of defining the scope of permissible regulations. Today judicial craftsmen have confidently asserted that a policy choice that denies a "law-abiding, responsible citize[n]" the right to keep and use weapons in the home for self-defense is "off the table." Given the presumption that most citizens are law abiding, and the reality that the need to defend oneself may suddenly arise in a host of locations outside the home, I fear that the District's policy choice may well be just the first of an unknown number of dominoes to be knocked off the table.

I do not know whether today's decision will increase the labor of federal judges to the "breaking point" envisioned by Justice Cardozo, but it will surely give rise to a far more active judicial role in making vitally important national policy decisions than was envisioned at any time in the 18th, 19th, or 20th centuries.

The Court properly disclaims any interest in evaluating the wisdom of the specific policy choice challenged in this case, but it fails to pay heed to a far more important policy choice—the choice made by the Framers themselves. The Court would have us believe that over 200 years ago, the Framers made a choice to limit the tools available to elected officials wishing to regulate civilian uses of weapons, and to authorize this Court to use the common-law process of case-by-case judicial lawmaking to define the contours of acceptable gun control policy. Absent compelling evidence that is nowhere to be found in the Court's opinion, I could not possibly conclude that the Framers made such a choice.

For these reasons, I respectfully dissent.

––––––

Justice BREYER, with whom Justice STEVENS, Justice SOUTER, and Justice GINSBURG join, dissenting.

I agree with Justice Stevens that the Second Amendment protects militia-related, not self-defense-related, interests], and I join his opinion. [But] the District's law is consistent with the Second Amendment even if that Amendment is interpreted as protecting a wholly separate interest in individual self-defense. That is so because the District's regulation, which focuses upon the presence of handguns in high-crime urban areas, represents a permissible legislative response to a serious, indeed life-threatening, problem. . . .

II

[Even if] the Second Amendment embodies a general concern about self-defense, [it does not] contain[] a specific untouchable right to keep guns in the house to shoot burglars. . . .

To the contrary, colonial history itself offers important examples of the kinds of gun regulation that citizens would then have thought compatible with the "right to keep and bear arms." . . . [T]hose examples include substantial regulation of firearms in urban areas, including regulations that imposed obstacles to the use of firearms for the protection of the home.

Boston, Philadelphia, and New York City, the three largest cities in America during that period, all restricted the firing of guns within city limits to at least some degree. . . . Furthermore, several towns and cities (including Philadelphia, New York, and Boston) regulated, for fire-safety reasons, the storage of gunpowder, a necessary component of an operational firearm. . . . Even assuming, as the majority does, that this law included an implicit self-defense exception, it would nevertheless have prevented a homeowner from keeping in his home a gun that he could immediately pick up and use against an intruder. Rather, the homeowner would have had to get the gunpowder and load it into the gun, an operation that would have taken a fair amount of time to perform.

Moreover, the law would, as a practical matter, have prohibited the carrying of loaded firearms anywhere in the city, unless the carrier had no plans to enter any building or was willing to unload or discard his weapons before going inside. . . .

This historical evidence demonstrates that a self-defense assumption is the *beginning,* rather than the *end,* of any constitutional inquiry. That the District law impacts self-defense merely raises *questions* about the law's constitutionality. . . .

III

[W]hat kind of constitutional standard should the court use? How high a protective hurdle does the Amendment erect? . . . The majority is wrong when it says that the District's law is unconstitutional "[u]nder any of the standards of scrutiny that we have applied to enumerated constitutional rights." . . . It certainly would not be unconstitutional under, for example, a "rational basis" standard . . . The law at issue here, which in part seeks to prevent gun-related accidents, at least bears a "rational relationship" to that "legitimate" life-saving objective. . . .

Respondent proposes that the Court adopt a "strict scrutiny" test, which would require reviewing with care each gun law to determine whether it is "narrowly tailored to achieve a compelling governmental interest." But the majority implicitly, and appropriately, rejects that suggestion by broadly approving a set of laws—prohibitions on concealed weapons, forfeiture by criminals of the Second Amendment right, prohibitions on firearms in certain locales, and governmental regulation of commercial firearm sales—whose constitutionality under a strict scrutiny standard would be far from clear.

Indeed, adoption of a true strict-scrutiny standard for evaluating gun regulations would be impossible. That is because almost every gun-control regulation will seek to advance (as the one here does) a "primary concern of every government—a concern for the safety and indeed the lives of its citizens." [In other cases] [t]he Court has deemed that interest, as well as "the Government's general interest in preventing crime," to be "compelling," and the Court has in a wide variety of constitutional contexts found such public-safety concerns sufficiently forceful to justify restrictions on individual liberties, see *e.g., Brandenburg v. Ohio,* 395 U.S. 444 (1969) *(per curiam)* (First Amendment free speech rights); *Sherbert v. Verner,* 374 U.S. 398 (1963) (First Amendment religious rights); *Brigham City v. Stuart,* 547 U.S. 398 (2006) (Fourth Amendment protection of the home); *New York v. Quarles,* 467 U.S. 649 (1984) (Fifth Amendment rights under *Miranda v. Arizona,* 384 U.S. 436 (1966)); [*United States v.*] *Salerno,* 481 U.S. 739 (1987) (Eighth Amendment bail rights). Thus, any attempt *in theory* to apply strict scrutiny to gun regulations will *in practice* turn into an interest-balancing inquiry, with the interests protected by the Second Amendment on one side and the governmental public-safety concerns on the other, the only question being whether the regulation at issue impermissibly burdens the former in the course of advancing the latter.

I would simply adopt such an interest-balancing inquiry explicitly. [R]eview of gun-control regulation is not a context in which a court should effectively presume either constitutionality (as in rational-basis review) or unconstitutionality (as in strict scrutiny). Rather, "where a law significantly implicates competing constitutionally protected interests in complex ways," the Court generally asks whether the statute burdens a protected interest in a way or to an extent that is out of proportion to the statute's salutary effects upon other important governmental interests. Any answer would take account both of the statute's effects upon the competing interests and the existence of any clearly superior less restrictive alternative. Contrary to the majority's unsupported suggestion that this sort of "proportionality" approach is unprecedented, the Court has applied it in various constitutional contexts, including election-law cases, speech cases, and due process cases.

In applying this kind of standard the Court normally defers to a legislature's empirical judgment in matters where a legislature is likely to have greater expertise and greater institutional factfinding capacity. See *Turner Broadcasting System, Inc. v. FCC,* 520 U.S. 180 (1997). Nonetheless, a court, not a legislature, must make the ultimate constitutional conclusion, exercising its "independent judicial judgment" in light of the whole record to determine whether a law exceeds constitutional boundaries.

[E]xperience as much as logic has led the Court to decide that in one area of constitutional law or another the interests are likely to prove stronger on one side of a typical constitutional case than on the other. Here, we have little prior experience. Courts that *do* have experience in these matters have uniformly taken an approach that treats empirically-based legislative judgment with a degree of deference. See Winkler, Scrutinizing the Second Amendment, 105 Mich. L. Rev. 683 (2007) (describing hundreds of gun-law decisions issued in the last half-century by Supreme Courts in 42 States, which courts with "surprisingly little variation," have adopted a standard more deferential than strict scrutiny). . . .

IV

The present suit involves challenges to three separate District firearm restrictions. . . . Because the District assures us that respondent could obtain . . . a license [for a handgun] so long as he meets the statutory eligibility criteria, and because respondent concedes that those criteria are facially constitutional, I, like the majority, see no need to address the constitutionality of the licensing requirement.

[The District also] requires that the lawful owner of a firearm keep his weapon "unloaded and disassembled or bound by a trigger lock or similar device" unless it is kept at his place of business or being used for lawful recreational purposes. The only dispute regarding this provision appears to be ⌐ whether the Constitution requires an exception that would allow someone to render a firearm operational when necessary for self-defense (*i.e.,* that the firearm may be operated under circumstances where the common law would normally permit a self-defense justification in defense against a criminal charge). The District concedes that such an exception exists. This Court has final authority (albeit not often used) to definitively interpret District law, which is, after all, simply a species of federal law. And because I see nothing in the District law that would *preclude* the existence of a background common-law self-defense exception, I would avoid the constitutional question by interpreting the statute to include it.

I am puzzled by the majority's unwillingness to adopt a similar approach. It ⌐ readily reads unspoken self-defense exceptions into every colonial law, but it refuses to accept the District's concession that this law has one. The one District case it cites to support that refusal [does not] say that the statute precludes a self-defense exception of the sort that I have just described. And even if it did, we are not bound by a lower court's interpretation of federal law.

The third District restriction prohibits (in most cases) the registration of a handgun within the District. Because registration is a prerequisite to firearm possession, the effect of this provision is generally to prevent people in the District from possessing handguns. . . . No one doubts the constitutional importance of the statute's basic objective, saving lives. But there is considerable debate about whether the District's statute helps to achieve that objective. . . .

1

First, consider the facts as the legislature saw them when it adopted the District statute. [T]he local council committee that recommended its adoption . . . concluded, on the basis of "extensive public hearings" and "lengthy research," that "[t]he easy availability of firearms in the United States has been a major factor contributing to the drastic increase in gun-related violence and crime over the past 40 years." . . .

The committee informed the Council that guns were "responsible for 69 deaths in this country each day," for a total of "[a]pproximately 25,000 gun-deaths . . . each year," along with an additional 200,000 gun-related injuries. Three thousand of these deaths, the report stated, were accidental. A quarter of the victims in those accidental deaths were children under the age of 14. And according to the committee, [f]or every intruder stopped by a homeowner with a firearm, there are 4 gun-related accidents within the home.

In respect to local crime, the committee observed that there were 285 murders in the District during 1974—a record number. The committee also stated that, "[c]ontrary to popular opinion on the subject, firearms are more frequently involved in deaths and violence among relatives and friends than in premeditated criminal activities." Citing an article from the American Journal of Psychiatry, the committee reported that "[m]ost murders are committed by previously law-abiding citizens, in situations where spontaneous violence is generated by anger, passion or intoxication, and where the killer and victim are acquainted." Twenty-five percent of these murders, "the committee informed the Council," occur within families.

The committee report furthermore presented statistics strongly correlating handguns with crime. Of the 285 murders in the District in 1974, 155 were committed with handguns. This did not appear to be an aberration, as the report revealed that "handguns [had been] used in roughly 54% of all murders" (and 87% of murders of law enforcement officers) nationwide over the preceding several years. Nor were handguns only linked to murders, as statistics showed that they were used in roughly 60% of robberies and 26% of assaults. "A crime committed with a pistol," the committee reported, "is 7 times more likely to be lethal than a crime committed with any other weapon." The committee furthermore presented statistics regarding the availability of handguns in the United States, and noted that they had "become easy for juveniles to obtain," even despite then-current District laws prohibiting juveniles from possessing them.

[I]n the absence of adequate federal gun legislation, the committee concluded, it "becomes necessary for local governments to act to protect their citizens, and certainly the District of Columbia as the only totally urban state-like jurisdiction should be strong in its approach." It recommended that the Council adopt a restriction on handgun registration to reflect "a legislative decision that, at this point in time and due to the gun-control tragedies and horrors enumerated previously" in the committee report, "pistols . . . are no longer justified in this jurisdiction."

The District's special focus on handguns thus reflects the fact that the committee report found them to have a particularly strong link to undesirable activities in the District's exclusively urban environment. The District did not seek to prohibit possession of other sorts of weapons deemed more suitable for an "urban area." Indeed, an original draft of the bill, and the original committee recommendations, had sought to prohibit registration of shotguns as well as handguns, but the Council as a whole decided to narrow the prohibition.

2

Next, consider the facts as a court must consider them looking at the matter as of today. Petitioners, and their *amici,* have presented us with more recent statistics that tell much the same story that the committee report told 30 years ago. At the least, they present nothing that would permit us to second-guess the Council in respect to the numbers of gun crimes, injuries, and deaths, or the role of handguns.

From 1993 to 1997, there were 180,533 firearm-related deaths in the United States, an average of over 36,000 per year. Fifty-one percent were suicides, 44% were homicides, 1% were legal interventions, 3% were unintentional accidents, and 1% were of undetermined causes. Over that same period there were an additional 411,800 nonfatal firearm-related injuries treated in U.S. hospitals, an average of over 82,000 per year. Of these, 62% resulted from assaults, 17% were unintentional, 6% were suicide attempts, 1% were legal interventions, and 13% were of unknown causes.

The statistics are particularly striking in respect to children and adolescents. In over one in every eight firearm-related deaths in 1997, the victim was someone under the age of 20. Firearm-related deaths account for 22.5% of all injury deaths between the ages of 1 and 19. More male teenagers die from firearms than from all natural causes combined. Persons under 25 accounted for 47% of hospital-treated firearm injuries between June 1, 1992 and May 31, 1993.

Handguns are involved in a majority of firearm deaths and injuries in the United States. From 1993 to 1997, 81% of firearm-homicide victims were killed by handgun. In the same period, for the 41% of firearm injuries for which the weapon type is known, 82% of them were from handguns. And among children under the age of 20, handguns account for approximately 70% of all unintentional firearm-related injuries and deaths. In particular, 70% of all firearm-related teenage suicides in 1996 involved a handgun.

Handguns also appear to be a very popular weapon among criminals. In a 1997 survey of inmates who were armed during the crime for which they were incarcerated, 83.2% of state inmates and 86.7% of federal inmates said that they were armed with a handgun. And handguns are not only popular tools for crime, but popular objects of it as well: the FBI received on average over 274,000 reports of stolen guns for each year between 1985 and 1994, and almost 60% of stolen guns are handguns. Department of Justice studies have concluded that stolen handguns in particular are an important source of weapons for both adult and juvenile offenders.

Statistics further suggest that urban areas, such as the District, have different experiences with gun-related death, injury, and crime, than do less densely populated rural areas. A disproportionate amount of violent and property crimes occur in urban areas, and urban criminals are more likely than other offenders to use a firearm during the commission of a violent crime. Homicide appears to be a much greater issue in urban areas; from 1985 to 1993, for example, "half of all homicides occurred in 63 cities with 16% of the nation's population." One study concluded that although the overall rate of gun death between 1989 and 1999 was roughly the same in urban than rural areas, the urban homicide rate was three times as high; even after adjusting for other variables, it was still twice as high. And a study of firearm injuries to children and adolescents in Pennsylvania between 1987 and 2000 showed an injury rate in urban counties 10 times higher than in nonurban counties.

Finally, the linkage of handguns to firearms deaths and injuries appears to be much stronger in urban than in rural areas. "[S]tudies to date generally support the hypothesis that the greater number of rural gun deaths are from rifles or shotguns, whereas the greater number of urban gun deaths are from handguns." And the Pennsylvania study reached a similar conclusion with respect to firearm injuries—they are much more likely to be caused by handguns in urban areas than in rural areas.

3

Respondent and his many *amici* for the most part do not disagree about the *figures* set forth in the preceding subsection, but they do disagree strongly with the District's *predictive judgment* that a ban on handguns will help solve the crime and accident problems that those figures disclose. In particular, they disagree with the District Council's assessment that "freezing the pistol . . . population within the District," will reduce crime, accidents, and deaths related to guns. And they provide facts and figures designed to show that it has not done so in the past, and hence will not do so in the future.

First, they point out that, since the ban took effect, violent crime in the District has increased, not decreased. Indeed, a comparison with 49 other major cities reveals that the District's homicide rate is actually substantially *higher* relative to these other cities than it was before the handgun restriction went into effect. Respondent's *amici* report similar results in comparing the District's homicide rates during that period to that of the neighboring States of Maryland and Virginia (neither of which restricts handguns to the same degree), and to the homicide rate of the Nation as a whole.

Second, respondent's *amici* point to a statistical analysis that regresses murder rates against the presence or absence of strict gun laws in 20 European nations. That analysis concludes that strict gun laws are correlated with *more* murders, not fewer. They also cite domestic studies, based on data from various cities, States, and the Nation as a whole, suggesting that a reduction in the number of guns does not lead to a reduction in the amount of violent crime. They further argue that handgun bans do not reduce suicide rates, or rates of accidents, even those involving children.

Third, they point to evidence indicating that firearm ownership does have a beneficial self-defense effect. Based on a 1993 survey, the authors of one study estimated that there were 2.2-to-2.5 million defensive uses of guns (mostly brandishing, about a quarter involving the actual firing of a gun) annually. Another study estimated that for a period of 12 months ending in 1994, there were 503,481 incidents in which a burglar found himself confronted by an armed homeowner, and that in 497,646 (98.8%) of them, the intruder was successfully scared away. A third study suggests that gun-armed victims are substantially less likely than non-gun-armed victims to be injured in resisting robbery or assault. And additional evidence suggests that criminals are likely to be deterred from burglary and other crimes if they know the victim is likely to have a gun.

Fourth, respondent's *amici* argue that laws criminalizing gun possession are self-defeating, as evidence suggests that they will have the effect only of restricting law-abiding citizens, but not criminals, from acquiring guns. That effect, they argue, will be especially pronounced in the District, whose proximity to Virginia and Maryland will provide criminals with a steady supply of guns.

In the view of respondent's *amici,* this evidence shows that other remedies— such as *less* restriction on gun ownership, or liberal authorization of law-abiding citizens to carry concealed weapons—better fit the problem. They further suggest that at a minimum the District fails to show that its *remedy,* the gun ban, bears a reasonable relation to the crime and accident *problems* that the District seeks to solve.

These empirically based arguments may have proved strong enough to convince many legislatures, as a matter of legislative policy, not to adopt total handgun bans. But the question here is whether they are strong enough to destroy judicial confidence in the reasonableness of a legislature that rejects them. And that they are not. For one thing, they can lead us more deeply into the uncertainties that surround any effort to reduce crime, but they cannot prove either that handgun possession diminishes crime or that handgun bans are ineffective. The statistics do show a soaring District crime rate. And the District's crime rate went up after the District adopted its handgun ban. But, as students of elementary logic know, *after it* does not mean *because of it.* What would the District's crime rate have looked like without the ban? Higher? Lower? The same? Experts differ; and we, as judges, cannot say.

What about the fact that foreign nations with strict gun laws have higher crime rates? Which is the cause and which the effect? The proposition that strict gun laws *cause* crime is harder to accept than the proposition that strict gun laws in part grow out of the fact that a nation already has a higher crime rate. And we are then left with the same question as before: What would have happened to crime without the gun laws—a question that respondent and his *amici* do not convincingly answer.

Further, suppose that respondent's *amici* are right when they say that house-holders' possession of loaded handguns help to frighten away intruders. On that assumption, one must still ask whether that benefit is worth the potential death-related cost. And that is a question without a directly provable answer.

Finally, consider the claim of respondent's *amici* that handgun bans *cannot* work; there are simply too many illegal guns already in existence for a ban on legal guns to make a difference. In a word, they claim that, given the urban sea of pre-existing legal guns, criminals can readily find arms regardless. Nonetheless, a legislature might respond, we want to make an effort to try to dry up that urban sea, drop by drop. And none of the studies can show that effort is not worthwhile.

In a word, the studies to which respondent's *amici* point raise policy-related questions. They succeed in proving that the District's predictive judgments are controversial. But they do not by themselves show that those judgments are incorrect; nor do they demonstrate a consensus, academic or otherwise, support-ing that conclusion.

Thus, it is not surprising that the District and its *amici* support the District's handgun restriction with studies of their own. One in particular suggests that, statistically speaking, the District's law has indeed had positive life-saving effects. Others suggest that firearm restrictions as a general matter reduce homicides, suicides, and accidents in the home. Still others suggest that the defensive uses of handguns are not as great in number as respondent's *amici* claim.

Respondent and his *amici* reply to these responses; and in doing so, they seek to discredit as methodologically flawed the studies and evidence relied upon by the District. And, of course, the District's *amici* produce counter-rejoinders, referring to articles that defend their studies.

The upshot is a set of studies and counterstudies that, at most, could leave a judge uncertain about the proper policy conclusion. But from respondent's perspective any such uncertainty is not good enough. That is because legislators, not judges, have primary responsibility for drawing policy conclusions from empirical fact. And, given that constitutional allocation of decisionmaking responsibility, the empirical evidence presented here is sufficient to allow a judge to reach a firm *legal* conclusion.

In particular this Court, in First Amendment cases applying intermediate scrutiny, has said that our "sole obligation" in reviewing a legislature's "predictive judgments" is "to assure that, in formulating its judgments," the legislature "has drawn reasonable inferences based on substantial evidence." *Turner*. And judges, looking at the evidence before us, should agree that the District legislature's predictive judgments satisfy that legal standard. That is to say, the District's judgment, while open to question, is nevertheless supported by "substantial evidence."

There is no cause here to depart from the standard set forth in *Turner,* for the District's decision represents the kind of empirically based judgment that legislatures, not courts, are best suited to make. In fact, deference to legislative judgment seems particularly appropriate here, where the judgment has been made by a local legislature, with particular knowledge of local problems and insight into appropriate local solutions. Different localities may seek to solve similar problems in different ways, and a "city must be allowed a reasonable opportunity to experiment with solutions to admittedly serious problems." The Framers recognized that the most effective democracy occurs at local levels of government, where people with firsthand knowledge of local problems have more ready access to public officials responsible for dealing with them. *Garcia v. San Antonio Metropolitan Transit Authority,* 469 U.S. 528 (1985) (Powell, J., dissenting) (citing The Federalist No. 17 (A. Hamilton). We owe that democratic process some substantial weight in the constitutional calculus. . . .

B

I next assess the extent to which the District's law burdens the interests that the Second Amendment seeks to protect. Respondent and his *amici,* as well as the majority, suggest that those interests include: (1) the preservation of a "well regulated Militia"; (2) safeguarding the use of firearms for sporting purposes, *e.g.,* hunting and marksmanship; and (3) assuring the use of firearms for self-defense. . . .

1

The District's statute burdens the Amendment's first and primary objective [the preservation of a "well regulated Militia"] hardly at all. . . . [T]he present case has nothing to do with *actual* military service. I am aware of no indication that the District either now or in the recent past has called up its citizenry to serve in a militia, that it has any inkling of doing so anytime in the foreseeable future, or that this law must be construed to prevent the use of handguns during legitimate militia activities. Moreover, even if the District were to call up its militia, respondent would not be among the citizens whose service would be requested. The District does not consider him, at 66 years of age, to be a member of its militia. . . . [T]he District's law does not seriously affect military training interests. The law permits residents to engage in activities that will increase their familiarity with firearms. They may register (and thus possess in their homes) weapons other than handguns, such as rifles and shotguns. . . . And while the District law prevents citizens from training with handguns *within the District,* the District consists of only 61.4 square miles of urban area. The adjacent States do permit the use of handguns for target practice, and those States are only a brief subway ride away. . . .

The majority briefly suggests that the "right to keep and bear Arms" might encompass an interest in hunting. But in enacting the present provisions, the District sought "to take nothing away from sportsmen." [T]he District's law does not prohibit possession of rifles or shotguns. . . .

The District's law does prevent a resident from keeping a loaded handgun in his home. And it consequently makes it more difficult for the householder to use the handgun for self-defense in the home against intruders, such as burglars. As the Court of Appeals noted, statistics suggest that handguns are the most popular weapon for self defense. And there are some legitimate reasons why that would be the case: *Amici* suggest (with some empirical support) that handguns are easier to hold and control (particularly for persons with physical infirmities), easier to carry, easier to maneuver in enclosed spaces, and that a person using one will still have a hand free to dial 911. . . .

In weighing needs and burdens, we must take account of the possibility that ‒ there are reasonable, but less restrictive alternatives. Are there *other* potential measures that might similarly promote the same goals while imposing lesser restrictions? Here I see none.

The reason there is no clearly superior, less restrictive alternative to the District's handgun ban is that the ban's very objective is to reduce significantly ‒ the number of handguns in the District, say, for example, by allowing a law enforcement officer immediately to assume that *any* handgun he sees is an *illegal* handgun. And there is no plausible way to achieve that objective other than to ban the guns.

It does not help respondent's case to describe the District's objective more generally as an "effort to diminish the dangers associated with guns." That is because the very attributes that make handguns particularly useful for self-defense are also what make them particularly dangerous. That they are easy to hold and control means that they are easier for children to use. That they are maneuverable and permit a free hand likely contributes to the fact that they are by far the firearm of choice for crimes such as rape and robbery. That they are small and light makes them easy to steal, and concealable.

This symmetry suggests that any measure less restrictive in respect to the use of handguns for self-defense will, to that same extent, prove less effective in preventing the use of handguns for illicit purposes. If a resident has a handgun in the home that he can use for self-defense, then he has a handgun in the home that he can use to commit suicide or engage in acts of domestic violence. If it is indeed the case, as the District believes, that the number of guns contributes to the number of gun-related crimes, accidents, and deaths, then, although there may be less restrictive, *less effective* substitutes for an outright ban, there is no less restrictive *equivalent* of an outright ban.

Licensing restrictions would not similarly reduce the handgun population, and the District may reasonably fear that even if guns are initially restricted to law-abiding citizens, they might be stolen and thereby placed in the hands of criminals. Permitting certain types of handguns, but not others, would affect the commercial market for handguns, but not their availability. And requiring safety devices such as trigger locks, or imposing safe-storage requirements would interfere with any self-defense interest while simultaneously leaving operable weapons in the hands of owners (or others capable of acquiring the weapon and disabling the safety device) who might use them for domestic violence or other crimes.

The absence of equally effective alternatives to a complete prohibition finds support in the empirical fact that other States and urban centers prohibit particular types of weapons. Chicago has a law very similar to the District's, and many of its suburbs also ban handgun possession under most circumstances. Toledo bans certain types of handguns. And San Francisco in 2005 enacted by popular referendum a ban on most handgun possession by city residents; it has been precluded from enforcing that prohibition, however, by state-court decisions deeming it pre-empted by state law. (Indeed, the fact that as many as 41 States may pre-empt local gun regulation suggests that the absence of more regulation like the District's may perhaps have more to do with state law than with a lack of locally perceived need for them.

In addition, at least six States and Puerto Rico impose general bans on certain types of weapons, in particular assault weapons or semiautomatic weapons. And at least 14 municipalities do the same. These bans, too, suggest that there may be no substitute to an outright prohibition in cases where a governmental body has deemed a particular type of weapon especially dangerous.

D

The upshot is that the District's objectives are compelling; its predictive judgments as to its law's tendency to achieve those objectives are adequately supported; the law does impose a burden upon any self-defense interest that the

Amendment seeks to secure; and there is no clear less restrictive alternative. I turn now to the final portion of the "permissible regulation" question: Does the District's law *disproportionately* burden Amendment-protected interests? Several considerations, taken together, convince me that it does not.

First, the District law is tailored to the life-threatening problems it attempts to address. The law concerns one class of weapons, handguns, leaving residents free to possess shotguns and rifles, along with ammunition. The area that falls within its scope is totally urban. That urban area suffers from a serious handgun-fatality problem. The District's law directly aims at that compelling problem. And there is no less restrictive way to achieve the problem-related benefits that it seeks.

Second, the self-defense interest in maintaining loaded handguns in the home to shoot intruders is not the *primary* interest, but at most a subsidiary interest, that the Second Amendment seeks to serve. The Second Amendment's language, while speaking of a "Militia," says nothing of "self-defense." As Justice Stevens points out, the Second Amendment's drafting history shows that the language reflects the Framers' primary, if not exclusive, objective. And the majority itself says that "the threat that the new Federal Government would destroy the citizens' militia by taking away their arms was *the* reason that right . . . was codified in a written Constitution." (emphasis added). The *way* in which the Amendment's operative clause seeks to promote that interest—by protecting a right "to keep and bear Arms"—may *in fact* help further an interest in self-defense. But a factual connection falls far short of a primary objective. The Amendment itself tells us that militia preservation was first and foremost in the Framers' minds.

Further, any self-defense interest at the time of the Framing could not have focused exclusively upon urban-crime related dangers. Two hundred years ago, most Americans, many living on the frontier, would likely have thought of self-defense primarily in terms of outbreaks of fighting with Indian tribes, rebellions such as Shays' Rebellion, marauders, and crime-related dangers to travelers on the roads, on footpaths, or along waterways. Insofar as the Framers focused at all on the tiny fraction of the population living in large cities, they would have been aware that these city dwellers were subject to firearm restrictions that their rural counterparts were not. They are unlikely then to have thought of a right to keep loaded handguns in homes to confront intruders in urban settings as *central*. And the subsequent development of modern urban police departments, by diminishing the need to keep loaded guns nearby in case of intruders, would have moved any such right even further away from the heart of the amendment's more basic protective ends. See, *e.g.,* Sklansky, The Private Police, 46 UCLA L. Rev. 1165 (1999) (professional urban police departments did not develop until roughly the mid-19th century).

Nor, for that matter, am I aware of any evidence that *handguns* in particular were central to the Framers' conception of the Second Amendment. The lists of militia-related weapons in the late 18th-century state statutes appear primarily to refer to other sorts of weapons, muskets in particular. Respondent points out in his brief that the Federal Government and two States at the time of the founding had enacted statutes that listed handguns as "acceptable" militia weapons. But these statutes apparently found them "acceptable" only for certain special militiamen (generally, certain soldiers on horseback), while requiring muskets or rifles for the general infantry.

Third, irrespective of what the Framers *could have thought,* we know what they *did think.* Samuel Adams, who lived in Boston, advocated a constitutional amendment that would have precluded the Constitution from ever being "construed" to "prevent the people of the United States, who are peaceable citizens, from keeping their own arms." Samuel Adams doubtless knew that the Massachusetts Constitution contained somewhat similar protection. And he doubtless knew that Massachusetts law prohibited Bostonians from keeping loaded guns in the house. So how could Samuel Adams have advocated such protection *unless* he thought that the protection was *consistent* with local regulation that seriously impeded urban residents from using their arms against intruders? It seems unlikely that he meant to deprive the Federal Government of power (to enact Boston-type weapons regulation) that he kn[e]w Boston had and (as far as we know) he would have thought constitutional under the Massachusetts Constitution. Indeed, since the District of Columbia (the subject of the Seat of Government Clause, U.S. Const., Art. I, §8, cl. 17) was the only *urban* area under direct federal control, it seems unlikely that the Framers thought about *urban* gun control at all.

Of course the District's law and the colonial Boston law are not identical. But the Boston law disabled an even wider class of weapons (indeed, all firearms). And its existence shows at the least that local legislatures could impose (as here) serious restrictions on the right to use firearms. Moreover, as I have said, Boston's law, though highly analogous to the District's, was not the *only* colonial law that could have impeded a homeowner's ability to shoot a burglar. Pennsylvania's and New York's laws could well have had a similar effect. And the Massachusetts and Pennsylvania laws were not only thought consistent with an *unwritten* common-law gun-possession right, but also consistent with *written* state constitutional provisions providing protections similar to those provided by the Federal Second Amendment. I cannot agree with the majority that these laws are largely uninformative because the penalty for violating them was civil, rather than criminal. The Court has long recognized that the exercise of a constitutional right can be burdened by penalties far short of jail time. See, *e.g., Murdock v. Pennsylvania,* 319 U.S. 105 (1943) (invalidating $7 per week solicitation fee as applied to religious group); see also *Forsyth County v. Nationalist Movement,* 505 U.S. 123 (1992) ("A tax based on the content of speech does not become more constitutional because it is a small tax").

Regardless, why would the majority require a precise colonial regulatory analogue in order to save a modern gun regulation from constitutional challenge? After all, insofar as we look to history to discover how we can constitutionally regulate a right to self-defense, we must look, not to what 18th-century legislatures actually *did* enact, but to what they would have thought they *could* enact. . . . The question should not be whether a modern restriction on a right to self-defense *duplicates* a past one, but whether that restriction, when compared with restrictions originally thought possible, enjoys a similarly strong justification. At a minimum that similarly strong justification is what the District's modern law, compared with Boston's colonial law, reveals.

Fourth, a contrary view, as embodied in today's decision, will have unfortunate consequences. The decision will encourage legal challenges to gun regulation throughout the Nation. Because it says little about the standards used to evaluate regulatory decisions, it will leave the Nation without clear standards for resolving those challenges. And litigation over the course of many years, or the mere specter of such litigation, threatens to leave cities without effective protection against gun violence and accidents during that time.

As important, the majority's decision threatens severely to limit the ability of more knowledgeable, democratically elected officials to deal with gun-related problems. The majority says that it leaves the District "a variety of tools for combating" such problems. It fails to list even one seemingly adequate replacement for the law it strikes down. I can understand how reasonable individuals can disagree about the merits of strict gun control as a crime-control measure, even in a totally urbanized area. But I cannot understand how one can take from the elected branches of government the right to decide whether to insist upon a handgun-free urban populace in a city now facing a serious crime problem and which, in the future, could well face environmental or other emergencies that threaten the breakdown of law and order.

V

The majority derides my approach as "judge-empowering." I take this criticism seriously, but I do not think it accurate. As I have previously explained, this is an approach that the Court has taken in other areas of constitutional law. Application of such an approach, of course, requires judgment, but the very nature of the approach—requiring careful identification of the relevant interests and evaluating the law's effect upon them—limits the judge's choices; and the method's necessary transparency lays bare the judge's reasoning for all to see and to criticize.

The majority's methodology is, in my view, substantially less transparent than mine. At a minimum, I find it difficult to understand the reasoning that seems to underlie certain conclusions that it reaches.

[I]n the majority's view, the Amendment also protects an interest in armed personal self-defense, at least to some degree. But the majority does not tell us precisely what that interest is. "Putting all of [the Second Amendment's] textual elements together," the majority says, "we find that they guarantee the individual right to possess and carry weapons in case of confrontation." Then, three pages later, it says that "we do not read the Second Amendment to permit citizens to carry arms for *any sort* of confrontation." Yet, with one critical exception, it does not explain which confrontations count. It simply leaves that question unanswered.

The majority does, however, point to one type of confrontation that counts, for it describes the Amendment as "elevat[ing] above all other interests the right of law-abiding, responsible citizens to use arms in defense of hearth and home." What is its basis for finding that to be the core of the Second Amendment right? The only historical sources identified by the majority that even appear to touch upon that specific matter consist of an 1866 newspaper editorial discussing the Freedmen's Bureau Act, two quotations from that 1866 Act's legislative history, and a 1980 state court opinion saying that in colonial times the same were used to defend the home as to maintain the militia. How can citations such as these support the far-reaching proposition that the Second Amendment's primary concern is not its stated concern about the militia, but rather a right to keep loaded weapons at one's bedside to shoot intruders?

Nor is it at all clear to me how the majority decides *which* loaded "arms" a homeowner may keep. The majority says that that Amendment protects those weapons "typically possessed by law-abiding citizens for lawful purposes." This definition conveniently excludes machineguns, but permits handguns, which the majority describes as "the most popular weapon chosen by Americans for self-defense in the home." But what sense does this approach make? According to the majority's reasoning, if Congress and the States lift restrictions on the possession and use of machineguns, and people buy machineguns to protect their homes, the Court will have to reverse course and find that the Second Amendment *does,* in fact, protect the individual self-defense-related right to possess a machinegun. On the majority's reasoning, if tomorrow someone invents a particularly useful, highly dangerous self-defense weapon, Congress and the States had better ban it immediately, for once it becomes popular Congress will no longer possess the constitutional authority to do so. In essence, the majority determines what regulations are permissible by looking to see what existing regulations permit. There is no basis for believing that the Framers intended such circular reasoning.

I am similarly puzzled by the majority's list, in Part III of its opinion, of provisions that in its view would survive Second Amendment scrutiny. These consist of (1) "prohibitions on carrying concealed weapons"; (2) "prohibitions on the possession of firearms by felons"; (3) "prohibitions on the possession of firearms by . . . the mentally ill"; (4) "laws forbidding the carrying of firearms in sensitive places such as schools and government buildings"; and (5) government "conditions and qualifications" attached "to the commercial sale of arms." Why these? Is it that similar restrictions existed in the late 18th century? The majority fails to cite any colonial analogues. And even were it possible to find analogous colonial laws in respect to all these restrictions, why should these colonial laws count, while the Boston loaded-gun restriction (along with the other laws I have identified) apparently does not count?

At the same time the majority ignores a more important question: Given the purposes for which the Framers enacted the Second Amendment, how should it be applied to modern-day circumstances that they could not have anticipated? Assume, for argument's sake, that the Framers did intend the Amendment to offer a degree of self-defense protection. Does that mean that the Framers also intended to guarantee a right to possess a loaded gun near swimming pools, parks, and playgrounds? That they would not have cared about the children who might pick up a loaded gun on their parents' bedside table? That they (who certainly showed concern for the risk of fire) would have lacked concern for the risk of accidental deaths or suicides that readily accessible loaded handguns in urban areas might bring? Unless we believe that they intended future generations to ignore such matters, answering questions such as the questions in this case requires judgment—judicial judgment exercised within a framework for constitutional analysis that guides that judgment and which makes its exercise transparent. One cannot answer those questions by combining inconclusive historical research with judicial *ipse dixit*.

The argument about method, however, is by far the less important argument surrounding today's decision. Far more important are the unfortunate consequences that today's decision is likely to spawn. Not least of these, as I have said, is the fact that the decision threatens to throw into doubt the constitutionality of gun laws throughout the United States. I can find no sound legal basis for launching the courts on so formidable and potentially dangerous a mission. In my view, there simply is no untouchable constitutional right guaranteed by the Second Amendment to keep loaded handguns in the house in crime-ridden urban areas. . . .

Discussion

1. *Textualism and purposivism.* Note carefully Justice Scalia's methods for interpreting the Second Amendment. He delays discussing the so-called "purposive clause" of the Second Amendment until after parsing what he calls the "operative clause," which mentions the right to keep and bear arms. From the "operative clause" he derives an individual right to "possess and carry weapons in case of confrontation." Why does he proceed in this way?

Justice Scalia notes that the Second Amendment is equivalent to the statement that "Because a well regulated Militia is necessary to the security of a free State, the right of the people to keep and bear Arms shall not be infringed." He argues that "apart from [its] clarifying function, a prefatory clause does not limit or expand the scope of the operative clause." Why should this be? Suppose someone says, "Because I need someone to drive my parents around, you may use my car." Does this give permission to use the car other than as a chauffeur? Does it give permission to use the car if the parents move out of state or to a different country? Suppose the Constitution had said, "Freedom of discussion on public issues being necessary to a free state, Congress shall not abridge the right of free speech." Should this have affected what kinds of speech (e.g., music, painting, pornography, advertisements) are protected and unprotected?

With the Second Amendment, compare the Progress Clause of Article I, section 8, clause 8, which gives Congress the power "[t]o promote the progress of science and useful arts, by securing for limited times to authors and inventors the exclusive right to their respective writings and discoveries." The structure of the Progress Clause is somewhat different than the Second Amendment: the first clause offers a grant of power (to promote progress) that is limited by the second clause as to the means (granting exclusive rights for limited times). Conversely, the power to grant exclusive rights that appears in the second clause is glossed by the purpose (promoting progress) stated in the first clause.

2. *Dueling theories.* Justice Scalia argues that the Second Amendment was placed in the Constitution because of "the threat that the new Federal Government would destroy the citizens' militia by taking away their arms" and that the purpose of the citizen's militia, in turn, was "to oppose an oppressive military force if the constitutional order broke down." The common law right to keep and bear arms for self-defense and for hunting, Scalia argues, was codified in order to prevent such disarmament.

Justice Stevens, by contrast, argues that the common law right was not constitutionalized, at least at this point in history. Instead, the Second Amendment guaranteed "the right of the people of each of the several States to maintain a well-regulated militia" so as to prevent the Federal government from disarming state militias. Under Stevens' theory, what rights, if any, do individual Americans have under the Second Amendment? Presumably they have the right to the military use of weapons in state militias. But if the state no longer has a militia, or if the state excludes people from its organized militia, is there any remaining individual right? Under Stevens' account, do citizens have the right to form their own militias outside of state control?

In fact, Scalia argues that a major flaw with Stevens' theory is that it allows states (and the federal government) to disarm their citizens by closing down the militia or excluding most people from it. Does this mean that under Scalia's account, citizens have the right to form militias free from federal or state control or supervision? Such militias might be formed not only for mutual self-defense but also to ensure that federal and state law enforcement do not oppress the people or violate the Constitution as members of these militias understand it. Suppose the government considers such private armies (which we assume employ nothing other than weapons permitted to ordinary citizens) a danger to public safety. May it disband them as long as it allows citizens to retain ordinary weapons for self-defense? Cf. Presser v. Illinois, 116 U.S. 252 (1886)(upholding a law banning private militias, but holding that the Second Amendment did not apply to the states.). Suppose that the government proves that a group of citizens has formed a paramilitary organization designed to deter what the group regards as the potential for future government tyranny. May the government disarm those people? May it convict them of violating a ban on paramilitary organizations and then disarm them on the grounds that they are felons?

The history and the text of the Second Amendment focus on citizen militias because the Second Amendment was drafted in the context of a larger ideology of civic republicanism: citizens had duties to work together to promote the public good. Participating in citizen militias to resist or deter tyranny or invasion was one of the common duties of members of the community. See Sanford Levinson, The Embarrassing Second Amendment, 99 Yale L.J. 637 (1989). Thus, the right to keep and bear arms at the Founding was not a purely individualist or liberal right to be free from state interference, in the way we often think of rights today. Rather, it was a right that arose from a common political obligation and a common duty to fellow citizens and to the republic.

The need to preserve state militias to counteract federal tyranny, insurrection, and foreign invasion is a civic republican idea. So too is the preservation of an unorganized militia that could arise spontaneously to fight a tyrannical federal government, tyrannical state government, anti-republican insurrection, or foreign invasion. Citizens would band together, either organized by states, or spontaneously, to protect each other and the republic from invaders or tyrants.

3. *A Vestigial Right?* Scalia's argument is that in order to secure the militia to battle tyranny, the citizenry must have the sort of arms they would ordinarily use in self-defense of the home. In the 1790s, weapons commonly used in combat and weapons commonly used for self-defense overlapped considerably. They do no longer. As Scalia notes, a citizenry armed with handguns might be no match for today's heavy weaponry. Nevertheless, Scalia argues that the right to bear arms in defense of self and home endures even if it no longer effectively serves the original purpose for which it was codified in the Constitution—defending the people against tyranny. Why? Justice Scalia argues that originalism is consistent with responding to technological change, citing the First and Fourth Amendments as examples. Compare the effect of technological change on interpretations of federal power to regulate the economy. Industrialization, changes in transportation technology, economies of scale, and the growth of national markets eventually led courts to cut back on judicial restrictions on government power following the New Deal. What is the best response to technological change in this context?

4. *Which tyranny?* Scalia's historical account puts the best possible face on a tension inherent in the 1791 Constitution raised by the possibility of unorganized militias. On the one hand, the militia had the right to keep and bear arms to prevent tyranny, including a tyrannical federal government (or state government, in the case of state constitutions). On the other hand, the federal government had the obligation to put down insurrections and invasions (see the Guarantee Clause of Article IV), and it had the right to organize and take over state militias for this purpose. See the Militia clauses, Article I, section 8, clauses 15 and 16.

This balance of powers did not decide which group—the "insurrectionists" or the "government"—was the problem and which was the solution. The government might be tyrannical, or it might be a republican government defending against a mob or a putsch. The (unorganized) militia exercising its Second Amendment rights might be rising up against a tyrannical government, or it might be a force threatening republican government. *Heller* resolves this problem largely by ignoring it; it reads the Second Amendment as guaranteeing the right to bear arms for self-defense, but not the right to possess "dangerous" weapons.

Consider a civic republican reading of the ban on "dangerous" weapons. Civic republicanism requires cooperation and mutual support. Some weapons, such as nuclear bombs, tanks, or machine guns, don't require many people to cooperate to inflict enormous damage. Other weapons, such as swords and muskets, can inflict much less damage individually, and require people to band together to resist oppression. Under a civic republican reading, handguns and shotguns might be "republican" and are constitutionally protected while machine guns might be "anti-republican" and may be proscribed. Does *Heller* contemplate this distinction or a different one that is unrelated to civic republican ideology?

Does Scalia's reading of the individual right to keep and bear arms allow government to criminalize caches of arms that might someday be used to resist an oppressive government? *Heller* assumes that licensing requirements are constitutional. Do citizens have a constitutional right to stockpile as many weapons as they like, subject to obtaining a license for each one?

Suppose citizens stockpile weapons and engage in military exercises to resist government tyranny. Does *Heller* allow governments to prosecute these citizens for criminal conspiracy to commit insurrection or terrorism? What if the basis of the charge of conspiracy is that the citizens are stockpiling weapons presumably, in order to allow them to resist future tyranny or invasion?

5. *The Uses of History, Originalism, and the Living Constitution.* Both Justices Scalia and Stevens state their historical conclusions confidently, asserting that that the historical record is clear. As is often the case with attempts to recapture the past, however, the same facts can often be interpreted in more than one way, a point made abundantly clear by juxtaposing Scalia's and Stevens' equally self-assured claims about identical texts and events.

Justice Scalia's argument is that the Second Amendment codified the English common law right to use weapons for self defense. There is some evidence for this position, but the historical record is mixed and can be read in several different ways. Different views about the nature of the right to keep and bear arms circulated during the Founding period, which is hardly surprising given that it was one of the most intellectually lively periods in American political thought. On the ambiguities of the historical record, see Mark V. Tushnet, Out of Range: Why the Constitution Can't End the Battle Over Guns. (New York: Oxford University Press, 2007); Saul Cornell, A Well-Regulated Militia: The Founding Fathers and the Origins of Gun Control in America. (New York: Oxford University Press, 2006); Sanford Levinson, Guns and the Constitution, A Complex Relationship, 36 Reviews in American History, 1-14 (2008)(reviewing Tushnet and Cornell).

On the other hand, as Scalia notes, there is fairly strong evidence that during the 19th century people believed that the Second Amendment guaranteed a right to use arms in self defense, and the evidence grows stronger as the century proceeds. As the casebook recounts (at p. 496) by the time of the Civil War, it was widely assumed that the common law right to keep and bear arms for self defense was a fundamental constitutional right, whether it was protected by the

Privileges and Immunities Clause of Article IV, the Second Amendment, or the Ninth Amendment.

Justice Scalia reads this history as evidence not of evolving views about basic rights, but as evidence of the common understandings of 1791. Scalia does this because his originalist theory of interpretation requires it. The danger, of course, is that his use of history is anachronistic. For the same reason, Scalia scoffs at "the proposition, unsupported by any evidence, that different people of the founding period had vastly different conceptions of the right to keep and bear arms. That simply does not comport with our longstanding view that the Bill of Rights codified venerable, widely understood liberties." But surely it is likely that people disagreed about the meaning of the right to bear arms in 1791 just as they disagree about basic rights today.

Does a sophisticated version of originalism require the degree of historical certainty and consensus that Scalia seems to assume? One potential problem is that if we assume that more than one view was circulating at the time, present day judges must pick one reading as more faithful than the others. Would doing this pose any problems for originalism's conception of the judicial role, or with the democratic legitimacy of judicial review?

A far more plausible reading of the history is that views about the purposes of the Amendment were in flux at the Founding and changed over the course of a century, and that by the time of Reconstruction, it was widely accepted that the right to self-defense was a constitutional liberty identified with the Second Amendment. Even if there was no consensus about whether the English common law right was constitutionalized in 1791, such a consensus had developed by Reconstruction. Hence the framers of the Fourteenth Amendment believed that the right to use arms in self-defense was one of the "Privileges or Immunities of Citizens of the United States" protected by the Fourteenth Amendment. (For example, see Senator Jacob Howard's Speech introducing the Fourteenth Amendment before the Senate in May 1866, reprinted in this supplement).

Given this evidence, could a court read the text of the Second Amendment consistent with these 19th century views, and particularly those widely held at the time of the Fourteenth Amendment? This would not be a necessary implication of the original meaning of the Second Amendment. Rather, it would be a constitutional *construction* of the original meaning that became commonplace in the 19th century. The original meaning of the text can easily bear this construction and, so the argument would go, we should accept it today, especially because it was assumed in the debates leading up to the ratification of the Fourteenth Amendment.

This reading of history, however, would require a "living Constitution" approach. It would maintain that a later generation's views on the scope of the Second Amendment can be accepted as part of the Constitution as long as those views are consistent with the original meaning of the words of the text. Why does the majority not adopt this model of interpretation? Equally important, why doesn't Justice Stevens' dissent?

What are the problems with accepting the 19th century's construction of the Second Amendment as the best interpretation? Does it commit us to accept 19th century assumptions about the scope of other parts of the Bill of Rights, or, for that matter, the Fourteenth Amendment?

6. *Living Constitutionalism and the Role of Social Movements.* Justice Stevens makes much of the fact that for the better part of a century courts had assumed that the Second Amendment did not guarantee an individual right to use guns for self-defense. Indeed, this was the conventional wisdom for many years. In 1991, for example, retired Chief Justice Warren Burger, a conservative Republican, insisted that the individual rights view of the Second Amendment was "one of the greatest pieces of fraud—I repeat the word 'fraud'—on the American public by special interest groups that I have ever seen in my lifetime." Burger cast particular scorn on the efforts of the National Rifle Association (NRA) and other groups—which he pejoratively labeled "special interest groups"—to convince Americans otherwise. As we have seen elsewhere in this course, in the context of social movements like the women's movement and the gay rights movement, sustained political and social mobilization can persuade people to change their minds about what is "off the wall" and "on the wall" concerning legal and constitutional claims. For a history of how the work of social movements eventually led to the decision in *Heller*, see Reva B. Siegel, Dead or Alive: Originalism as Popular Constitutionalism in *Heller*, 122 Harv. L. Rev. 191, 201-246 (2008).

The modern movement for gun rights arose in reaction to increased political mobilization for stricter gun control laws, particularly after passage of the 1968 Crime Control Act, which Congress enacted following the assassinations of Martin Luther King and Robert F. Kennedy. Beginning in the 1970s, the NRA began national lobbying efforts to oppose gun control legislation, arguing that gun control laws violated Second Amendment rights and that the conventional wisdom about the Constitution was incorrect. The gun rights movement gained influence within the Republican Party, as gun rights became one of many interconnected issues in the culture wars. Movement conservatives who used originalism to attack liberal judicial decisions, also turned to originalism to defend Second Amendment rights. See, e.g., The Right to Keep and Bear Arms: Report of the Subcommittee on the Constitution of the Committee on the Judiciary 1 S. 97th Cong., 2d sess. (1982).

As conservatives gained increasing political influence during the last part of the twentieth century, the NRA's constitutional position gained increasing public support, and convinced members of a newer generation of conservative legal elites. In 1994, the Republicans took control of both Houses of Congress by making a key campaign issue of their opposition to recent gun control laws passed by a Democratic-controlled Congress. See Nicholas J. Johnson, A Second Amendment Moment: The Constitutional Politics of Gun Control, 71 Brooklyn L. Rev. 715 (2005). In May 2002, Attorney General John Ashcroft announced the Bush Justice Department's official position that the Second Amendment protected an individual right to use arms in self-defense.

As we have seen in Brown v. Board of Education and other cases, the Supreme Court tends to respond in the long run to the views of the dominant political coalition as well as to public opinion. The agendas of legal scholarship also tend to shift in response to political changes. An outpouring of new legal and historical scholarship began debating the individual rights interpretation in the 1990s and 2000s, and the Third Edition of Professor Laurence Tribe's Treatise, *American Constitutional Law*, published in 2000, argued—in contrast to the two previous editions—that the Second Amendment protected an individual right. See Laurence H. Tribe, American Constitutional Law §5-11, 901-02 n. 221 (3d ed., Foundation Press 2000).

In this sense, the result in *Heller* was not entirely surprising. As in *Brown v. Board of Education*, the 1970s sex equality cases, and *Lawrence v. Texas*, the Supreme Court has kept its interpretation of the Constitution in line with changing public values. Another name for this phenomenon is living constitutionalism.

The irony of course, is that the arguments for modifying constitutional doctrine to reflect changed political realities were all phrased in the language of fidelity to original meaning. However, this makes perfect sense. The best way for social movements to persuade others that their views are correct is to show how they follow ineluctably from the nation's deepest commitments. Appeals to the framers and the Constitution's original meaning are one way, although not the only way, to do that. For example, opponents of affirmative action have not made arguments from the original meaning of the Fourteenth Amendment, but rather argued that colorblindness follows from the meaning of Brown v. Board of Education and the civil rights movement.

This account of *Heller* assumes a very different theory of the democratic legitimacy of judicial review than the one offered in Scalia's opinion. The implicit theory in *Heller* is that judges are simply bound by the original meaning and original understanding of the Constitution. That meaning is clear: it protects an individual right to use arms in self-defense. Therefore it is the duty of judges to enforce that meaning. But if we understand *Heller* as the result of a long process of mobilization seeking to change conventional wisdom, first among the general public and later among legal elites, we can offer a different account of the democratic legitimacy of judicial review. The American people today understand these rights as their rights, and the text can bear this construction.

The first theory views the judges' role as faithfully following an ancient law of the framers as they would have understood and applied it. It asserts (or at least must assert) that the text is clear and there can be no other reasonable construction. The second views the judges' role as articulating and applying vague or ambiguous texts in light of contemporary social values, securing American's present-day understanding of their basic rights. Why are the opinions in *Heller* written according to the first theory rather than the second?

7. *Judicial scrutiny under the Second Amendment.* Justice Breyer suggests that Second Amendment rights should be determined according to a balancing

test, roughly akin to the intermediate scrutiny employed in the sex equality cases and in first amendment cases involving regulations of time, place and manner. He notes that state courts with analogous constitutional provisions have, by and large, used a balancing or intermediate scrutiny approach. For a review of the state cases, see Adam Winkler, Scrutinizing the Second Amendment, 105 Mich. L. Rev. 683 (2007). The majority, although striking down parts of the D.C. ordinance, leaves open the question of the appropriate level of scrutiny for a future case. However it seems to reject Breyer's approach. Is this because it rejects the idea of applying intermediate scrutiny or merely Breyer's application of it?

Consider Breyer's argument that the empirical studies on gun control laws point in different directions; given this uncertainty, courts should defer to legislatures about the best way to balance home owners' rights and public safety. Compare Breyer's views with the Court's application of the "undue burden" test in abortion cases, in particular *Casey* and *Carhart II*. Could the majority respond that the D.C. ban on handguns is a complete ban of a commonly used weapon rather than merely a regulation of handgun use? Does the Second Amendment prohibit complete bans on any weapons that are currently in common use? Does it allow the government to prevent new weapons from becoming commonly used?

8. *What Kind of Self Defense?* Justice Scalia reads the Second Amendment to protect the common law right of self-defense. What precisely is this right? Does it protect only the right to keep firearms in the home for self defense, or does it also include the right to keep them on one's person outside the home, for example, when one travels in dangerous neighborhoods? Does *Heller* protect the right to use weapons other than firearms for self-defense in the home? For example, are laws banning the possession of switchblades within the home constitutional under *Heller*? Does it protect the right to possess these weapons outside the home?

Does *Heller* protect the right of self-defense per se, whether with or without a firearm? Does it mean, for example, that states must, as a constitutional matter, have a doctrine of self-defense in their criminal and tort laws? If there is a constitutional right of self-defense, is it limited only to situations where a person is directly attacked by another? For example, would the constitutional right of self-defense extend to the use of drugs and surgeries that patients reasonably believe are necessary for their survival? See Eugene Volokh, Medical Self-defense, Prohibited Experimental Therapies, and Payment for Organs, 120 Harv. L. Rev. 1813 (2007)(discussing possible rights of self-defense under the Due Process Clause); Abigail Alliance for Better Access to Developmental Drugs v. von Eschenbach, 495 F.3d 695 (D.C. Cir. 2007) (en banc), cert. denied, 128 S. Ct. 1069 (2008) (holding that terminally ill patients have no fundamental right under the Due Process Clause to obtain potentially live-saving medications still undergoing testing required by the Food and Drug Administration). Would the constitutional guarantee of self-defense protect the right of women to have abortions to save their lives? Compare the guarantee of abortions to save the mother's life in Roe v. Wade, Chapter 8, supra. Or does *Heller* merely hold that people have a right to keep weapons in their homes for purposes of self-defense where such weapons are of the sort commonly available and that might be used in a state militia, if the state had such a militia?

McDONALD v. CITY OF CHICAGO
130 S.Ct. 3020 (2010), 2010 WL 2555188

Justice ALITO announced the judgment of the Court and delivered the opinion of the Court with respect to Parts I, II-A, II-B, II-D, III-A, and III-B, in which The CHIEF JUSTICE, Justice SCALIA, Justice KENNEDY, and Justice THOMAS join, and an opinion with respect to Parts II-C, IV, and V, in which The CHIEF JUSTICE, Justice SCALIA, and Justice KENNEDY join.

[Petitioners challenged city ordinances in Chicago and Oak Park that effectively banned handgun possession. Chicago's ordinance prohibits registration of most handguns and then provides that that "[n]o person shall ... possess ... any firearm unless such person is the holder of a valid registration certificate for such firearm." Chicago, Ill., Municipal Code §8-20-040(a) (2009). Oak Park makes it "unlawful for any person to possess ... any firearm," a term that includes "pistols, revolvers, guns and small arms ... commonly known as handguns." Oak Park, Ill., Municipal Code §§27-2-1 (2007), 27-1-1 (2009). Petitioners argued that that the Second Amendment right to keep and bear arms for the purpose of self defense recognized in *Heller* applied to the states through the Fourteenth Amendment.]

II

A (м|

Three years after the decision in the *Slaughter-House Cases,* the Court decided [*United States v.*] *Cruikshank*, [which held] that the right of bearing arms for a lawful purpose "is not a right granted by the Constitution" and is not "in any manner dependent upon that instrument for its existence." "The second amendment," the Court continued, "declares that it shall not be infringed; but this ... means no more than that it shall not be infringed by Congress." Our later decisions in *Presser v. Illinois,* 116 U.S. 252, 265 (1886), and *Miller v. Texas,* 153 U.S. 535 (1894), reaffirmed that the Second Amendment applies only to the Federal Government. ... Petitioners argue ... that we should overrule those decisions and hold that the right to keep and bear arms is one of the "privileges or immunities of citizens of the United States." In petitioners' view, the Privileges or Immunities Clause protects all of the rights set out in the Bill of Rights, as well as some others, but petitioners are unable to identify the Clause's full scope. Nor is there any consensus on that question among the scholars who agree that the *Slaughter-House Cases'* interpretation is flawed.

We see no need to reconsider that interpretation here. For many decades, the question of the rights protected by the Fourteenth Amendment against state infringement has been analyzed under the Due Process Clause of that Amendment and not under the Privileges or Immunities Clause. We therefore decline to disturb the *Slaughter-House* holding.

At the same time, however, this Court's decisions in *Cruikshank, Presser,* and *Miller* do not preclude us from considering whether the Due Process Clause of the Fourteenth Amendment makes the Second Amendment right binding on the States. . . . Indeed, *Cruikshank* has not prevented us from holding that other rights that were at issue in that case are binding on the States through the Due Process Clause. In *Cruikshank,* the Court held that the general "right of the people peaceably to assemble for lawful purposes," which is protected by the First Amendment, applied only against the Federal Government and not against the States. Nonetheless, over 60 years later the Court held that the right of peaceful assembly was a "fundamental righ[t] . . . safeguarded by the due process clause of the Fourteenth Amendment." *De Jonge v. Oregon,* 299 U.S. 353, 364 (1937). . . .

D (η)

In the late 19th century, the Court began to consider whether the Due Process Clause prohibits the States from infringing rights set out in the Bill of Rights. See *Hurtado v. California,* 110 U.S. 516 (1884) (due process does not require grand jury indictment); *Chicago, B. & Q.R. Co. v. Chicago,* 166 U.S. 226 (1897) (due process prohibits States from taking of private property for public use without just compensation). [During this period] the Court viewed the due process question as entirely separate from the question whether a right was a privilege or immunity of national citizenship. [It] explained that the only rights protected against state infringement by the Due Process Clause were those rights "of such a nature that they are included in the conception of due process of law." [*Twining v. New Jersey,* 211 U.S. 78, 99 (1908)]. . . . The Court used different formulations in describing the boundaries of due process. For example, in *Twining,* the Court referred to "immutable principles of justice which inhere in the very idea of free government which no member of the Union may disregard." 211 U.S., at 102. In *Snyder v. Massachusetts,* 291 U.S. 97, 105 (1934), the Court spoke of rights that are "so rooted in the traditions and conscience of our people as to be ranked as fundamental." And in *Palko* [*v. Connecticut,* 302 U.S. 319 (1937)], the Court famously said that due process protects those rights that are "the very essence of a scheme of ordered liberty" and essential to "a fair and enlightened system of justice." [In] some cases decided during this era the Court "can be seen as having asked, when inquiring into whether some particular procedural safeguard was required of a State, if a civilized system could be imagined that would not accord the particular protection." [For example,] the Court found that due process did not provide a right against compelled incrimination in part because this right "has no place in the jurisprudence of civilized and free countries outside the domain of the common law." *Twining*.

Finally, even when a right set out in the Bill of Rights was held to fall within the conception of due process, the protection or remedies afforded against state infringement sometimes differed from the protection or remedies provided against abridgment by the Federal Government. To give one example, in *Betts* [*v. Brady*, 316 U.S. 455 (1942)] the Court held that, although the Sixth Amendment required the appointment of counsel in all federal criminal cases in which the defendant was unable to retain an attorney, the Due Process Clause required appointment of counsel in state criminal proceedings only where "want of counsel in [the] particular case . . . result[ed] in a conviction lacking in . . . fundamental fairness." Similarly, in *Wolf v. Colorado,* 338 U.S. 25 (1949), the Court held that the "core of the Fourth Amendment" was implicit in the concept of ordered liberty and thus "enforceable against the States through the Due Process Clause" but that the exclusionary rule, which applied in federal cases, did not apply to the States. . . .

Justice Black [argued] that §1 of the Fourteenth Amendment totally incorporated all of the provisions of the Bill of Rights [noting that] the chief congressional proponents of the Fourteenth Amendment espoused [this] view. [T]he Court never has embraced Justice Black's "total incorporation" theory. [Nevertheless,] the Court eventually moved in that direction [through] a process of "selective incorporation," *i.e.*, the Court began to hold that the Due Process Clause fully incorporates particular rights contained in the first eight Amendments.

The decisions during this time abandoned three of the previously noted characteristics of the earlier period. The Court made it clear that the governing — standard is not whether *any* "civilized system [can] be imagined that would not accord the particular protection." *Duncan v. Louisiana,* 391 U.S. 145, 149, n. 14 (1968). Instead, the Court inquired whether a particular Bill of Rights guarantee is fundamental to *our* scheme of ordered liberty and system of justice. . . . The Court eventually incorporated almost all of the provisions of the Bill of Rights. Only a handful of the Bill of Rights protections remain unincorporated.[a]

Finally, the Court abandoned "the notion that the Fourteenth Amendment applies to the States only a watered-down, subjective version of the individual guarantees of the Bill of Rights," stating that it would be "incongruous" to apply different standards "depending on whether the claim was asserted in a state or

---

a. In addition to the right to keep and bear arms (and the Sixth Amendment right to a unanimous jury verdict), the only rights not fully incorporated are (1) the Third Amendment's protection against quartering of soldiers; (2) the Fifth Amendment's grand jury indictment requirement; (3) the Seventh Amendment right to a jury trial in civil cases; and (4) the Eighth Amendment's prohibition on excessive fines. We never have decided whether the Third Amendment or the Eighth Amendment's prohibition of excessive fines applies to the States through the Due Process Clause. Our governing decisions regarding the Grand Jury Clause of the Fifth Amendment and the Seventh Amendment's civil jury requirement long predate the era of selective incorporation.

federal court." *Malloy v. Hogan,* 378 U.S. [1,10-11 (1964).] Instead, the Court decisively held that incorporated Bill of Rights protections "are all to be enforced against the States under the Fourteenth Amendment according to the same standards that protect those personal rights against federal encroachment."[b]

III

[W]e must decide whether the right to keep and bear arms is fundamental to *our* scheme of ordered liberty, *Duncan,* or as we have said in a related context, whether this right is "deeply rooted in this Nation's history and tradition," *Washington v. Glucksberg,* 521 U.S. 702, 721 (1997).

A (м)

Our decision in *Heller* points unmistakably to the answer. Self-defense is a basic right, recognized by many legal systems from ancient times to the present day, and in *Heller,* we held that individual self-defense is "the *central component*" of the Second Amendment right. Explaining that "the need for defense of self, family, and property is most acute" in the home, we found that this right applies to handguns because they are "the most preferred firearm in the nation to 'keep' and use for protection of one's home and family." . . . *Heller* makes it clear that this right is "deeply rooted in this Nation's history and tradition." *Glucksberg. Heller* explored the right's origins, noting that the 1689 English Bill of Rights explicitly protected a right to keep arms for self-defense, and that by 1765, Blackstone was able to assert that the right to keep and bear arms was "one of the fundamental rights of Englishmen."

Blackstone's assessment was shared by the American colonists. As we noted in *Heller,* King George III's attempt to disarm the colonists in the 1760's and 1770's "provoked polemical reactions by Americans invoking their rights as Englishmen to keep arms." The right to keep and bear arms was considered no less fundamental by those who drafted and ratified the Bill of Rights. "During the 1788 ratification debates, the fear that the federal government would disarm the people in order to impose rule through a standing army or select militia was

---

b. There is one exception to this general rule. The Court has held that although the Sixth Amendment right to trial by jury requires a unanimous jury verdict in federal criminal trials, it does not require a unanimous jury verdict in state criminal trials. See *Apodaca v. Oregon,* 406 U.S. 404, (1972); see also *Johnson v. Louisiana,* 406 U.S. 356 (1972) (holding that the Due Process Clause does not require unanimous jury verdicts in state criminal trials). But that ruling was the result of an unusual division among the Justices, not an endorsement of the two-track approach to incorporation. In *Apodaca,* eight Justices agreed that the Sixth Amendment applies identically to both the Federal Government and the States. Nonetheless, among those eight, four Justices took the view that the Sixth Amendment does not require unanimous jury verdicts in either federal or state criminal trials, and four other Justices took the view that the Sixth Amendment requires unanimous jury verdicts in federal and state criminal trials. Justice Powell's concurrence in the judgment broke the tie, and he concluded that the Sixth Amendment requires juror unanimity in federal, but not state, cases. *Apodaca,* therefore, does not undermine the well-established rule that incorporated Bill of Rights protections apply identically to the States and the Federal Government.

pervasive in Antifederalist rhetoric." Federalists responded, not by arguing that the right was insufficiently important to warrant protection but by contending that the right was adequately protected by the Constitution's assignment of only limited powers to the Federal Government. Thus, Antifederalists and Federalists alike agreed that the right to bear arms was fundamental to the newly formed system of government. But those who were fearful that the new Federal Government would infringe traditional rights such as the right to keep and bear arms insisted on the adoption of the Bill of Rights as a condition for ratification of the Constitution. This is surely powerful evidence that the right was regarded as fundamental in the sense relevant here.

This understanding persisted in the years immediately following the ratification of the Bill of Rights. In addition to the four States that had adopted Second Amendment analogues before ratification, nine more States adopted state constitutional provisions protecting an individual right to keep and bear arms between 1789 and 1820. Founding-era legal commentators confirmed the importance of the right to early Americans. St. George Tucker, for example, described the right to keep and bear arms as "the true palladium of liberty" and explained that prohibitions on the right would place liberty "on the brink of destruction." 1 Blackstone's Commentaries, Editor's App. 300 (S. Tucker ed. 1803); see also W. Rawle, A View of the Constitution of the United States of America, 125-126 (2d ed. 1829) (reprint 2009); 3 J. Story, Commentaries on the Constitution of the United States §1890, p. 746 (1833) ("The right of the citizens to keep and bear arms has justly been considered, as the palladium of the liberties of a republic; since it offers a strong moral check against the usurpation and arbitrary power of rulers; and will generally, even if these are successful in the first instance, enable the people to resist and triumph over them").

B (m)

By the 1850's, the perceived threat that had prompted the inclusion of the Second Amendment in the Bill of Rights—the fear that the National Government would disarm the universal militia—had largely faded as a popular concern, but the right to keep and bear arms was highly valued for purposes of self-defense. Abolitionist authors wrote in support of the right. And when attempts were made to disarm "Free-Soilers" in "Bloody Kansas," Senator Charles Sumner, who later played a leading role in the adoption of the Fourteenth Amendment, proclaimed that "[n]ever was [the rifle] more needed in just self-defense than now in Kansas." Indeed, the 1856 Republican Party Platform protested that in Kansas the constitutional rights of the people had been "fraudulently and violently taken from them" and the "right of the people to keep and bear arms" had been "infringed."[c]

---

c. Abolitionists and Republicans were not alone in believing that the right to keep and bear arms was a fundamental right. The 1864 Democratic Party Platform complained that the confiscation of firearms by Union troops occupying parts of the South constituted "the interference with and denial of the right of the people to bear arms in their defense."

After the Civil War, many of the over 180,000 African Americans who served in the Union Army returned to the States of the old Confederacy, where systematic efforts were made to disarm them and other blacks. The laws of some States formally prohibited African Americans from possessing firearms. . . . Throughout the South, armed parties, often consisting of ex-Confederate soldiers serving in the state militias, forcibly took firearms from newly freed slaves. In the first session of the 39th Congress, Senator Wilson told his colleagues: "In Mississippi rebel State forces, men who were in the rebel armies, are traversing the State, visiting the freedmen, disarming them, perpetrating murders and outrages upon them; and the same things are done in other sections of the country." The Report of the Joint Committee on Reconstruction—which was widely reprinted in the press and distributed by Members of the 39th Congress to their constituents shortly after Congress approved the Fourteenth Amendment—contained numerous examples of such abuses. . . . As Senator Wilson put it during the debate on a failed proposal to disband Southern militias: "There is one unbroken chain of testimony from all people that are loyal to this country, that the greatest outrages are perpetrated by armed men who go up and down the country searching houses, disarming people, committing outrages of every kind and description."

Union Army commanders took steps to secure the right of all citizens to keep and bear arms, but the 39th Congress concluded that legislative action was necessary. Its efforts to safeguard the right to keep and bear arms demonstrate that the right was still recognized to be fundamental.

The most explicit evidence of Congress' aim appears in §14 of the Freedmen's Bureau Act of 1866, which provided that "the right . . . to have full and equal benefit of all laws and proceedings concerning personal liberty, personal security, and the acquisition, enjoyment, and disposition of estate, real and personal, *including the constitutional right to bear arms,* shall be secured to and enjoyed by all the citizens . . . without respect to race or color, or previous condition of slavery." 14 Stat. 176-177 (emphasis added). Section 14 thus explicitly guaranteed that "all the citizens," black and white, would have "the constitutional right to bear arms."

The Civil Rights Act of 1866, 14 Stat. 27, which was considered at the same time as the Freedmen's Bureau Act, similarly sought to protect the right of all citizens to keep and bear arms. Section 1 of the Civil Rights Act guaranteed the "full and equal benefit of all laws and proceedings for the security of person and property, as is enjoyed by white citizens." This language was virtually identical to language in §14 of the Freedmen's Bureau Act. . . . Representative Bingham believed that the Civil Rights Act protected the same rights as enumerated in the Freedmen's Bureau bill, which of course explicitly mentioned the right to keep and bear arms. The unavoidable conclusion is that the Civil Rights Act, like the Freedmen's Bureau Act, aimed to protect "the constitutional right to bear arms" and not simply to prohibit discrimination. . . .

Today, it is generally accepted that the Fourteenth Amendment was under-stood to provide a constitutional basis for protecting the rights set out in the Civil Rights Act of 1866. In debating the Fourteenth Amendment, the 39th Congress referred to the right to keep and bear arms as a fundamental right deserving of protection. Senator Samuel Pomeroy described three "indispens-able" "safeguards of liberty under our form of Government." Cong. Globe, 39th Cong., 1st Sess. 1182. One of these, he said, was the right to keep and bear arms: "Every man . . . should have the right to bear arms for the defense of himself and family and his homestead. And if the cabin door of the freedman is broken open and the intruder enters for purposes as vile as were known to slavery, then should a well-loaded musket be in the hand of the occupant to send the polluted wretch to another world, where his wretchedness will forever remain complete." *Ibid*. Even those who thought the Fourteenth Amendment unnecessary believed that blacks, as citizens, "have equal right to protection, and to keep and bear arms for self-defense." *Id*., at 1073 (Sen. James Nye).

. . . The right to keep and bear arms was also widely protected by state constitutions at the time when the Fourteenth Amendment was ratified. In 1868, 22 of the 37 States in the Union had state constitutional provisions explicitly protecting the right to keep and bear arms. . . . In sum, it is clear that the Framers and ratifiers of the Fourteenth Amendment counted the right to keep and bear arms among those fundamental rights necessary to our system of ordered liberty.

Despite all this evidence, municipal respondents contend that Congress, in the years immediately following the Civil War, merely sought to outlaw "dis-criminatory measures taken against freedmen, which it addressed by adopting a non-discrimination principle" and that even an outright ban on the possession of firearms was regarded as acceptable, "so long as it was not done in a discrimi-natory manner." They argue that Members of Congress overwhelmingly viewed §1 of the Fourteenth Amendment "as an antidiscrimination rule," and they cite statements to the effect that the section would outlaw discriminatory measures. This argument is implausible.

First, while §1 of the Fourteenth Amendment contains "an antidiscrimination rule," namely, the Equal Protection Clause, municipal respondents can hardly mean that §1 does no more than prohibit discrimination. If that were so, then the First Amendment, as applied to the States, would not prohibit nondiscriminatory abridgments of the rights to freedom of speech or freedom of religion; the Fourth Amendment, as applied to the States, would not prohibit all unreasonable searches and seizures but only discriminatory searches and seizures—and so on. We assume that this is not municipal respondents' view, so what they must mean is that the Second Amendment should be singled out for special—and specially unfavorable—treatment. We reject that suggestion.

Second, municipal respondents' argument ignores the clear terms of the Freedmen's Bureau Act of 1866 . . . §14 speaks of and protects "the constitu-tional right to bear arms," an unmistakable reference to the right protected by the Second Amendment. And it protects the "full and equal benefit" of this right in the States. It would have been nonsensical for Congress to guarantee the full and equal benefit of a constitutional right that does not exist.

Third, if the 39th Congress had outlawed only those laws that discriminate on the basis of race or previous condition of servitude, African Americans in the South would likely have remained vulnerable to attack by many of their worst abusers: the state militia and state peace officers. In the years immediately following the Civil War, a law banning the possession of guns by all private citizens would have been nondiscriminatory only in the formal sense. Any such law—like the Chicago and Oak Park ordinances challenged here—presumably would have permitted the possession of guns by those acting under the authority of the State and would thus have left firearms in the hands of the militia and local peace officers. And as the Report of the Joint Committee on Reconstruction revealed, those groups were widely involved in harassing blacks in the South.

Fourth, municipal respondents' purely antidiscrimination theory of the Fourteenth Amendment disregards the plight of whites in the South who opposed the Black Codes. If the 39th Congress and the ratifying public had simply prohibited racial discrimination with respect to the bearing of arms, opponents of the Black Codes would have been left without the means of self-defense—as had abolitionists in Kansas in the 1850's. . . .

IV (no T)

[M]unicipal respondents, in effect, ask us to treat the right recognized in *Heller* as a second-class right, subject to an entirely different body of rules than the other Bill of Rights guarantees that we have held to be incorporated into the Due Process Clause. . . . According to municipal respondents, if it is possible to imagine *any* civilized legal system that does not recognize a particular right, then the Due Process Clause does not make that right binding on the States. . . . Therefore, the municipal respondents continue, because such countries as England, Canada, Australia, Japan, Denmark, Finland, Luxembourg, and New Zealand either ban or severely limit handgun ownership, it must follow that no right to possess such weapons is protected by the Fourteenth Amendment.

This line of argument is, of course, inconsistent with the long-established standard we apply in incorporation cases. And the present-day implications of municipal respondents' argument are stunning. For example, many of the rights that our Bill of Rights provides for persons accused of criminal offenses are virtually unique to this country. If *our* understanding of the right to a jury trial, the right against self-incrimination, and the right to counsel were necessary attributes of *any* civilized country, it would follow that the United States is the only civilized Nation in the world.

Municipal respondents attempt to salvage their position by suggesting that their argument applies only to substantive as opposed to procedural rights. [But] several of the countries that municipal respondents recognize as civilized have established state churches. If we were to adopt municipal respondents' theory, all of this Court's Establishment Clause precedents involving actions taken by state and local governments would go by the boards.

Municipal respondents maintain that the Second Amendment differs from all of the other provisions of the Bill of Rights because it concerns the right to possess a deadly implement and thus has implications for public safety. And they note that there is intense disagreement on the question whether the private possession of guns in the home increases or decreases gun deaths and injuries.

The right to keep and bear arms, however, is not the only constitutional right ⌐ that has controversial public safety implications. All of the constitutional provisions that impose restrictions on law enforcement and on the prosecution of crimes fall into the same category. Municipal respondents cite no case in which we have refrained from holding that a provision of the Bill of Rights is binding on the States on the ground that the right at issue has disputed public safety implications.

We likewise reject municipal respondents' argument that we should depart from our established incorporation methodology on the ground that making the Second Amendment binding on the States and their subdivisions is inconsistent with principles of federalism and will stifle experimentation. Municipal respondents point out—quite correctly—that conditions and problems differ from locality to locality and that citizens in different jurisdictions have divergent views on the issue of gun control. Municipal respondents therefore urge us to allow state and local governments to enact any gun control law that they deem to be reasonable, including a complete ban on the possession of handguns in the home for self-defense.

There is nothing new in the argument that, in order to respect federalism and allow useful state experimentation, a federal constitutional right should not be fully binding on the States. This argument was made repeatedly and eloquently by Members of this Court who rejected the concept of incorporation and urged retention of the two-track approach to incorporation. Throughout the era of "selective incorporation," Justice Harlan in particular, invoking the values of federalism and state experimentation, fought a determined rearguard action to preserve the two-track approach. Time and again, however, those pleas failed. Unless we turn back the clock or adopt a special incorporation test applicable only to the Second Amendment, municipal respondents' argument must be rejected. Under our precedents, if a Bill of Rights guarantee is fundamental from an American perspective, then, unless *stare decisis* counsels otherwise,[d] that guarantee is fully binding on the States and thus *limits* (but by no means

---

d. As noted above, cases that predate the era of selective incorporation held that the Grand Jury Clause of the Fifth Amendment and the Seventh Amendment's civil jury requirement do not apply to the States. See *Hurtado v. California,* 110 U.S. 516 (1884) (indictment); *Minneapolis & St. Louis R. Co. v. Bombolis,* 241 U.S. 211 (1916) (civil jury). As a result of *Hurtado,* most States do not require a grand jury indictment in all felony cases, and many have no grand juries. As a result of *Bombolis,* cases that would otherwise fall within the Seventh Amendment are now tried without a jury in state small claims courts.

eliminates) their ability to devise solutions to social problems that suit local needs and values.

Municipal respondents and their *amici* complain that incorporation of the Second Amendment right will lead to extensive and costly litigation, but this argument applies with even greater force to constitutional rights and remedies that have already been held to be binding on the States. Consider the exclusionary rule[, which] is said to result in "tens of thousands of contested suppression motions each year."

Municipal respondents assert that, although most state constitutions protect firearms rights, state courts have held that these rights are subject to "interest-balancing" and have sustained a variety of restrictions. In *Heller,* however, we expressly rejected the argument that the scope of the Second Amendment right should be determined by judicial interest balancing, and this Court decades ago abandoned "the notion that the Fourteenth Amendment applies to the States only a watered-down, subjective version of the individual guarantees of the Bill of Rights."

It is important to keep in mind that *Heller,* while striking down a law that prohibited the possession of handguns in the home, recognized that the right to keep and bear arms is not "a right to keep and carry any weapon whatsoever in any manner whatsoever and for whatever purpose." We made it clear in *Heller* that our holding did not cast doubt on such longstanding regulatory measures as "prohibitions on the possession of firearms by felons and the mentally ill," "laws forbidding the carrying of firearms in sensitive places such as schools and government buildings, or laws imposing conditions and qualifications on the commercial sale of arms." We repeat those assurances here. Despite municipal respondents' doomsday proclamations, incorporation does not imperil every law regulating firearms.

Municipal respondents argue, finally, that the right to keep and bear arms is unique among the rights set out in the first eight Amendments "because the reason for codifying the Second Amendment (to protect the militia) differs from the purpose (primarily, to use firearms to engage in self-defense) that is claimed to make the right implicit in the concept of ordered liberty." Municipal respondents suggest that the Second Amendment right differs from the rights heretofore incorporated because the latter were "valued for [their] own sake." But we have never previously suggested that incorporation of a right turns on whether it has intrinsic as opposed to instrumental value, and quite a few of the rights previously held to be incorporated—for example the right to counsel and the right to confront and subpoena witnesses—are clearly instrumental by any measure. Moreover, this contention repackages one of the chief arguments that we rejected in *Heller, i.e.,* that the scope of the Second Amendment right is defined by the immediate threat that led to the inclusion of that right in the Bill of Rights. In *Heller,* we recognized that the codification of this right was prompted by fear that the Federal Government would disarm and thus disable the militias, but we rejected the suggestion that the right was valued only as a means of preserving the militias. On the contrary, we stressed that the right was also valued because the possession of firearms was thought to be essential for self-defense. As we put it, self-defense was "the *central component* of the right itself."

V (no T)

Justice Stevens would "'ground the prohibitions against state action squarely on due process, without intermediate reliance on any of the first eight Amendments.'" . . . He would hold that "[t]he rights protected against state infringement by the Fourteenth Amendment's Due Process Clause need not be identical in shape or scope to the rights protected against Federal Government infringement by the various provisions of the Bill of Rights." . . . The relationship between the Bill of Rights' guarantees and the States must be governed by a single, neutral principle. It is far too late to exhume what Justice Brennan, writing for the Court 46 years ago, derided as "the notion that the Fourteenth Amendment applies to the States only a watered-down, subjective version of the individual guarantees of the Bill of Rights." . . .

Justice Breyer's conclusion that the Fourteenth Amendment does not incorporate the right to keep and bear arms appears to rest primarily on four factors: First, "there is no popular consensus" that the right is fundamental; second, the right does not protect minorities or persons neglected by those holding political power; third, incorporation of the Second Amendment right would "amount to a significant incursion on a traditional and important area of state concern, altering the constitutional relationship between the States and the Federal Government" and preventing local variations; and fourth, determining the scope of the Second Amendment right in cases involving state and local laws will force judges to answer difficult empirical questions regarding matters that are outside their area of expertise. . . .

First, we have never held that a provision of the Bill of Rights applies to the States only if there is a "popular consensus" that the right is fundamental, and we see no basis for such a rule. But in this case, as it turns out, there is evidence of such a consensus. An *amicus* brief submitted by 58 Members of the Senate and 251 Members of the House of Representatives urges us to hold that the right to keep and bear arms is fundamental. Another brief submitted by 38 States takes the same position.

Second, petitioners and many others who live in high-crime areas dispute the proposition that the Second Amendment right does not protect minorities and those lacking political clout. The plight of Chicagoans living in high-crime areas was recently highlighted when two Illinois legislators representing Chicago districts called on the Governor to deploy the Illinois National Guard to patrol the City's streets. The legislators noted that the number of Chicago homicide victims during the current year equaled the number of American soldiers killed during that same period in Afghanistan and Iraq and that 80% of the Chicago victims were black. *Amici* supporting incorporation of the right to keep and bear arms contend that the right is especially important for women and members of other groups that may be especially vulnerable to violent crime. If, as petitioners believe, their safety and the safety of other law-abiding members of the community would be enhanced by the possession of handguns in the home for self-defense, then the Second Amendment right protects the rights of minorities and other residents of high-crime areas whose needs are not being met by elected public officials.

Third, Justice Breyer is correct that incorporation of the Second Amendment right will to some extent limit the legislative freedom of the States, but this is always true when a Bill of Rights provision is incorporated. Incorporation always restricts experimentation and local variations, but that has not stopped the Court from incorporating virtually every other provision of the Bill of Rights. . . .

Finally, Justice Breyer is incorrect that incorporation will require judges to assess the costs and benefits of firearms restrictions and thus to make difficult empirical judgments in an area in which they lack expertise. As we have noted, while his opinion in *Heller* recommended an interest-balancing test, the Court specifically rejected that suggestion.

In *Heller,* we held that the Second Amendment protects the right to possess a handgun in the home for the purpose of self-defense. Unless considerations of *stare decisis* counsel otherwise, a provision of the Bill of Rights that protects a right that is fundamental from an American perspective applies equally to the Federal Government and the States. We therefore hold that the Due Process Clause of the Fourteenth Amendment incorporates the Second Amendment right recognized in *Heller.* The judgment of the Court of Appeals is reversed, and the case is remanded for further proceedings.

It is so ordered.

Justice SCALIA, concurring.

I join the Court's opinion. Despite my misgivings about Substantive Due Process as an original matter, I have acquiesced in the Court's incorporation of certain guarantees in the Bill of Rights "because it is both long established and narrowly limited." This case does not require me to reconsider that view, since straightforward application of settled doctrine suffices to decide it. . . .

Justice Stevens . . . urge[s] readoption of the theory of incorporation articulated in *Palko v. Connecticut,* [but] whether *Palko* requires only that "a fair and enlightened system of justice would be impossible without" the right sought to be incorporated, or requires in addition that the right be rooted in the "traditions and conscience of our people," many of the rights Justice STEVENS thinks are incorporated could not past muster under either test: abortion, (*Planned Parenthood of Southeastern Pa. v. Casey*); homosexual sodomy (*Lawrence v. Texas*); the right to have excluded from criminal trials evidence obtained in violation of the Fourth Amendment (*Mapp v. Ohio*); and the right to teach one's children foreign languages (*Meyer v. Nebraska*), among others.

Justice Thomas, concurring in part and concurring in the judgment.

I agree with the Court that the Fourteenth Amendment makes the right to keep and bear arms set forth in the Second Amendment "fully applicable to the States." I write separately because I believe there is a more straightforward path to this conclusion, one that is more faithful to the Fourteenth Amendment's text and history. . . . [T]he right to keep and bear arms is a privilege of American citizenship that applies to the States through the Fourteenth Amendment's Privileges or Immunities Clause. . . .

While this Court has at times concluded that a right gains "fundamental" status only if it is essential to the American "scheme of ordered liberty" or "'deeply rooted in this Nation's history and tradition,'" the Court has just as often held that a right warrants Due Process Clause protection if it satisfies a far less measurable range of criteria, see *Lawrence v. Texas,* 539 U.S. 558, 562 (2003) (concluding that the Due Process Clause protects "liberty of the person both in its spatial and in its more transcendent dimensions"). Using the latter approach, the Court has determined that the Due Process Clause applies rights against the States that are not mentioned in the Constitution at all, even without seriously arguing that the Clause was originally understood to protect such rights. See, *e.g., Lochner v. New York,* 198 U.S. 45 (1905); *Roe v. Wade,* 410 U.S. 113 (1973); *Lawrence, supra.*

All of this is a legal fiction. The notion that a constitutional provision that guarantees only "process" before a person is deprived of life, liberty, or property could define the substance of those rights strains credulity for even the most casual user of words. Moreover, this fiction is a particularly dangerous one. The one theme that links the Court's substantive due process precedents together is their lack of a guiding principle to distinguish "fundamental" rights that warrant protection from nonfundamental rights that do not. Today's decision illustrates the point. Replaying a debate that has endured from the inception of the Court's substantive due process jurisprudence, the dissents laud the "flexibility" in this Court's substantive due process doctrine, while the plurality makes yet another effort to impose principled restraints on its exercise. But neither side argues that the meaning they attribute to the Due Process Clause was consistent with public understanding at the time of its ratification.

To be sure, the plurality's effort to cabin the exercise of judicial discretion under the Due Process Clause by focusing its inquiry on those rights deeply rooted in American history and tradition invites less opportunity for abuse than the alternatives. But any serious argument over the scope of the Due Process Clause must acknowledge that neither its text nor its history suggests that it protects the many substantive rights this Court's cases now claim it does.

I cannot accept a theory of constitutional interpretation that rests on such tenuous footing. This Court's substantive due process framework fails to account for both the text of the Fourteenth Amendment and the history that led to its adoption, filling that gap with a jurisprudence devoid of a guiding principle. I believe the original meaning of the Fourteenth Amendment offers a superior alternative, and that a return to that meaning would allow this Court to enforce the rights the Fourteenth Amendment is designed to protect with greater clarity and predictability than the substantive due process framework has so far managed.

I acknowledge the volume of precedents that have been built upon the substantive due process framework, and I further acknowledge the importance of *stare decisis* to the stability of our Nation's legal system. But *stare decisis* is only an "adjunct" of our duty as judges to decide by our best lights what the Constitution means. It is not "an inexorable command." *Lawrence.* Moreover, as judges, we interpret the Constitution one case or controversy at a time. The question presented in this case is not whether our entire Fourteenth Amendment jurisprudence must be preserved or revised, but only whether, and to what extent, a particular clause in the Constitution protects the particular right at issue here. With the inquiry appropriately narrowed, I believe this case presents an opportunity to reexamine, and begin the process of restoring, the meaning of the Fourteenth Amendment agreed upon by those who ratified it.

II

[T]he objective . . . is to discern what "ordinary citizens" at the time of ratification would have understood the Privileges or Immunities Clause to mean.

At the time of Reconstruction, the terms "privileges" and "immunities" had an established meaning as synonyms for "rights." The two words, standing alone or paired together, were used interchangeably with the words "rights," "liberties," and "freedoms," and had been since the time of Blackstone . . . By the time of Reconstruction, it had long been established that both the States and the Federal Government existed to preserve their citizens' inalienable rights, and that these rights were considered "privileges" or "immunities" of citizenship . . .

Section 1 protects the rights of citizens "of the United States" specifically. The evidence overwhelmingly demonstrates that the privileges and immunities of such citizens included individual rights enumerated in the Constitution, including the right to keep and bear arms.

Nineteenth-century treaties through which the United States acquired territory from other sovereigns routinely promised inhabitants of the newly acquired territories that they would enjoy all of the "rights," "privileges," and "immunities" of United States citizens. . . . Commentators of the time explained that the rights and immunities of "citizens of the United States" recognized in these treaties "undoubtedly mean[t] those privileges that are common to all citizens of this republic." It is therefore altogether unsurprising that several of these treaties identify liberties enumerated in the Constitution as privileges and immunities common to all United States citizens. . . .

Evidence from the political branches in the years leading to the Fourteenth Amendment's adoption demonstrates broad public understanding that the privileges and immunities of United States citizenship included rights set forth in the Constitution, . . . In 1868, President Andrew Johnson issued a proclamation granting amnesty to former Confederates, guaranteeing "to all and to every person who directly or indirectly participated in the late insurrection or rebellion, a full pardon and amnesty for the offence of treason . . . with restoration of *all rights, privileges, and immunities under the Constitution* and the laws which have been made in pursuance thereof." 15 Stat. 712. . . .

After the Civil War, Congress established the Joint Committee on Reconstruction to investigate circumstances in the Southern States and to determine whether, and on what conditions, those States should be readmitted to the Union. That Committee would ultimately recommend the adoption of the Fourteenth Amendment, justifying its recommendation by submitting a report to Congress that extensively catalogued the abuses of civil rights in the former slave States and argued that "adequate security for future peace and safety . . . can only be found in such changes of the organic law as shall determine the civil rights and privileges of all citizens in all parts of the republic." As the Court notes, the Committee's Report "was widely reprinted in the press and distributed by members of the 39th Congress to their constituents." In addition, newspaper coverage suggests that the wider public was aware of the Committee's work even before the Report was issued. . . .

Statements made by Members of Congress leading up to, and during, the debates on the Fourteenth Amendment point in the same direction. . . . When interpreting constitutional text, the goal is to discern the most likely public understanding of a particular provision at the time it was adopted. Statements by legislators can assist in this process to the extent they demonstrate the manner in which the public used or understood a particular word or phrase. They can further assist to the extent there is evidence that these statements were disseminated to the public. In other words, this evidence is useful not because it demonstrates what the draftsmen of the text may have been thinking, but only insofar as it illuminates what the public understood the words chosen by the draftsmen to mean.

[Justice Thomas discusses speeches by John Bingham, the primary drafter of the Fourteenth Amendment, and Jacob Howard, the Amendment's floor manager in the Senate, stating that the Privileges or Immunities Clause would enforce the Bill of Rights against the states.] As a whole, these well-circulated speeches indicate that §1 was understood to enforce constitutionally declared rights against the States, and they provide no suggestion that any language in — the section other than the Privileges or Immunities Clause would accomplish that task. [T]he civil rights legislation adopted by the 39th Congress in 1866 further supports this view. . . . Both proponents and opponents of [the 1866 Civil Rights] Act described it as providing the "privileges" of citizenship to freedmen, and defined those privileges to include constitutional rights, such as the right to keep and bear arms. . . . Three months later, Congress passed the Freedmen's Bureau Act, which also entitled all citizens to the "full and equal benefit of all laws and proceedings concerning personal liberty" and "personal security." Act of July 16, 1866, ch. 200, §14, 14 Stat. 176. The Act stated expressly that the rights of personal liberty and security protected by the Act "includ[ed] the constitutional right to bear arms." . . .

Many statements by Members of Congress corroborate the view that the Privileges or Immunities Clause enforced constitutionally enumerated rights against the States. I am not aware of any statement that directly refutes that proposition. That said, the record of the debates—like most legislative history—is less than crystal clear. In particular, much ambiguity derives from the fact that at least several Members described §1 as protecting the privileges and immunities of citizens "in the several States," harkening back to Article IV, §2. These statements can be read to support the view that the Privileges or Immunities Clause protects some or all the fundamental rights of "citizens" described in *Corfield*. They can also be read to support the view that the Privileges or Immunities Clause, like Article IV, §2, prohibits only state discrimination with respect to those rights it covers, but does not deprive States of the power to deny those rights to all citizens equally. [Nevertheless,] it is significant that the most widely publicized statements by the legislators who voted on §1 . . . point unambiguously toward the conclusion that the Privileges or Immunities Clause enforces at least those fundamental rights enumerated in the Constitution against the States, including the Second Amendment right to keep and bear arms. . . . As the Court demonstrates, there can be no doubt that §1 was understood to enforce the Second Amendment against the States. In my view, this is because the right to keep and bear arms was understood to be a privilege of American citizenship guaranteed by the Privileges or Immunities Clause. . . .

III

[T]here was no reason [for the Court in *Slaughter-House*] to interpret the Privileges or Immunities Clause as putting the Court to the extreme choice of interpreting the "privileges and immunities" of federal citizenship to mean either all those rights listed in *Corfield* [*v. Coryell*], or almost no rights at all. The record is scant that the public understood the Clause to make the Federal Government "a perpetual censor upon all legislation of the States" as the *Slaughter-House* majority feared. For one thing, *Corfield* listed the "elective franchise" as one of the privileges and immunities of "citizens of the several states," yet Congress and the States still found it necessary to adopt the Fifteenth Amendment—which protects "[t]he right of citizens of the United States to vote"—two years after the Fourteenth Amendment's passage. If the Privileges or Immunities Clause were understood to protect every conceivable civil right from state abridgment, the Fifteenth Amendment would have been redundant.

The better view, in light of the States and Federal Government's shared history of recognizing certain inalienable rights in their citizens, is that the privileges and immunities of state and federal citizenship overlap. This is not to say that the privileges and immunities of state and federal citizenship are the same. At the time of the Fourteenth Amendment's ratification, States performed many more functions than the Federal Government, and it is unlikely that, simply by referring to "privileges or immunities," the Framers of §1 meant to transfer every right mentioned in *Corfield* to congressional oversight. . . . Because the privileges and immunities of American citizenship include rights enumerated in the Constitution, they overlap to at least some extent with the privileges and immunities traditionally recognized in citizens in the several States.

A separate question is whether the privileges and immunities of American citizenship include any rights besides those enumerated in the Constitution. The four dissenting Justices in *Slaughter-House* would have held that the Privileges or Immunities Clause protected the unenumerated right that the butchers in that case asserted. Because this case does not involve an unenumerated right, it is — not necessary to resolve the question whether the Clause protects such rights, or whether the Court's judgment in *Slaughter-House* was correct.

Still, it is argued that the mere possibility that the Privileges or Immunities Clause may enforce unenumerated rights against the States creates "'special hazards'" that should prevent this Court from returning to the original meaning of the Clause. Ironically, the same objection applies to the Court's substantive due process jurisprudence, which illustrates the risks of granting judges broad discretion to recognize individual constitutional rights in the absence of textual or historical guideposts. But I see no reason to assume that such hazards apply to the Privileges or Immunities Clause. The mere fact that the Clause does not — expressly list the rights it protects does not render it incapable of principled judicial application. The Constitution contains many provisions that require an examination of more than just constitutional text to determine whether a particular act is within Congress' power or is otherwise prohibited. See, *e.g.,* Art. I, §8, cl. 18 (Necessary and Proper Clause); Amdt. 8 (Cruel and Unusual Punishments Clause). When the inquiry focuses on what the ratifying era understood the Privileges or Immunities Clause to mean, interpreting it should be no more "hazardous" than interpreting these other constitutional provisions by using the same approach. To be sure, interpreting the Privileges or Immunities Clause may produce hard questions. But they will have the advantage of being questions the Constitution asks us to answer. I believe those questions are more worthy of this Court's attention—and far more likely to yield discernable answers—than the substantive due process questions the Court has for years created on its own, with neither textual nor historical support. . . .

. . . . *Cruikshank* squarely held that the right to keep and bear arms was not a privilege of American citizenship, thereby overturning the convictions of militia members responsible for the brutal Colfax Massacre. *Cruikshank* is not a precedent entitled to any respect. . . . *Cruikshank*'s holding that blacks could — look only to state governments for protection of their right to keep and bear arms enabled private forces, often with the assistance of local governments, to subjugate the newly freed slaves and their descendants through a wave of private violence designed to drive blacks from the voting booth and force them into peonage, an effective return to slavery. Without federal enforcement of the inalienable right to keep and bear arms, these militias and mobs were tragically successful in waging a campaign of terror against the very people the Fourteenth Amendment had just made citizens.

Organized terrorism . . . proliferated in the absence of federal enforcement of constitutional rights. Militias such as the Ku Klux Klan, the Knights of the White Camellia, the White Brotherhood, the Pale Faces, and the '76 Association spread terror among blacks and white Republicans by breaking up Republican meetings, threatening political leaders, and whipping black militiamen. These groups raped, murdered, lynched, and robbed as a means of intimidating, and instilling pervasive fear in, those whom they despised. . . . Klan tactics remained a constant presence in the lives of Southern blacks for decades. Between 1882 and 1968, there were at least 3,446 reported lynchings of blacks in the South. They were tortured and killed for a wide array of alleged crimes, without even the slightest hint of due process. . . . The use of firearms for self-defense was often the only way black citizens could protect themselves from mob violence. . . .

In my view, the record makes plain that the Framers of the Privileges or Immunities Clause and the ratifying-era public understood—just as the Framers of the Second Amendment did—that the right to keep and bear arms was essential to the preservation of liberty. The record makes equally plain that they deemed this right necessary to include in the minimum baseline of federal rights that the Privileges or Immunities Clause established in the wake of the War over slavery. There is nothing about *Cruikshank*'s contrary holding that warrants its retention. . . .

Justice Stevens, dissenting.

[T]he question we should be answering in this case is whether the Constitution "guarantees individuals a fundamental right," enforceable against the States, "to possess a functional, personal firearm, including a handgun, within the home." That is a different—and more difficult—inquiry than asking if the Fourteenth Amendment "incorporates" the Second Amendment. The so-called incorporation question was squarely and, in my view, correctly resolved in the late 19th century. . . .

[Petitioners] marshal an impressive amount of historical evidence for their argument that the Court interpreted the Privileges or Immunities Clause too narrowly in the *Slaughter-House Cases*. But the original meaning of the Clause is not as clear as they suggest—and not nearly as clear as it would need to be to dislodge 137 years of precedent. The burden is severe for those who seek radical change in such an established body of constitutional doctrine. Moreover, the suggestion that invigorating the Privileges or Immunities Clause will reduce judicial discretion, strikes me as implausible, if not exactly backwards. "For the very reason that it has so long remained a clean slate, a revitalized Privileges or Immunities Clause holds special hazards for judges who are mindful that their proper task is not to write their personal views of appropriate public policy into the Constitution."

I further agree with the plurality that there are weighty arguments supporting petitioners' second submission, insofar as it concerns the possession of firearms for lawful self-defense in the home. But these arguments are less compelling than the plurality suggests; they are much less compelling when applied outside the home; and their validity does not depend on the Court's holding in *Heller*. For that holding sheds no light on the meaning of the Due Process Clause of the Fourteenth Amendment. Our decisions construing that Clause to render various procedural guarantees in the Bill of Rights enforceable against the States likewise tell us little about the meaning of the word "liberty" in the Clause or about the scope of its protection of nonprocedural rights. This is a substantive due process case. . . .

The rights protected against state infringement by the Fourteenth Amendment's Due Process Clause need not be identical in shape or scope to the rights protected against Federal Government infringement by the various provisions of the Bill of Rights. . . . Elementary considerations of constitutional text and structure suggest there may be legitimate reasons to hold state governments to different standards than the Federal Government in certain areas. . . . [W]e have never accepted a "total incorporation" theory of the Fourteenth Amendment. . . . We have, moreover, resisted a uniform approach to the Sixth Amendment's criminal jury guarantee, demanding 12-member panels and unanimous verdicts in federal trials, yet not in state trials. See *Apodaca v. Oregon,* 406 U.S. 404 (1972) (plurality opinion) . . . [T]the "incorporation" of a provision of the Bill of Rights into the Fourteenth Amendment does not, in itself, mean the provision must have precisely the same meaning in both contexts.

It is true, as well, that during the 1960's the Court decided a number of cases involving procedural rights in which it treated the Due Process Clause as if it transplanted language from the Bill of Rights into the Fourteenth Amendment. . . . "Jot-for-jot" incorporation was the norm in this expansionary era. Yet at least one subsequent opinion suggests that these precedents require perfect state/federal congruence only on matters "'at the core'" of the relevant constitutional guarantee. In my judgment, this line of cases is best understood as having concluded that, to ensure a criminal trial satisfies essential standards of fairness, some procedures should be the same in state and federal courts: The need for certainty and uniformity is more pressing, and the margin for error slimmer, when criminal justice is at issue. That principle has little relevance to the question whether a *non* procedural rule set forth in the Bill of Rights qualifies as an aspect of the liberty protected by the Fourteenth Amendment.

Notwithstanding some overheated dicta in *Malloy*, it is therefore an overstatement to say that the Court has "abandoned," a "two-track approach to incorporation." The Court moved away from that approach in the area of criminal procedure. But the Second Amendment differs in fundamental respects from its neighboring provisions in the Bill of Rights, and if some 1960's opinions purported to establish a general method of incorporation, that hardly binds us in this case. The Court has not hesitated to cut back on perceived Warren Court excesses in more areas than I can count.

I do not mean to deny that there can be significant practical, as well as esthetic, benefits from treating rights symmetrically with regard to the State and Federal Governments. Jot-for-jot incorporation of a provision may entail greater protection of the right at issue and therefore greater freedom for those who hold it; jot-for-jot incorporation may also yield greater clarity about the contours of the legal rule. In a federalist system such as ours, however, this approach can carry substantial costs. When a federal court insists that state and local authorities follow its dictates on a matter not critical to personal liberty or procedural justice, the latter may be prevented from engaging in the kind of beneficent "experimentation in things social and economic" that ultimately redounds to the benefit of all Americans. *New State Ice Co. v. Liebmann,* 285 U.S. 262, 311 (1932) (Brandeis, J., dissenting). The costs of federal courts' imposing a uniform national standard may be especially high when the relevant regulatory interests vary significantly across localities, and when the ruling implicates the States' core police powers.

Furthermore, there is a real risk that, by demanding the provisions of the Bill of Rights apply identically to the States, federal courts will cause those provisions to "be watered down in the needless pursuit of uniformity." When one legal standard must prevail across dozens of jurisdictions with disparate needs and customs, courts will often settle on a relaxed standard. This watering-down risk is particularly acute when we move beyond the narrow realm of criminal procedure and into the relatively vast domain of substantive rights. So long as the requirements of fundamental fairness are always and everywhere respected, it is not clear that greater liberty results from the jot-for-jot application of a provision of the Bill of Rights to the States. Indeed, it is far from clear that proponents of an individual right to keep and bear arms ought to celebrate today's decision. . . .

IV

The question in this case, then, is not whether the Second Amendment right to keep and bear arms (whatever that right's precise contours) applies to the States because the Amendment has been incorporated into the Fourteenth Amendment. It has not been. The question, rather, is whether the particular right asserted by petitioners applies to the States because of the Fourteenth Amendment itself, standing on its own bottom. . . . [T]he liberty interest petitioners have asserted is the "right to possess a functional, personal firearm, including a handgun, within the home." . . . Petitioners now frame the question that confronts us as "[w]hether the Second Amendment right to keep and bear arms is incorporated as against the States by the Fourteenth Amendment's Privileges or Immunities or Due Process Clauses." But it is our duty "to focus on the allegations in the complaint to determine how petitioner describes the constitutional right at stake," and the gravamen of this complaint is plainly an appeal to keep a handgun or other firearm of one's choosing in the home. . . . The majority opinion [in *Heller*] contained some dicta suggesting the possibility of a more expansive arms-bearing right, one that would travel with the individual to an extent into public places, as "in case of confronta- tion." But the *Heller* plaintiff sought only dispensation to keep an operable – firearm in his home for lawful self-defense, and the Court's opinion was book- ended by reminders that its holding was limited to that one issue. The distinction between the liberty right these petitioners have asserted and the Second Amendment right identified in *Heller* is therefore evanescent . . .

In their briefs to this Court, several *amici* have sought to bolster petitioners' claim still further by invoking a right to individual self-defense. As petitioners note, the *Heller* majority discussed this subject extensively and remarked that "[t]he inherent right of self-defense has been central to the Second Amendment right." . . . But that is not the case before us. Petitioners have not asked that we establish a constitutional right to individual self-defense; neither their pleadings in the District Court nor their filings in this Court make any such request. Nor do petitioners contend that the city of Chicago—which, recall, allows its residents to keep most rifles and shotguns, and to keep them loaded—has unduly burdened any such right. What petitioners have asked is that we "in- corporate" the Second Amendment and thereby establish a constitutional entitlement, enforceable against the States, to keep a handgun in the home. . . .

Of course, owning a handgun may be useful for practicing self-defense. But the right to take a certain type of action is analytically distinct from the right to acquire and utilize specific instrumentalities in furtherance of that action. And while some might favor handguns, it is not clear that they are a superior weapon for lawful self-defense, and nothing in petitioners' argument turns on that being the case. The notion that a right of self-defense *implies* an auxiliary right to own a certain type of firearm presupposes not only controversial judgments about the strength and scope of the (posited) self-defense right, but also controversial assumptions about the likely effects of making that type of firearm more broadly available. It is a very long way from the proposition that the Fourteenth Amendment protects a basic individual right of self-defense to the conclusion that a city may not ban handguns. . . .

V

While I agree with the Court that our substantive due process cases offer a principled basis for holding that petitioners have a constitutional right to possess a usable firearm in the home, I am ultimately persuaded that a better reading of our case law supports the city of Chicago. I would not foreclose the possibility that a particular plaintiff—say, an elderly widow who lives in a dangerous neighborhood and does not have the strength to operate a long gun—may have a cognizable liberty interest in possessing a handgun. But I cannot accept petitioners' broader submission. A number of factors, taken together, lead me to this conclusion.

First, firearms have a fundamentally ambivalent relationship to liberty. Just as they can help homeowners defend their families and property from intruders, they can help thugs and insurrectionists murder innocent victims. The threat that firearms will be misused is far from hypothetical, for gun crime has devastated many of our communities. *Amici* calculate that approximately one million Americans have been wounded or killed by gunfire in the last decade. Urban areas such as Chicago suffer disproportionately from this epidemic of violence. Handguns contribute disproportionately to it. Just as some homeowners may prefer handguns because of their small size, light weight, and ease of operation, some criminals will value them for the same reasons. In recent years, handguns were reportedly used in more than four-fifths of firearm murders and more than half of all murders nationwide.

Hence, in evaluating an asserted right to be free from particular gun-control regulations, liberty is on both sides of the equation. Guns may be useful for self-defense, as well as for hunting and sport, but they also have a unique potential to facilitate death and destruction and thereby to destabilize ordered liberty. *Your* interest in keeping and bearing a certain firearm may diminish *my* interest in being and feeling safe from armed violence. And while granting you the right to own a handgun might make you safer on any given day—assuming the handgun's marginal contribution to self-defense outweighs its marginal contribution to the risk of accident, suicide, and criminal mischief—it may make you and the community you live in less safe overall, owing to the increased number of handguns in circulation. It is at least reasonable for a democratically elected legislature to take such concerns into account in considering what sorts of regulations would best serve the public welfare.

The practical impact of various gun-control measures may be highly controversial, but this basic insight should not be. The idea that deadly weapons pose a distinctive threat to the social order—and that reasonable restrictions on their usage therefore impose an acceptable burden on one's personal liberty—is as old as the Republic. . . .

Limiting the federal constitutional right to keep and bear arms to the home complicates the analysis but does not dislodge this conclusion. Even though the Court has long afforded special solicitude for the privacy of the home, we have never understood that principle to "infring[e] upon" the authority of the States to proscribe certain inherently dangerous items, for "[i]n such cases, compelling reasons may exist for overriding the right of the individual to possess those materials." And, of course, guns that start out in the home may not stay in the home. Even if the government has a weaker basis for restricting domestic possession of firearms as compared to public carriage—and even if a blanket, statewide prohibition on domestic possession might therefore be unconstitutional—the line between the two is a porous one. A state or local legislature may determine that a prophylactic ban on an especially portable weapon is necessary to police that line.

Second, the right to possess a firearm of one's choosing is different in kind from the liberty interests we have recognized under the Due Process Clause. Despite the plethora of substantive due process cases that have been decided in the post-*Lochner* century, I have found none that holds, states, or even suggests that the term "liberty" encompasses either the common-law right of self-defense or a right to keep and bear arms. I do not doubt for a moment that many Americans feel deeply passionate about firearms, and see them as critical to their way of life as well as to their security. Nevertheless, it does not appear to be the case that the ability to own a handgun, or any particular type of firearm, is critical to leading a life of autonomy, dignity, or political equality: The market-place offers many tools for self-defense, even if they are imperfect substitutes, and neither petitioners nor their *amici* make such a contention. Petitioners' claim is not the kind of substantive interest, accordingly, on which a uniform, judicially enforced national standard is presumptively appropriate. . . .

The liberty interest asserted by petitioners is also dissimilar from those we have recognized in its capacity to undermine the security of others. To be sure, some of the Bill of Rights' procedural guarantees may place "restrictions on law enforcement" that have "controversial public safety implications." But those implications are generally quite attenuated. A defendant's invocation of *?* his right to remain silent, to confront a witness, or to exclude certain evidence cannot directly cause any threat. The defendant's liberty interest is constrained by (and is itself a constraint on) the adjudicatory process. The link between handgun ownership and public safety is much tighter. The handgun is itself a tool for crime; the handgun's bullets *are* the violence.

Similarly, it is undeniable that some may take profound offense at a remark made by the soapbox speaker, the practices of another religion, or a gay couple's choice to have intimate relations. But that offense is moral, psychological, or theological in nature; the actions taken by the rights-bearers do not actually threaten the physical safety of any other person. Firearms may be used to kill another person. If a legislature's response to dangerous weapons ends up imping-ing upon the liberty of any individuals in pursuit of the greater good, it invariably does so on the basis of more than the majority's "'own moral code,'" *Lawrence* (quoting *Casey*). While specific policies may of course be misguided, gun control is an area in which it "is quite wrong . . . to assume that regulation and liberty occupy mutually exclusive zones—that as one expands, the other must contract."

Third, the experience of other advanced democracies, including those that — share our British heritage, undercuts the notion that an expansive right to keep and bear arms is intrinsic to ordered liberty. Many of these countries place restrictions on the possession, use, and carriage of firearms far more onerous than the restrictions found in this Nation. See Municipal Respondents' Brief 21-23 (discussing laws of England, Canada, Australia, Japan, Denmark, Finland, Luxembourg, and New Zealand). That the United States is an interna-tional outlier in the permissiveness of its approach to guns does not suggest that our laws are bad laws. It does suggest that this Court may not need to assume responsibility for making our laws still more permissive.

Admittedly, these other countries differ from ours in many relevant respects, including their problems with violent crime and the traditional role that firearms have played in their societies. But they are not so different from the United States that we ought to dismiss their experience entirely. The fact that our oldest allies have almost uniformly found it appropriate to regulate firearms extensively tends to weaken petitioners' submission that the right to possess a gun of one's choosing is fundamental to a life of liberty. While the "American perspective" must always be our focus, it is silly—indeed, arrogant—to think we have nothing to learn about liberty from the billions of people beyond our borders.

Fourth, the Second Amendment differs in kind from the Amendments that surround it, with the consequence that its inclusion in the Bill of Rights is not merely unhelpful but positively harmful to petitioners' claim. Generally, the inclusion of a liberty interest in the Bill of Rights points toward the conclusion that it is of fundamental significance and ought to be enforceable against the States. But the Second Amendment plays a peculiar role within the Bill, as announced by its peculiar opening clause. Even accepting the *Heller* Court's view that the Amendment protects an individual right to keep and bear arms disconnected from militia service, it remains undeniable that "the purpose for which the right was codified" was "to prevent elimination of the militia." It was the States, not private persons, on whose immediate behalf the Second Amendment was adopted. Notwithstanding the *Heller* Court's efforts to write the Second Amendment's preamble out of the Constitution, the Amendment still serves the structural function of protecting the States from encroachment by an overreaching Federal Government.

The Second Amendment, in other words, "is a federalism provision." It is directed at preserving the autonomy of the sovereign States, and its logic therefore "resists" incorporation by a federal court *against* the States. *Ibid.* No one suggests that the Tenth Amendment, which provides that powers not given to the Federal Government remain with "the States," applies to the States; such a reading would border on incoherent, given that the Tenth Amendment exists (in significant part) to safeguard the vitality of state governance. The Second Amendment is no different.

The Court is surely correct that Americans' conceptions of the Second Amendment right evolved over time in a more individualistic direction; that Members of the Reconstruction Congress were urgently concerned about the safety of the newly freed slaves; and that some Members believed that, following ratification of the Fourteenth Amendment, the Second Amendment would apply to the States. But it is a giant leap from these data points to the conclusion that the Fourteenth Amendment "incorporated" the Second Amendment as a matter of original meaning or postenactment interpretation. Consider, for example, that the text of the Fourteenth Amendment says nothing about the Second Amendment or firearms; that there is substantial evidence to suggest that, when the Reconstruction Congress enacted measures to ensure newly freed slaves and Union sympathizers in the South enjoyed the right to possess firearms, it was motivated by antidiscrimination and equality concerns rather than arms-bearing concerns *per se* that many contemporaneous courts and commentators did not understand the Fourteenth Amendment to have had an "incorporating" effect; and that the States heavily regulated the right to keep and bear arms both before and after the Amendment's passage. The Court's narrative largely elides these facts. The complications they raise show why even the most dogged historical inquiry into the "fundamentality" of the Second Amendment right (or any other) necessarily entails judicial judgment—and therefore judicial discretion—every step of the way.

I accept that the evolution in Americans' understanding of the Second Amendment may help shed light on the question whether a right to keep and bear arms is comprised within Fourteenth Amendment "liberty." But the reasons that motivated the Framers to protect the ability of militiamen to keep muskets available for military use when our Nation was in its infancy, or that motivated the Reconstruction Congress to extend full citizenship to the freedmen in the wake of the Civil War, have only a limited bearing on the question that confronts the homeowner in a crime-infested metropolis today. The many episodes of brutal violence against African-Americans that blight our Nation's history, do not suggest that every American must be allowed to own whatever type of firearm he or she desires—just that no group of Americans should be — systematically and discriminatorily disarmed and left to the mercy of racial terrorists. And the fact that some Americans may have thought or hoped that the Fourteenth Amendment would nationalize the Second Amendment hardly suffices to justify the conclusion that it did.

Fifth, although it may be true that Americans' interest in firearm possession and state-law recognition of that interest are "deeply rooted" in some important senses, it is equally true that the States have a long and unbroken history of regulating firearms. The idea that States may place substantial restrictions on the right to keep and bear arms short of complete disarmament is, in fact, far more entrenched than the notion that the Federal Constitution protects any such right. Federalism is a far "older and more deeply rooted tradition than is a right to carry," or to own, "any particular kind of weapon."

From the early days of the Republic, through the Reconstruction era, to the present day, States and municipalities have placed extensive licensing requirements on firearm acquisition, restricted the public carriage of weapons, and banned altogether the possession of especially dangerous weapons, including handguns. After the 1860's just as before, the state courts almost uniformly upheld these measures: Apart from making clear that all regulations had to be constructed and applied in a nondiscriminatory manner, the Fourteenth Amendment hardly made a dent. And let us not forget that this Court did not recognize *any* non-militia-related interests under the Second Amendment until two Terms ago, in *Heller*. Petitioners do not dispute the city of Chicago's observation that "[n]o other substantive Bill of Rights protection has been regulated nearly as intrusively" as the right to keep and bear arms.

This history of intrusive regulation is not surprising given that the very text of the Second Amendment calls out for regulation, and the ability to respond to the social ills associated with dangerous weapons goes to the very core of the States' police powers. . . . Compared with today's ruling, most if not all of this Court's decisions requiring the States to comply with other provisions in the Bill of Rights did not exact nearly so heavy a toll in terms of state sovereignty.

Finally, even apart from the States' long history of firearms regulation and its location at the core of their police powers, this is a quintessential area in which federalism ought to be allowed to flourish without this Court's meddling. Whether or not we *can* assert a plausible constitutional basis for intervening, there are powerful reasons why we *should not* do so.

Across the Nation, States and localities vary significantly in the patterns and problems of gun violence they face, as well as in the traditions and cultures of lawful gun use they claim. The city of Chicago, for example, faces a pressing challenge in combating criminal street gangs. Most rural areas do not. The city of Chicago has a high population density, which increases the potential for a gunman to inflict mass terror and casualties. Most rural areas do not. The city of Chicago offers little in the way of hunting opportunities. Residents of rural communities are, one presumes, much more likely to stock the dinner table with game they have personally felled.

Given that relevant background conditions diverge so much across jurisdictions, the Court ought to pay particular heed to state and local legislatures' "right to experiment." So long as the regulatory measures they have chosen are not "arbitrary, capricious, or unreasonable," we should be allowing them to "try novel social and economic" policies. *Ibid.* It "is more in keeping . . . with our status as a court in a federal system," under these circumstances, "to avoid imposing a single solution . . . from the top down."

It is all the more unwise for this Court to limit experimentation in an area "where the best solution is far from clear." Few issues of public policy are subject to such intensive and rapidly developing empirical controversy as gun control. Chicago's handgun ban, in itself, has divided researchers. Of course, on some matters the Constitution requires that we ignore such pragmatic considerations. But the Constitution's text, history, and structure are not so clear on the matter before us—as evidenced by the groundbreaking nature of today's fractured decision—and this Court lacks both the technical capacity and the localized expertise to assess "the wisdom, need, and propriety" of most gun-control measures.

Nor will the Court's intervention bring any clarity to this enormously complex area of law. Quite to the contrary, today's decision invites an avalanche of litigation that could mire the federal courts in fine-grained determinations about which state and local regulations comport with the *Heller* right—the precise contours of which are far from pellucid—under a standard of review we have not even established. The plurality's "assuranc[e]" that "incorporation does not imperil every law regulating firearms," provides only modest comfort. For it is also an admission of just how many different types of regulations are potentially implicated by today's ruling, and of just how ad hoc the Court's initial attempt to draw distinctions among them was in *Heller*. The practical significance of the proposition that "the Second Amendment right is fully applicable to the States," remains to be worked out by this Court over many, many years.

Furthermore, and critically, the Court's imposition of a national standard is – still more unwise because the elected branches have shown themselves to be perfectly capable of safeguarding the interest in keeping and bearing arms. The strength of a liberty claim must be assessed in connection with its status in the democratic process. And in this case, no one disputes "that opponents of [gun] control have considerable political power and do not seem to be at a systematic disadvantage in the democratic process," or that "the widespread commitment to an individual right to own guns . . . operates as a safeguard against excessive or unjustified gun control laws." Indeed, there is a good deal of evidence to suggest that, if anything, American lawmakers tend to *under* regulate guns, relative to the policy views expressed by majorities in opinion polls. If a particular State or locality has enacted some "improvident" gun-control measures, as petitioners believe Chicago has done, there is no apparent reason to infer that the mistake will not "eventually be rectified by the democratic process."

This is not a case, then, that involves a "special condition" that "may call for a correspondingly more searching judicial inquiry." *Carolene Products,* 304 U.S., at 153, n. 4. Neither petitioners nor those most zealously committed to their views represent a group or a claim that is liable to receive unfair treatment at the hands of the majority. On the contrary, petitioners' views are supported by powerful participants in the legislative process. Petitioners have given us no reason to believe that the interest in keeping and bearing arms entails any special need for judicial lawmaking, or that federal judges are more qualified to craft appropriate rules than the people's elected representatives. Having failed to show why their asserted interest is intrinsic to the concept of ordered liberty or vulnerable to maltreatment in the political arena, they have failed to show why "the word liberty in the Fourteenth Amendment" should be "held to prevent the natural outcome of a dominant opinion" about how to deal with the problem of handgun violence in the city of Chicago. *Lochner,* 198 U.S., at 76 (Holmes, J., dissenting). . . .

Justice BREYER, with whom Justice GINSBURG and Justice SOTOMAYOR join, dissenting.

. . . I can find nothing in the Second Amendment's text, history, or underlying rationale that could warrant characterizing it as "fundamental" insofar as it seeks to protect the keeping and bearing of arms for private self-defense purposes. Nor can I find any justification for interpreting the Constitution as transferring ultimate regulatory authority over the private uses of firearms from democratically elected legislatures to courts or from the States to the Federal Government. I therefore conclude that the Fourteenth Amendment does not "incorporate" the Second Amendment's right "to keep and bear Arms." And I consequently dissent.

I

[T]he Court based its conclusions [in *Heller*] almost exclusively upon its reading of history. But the relevant history in *Heller* was far from clear: Four dissenting Justices disagreed with the majority's historical analysis. And subsequent scholarly writing reveals why disputed history provides treacherous ground on which to build decisions written by judges who are not expert at history.

Since *Heller*, historians, scholars, and judges have continued to express the view that the Court's historical account was flawed. . . . If history, and history alone, is what matters, why would the Court not now reconsider *Heller* in light of these more recently published historical views? At the least, where *Heller*'s historical foundations are so uncertain, why extend its applicability? . . . In my own view, the Court should not look to history alone but to other factors as well—above all, in cases where the history is so unclear that the experts themselves strongly disagree. It should, for example, consider the basic values that underlie a constitutional provision and their contemporary significance. And it should examine as well the relevant consequences and practical justifications that might, or might not, warrant removing an important question from the democratic decisionmaking process.

II

A

In my view, taking *Heller* as a given, the Fourteenth Amendment does not incorporate the Second Amendment right to keep and bear arms for purposes of private self-defense. Under this Court's precedents, to incorporate the private self-defense right the majority must show that the right is, *e.g.,* "fundamental to the American scheme of justice," *Duncan*. And this it fails to do. The majority here, like that in *Heller,* relies almost exclusively upon history to make the necessary showing. But to do so for incorporation purposes is both wrong and dangerous. [O]ur society has historically made mistakes—for example, when considering certain 18th- and 19th-century property rights to be fundamental. And in the incorporation context, as elsewhere, history often is unclear about the answers.

Accordingly, this Court, in considering an incorporation question, has never stated that the historical status of a right is the only relevant consideration. Rather, the Court has either explicitly or implicitly made clear in its opinions that the right in question has remained fundamental over time. . . . I thus think it proper, above all where history provides no clear answer, to look to other factors in considering whether a right is sufficiently "fundamental" to remove it from the political process in every State. I would include among those factors the nature of the right; any contemporary disagreement about whether the right is fundamental; the extent to which incorporation will further other, perhaps more basic, constitutional aims; and the extent to which incorporation will advance or hinder the Constitution's structural aims, including its division of powers among different governmental institutions (and the people as well). Is incorporation needed, for example, to further the Constitution's effort to ensure that the government treats each individual with equal respect? Will it help maintain the democratic form of government that the Constitution foresees? In a word, will incorporation prove consistent, or inconsistent, with the Constitution's efforts to create governmental institutions well suited to the carrying out of its constitutional promises? . . .

B

[I]t is difficult to see how a right that, as the majority concedes, has "largely faded as a popular concern" could possibly be so fundamental that it would warrant incorporation through the Fourteenth Amendment. Hence, the incorporation of the Second Amendment cannot be based on the militia-related aspect of what *Heller* found to be more extensive Second Amendment rights. [A]s *Heller* concedes, the private self-defense right that the Court would incorporate has nothing to do with "the *reason*" the Framers "codified" the right to keep and bear arms "in a written Constitution." *Heller* immediately adds that the self-defense right was nonetheless "the *central component* of the right." In my view, this is the historical equivalent of a claim that water runs uphill. . . .

Further, there is no popular consensus that the private self-defense right described in *Heller* is fundamental. The plurality suggests that two *amici* briefs filed in the case show such a consensus, but, of course, numerous *amici* briefs have been filed opposing incorporation as well. Moreover, every State regulates firearms extensively, and public opinion is sharply divided on the appropriate level of regulation. Much of this disagreement rests upon empirical considerations. One side believes the right essential to protect the lives of those attacked in the home; the other side believes it essential to regulate the right in order to protect the lives of others attacked with guns. It seems unlikely that definitive evidence will develop one way or the other. And the appropriate level of firearm regulation has thus long been, and continues to be, a hotly contested matter of political debate. See, *e.g.,* Siegel, Dead or Alive: Originalism as Popular Constitutionalism in *Heller,* 122 Harv. L. Rev. 191, 201-246 (2008).

Moreover, there is no reason here to believe that incorporation of the private self-defense right will further any other or broader constitutional objective. We are aware of no argument that gun-control regulations target or are passed with the purpose of targeting "discrete and insular minorities." *Carolene Products Co., supra,* at 153, n. 4. Nor will incorporation help to assure equal respect for individuals. Unlike the First Amendment's rights of free speech, free press, assembly, and petition, the private self-defense right does not comprise a necessary part of the democratic process that the Constitution seeks to establish. Unlike the First Amendment's religious protections, the Fourth Amendment's protection against unreasonable searches and seizures, the Fifth and Sixth Amendments' insistence upon fair criminal procedure, and the Eighth Amendment's protection against cruel and unusual punishments, the private self-defense right does not significantly seek to protect individuals who might otherwise suffer unfair or inhumane treatment at the hands of a majority. Unlike the protections offered by many of these same Amendments, it does not involve matters as to which judges possess a comparative expertise, by virtue of their close familiarity with the justice system and its operation. And, unlike the Fifth Amendment's insistence on just compensation, it does not involve a matter where a majority might unfairly seize for itself property belonging to a minority.

Finally, incorporation of the right *will* work a significant disruption in the constitutional allocation of decisionmaking authority, thereby interfering with the Constitution's ability to further its objectives.

First, on any reasonable accounting, the incorporation of the right recognized in *Heller* would amount to a significant incursion on a traditional and important area of state concern, altering the constitutional relationship between the States and the Federal Government. Private gun regulation is the quintessential exercise of a State's "police power"—*i.e.,* the power to "protec[t] . . . the lives, limbs, health, comfort, and quiet of all persons, and the protection of all property within the State," by enacting "all kinds of restraints and burdens" on both "persons and property." . . .

Second, determining the constitutionality of a particular state gun law requires finding answers to complex empirically based questions of a kind that legislatures are better able than courts to make. And it may require this kind of analysis in virtually every case. . . . With respect to other incorporated rights, this sort of inquiry is *sometimes* present. But here, this inquiry—calling for the fine tuning of protective rules—is likely to be part of a daily judicial diet. . . .

Perhaps the Court could lessen the difficulty of the mission it has created for itself by adopting a jurisprudential approach similar to the many state courts that administer a state constitutional right to bear arms. But the Court has not yet done so. Cf. *Heller* (rejecting an "'interest-balancing' approach" similar to that employed by the States). Rather, the Court has haphazardly created a few simple rules, such as that it will not touch "prohibitions on the possession of firearms by felons and the mentally ill," "laws forbidding the carrying of firearms in sensitive places such as schools and government buildings," or "laws imposing conditions and qualifications on the commercial sale of arms." *Heller.* But why these rules and not others? Does the Court know that these regulations are justified by some special gun-related risk of death? In fact, the Court does not know. It has simply invented rules that sound sensible without being able to explain why or how Chicago's handgun ban is different.

The fact is that judges do not know the answers to the kinds of empirically based questions that will often determine the need for particular forms of gun regulation. Nor do they have readily available "tools" for finding and evaluating the technical material submitted by others. Judges cannot easily make empirically based predictions; they have no way to gather and evaluate the data required to see if such predictions are accurate; and the nature of litigation and concerns about *stare decisis* further make it difficult for judges to change course if predictions prove inaccurate. Nor can judges rely upon local community views and values when reaching judgments in circumstances where prediction is difficult because the basic facts are unclear or unknown.

Legislators are able to "amass the stuff of actual experience and cull conclusions from it." They are far better suited than judges to uncover facts and to understand their relevance. And legislators, unlike Article III judges, can be held democratically responsible for their empirically based and value-laden conclusions. We have thus repeatedly affirmed our preference for "legislative not judicial solutions" to this kind of problem, just as we have repeatedly affirmed the Constitution's preference for democratic solutions legislated by those whom the people elect. . . .

Third, the ability of States to reflect local preferences and conditions—both key virtues of federalism—here has particular importance. The incidence of gun ownership varies substantially as between crowded cities and uncongested rural communities, as well as among the different geographic regions of the country. Thus, approximately 60% of adults who live in the relatively sparsely populated Western States of Alaska, Montana, and Wyoming report that their household keeps a gun, while fewer than 15% of adults in the densely populated Eastern States of Rhode Island, New Jersey, and Massachusetts say the same.

The nature of gun violence also varies as between rural communities and cities. Urban centers face significantly greater levels of firearm crime and homicide, while rural communities have proportionately greater problems with nonhomicide gun deaths, such as suicides and accidents. And idiosyncratic local factors can lead to two cities finding themselves in dramatically different circumstances: For example, in 2008, the murder rate was 40 times higher in New Orleans than it was in Lincoln, Nebraska. . . .

Given the empirical and local value-laden nature of the questions that lie at the heart of the issue, why, in a Nation whose Constitution foresees democratic decisionmaking, is it so *fundamental* a matter as to require taking that power from the people? What is it here that the people did not know? What is it that a judge knows better? . . .

I can find much in the historical record that shows that some Americans in some places at certain times thought it important to keep and bear arms for private self-defense. For instance, the reader will see that many States have constitutional provisions protecting gun possession. But, as far as I can tell, those provisions typically do no more than guarantee that a gun regulation will be a *reasonable* police power regulation. It is thus altogether unclear whether such provisions would prohibit cities such as Chicago from enacting laws, such as the law before us, banning handguns. . . . States and localities have consistently enacted firearms regulations, including regulations similar to those at issue here, throughout our Nation's history. Courts have repeatedly upheld such regulations. And it is, at the very least, possible, and perhaps likely, that incorporation will impose on every, or nearly every, State a different right to bear arms than they currently recognize—a right that threatens to destabilize settled state legal principles. . . .

Discussion

1. *Changing places.* The result in *McDonald* was widely expected following the 2008 decision in *Heller.* One remarkable feature of the opinion is how fairly standard arguments made by in the past by conservative judges against incorporation and broad readings of the Bill of Rights have become the arguments of liberal judges and vice versa. Justice Stevens argues (as the second Justice Harlan did before him) that the provisions of the Bill of Rights need not apply fully to the states. Justices Stevens and Breyer make standard arguments for judicial restraint and emphasize the inability of judges to fully consider the consequences of new rights; both emphasize that courts should not attempt to intervene in difficult and contested social controversies, and both make standard arguments for respecting states' rights and for the ability of states to experiment with forms of regulation best attuned to local conditions. Justice Alito, on the other hand, emphasizes that constitutional rights must be respected whether or not they may make law enforcement more difficult or even put lives at risk. (Compare Justice Alito's willingness to sacrifice public safety to ensure constitutional liberty with the arguments of the conservative Justices in *Boumediene* a few years previously.) Justice Scalia, for his part, argues that stare decisis must trump originalist considerations.

2. *Deeply rooted in our nation's traditions.* While Justice Thomas' concurrence is strongly originalist, Justice Alito's plurality opinion offers an interesting mix of modalities. Justice Alito's approach is not strictly originalist, because he employs the Due Process Clause to incorporate the Second Amendment. On the other hand, he asks whether people in 1791 and 1868 considered the right to keep arms in the home for self-defense to be fundamental, which resembles an originalist inquiry into understandings at the time of the Founding and Reconstruction. But if the test is one of tradition, then Justice Alito should be concerned about a continuous regard for the right up to the present day. Why does he not focus more on respect for this right during the twentieth century?

3. *The Civil Rights Act and the Freedman's Bureau Act.* Both Justice Alito and Justice Thomas emphasize congressional intent to protect individual rights to bear arms in self-defense in the Civil Rights Act of 1866 and the Freedman's Bureau Act of 1866. They argue that these acts protected not only equal rights but also substantive guarantees of liberty. The Civil Rights Act of 1866, reenacted as part of the 1870 Enforcement Act under Congress's powers to enforce the Fourteenth Amendment, currently appears at 42 U.S.C. §1981.

According to *McDonald*, then, does §1981 already apply the right to bear arms against the states? If so, the constitutional holding of *McDonald* was unnecessary, because the Chicago ordinance (and any other state and local laws violating the right recognized in *Heller*) would be preempted by §1981. (Of course, the Court would still have to decide whether the Civil Rights Act of

1866 and the Enforcement Act of 1870 were constitutional exercises of Congress's powers under the Thirteenth and Fourteenth amendments, respectively.)

Michael Kent Curtis points out that the intent of Congressional Republicans —
was not only to protect Second Amendment rights, but the individual rights guarantees of the Bill of Rights generally. See Michael Kent Curtis, No State Shall Abridge: The Fourteenth Amendment and the Bill of Rights 71-83, 104 (1986). If that is so, then Section 1981 already "incorporated" the Bill of Rights against the states in 1866, including portions that the Supreme Court has not yet incorporated. See Jack M. Balkin, "Supreme Court Holds That Congress Has Incorporated Entire Bill of Rights," Balkinization, July 2, 2010, at http://balkin. blogspot.com/2010/07/supreme-court-holds-that-congress-has.html.

4. *No privileges or immunities for you.* Justice Thomas is the only Justice willing to take seriously the original design of the Fourteenth Amendment. He argues that the Privileges or Immunities Clause was the primary vehicle for protecting substantive rights, not the Due Process Clause. The other eight Justices reject this idea, including Justice Scalia, the Court's other originalist judge. Why is this? One possibility is that the Justices do not know what would happen if the Court used the Privileges or Immunities Clause. Some Justices might fear that implied fundamental rights (like the rights recognized in *Lawrence* and *Casey*) would no longer be protected. Other Justices might fear, to the contrary, that moving to a clause that seems on its face to protect substantive rights would give judges greater discretion to protect new implied fundamental rights. Still other Justices might fear that reviving the Privileges or Immunities Clause would revive *Lochner*-style rights. And still others might fear that this would require incorporating the entire Bill of Rights, including the Seventh Amendment civil jury right and the Fifth Amendment right to grand jury indictments.

Given what you know about the path of doctrinal development in the United States Supreme Court in American history, how realistic are these fears? Is there any reason to think that a Justice who believes there is a right to abortion under the Due Process Clause would believe that such a right is not protected by the Privileges or Immunities Clause? Conversely, is there any reason to think that a Justice who does not think that abortion is a fundamental right under the Due Process Clause would conclude that it is protected as a privilege or immunity? Is there any reason to believe that a shift to the Privileges or Immunities Clause would cause a majority of the Justices (or even Justice Thomas) to reconsider *Lochner v. New York*? If constitutional protection of such rights came back into fashion, it is far more likely that it would be because of large-scale changes in American politics than because of a change in the relevant constitutional language.

Would a shift in focus to the Privileges or Immunities Clause require any significant changes in doctrine? One possibility concerns the rights of non-citizens. The Due Process Clause protects persons as well as citizens. Therefore the Court would have to use the Due Process and Equal Protection Clauses together to explain why non-citizens enjoy the same fundamental rights as citizens. However, this result is consistent with the views of the Reconstruction Era framers. See Akhil Amar, The Bill of Rights: Creation and Reconstruction 172-74 (1998). Another possibility is that the Court would be required to incorporate the remaining individual rights mentioned in the Bill of Rights, including the Third Amendment, the Eighth Amendment's ban on excessive fines, and the Fifth Amendment's guarantee of grand jury indictments. (Of course, as noted above, if the Court's construction of congressional intent in §1981 is correct, that horse may already be out of the barn door.) It is unclear, however, whether the Seventh Amendment right to civil juries is such an individual right or is rather a structural *Erie*-like provision, requiring federal courts to provide litigants the same right to trial by jury they would receive in the state in which the federal court sits. See *id.* at. 275-76.

5. <u>*Scrutiny?*</u> Justice Alito repeatedly refers to the right incorporated in *McDonald* as "fundamental." Does this mean that strict scrutiny applies to any regulations of the right to keep handguns in the home for self-defense? Does it mean that any other aspect of the right to keep and bear arms is equally fundamental and therefore equally subject to strict scrutiny? Should the Court employ the "undue burden" test employed in *Casey* for protection of liberty interests under the Due Process Clause?

Note that most states apply a reasonableness or balancing test to regulations of firearms. In both *Heller* and *McDonald* the Court rejects an "interest-balancing" test. But one must take this language with a grain of salt, since all scrutiny tests inevitably involve some form of balancing. Do either *Heller* or *McDonald* tell us anything about the level of scrutiny the Court will eventually adopt? Consider a few possibilities:

(1)   All regulations of firearms other than "dangerous" or "unusual" fire-arms are subject to strict scrutiny.

(2)   All regulations of handguns and other commonly available firearms used for self defense are subject to strict scrutiny, whether or not kept in the home and used for self-defense. Exceptions are limited to the list offered in *Heller* and *McDonald*: "prohibitions on the possession of firearms by felons and the mentally ill," "laws forbidding the carrying of firearms in sensitive places such as schools and government build-ings, or laws imposing conditions and qualifications on the commercial sale of arms." These are subject to a test of reasonableness.

(3)   Regulations banning possession in the home of handguns and other commonly available firearms used for self defense are subject to strict scrutiny; all other regulations are treated according to a test of reason-ableness or to a test of undue burden (borrowed from *Casey*).

6. *The effect of a national standard. McDonald* imposes a national standard on gun control measures. What effect will this have? Consider the following analysis:

The big difference between applying a constitutional right only against the federal government and applying it against state and local governments is that there are many more state and local regulations of firearms than federal regulations, and these regulations occur in many different varieties. This increases the number of possible constitutional claims, and it also increases the opportunities for litigation. It does not, however, guarantee that Second Amendment rights will become too robust over time.

We can guess what is likely to happen from the way that courts have protected other federal constitutional rights against states and local governments in the past. Federal judicial protection of fundamental rights tends to converge toward the preferences of the national political coalition, which includes executive branch and law enforcement officials. Federal courts tend to strike down mostly laws in outlier jurisdictions that are markedly different from the norm. That is what happened in the District of Columbia, and will likely happen in Chicago. More than 40 states already recognize an individual right to bear arms under their own constitutions. By and large, they have upheld most gun control laws under a loose standard of reasonableness. The federal courts will probably follow suit.

Gun control advocates are concerned that a single federal rule for gun rights will leave urban areas defenseless. Ironically, however, a national standard that lumps cities and rural areas together is far more likely to produce moderation than radical change. That is because many more people live in metropolitan than in rural areas, and in the long run their preferences will shape the national political coalition.

Jack M. Balkin, "Creating a National Norm," New York Times, June 28, 2010, at http://roomfordebate.blogs.nytimes.com/2010/06/28/what-bolstering-gun-rights-will-mean/#jack. In a footnote in his dissenting opinion, Justice Stevens argues that following incorporation, "federal courts will face a profound pressure to reconcile [a single national] standard with the diverse interests of the States and their long history of regulating in this sensitive area. . . . [F]ederal courts will have little choice but to fix a highly flexible standard of review if they are to avoid leaving federalism and the separation of powers—not to mention gun policy—in shambles."

Do you agree? Another lesson of political science studies is that rights protections tend to expand if there are well-funded and continuous litigation campaigns assisted by other forms of grass-roots political organization. See generally Charles R. Epp, The Rights Revolution: Lawyers, Activists, and Supreme Courts in Comparative Perspective (1998). Why won't a sustained litigation campaign by conservative public interest organizations and by interest groups such as the National Rifle Association lead to increasingly stronger gun rights?

Chapter 5

Economic Regulation, Federalism, and Separation of Powers in the Modern Era

Insert the following before section 2 on p. 627:

UNITED STATES v. COMSTOCK, 130 S. Ct. 1949 (2010). By a 7-2 vote, the Supreme Court upheld a federal civil commitment statute as within Congress's powers under the Necessary and Proper Clause without reaching any questions of its constitutionality under the Bill of Rights. 18 U.S.C. §4248 allows a district court to order the civil commitment of a mentally ill, sexually dangerous federal prisoner beyond the date he would otherwise be released. The statute authorizes the federal government to request civil commitment if neither the State of a prisoner's domicile nor the State in which the prisoner was tried will assume the responsibility for the prisoner's "custody, care, and treatment." §4248(d). The individual must (1) currently be "in the custody of the [Federal] Bureau of Prisons;" (2) have previously "engaged or attempted to engage in sexually violent conduct or child molestation;" (3) currently "suffer from a serious mental illness, abnormality, or disorder;" and (4) "as a result of" that mental illness, abnormality, or disorder be "sexually dangerous to others," in that "he would have serious difficulty in refraining from sexually violent conduct or child molestation if released." §§4247(a)(5)-(6).

Justice Breyer's majority opinion explained that "in determining whether the Necessary and Proper Clause grants Congress the legislative authority to enact a particular federal statute, we look to see whether the statute constitutes a means — that is rationally related to the implementation of a constitutionally enumerated power. Sabri v. United States, 541 U.S. 600 (2004) (using term 'means-ends rationality' to describe the necessary relationship)."

"Neither Congress' power to criminalize conduct, nor its power to imprison individuals who engage in that conduct, nor its power to enact laws governing prisons and prisoners, is explicitly mentioned in the Constitution. But Congress nonetheless possesses broad authority to do each of those things" by the "authority granted by the Necessary and Proper Clause."

Justice Breyer pointed out that "Congress has long been involved in the delivery of mental health care to federal prisoners, and has long provided for their civil commitment." In the 1940s, for example, Congress amended its civil commitment regime to take account of mentally ill and mentally incompetent prisoners whose terms have expired, responding to concerns that long sentences of prisoners might sever their connection to any state so that no state would be willing to assume responsibility for them upon release. It was reasonable for Congress to extend its system to mentally ill sexually dangerous prisoners because "the Federal Government is the custodian of its prisoners" and "[a]s federal custodian, it has the constitutional power to act in order to protect nearby (and other) communities from the danger federal prisoners may pose." Section 4248 did not violate state sovereignty protected by the Tenth Amendment because "[t]he powers delegated to the United States by the Constitution include those specifically enumerated powers listed in Article I along with the implementation authority granted by the Necessary and Proper Clause. Virtually by definition, these powers are not powers that the Constitution reserved to the States."

Nor did §4248 "invade state sovereignty or otherwise improperly limit the scope of powers that remain with the States. . . . To the contrary, it requires *accommodation* of state interests: The Attorney General must inform the State in which the federal prisoner 'is domiciled or was tried' that he is detaining someone with respect to whom those States may wish to assert their authority, and he must encourage those States to assume custody of the individual. He must also immediately 'release' that person 'to the appropriate official of' either State 'if such State will assume [such] responsibility.' And either State has the right, at any time, to assert its authority over the individual, which will prompt the individual's immediate transfer to State custody."

Finally, Justice Breyer rejected respondents' argument "that, when legislating pursuant to the Necessary and Proper Clause, Congress' authority can be no more than one step removed from a specifically enumerated power. . . . [E]ven the dissent acknowledges that Congress has the implied power to criminalize any conduct that might interfere with the exercise of an enumerated power, and also the additional power to imprison people who violate those (inferentially authorized) laws, and the additional power to provide for the safe and reasonable management of those prisons, and the additional power to regulate the prisoners' behavior even after their release."

Justice Kennedy concurred in the judgment, arguing that the proper test is not the highly deferential minimum rationality test of Williamson v. Lee Optical. "Rather, under the Necessary and Proper Clause, application of a rational basis test should be at least as exacting as it has been in the Commerce Clause cases, if not more so." Commerce Clause precedents like United States v. Lopez, Justice Kennedy argued, "require a tangible link to commerce, not a mere conceivable rational relation, as in *Lee Optical*." They require "a demonstrated link in fact, based on empirical demonstration." Moreover, Justice Kennedy argued, "[i]t is of fundamental importance to consider whether essential attributes of state sovereignty are compromised by the assertion of federal power under the Necessary and Proper Clause; if so, that is a factor suggesting that the power is not one properly within the reach of federal power."

Justice Alito also concurred in the judgment, although stating "I am concerned about the breadth of the Court's language, and the ambiguity of the standard that the Court applies." Nevertheless, "[m]ost federal criminal statutes rest upon a congressional judgment that, in order to execute one or more of the powers conferred on Congress, it is necessary and proper to criminalize certain conduct, and in order to do that it is obviously necessary and proper to provide for the operation of a federal criminal justice system and a federal prison system. . . . Just as it is necessary and proper for Congress to provide for the apprehension of escaped federal prisoners, it is necessary and proper for Congress to provide for the civil commitment of dangerous federal prisoners who would otherwise escape civil commitment as a result of federal imprisonment."

"Some years ago, a distinguished study group created by the Judicial Conference of the United States found that, in a disturbing number of cases, no State was willing to assume the financial burden of providing for the civil commitment of federal prisoners who, if left at large after the completion of their sentences, would present a danger to any communities in which they chose to live or visit. These federal prisoners, having been held for years in a federal prison, often had few ties to any State; it was a matter of speculation where they would choose to go upon release; and accordingly no State was enthusiastic about volunteering to shoulder the burden of civil commitment. . . . This is not a case in which it is merely possible for a court to think of a rational basis on which Congress might have perceived an attenuated link between the powers underlying the federal criminal statutes and the challenged civil commitment provision. Here, there is a substantial link to Congress' constitutional powers."

Justice Thomas, joined by Justice Scalia, dissented: "[T]he power to care for the mentally ill and, where necessary, the power to protect the community from the dangerous tendencies of some mentally ill persons, are among the numerous powers that remain with the States. . . . Section 4248 closely resembles the involuntary civil-commitment laws that States have enacted under their *parens patriae* and general police powers. Indeed, it is clear, on the face of the Act and — in the Government's arguments urging its constitutionality, that §4248 is aimed at protecting society from acts of sexual violence, not toward carrying into Execution any enumerated power or powers of the Federal Government."

"[P]rotecting society from violent sexual offenders is certainly an important end. . . . But the Constitution does not vest in Congress the authority to protect society from every bad act that might befall it. In my view, this should decide the question. Section 4248 runs afoul of our settled understanding of Congress' power under the Necessary and Proper Clause. Congress may act under that Clause only when its legislation 'carr[ies] into Execution one of the Federal Government's enumerated powers.' Section 4248 does not execute *any* enumerated power. Section 4248 is therefore unconstitutional. . . . "

"The absence of a constitutional delegation of general police power to Congress does not leave citizens vulnerable to the harms Congress seeks to regulate in §4248 because, as recent legislation indicates, the States have the capacity to address the threat that sexual offenders pose. . . . States plainly have the constitutional authority to take charge of a federal prisoner released within their jurisdiction. In addition, the assumption that a State knowingly would fail to exercise that authority is, in my view, implausible. . . . [N]either the Court nor the concurrences argue that a State has the power to refuse such a person domicile within its borders. Thus, they appear to assume that, in the absence of 18 U.S.C. §4248, a State would take no action when informed by the BOP [Bureau of Prisons] that a sexually dangerous federal prisoner was about to be released within its jurisdiction. In light of the plethora of state laws enacted in recent decades to protect communities from sex offenders, the likelihood of such an occurrence seems quite remote. But even in the event a State made such a decision, the Constitution assigns the responsibility for that decision, and its consequences, to the state government alone."

In a portion of the dissent not joined by Justice Scalia, Justice Thomas added: "The Necessary and Proper Clause does not provide Congress with authority to enact any law simply because it furthers *other laws* Congress has enacted in the exercise of its incidental authority; the Clause plainly requires a showing that every federal statute 'carr[ies] into Execution' one or more of the Federal Government's *enumerated* powers. . . . Federal laws that criminalize conduct that interferes with enumerated powers, establish prisons for those who engage in that conduct, and set rules for the care and treatment of prisoners awaiting trial or serving a criminal sentence satisfy this test because each helps to 'carr[y] into Execution' the enumerated powers that justify a criminal defendant's arrest or conviction. For example, Congress' enumerated power '[t]o establish Post Offices and post Roads,' Art. I, §8, cl. 7, would lack force or practical effect if Congress lacked the authority to enact criminal laws 'to punish those who steal letters from the post office, or rob the mail.' Similarly, that enumerated power would be compromised if there were no prisons to hold persons who violate those laws, or if those prisons were so poorly managed that prisoners could escape or demand their release on the grounds that the conditions of their confinement violate their constitutional rights, at least as we have defined them. Civil detention under §4248, on the other hand, lacks any such connection to an enumerated power."

Discussion

1. *Comstock* is based on a familiar justification for federal power: a collective action problem among the states, in this case what is sometimes called a NIMBY ("not in my back yard") problem. Once a known mentally ill sexual predator is released into a state's custody, the state is under enormous pressure to institute its own civil commitment proceedings, at which point the state will be stuck with the costs of taking care of the former prisoner, possibly indefinitely. Therefore no state has an incentive to ask for custody; each hopes that some other state will foot the bill. As Justice Alito puts it, "[t]he statute recognizes that, in many cases, no State will assume the heavy financial burden of civilly committing a dangerous federal prisoner who, as a result of lengthy

federal incarceration, no longer has any substantial ties to any State." Most states would be happier if the federal government simply solved this problem for them (using federal tax money), and that is why 29 states as amicus curiae argued for the constitutionality of the statute. Justices Thomas and Scalia counter that if the federal government simply releases a prisoner into some state's custody, that state will have ample incentives to assume responsibility. This solves the collective action problem a different way, by giving the federal government the power to choose which state will have to bear the costs of long term care and custody. Is this solution more or less respectful of state interests?

2. In its arguments before the Supreme Court, the government declined to base Congress's authority for the civil commitment scheme on the Commerce Clause, relying instead on the Necessary and Proper Clause. Why do you think the government made this choice? Was it correct to do so in light of *Lopez* and *Morrison*?

Consider possible theories under the commerce power: (1) The civil commitment system is "part of a broader regulatory scheme" under *Raich* that would be otherwise undermined; (2) the civil commitment scheme regulates the consumption and travel activities of former federal prisoners; (3) the civil commitment scheme is a reasonable means of preventing states from attempting to dump dangerous former prisoners on other states. Do you think the Court would accept any of these theories, or any other theories under the commerce power?

Insert the following after section 2 on p. 629:

NATIONAL FEDERATION OF INDEPENDENT BUSINESS v. SEBELIUS
[The Health Care Cases]
132 S. Ct. 1161 (2012), 2012 WL 2427810 (U.S.)

[In March 2010, Congress enacted the Patient Protection and Affordable Care Act in order to increase the number of Americans covered by health insurance and decrease the cost of health care. Twenty-six states, several individuals, and the National Federation of Independent Business challenged two key provisions of the Act as unconstitutional, and argued that, because the Affordable Care Act lacked a severability clause, the entire Act should be declared unconstitutional.

The first provision is the individual mandate, which requires most Americans to maintain "minimum essential" health insurance coverage. 26 U.S.C. §5000A. Individuals are exempted if they have qualifying health insurance through their employer or otherwise, receive health care through Medicare or Medicaid, are below the poverty line, live outside the country, serve in the military, are dependents, or have a religious objection.

Beginning in 2014, those not exempted who have not purchased qualifying health insurance must make a "[s]hared responsibility payment" to the federal government. In 2016, for example, the payment will be 2.5 percent of an individual's household income, but no less than $695 and no more than the average yearly premium for insurance that covers 60 percent of the cost of ten specified services (for example, prescription drugs and hospitalization).

The Act provides that this "penalty" will be paid by the "taxpayer" to the Internal Revenue Service with "a taxpayer's return," and "shall be assessed and collected in the same manner" as tax penalties, such as the penalty for claiming too large an income tax refund. The Act, however, bars the IRS from using several of its normal enforcement tools, such as criminal prosecutions and levies. And some individuals who are subject to the mandate are nonetheless exempt from the penalty—for example, those with income below a certain threshold and members of Indian tribes.

The second challenged provision is the expansion of Medicaid. The preexisting Medicaid program offers federal funding to states to assist pregnant women, children, needy families, the blind, the elderly, and the disabled in obtaining medical care. The Affordable Care Act expands the scope of the Medicaid program and increases the number of individuals the states must cover. For example, the Act requires state programs to provide Medicaid coverage by 2014 to adults with incomes up to 133 percent of the federal poverty level. Many states before the Act cover adults with children only if their income is considerably lower, and do not cover childless adults at all. The Act increases federal funding to cover the states' costs in expanding Medicaid coverage. Until 2016 the federal government will cover 100 percent of the new costs, reducing gradually to 90 percent. (The percentages that the federal government covers under the existing Medicaid plan vary by state between 50 to 83 percent.) If a state does not comply with the Act's new coverage requirements, it may lose not only the federal funding for those requirements but also all of its federal Medicaid funds.]

Chief Justice ROBERTS announced the judgment of the Court and delivered the opinion of the Court with respect to Parts I, II, and III-C, an opinion with respect to Part IV, in which Justice BREYER and Justice KAGAN join, and an opinion with respect to Parts III-A, III-B, and III-D.

II

[The Tax Anti-Injunction Act provides that "no suit for the purpose of restraining the assessment or collection of any tax shall be maintained in any court by any person, whether or not such person is the person against whom such tax was assessed." 26 U.S.C. §7421(a). Because of the Anti-Injunction Act, taxes can ordinarily be challenged only after they are paid, by suing for a refund, which in this case would prevent courts from hearing challenges to the individual mandate until 2014. Chief Justice Roberts held that Congress did not intend for this provision to apply to the individual mandate, in part because Congress had designated the mandate as a "penalty" rather than as a "tax." Although some "penalties" are subject to the Anti-Injunction Act, Congress had not indicated that the mandate would be one of them. Therefore, the Anti-Injunction Act did not prevent proceeding to the merits.]

III

A

The Government's first argument is that the individual mandate is a valid exercise of Congress's power under the Commerce Clause and the Necessary and Proper Clause. According to the Government, the health care market is characterized by a significant cost-shifting problem. Everyone will eventually need health care at a time and to an extent they cannot predict, but if they do not have insurance, they often will not be able to pay for it. Because state and federal laws nonetheless require hospitals to provide a certain degree of care to individuals without regard to their ability to pay, hospitals end up receiving compensation for only a portion of the services they provide. To recoup the losses, hospitals pass on the cost to insurers through higher rates, and insurers, in turn, pass on the cost to policy holders in the form of higher premiums. Congress estimated that the cost of uncompensated care raises family health insurance premiums, on average, by over $1,000 per year.

In the Affordable Care Act, Congress addressed the problem of those who cannot obtain insurance coverage because of preexisting conditions or other health issues. It did so through the Act's "guaranteed-issue" and "community rating" provisions. These provisions together prohibit insurance companies from denying coverage to those with such conditions or charging unhealthy individuals higher premiums than healthy individuals.

The guaranteed-issue and community-rating reforms do not, however, address the issue of healthy individuals who choose not to purchase insurance to cover potential health care needs. In fact, the reforms sharply exacerbate that problem, by providing an incentive for individuals to delay purchasing health insurance until they become sick, relying on the promise of guaranteed and affordable coverage. The reforms also threaten to impose massive new costs on insurers, who are required to accept unhealthy individuals but prohibited from charging them rates necessary to pay for their coverage. This will lead insurers to significantly increase premiums on everyone.

The individual mandate was Congress's solution to these problems. By requiring that individuals purchase health insurance, the mandate prevents cost-shifting by those who would otherwise go without it. In addition, the mandate forces into the insurance risk pool more healthy individuals, whose premiums on average will be higher than their health care expenses. This allows insurers to subsidize the costs of covering the unhealthy individuals the reforms require them to accept. The Government claims that Congress has power under the Commerce and Necessary and Proper Clauses to enact this solution.

1

The Government contends that the individual mandate is within Congress's power because the failure to purchase insurance "has a substantial and deleterious effect on interstate commerce" by creating the cost-shifting problem. . . .

— We have recognized, for example, that "[t]he power of Congress over interstate commerce is not confined to the regulation of commerce among the states," but extends to activities that "have a substantial effect on interstate commerce." *United States v. Darby*. Congress's power, moreover, is not limited to regulation of an activity that by itself substantially affects interstate commerce, but also extends to activities that do so only when aggregated with similar activities of others. *Wickard*.

—   [C]ongress has never attempted to rely on that power to compel individuals not engaged in commerce to purchase an unwanted product.[a] Legislative novelty is not necessarily fatal; there is a first time for everything. But sometimes "the most telling indication of [a] severe constitutional problem . . . is the lack of historical precedent" for Congress's action. . . .

The Constitution grants Congress the power to "*regulate* Commerce." Art. I, §8, cl. 3 (emphasis added). The power to *regulate* commerce presupposes the
— existence of commercial activity to be regulated. If the power to "regulate" something included the power to create it, many of the provisions in the Constitution would be superfluous. For example, the Constitution gives Congress the power to "coin Money," in addition to the power to "regulate the Value thereof." *Id.*, cl. 5. And it gives Congress the power to "raise and support Armies" and to "provide and maintain a Navy," in addition to the power to "make Rules for the Government and Regulation of the land and naval Forces." *Id.*, cls. 12-14. If the power to regulate the armed forces or the value of money included the power to bring the subject of the regulation into existence, the specific grant of such powers would have been unnecessary. The language of the Constitution reflects the natural understanding that the power to regulate assumes there is already something to be regulated. See *Gibbons* ("[T]he enlightened patriots who framed our constitution, and the people who adopted it, must be understood to have employed words in their natural sense, and to have intended what they have said").[b]

Our precedent also reflects this understanding. As expansive as our cases construing the scope of the commerce power have been, they all have one thing

---

a. The examples of other congressional mandates cited by JUSTICE GINSBURG . . . are not to the contrary. Each of those mandates—to report for jury duty, to register for the draft, to purchase firearms in anticipation of militia service, to exchange gold currency for paper currency, and to file a tax return—are based on constitutional provisions other than the Commerce Clause. See Art. I, § 8, cl. 9 (to "constitute Tribunals inferior to the supreme Court"); *id.*, cl. 12 (to "raise and support Armies"); *id.*, cl. 16 (to "provide for organizing, arming, and disciplining, the Militia"); *id.*, cl. 5 (to "coin Money"); *id.*, cl. 1 (to "lay and collect Taxes").

—   b. Justice Ginsburg suggests that "at the time the Constitution was framed, to 'regulate' meant, among other things, to require action," [relying] on a dictionary in which "[t]o order; to command" was the fifth-alternative definition of "to direct," which was itself the second-alternative definition of "to regulate." (citing S. Johnson, Dictionary of the English Language (4th ed. 1773) (reprinted 1978)). It is unlikely that the Framers had such an obscure meaning in mind when they used the word "regulate." Far more commonly, "[t]o regulate" meant "[t]o adjust by rule or method," which presupposes something to adjust. 2 Johnson, *supra*; see also *Gibbons* (defining the commerce power as the power "to prescribe the rule by which commerce is to be governed").

in common: They uniformly describe the power as reaching "activity." It is nearly impossible to avoid the word when quoting them. See, *e.g., Lopez* ("Where economic activity substantially affects interstate commerce, legislation regulating that activity will be sustained"); *Perez* ("Where the *class of activities* is regulated and that *class* is within the reach of federal power, the courts have no power to excise, as trivial, individual instances of the class" (emphasis in original; internal quotation marks omitted)); *Wickard* ("[E]ven if appellee's activity be local and though it may not be regarded as commerce, it may still, whatever its nature, be reached by Congress if it exerts a substantial economic effect on interstate commerce"); *NLRB v. Jones & Laughlin Steel Corp.* ("Although activities may be intrastate in character when separately considered, if they have such a close and substantial relation to interstate commerce that their control is essential or appropriate to protect that commerce from burdens and obstructions, Congress cannot be denied the power to exercise that control").

The individual mandate, however, does not regulate existing commercial activity. It instead compels individuals to *become* active in commerce by purchasing a product, on the ground that their failure to do so affects interstate commerce. Construing the Commerce Clause to permit Congress to regulate individuals precisely *because* they are doing nothing would open a new and potentially vast domain to congressional authority. Every day individuals do not do an infinite number of things. In some cases they decide not to do something; in others they simply fail to do it. Allowing Congress to justify federal regulation by pointing to the effect of inaction on commerce would bring countless decisions an individual could *potentially* make within the scope of federal regulation, and—under the Government's theory—empower Congress to make those decisions for him.

Applying the Government's logic to the familiar case of *Wickard v. Filburn* shows how far that logic would carry us from the notion of a government of limited powers. . . . Under *Wickard* it is within Congress's power to regulate the market for wheat by supporting its price. But price can be supported by increasing demand as well as by decreasing supply. The aggregated decisions of some consumers not to purchase wheat have a substantial effect on the price of wheat, just as decisions not to purchase health insurance have on the price of insurance. Congress can therefore command that those not buying wheat do so, just as it argues here that it may command that those not buying health insurance do so. The farmer in *Wickard* was at least actively engaged in the production of wheat, and the Government could regulate that activity because of its effect on commerce. The Government's theory here would effectively override that limitation, by establishing that individuals may be regulated under the Commerce Clause whenever enough of them are not doing something the Government would have them do.

Indeed, the Government's logic would justify a mandatory purchase to solve almost any problem. To consider a different example in the health care market, many Americans do not eat a balanced diet. That group makes up a larger percentage of the total population than those without health insurance. The failure of that group to have a healthy diet increases health care costs, to a greater extent than the failure of the uninsured to purchase insurance. Those increased costs are borne in part by other Americans who must pay more, just as the uninsured shift costs to the insured. Congress addressed the insurance problem by ordering everyone to buy insurance. Under the Government's theory, Congress could address the diet problem by ordering everyone to buy vegetables.

People, for reasons of their own, often fail to do things that would be good for them or good for society. Those failures—joined with the similar failures of others—can readily have a substantial effect on interstate commerce. Under the Government's logic, that authorizes Congress to use its commerce power to compel citizens to act as the Government would have them act.

That is not the country the Framers of our Constitution envisioned. James Madison explained that the Commerce Clause was "an addition which few oppose and from which no apprehensions are entertained." The Federalist No. 45. While Congress's authority under the Commerce Clause has of course expanded with the growth of the national economy, our cases have "always recognized that the power to regulate commerce, though broad indeed, has limits." *Maryland v. Wirtz.* The Government's theory would erode those limits, permitting Congress to reach beyond the natural extent of its authority, "everywhere extending the sphere of its activity and drawing all power into its impetuous vortex." The Federalist No. 48 (J. Madison). Congress already enjoys vast power to regulate much of what we do. Accepting the Government's theory would give Congress the same license to regulate what we do not do, fundamentally changing the relation between the citizen and the Federal Government.[c]

To an economist, perhaps, there is no difference between activity and inactivity; both have measurable economic effects on commerce. But the distinction between doing something and doing nothing would not have been lost on the Framers, who were "practical statesmen," not metaphysical philosophers. . . . The Framers gave Congress the power to *regulate* commerce, not to *compel* it, and for over 200 years both our decisions and Congress's actions have reflected this understanding. There is no reason to depart from that understanding now.

The Government sees things differently. It argues that because sickness and injury are unpredictable but unavoidable, "the uninsured as a class are active in the market for health care, which they regularly seek and obtain." The individual mandate "merely regulates how individuals finance and pay for that active

c. In an attempt to recast the individual mandate as a regulation of commercial activity, Justice Ginsburg suggests that "[a]n individual who opts not to purchase insurance from a private insurer can be seen as actively selecting another form of insurance: self-insurance." But "self-insurance" is, in this context, nothing more than a description of the failure to purchase insurance. Individuals are no more "activ[e] in the self-insurance market" when they fail to purchase insurance, than they are active in the "rest" market when doing nothing.

participation—requiring that they do so through insurance, rather than through attempted self-insurance with the back-stop of shifting costs to others."

[T]he phrase "active in the market for health care" . . . has no constitutional significance. An individual who bought a car two years ago and may buy another in the future is not "active in the car market" in any pertinent sense. The phrase "active in the market" cannot obscure the fact that most of those — regulated by the individual mandate are not currently engaged in any commercial activity involving health care, and that fact is fatal to the Government's effort to "regulate the uninsured as a class." Our precedents recognize Congress's power to regulate "class[es] of *activities,*" *Gonzales v. Raich* (emphasis added), not classes of *individuals,* apart from any activity in which they are engaged.

The individual mandate's regulation of the uninsured as a class is, in fact, particularly divorced from any link to existing commercial activity. The mandate primarily affects healthy, often young adults who are less likely to need significant health care and have other priorities for spending their money. It is precisely because these individuals, as an actuarial class, incur relatively low health care costs that the mandate helps counter the effect of forcing insurance companies to cover others who impose greater costs than their premiums are allowed to reflect. If the individual mandate is targeted at a class, it is a class whose commercial inactivity rather than activity is its defining feature.

The Government, however, claims that this does not matter. The Government regards it as sufficient to trigger Congress's authority that almost all those who are uninsured will, at some unknown point in the future, engage in a health care transaction. Asserting that "[t]here is no temporal limitation in the Commerce Clause," the Government argues that because "[e]veryone subject to this regulation is in or will be in the health care market," they can be "regulated in advance."

The proposition that Congress may dictate the conduct of an individual today because of prophesied future activity finds no support in our precedent. We — have said that Congress can anticipate the *effects* on commerce of an economic activity. But we have never permitted Congress to anticipate that activity itself in order to regulate individuals not currently engaged in commerce. Each one of our cases . . . involved preexisting economic activity. See, *e.g., Wickard* (producing wheat); *Raich* (growing marijuana).

Everyone will likely participate in the markets for food, clothing, transportation, shelter, or energy; that does not authorize Congress to direct them to purchase particular products in those or other markets today. The Commerce — Clause is not a general license to regulate an individual from cradle to grave, simply because he will predictably engage in particular transactions. Any police power to regulate individuals as such, as opposed to their activities, remains vested in the States.

The Government argues that the individual mandate can be sustained as a sort of exception to this rule, because health insurance is a unique product. According to the Government, upholding the individual mandate would not justify mandatory purchases of items such as cars or broccoli because, as the Government puts it, "[h]ealth insurance is not purchased for its own sake like a car or broccoli; it is a means of financing healthcare consumption and covering universal risks." But cars and broccoli are no more purchased for their "own sake" than health insurance. They are purchased to cover the need for transportation and food.

The Government says that health insurance and health care financing are "inherently integrated." But that does not mean the compelled purchase of the first is properly regarded as a regulation of the second. No matter how "inherently integrated" health insurance and health care consumption may be, they are not the same thing: They involve different transactions, entered into at different times, with different providers. And for most of those targeted by the mandate, significant health care needs will be years, or even decades, away. The proximity and degree of connection between the mandate and the subsequent commercial activity is too lacking to justify an exception of the sort urged by the Government. The individual mandate forces individuals into commerce precisely because they elected to refrain from commercial activity. Such a law cannot be sustained under a clause authorizing Congress to "regulate Commerce."

2

The Government next contends that Congress has the power under the Necessary and Proper Clause to enact the individual mandate because the mandate is an "integral part of a comprehensive scheme of economic regulation"—the guaranteed-issue and community-rating insurance reforms. Under this argument, it is not necessary to consider the effect that an individual's inactivity may have on interstate commerce; it is enough that Congress regulate commercial activity in a way that requires regulation of inactivity to be effective.

The power to "make all Laws which shall be necessary and proper for carrying into Execution" the powers enumerated in the Constitution, Art. I, § 8, cl. 18, vests Congress with authority to enact provisions "incidental to the [enumerated] power, and conducive to its beneficial exercise," *McCulloch*. Although the Clause gives Congress authority to "legislate on that vast mass of incidental powers which must be involved in the constitution," it does not license the exercise of any "great substantive and independent power[s]" beyond those specifically enumerated. Instead, the Clause is "'merely a declaration, for the removal of all uncertainty, that the means of carrying into execution those [powers] otherwise granted are included in the grant.'"

As our jurisprudence under the Necessary and Proper Clause has developed, we have been very deferential to Congress's determination that a regulation is "necessary." We have thus upheld laws that are "'convenient, or useful' or 'conducive' to the authority's 'beneficial exercise.'" *Comstock*. But we have also carried out our responsibility to declare unconstitutional those laws that undermine the structure of government established by the Constitution. Such laws, which are not "consist[ent] with the letter and spirit of the constitution," *McCulloch*, are not "*proper* [means] for carrying into Execution" Congress's enumerated powers. Rather, they are, "in the words of The Federalist, 'merely acts of usurpation' which 'deserve to be treated as such.'"

Applying these principles, the individual mandate cannot be sustained under the Necessary and Proper Clause as an essential component of the insurance reforms. Each of our prior cases upholding laws under that Clause involved ⁓ exercises of authority derivative of, and in service to, a granted power. For example, we have upheld provisions permitting continued confinement of those *already in federal custody* when they could not be safely released, *Comstock*; criminalizing bribes involving organizations *receiving federal funds, Sabri v. United States,* 541 U.S. 600 (2004); and tolling state statutes of limitations while cases are *pending in federal court, Jinks v. Richland County,* 538 U.S. 456 (2003). The individual mandate, by contrast, vests Congress with the ⁓ extraordinary ability to create the necessary predicate to the exercise of an enumerated power.

This is in no way an authority that is "narrow in scope," or "incidental" to the exercise of the commerce power. Rather, such a conception of the Necessary and Proper Clause would work a substantial expansion of federal authority. No longer would Congress be limited to regulating under the Commerce Clause those who by some preexisting activity bring themselves within the sphere of federal regulation. Instead, Congress could reach beyond the natural limit of its authority and draw within its regulatory scope those who otherwise would be outside of it. Even if the individual mandate is "necessary" to the Act's insurance reforms, such an expansion of federal power is not a "proper" means for making those reforms effective.

[I]n [*Gonzales v.*] *Raich,* we considered "comprehensive legislation to regulate the interstate market" in marijuana. Certain individuals sought an exemption from that regulation on the ground that they engaged in only intrastate possession and consumption. We denied any exemption, on the ground that marijuana is a fungible commodity, so that any marijuana could be readily diverted into the interstate market. Congress's attempt to regulate the interstate market for marijuana would therefore have been substantially undercut if it could not also regulate intrastate possession and consumption. Accordingly, we recognized that "Congress was acting well within its authority" under the Necessary and Proper Clause even though its "regulation ensnare[d] some purely intrastate activity." *Raich* thus did not involve the exercise of any "great substantive and independent power," *McCulloch,* of the sort at issue here. Instead, it concerned only the constitutionality of "individual *applications* of a concededly valid statutory scheme." *Raich* (emphasis added).

Just as the individual mandate cannot be sustained as a law regulating the substantial effects of the failure to purchase health insurance, neither can it be upheld as a "necessary and proper" component of the insurance reforms. The commerce power thus does not authorize the mandate. Accord, *post,* at 4-16 (joint opinion of Scalia, Kennedy, Thomas, and Alito, JJ., dissenting).

B

That is not the end of the matter. Because the Commerce Clause does not support the individual mandate, it is necessary to turn to the Government's second argument: that the mandate may be upheld as within Congress's enumerated power to "lay and collect Taxes." Art. I, §8, cl. 1.

A   The Government's tax power argument asks us to view the statute differently than we did in considering its commerce power theory. In making its Commerce Clause argument, the Government defended the mandate as a regulation requiring individuals to purchase health insurance. The Government does not claim that the taxing power allows Congress to issue such a command. Instead, the Government asks us to read the mandate not as ordering individuals to buy insurance, but rather as imposing a tax on those who do not buy that product.

The text of a statute can sometimes have more than one possible meaning. To take a familiar example, a law that reads "no vehicles in the park" might, or might not, ban bicycles in the park. And it is well established that if a statute has two possible meanings, one of which violates the Constitution, courts should adopt the meaning that does not do so. Justice Story said that 180 years ago: "No court ought, unless the terms of an act rendered it unavoidable, to give a construction to it which should involve a violation, however unintentional, of the constitution." Justice Holmes made the same point a century later: "[T]he rule is settled that as between two possible interpretations of a statute, by one of which it would be unconstitutional and by the other valid, our plain duty is to adopt that which will save the Act."

The most straightforward reading of the mandate is that it commands individuals to purchase insurance. After all, it states that individuals "shall" maintain health insurance. 26 U.S.C. §5000A(a). Congress thought it could enact such a command under the Commerce Clause, and the Government primarily defended the law on that basis. But, for the reasons explained above, the Commerce Clause does not give Congress that power. Under our precedent, it is therefore necessary to ask whether the Government's alternative reading of the statute—that it only imposes a tax on those without insurance—is a reasonable one.

Under the mandate, if an individual does not maintain health insurance, the only consequence is that he must make an additional payment to the IRS when he pays his taxes. See §5000A(b). That, according to the Government, means the mandate can be regarded as establishing a condition—not owning health insurance—that triggers a tax—the required payment to the IRS. Under that theory, the mandate is not a legal command to buy insurance. Rather, it makes going without insurance just another thing the Government taxes, like buying gasoline or earning income. And if the mandate is in effect just a tax hike on certain taxpayers who do not have health insurance, it may be within Congress's constitutional power to tax.

The question is not whether that is the most natural interpretation of the mandate, but only whether it is a "fairly possible" one. As we have explained, "every reasonable construction must be resorted to, in order to save a statute from unconstitutionality." The Government asks us to interpret the mandate as imposing a tax, if it would otherwise violate the Constitution. Granting the Act the full measure of deference owed to federal statutes, it can be so read, for the reasons set forth below.

C

The exaction the Affordable Care Act imposes on those without health insurance looks like a tax in many respects. The "[s]hared responsibility payment," as the statute entitles it, is paid into the Treasury by "taxpayer[s]" when they file their tax returns. 26 U.S.C. §5000A(b). It does not apply to individuals who do not pay federal income taxes because their household income is less than the filing threshold in the Internal Revenue Code. For taxpayers who do owe the payment, its amount is determined by such familiar factors as taxable income, number of dependents, and joint filing status. The requirement to pay is found in the Internal Revenue Code and enforced by the IRS, which—as we previously explained—must assess and collect it "in the same manner as taxes." This process yields the essential feature of any tax: it produces at least some revenue for the Government. *United States v. Kahriger,* 345 U.S. 22 (1953). Indeed, the payment is expected to raise about $4 billion per year by 2017.

It is of course true that the Act describes the payment as a "penalty," not a "tax." But while that label is fatal to the application of the Anti-Injunction Act, it does not determine whether the payment may be viewed as an exercise of Congress's taxing power. It is up to Congress whether to apply the Anti-Injunction Act to any particular statute, so it makes sense to be guided by Congress's choice of label on that question. That choice does not, however, control whether an exaction is within Congress's constitutional power to tax.

Our precedent reflects this: In 1922, we decided two challenges to the "Child Labor Tax" on the same day. In the first, we held that a suit to enjoin collection of the so-called tax was barred by the Anti-Injunction Act. [*Bailey v.*] *George,* 259 U.S. 16 (1922). Congress knew that suits to obstruct taxes had to await payment under the Anti-Injunction Act; Congress called the child labor tax a tax; Congress therefore intended the Anti-Injunction Act to apply. In the second case, however, we held that the same exaction, although labeled a tax, was not in fact authorized by Congress's taxing power. [*Bailey v.*] *Drexel Furniture,* 259 U.S., at 38 (1922). That constitutional question was not controlled by Congress's choice of label.

We have similarly held that exactions not labeled taxes nonetheless were authorized by Congress's power to tax. In the *License Tax Cases,* for example, we held that federal licenses to sell liquor and lottery tickets—for which the licensee had to pay a fee—could be sustained as exercises of the taxing power. And in *New York v. United States* we upheld as a tax a "surcharge" on out-of-state nuclear waste shipments, a portion of which was paid to the Federal Treasury. We thus ask whether the shared responsibility payment falls within Congress's taxing power, "[d]isregarding the designation of the exaction, and viewing its substance and application." *United States v. Constantine,* 296 U.S.

287 (1935); cf. *Quill Corp. v. North Dakota,* 504 U.S. 298 (1992) ("[M]agic words or labels" should not "disable an otherwise constitutional levy" (internal quotation marks omitted)); *Nelson v. Sears, Roebuck & Co.,* 312 U.S. 359 (1941) ("In passing on the constitutionality of a tax law, we are concerned only with its practical operation, not its definition or the precise form of descriptive words which may be applied to it" (internal quotation marks omitted)); *United States v. Sotelo,* 436 U.S. 268 (1978) ("That the funds due are referred to as a 'penalty' . . . does not alter their essential character as taxes").

Our cases confirm this functional approach. For example, in *Drexel Furniture,* we focused on three practical characteristics of the so-called tax on employing child laborers that convinced us the "tax" was actually a penalty. First, the tax imposed an exceedingly heavy burden—10 percent of a company's net income—on those who employed children, no matter how small their infraction. Second, it imposed that exaction only on those who knowingly employed underage laborers. Such scienter requirements are typical of punitive statutes, because Congress often wishes to punish only those who intentionally break the law. Third, this "tax" was enforced in part by the Department of Labor, an agency responsible for punishing violations of labor laws, not collecting revenue. 259 U.S., at 36-37; see also, *e.g.,* [*Department of Revenue of Mont. v.*] *Kurth Ranch,* [511 U.S. 767 (1994)] (considering, *inter alia,* the amount of the exaction, and the fact that it was imposed for violation of a separate criminal law); *Constantine* (same).

The same analysis here suggests that the shared responsibility payment may for constitutional purposes be considered a tax, not a penalty: First, for most Americans the amount due will be far less than the price of insurance, and, by statute, it can never be more.[d] It may often be a reasonable financial decision to make the payment rather than purchase insurance, unlike the "prohibitory" financial punishment in *Drexel Furniture.* Second, the individual mandate contains no scienter requirement. Third, the payment is collected solely by the IRS through the normal means of taxation—except that the Service is *not* allowed to use those means most suggestive of a punitive sanction, such as criminal prosecution. The reasons the Court in *Drexel Furniture* held that what was called a "tax" there was a penalty support the conclusion that what is called a "penalty" here may be viewed as a tax.[e]

---

d. In 2016, for example, individuals making $35,000 a year are expected to owe the IRS about $60 for any month in which they do not have health insurance. Someone with an annual income of $100,000 a year would likely owe about $200. The price of a qualifying insurance policy is projected to be around $400 per month.

e. We do not suggest that any exaction lacking a scienter requirement and enforced by the IRS is within the taxing power. Congress could not, for example, expand its authority to impose criminal fines by creating strict liability offenses enforced by the IRS rather than the FBI. But the fact that the exaction here is paid like a tax, to the agency that collects taxes—rather than, for example, exacted by Department of Labor inspectors after ferreting out willful malfeasance—suggests that this exaction may be viewed as a tax.

None of this is to say that the payment is not intended to affect individual conduct. Although the payment will raise considerable revenue, it is plainly designed to expand health insurance coverage. But taxes that seek to influence — conduct are nothing new. Some of our earliest federal taxes sought to deter the purchase of imported manufactured goods in order to foster the growth of domestic industry. Today, federal and state taxes can compose more than half the retail price of cigarettes, not just to raise more money, but to encourage people to quit smoking. And we have upheld such obviously regulatory measures as taxes on selling marijuana and sawed-off shotguns. Indeed, "[e]very tax is in some measure regulatory. To some extent it interposes an economic impediment to the activity taxed as compared with others not taxed." *Sonzinsky* [*v. United States,* 300 U.S. 506 (1937).] That §5000A seeks to shape decisions about whether to buy health insurance does not mean that it cannot be a valid exercise of the taxing power.

In distinguishing penalties from taxes, this Court has explained that "if the concept of penalty means anything, it means punishment for an unlawful act or omission." *United States v. Reorganized CF & I Fabricators of Utah, Inc.,* 518 U.S. 213 (1996); see also *United States v. La Franca,* 282 U.S. 568 (1931) ("[A] penalty, as the word is here used, is an exaction imposed by statute as punishment for an unlawful act"). While the individual mandate clearly aims to induce the purchase of health insurance, it need not be read to declare that failing to do so is unlawful. Neither the Act nor any other law attaches negative legal consequences — to not buying health insurance, beyond requiring a payment to the IRS. The Government agrees with that reading, confirming that if someone chooses to pay rather than obtain health insurance, they have fully complied with the law.

Indeed, it is estimated [by the Congressional Budget Office] that four million people each year will choose to pay the IRS rather than buy insurance. We would expect Congress to be troubled by that prospect if such conduct were unlawful. That Congress apparently regards such extensive failure to comply with the mandate as tolerable suggests that Congress did not think it was creating four million outlaws. It suggests instead that the shared responsibility payment merely imposes a tax citizens may lawfully choose to pay in lieu of buying health insurance.

The plaintiffs contend that Congress's choice of language—stating that individuals "shall" obtain insurance or pay a "penalty"—requires reading §5000A as punishing unlawful conduct, even if that interpretation would render the law unconstitutional. We have rejected a similar argument before. In *New York v.* — *United States* we examined a statute providing that "'[e]ach State shall be responsible for providing . . . for the disposal of . . . low-level radioactive waste.'" A State that shipped its waste to another State was exposed to surcharges by the receiving State, a portion of which would be paid over to the Federal Government. And a State that did not adhere to the statutory scheme faced "[p]enalties for failure to comply," including increases in the surcharge. New York urged us to read the statute as a federal command that the state legislature enact legislation to dispose of its waste, which would have violated the Constitution. To avoid that outcome, we interpreted the statute to impose only "a series of incentives" for the State to take responsibility for its waste. We then sustained the charge paid to the Federal Government as an exercise of the taxing power. We see no insurmountable obstacle to a similar approach here.

The joint dissenters argue that we cannot uphold §5000A as a tax because Congress did not "frame" it as such. In effect, they contend that even if the Constitution permits Congress to do exactly what we interpret this statute to do, the law must be struck down because Congress used the wrong labels. An — example may help illustrate why labels should not control here. Suppose Congress enacted a statute providing that every taxpayer who owns a house without energy efficient windows must pay $50 to the IRS. The amount due is adjusted based on factors such as taxable income and joint filing status, and is paid along with the taxpayer's income tax return. Those whose income is below the filing threshold need not pay. The required payment is not called a "tax," a "penalty," or anything else. No one would doubt that this law imposed a tax, and was within Congress's power to tax. That conclusion should not change simply because Congress used the word "penalty" to describe the payment. . . .

Our precedent demonstrates that Congress had the power to impose the exaction in §5000A under the taxing power, and that §5000A need not be read to do more than impose a tax. That is sufficient to sustain it. The "question of the constitutionality of action taken by Congress does not depend on recitals of the power which it undertakes to exercise." *Woods v. Cloyd W. Miller Co.,* 333 U.S. 138 (1948).

Even if the taxing power enables Congress to impose a tax on not obtaining health insurance, any tax must still comply with other requirements in the Constitution. Plaintiffs argue that the shared responsibility payment does not do so, citing Article I, §9, clause 4. That clause provides: "No Capitation, or other direct, Tax shall be laid, unless in Proportion to the Census or Enumeration herein before directed to be taken." This requirement means that any "direct Tax" must be apportioned so that each State pays in proportion to its population. According to the plaintiffs, if the individual mandate imposes a tax, it is a direct tax, and it is unconstitutional because Congress made no effort to apportion it among the States.

— Even when the Direct Tax Clause was written it was unclear what else, other than a capitation (also known as a "head tax" or a "poll tax"), might be a direct tax. See *Springer v. United States,* 102 U.S. 586 (1881). Soon after the framing, Congress passed a tax on ownership of carriages, over James Madison's objection that it was an unapportioned direct tax. This Court upheld the tax, in part reasoning that apportioning such a tax would make little sense, because it would have required taxing carriage owners at dramatically different rates depending on how many carriages were in their home State. See *Hylton v. United States,* 3 Dall. 171 (1796) (opinion of Chase, J.). The Court was unanimous, and those Justices who wrote opinions either directly asserted or strongly suggested that only two forms of taxation were direct: capitations and land taxes. See *id.,* at 175; *id.,* at 177 (opinion of Paterson, J.); *id.,* at 183 (opinion of Iredell, J.).

That narrow view of what a direct tax might be persisted for a century. In 1880, for example, we explained that *"direct taxes,* within the meaning of the Constitution, are only capitation taxes, as expressed in that instrument, and taxes on real estate." *Springer.* In 1895, we expanded our interpretation to – include taxes on personal property and income from personal property, in the course of striking down aspects of the federal income tax. *Pollock v. Farmers' Loan & Trust Co.,* 158 U.S. 601 (1895). That result was overturned by the – Sixteenth Amendment, although we continued to consider taxes on personal property to be direct taxes. See *Eisner v. Macomber,* 252 U.S. 189 (1920).

A tax on going without health insurance does not fall within any recognized category of direct tax. It is not a capitation. Capitations are taxes paid by every person, "without regard to property, profession, or *any other circumstance."* *Hylton, supra,* at 175 (opinion of Chase, J.) (emphasis altered). The whole point of the shared responsibility payment is that it is triggered by specific circumstances—earning a certain amount of income but not obtaining health insurance. The payment is also plainly not a tax on the ownership of land or personal property. The shared responsibility payment is thus not a direct tax that must be apportioned among the several States.

There may, however, be a more fundamental objection to a tax on those who lack health insurance. Even if only a tax, the payment under §5000A(b) remains a burden that the Federal Government imposes for an omission, not an act. If it is troubling to interpret the Commerce Clause as authorizing Congress to regulate those who abstain from commerce, perhaps it should be similarly troubling to permit Congress to impose a tax for not doing something.

Three considerations allay this concern. First, and most importantly, it is – abundantly clear the Constitution does not guarantee that individuals may avoid taxation through inactivity. A capitation, after all, is a tax that everyone must pay simply for existing, and capitations are expressly contemplated by the Constitution. The Court today holds that our Constitution protects us from federal regulation under the Commerce Clause so long as we abstain from the regulated activity. But from its creation, the Constitution has made no such promise with respect to taxes. See Letter from Benjamin Franklin to M. Le Roy (Nov. 13, 1789) ("Our new Constitution is now established . . . but in this world nothing can be said to be certain, except death and taxes").

Whether the mandate can be upheld under the Commerce Clause is a question about the scope of federal authority. Its answer depends on whether Congress can exercise what all acknowledge to be the novel course of directing individuals to purchase insurance. Congress's use of the Taxing Clause to ‒ encourage buying something is, by contrast, not new. Tax incentives already promote, for example, purchasing homes and professional educations. Sustaining the mandate as a tax depends only on whether Congress *has* properly exercised its taxing power to encourage purchasing health insurance, not whether it *can.* Upholding the individual mandate under the Taxing Clause thus does not recognize any new federal power. It determines that Congress has used an existing one.

Second, Congress's ability to use its taxing power to influence conduct is not without <u>limits</u>. A few of our cases policed these limits aggressively, invalidating punitive exactions obviously designed to regulate behavior otherwise regarded at the time as beyond federal authority. See, *e.g., United States v. Butler,* 297 U.S. 1 (1936); [*Bailey v.*] *Drexel Furniture.* More often and more recently we have declined to closely examine the regulatory motive or effect of revenue-raising measures. See *Kahriger* (collecting cases). We have nonetheless maintained that "'there comes a time in the extension of the penalizing features of the so-called tax when it loses its character as such and becomes a mere penalty with the characteristics of regulation and punishment.'" *Kurth Ranch* (quoting *Drexel Furniture*).

We have already explained that the shared responsibility payment's practical characteristics pass muster as a tax under our narrowest interpretations of the taxing power. Because the tax at hand is within even those strict limits, we need not here decide the precise point at which an exaction becomes so punitive that the taxing power does not authorize it. It remains true, however, that the "'power to tax is not the power to destroy while this Court sits.'" *Oklahoma Tax Comm'n v. Texas Co.,* 336 U.S. 342 (1949) (quoting *Panhandle Oil Co. v. Mississippi ex rel. Knox,* 277 U.S. 218 (1928) (Holmes, J., dissenting)).

Third, although the breadth of Congress's power to tax is greater than its power to regulate commerce, the taxing power does not give Congress the same degree of control over individual behavior. Once we recognize that Congress may regulate a particular decision under the Commerce Clause, the Federal Government can bring its full weight to bear. Congress may simply command individuals to do as it directs. An individual who disobeys may be subjected to criminal sanctions. Those sanctions can include not only fines and imprisonment, but all the attendant consequences of being branded a criminal: deprivation of otherwise protected civil rights, such as the right to bear arms or vote in elections; loss of employment opportunities; social stigma; and severe disabilities in other controversies, such as custody or immigration disputes.

By contrast, Congress's authority under the taxing power is limited to requiring an individual to pay money into the Federal Treasury, no more. If a tax is properly paid, the Government has no power to compel or punish individuals subject to it. We do not make light of the severe burden that taxation—especially taxation motivated by a regulatory purpose—can impose. But imposition of a tax nonetheless leaves an individual with a lawful choice to do or not do a certain act, so long as he is willing to pay a tax levied on that choice.[f]

---

f. Of course, individuals do not have a lawful choice not to pay a tax due, and may sometimes face prosecution for failing to do so (although not for declining to make the shared responsibility payment, see 26 U.S.C. § 5000A(g)(2)). But that does not show that the tax restricts the lawful choice whether to undertake or forgo the activity on which the tax is predicated. Those subject to the individual mandate may lawfully forgo health insurance and pay higher taxes, or buy health insurance and pay lower taxes. The only thing they may not lawfully do is not buy health insurance and not pay the resulting tax.

The Affordable Care Act's requirement that certain individuals pay a financial penalty for not obtaining health insurance may reasonably be characterized as a tax. Because the Constitution permits such a tax, it is not our role to forbid it, or to pass upon its wisdom or fairness.

D

Justice Ginsburg questions the necessity of rejecting the Government's commerce power argument, given that §5000A can be upheld under the taxing power. But the statute reads more naturally as a command to buy insurance than as a tax, and I would uphold it as a command if the Constitution allowed it. It is only because the Commerce Clause does not authorize such a command that it is necessary to reach the taxing power question. And it is only because we have — a duty to construe a statute to save it, if fairly possible, that §5000A can be interpreted as a tax. Without deciding the Commerce Clause question, I would find no basis to adopt such a saving construction.

The Federal Government does not have the power to order people to buy health insurance. Section 5000A would therefore be unconstitutional if read as a command. The Federal Government does have the power to impose a tax on those without health insurance. Section 5000A is therefore constitutional, because it can reasonably be read as a tax.

IV

A

The States also contend that the Medicaid expansion exceeds Congress's authority under the Spending Clause. They claim that Congress is coercing the States to adopt the changes it wants by threatening to withhold all of a State's Medicaid grants, unless the State accepts the new expanded funding and complies with the conditions that come with it. This, they argue, violates the basic principle that the "Federal Government may not compel the States to enact or administer a federal regulatory program."

There is no doubt that the Act dramatically increases state obligations under Medicaid. The current Medicaid program requires States to cover only certain discrete categories of needy individuals—pregnant women, children, needy families, the blind, the elderly, and the disabled. There is no mandatory coverage for most childless adults, and the States typically do not offer any such coverage. The States also enjoy considerable flexibility with respect to the coverage levels for parents of needy families. On average States cover only those unemployed parents who make less than 37 percent of the federal poverty level, and only those employed parents who make less than 63 percent of the poverty line.

The Medicaid provisions of the Affordable Care Act, in contrast, require States to expand their Medicaid programs by 2014 to cover *all* individuals under the age of 65 with incomes below 133 percent of the federal poverty line. The Act also establishes a new "[e]ssential health benefits" package, which States must provide to all new Medicaid recipients—a level sufficient to satisfy a recipient's obligations under the individual mandate. The Affordable Care Act provides that the Federal Government will pay 100 percent of the costs of covering these newly eligible individuals through 2016. In the following years, the federal payment level gradually decreases, to a minimum of 90 percent. In light of the expansion in coverage mandated by the Act, the Federal Government estimates that its Medicaid spending will increase by approximately $100 billion per year, nearly 40 percent above current levels.

The Spending Clause grants Congress the power "to pay the Debts and provide for the . . . general Welfare of the United States." U.S. Const., Art. I, §8, cl. 1. We have long recognized that Congress may use this power to grant federal funds to the States, and may condition such a grant upon the States' "taking certain actions that Congress could not require them to take." Such measures "encourage a State to regulate in a particular way, [and] influenc[e] a State's policy choices." *New York*. The conditions imposed by Congress ensure that the funds are used by the States to "provide for the . . . general Welfare" in the manner Congress intended.

At the same time, our cases have recognized limits on Congress's power under the Spending Clause to secure state compliance with federal objectives. "We have repeatedly characterized . . . Spending Clause legislation as 'much in the nature of a *contract.*'" *Barnes v. Gorman*, 536 U.S. 181 (2002) (quoting *Pennhurst State School and Hospital v. Halderman*, 451 U.S. 1 (1981)). The legitimacy of Congress's exercise of the spending power "thus rests on whether the State voluntarily and knowingly accepts the terms of the 'contract.'" *Pennhurst*. Respecting this limitation is critical to ensuring that Spending Clause legislation does not undermine the status of the States as independent sovereigns in our federal system. That system "rests on what might at first seem a counterintuitive insight, that 'freedom is enhanced by the creation of two governments, not one.'" For this reason, "the Constitution has never been understood to confer upon Congress the ability to require the States to govern according to Congress' instructions." *New York*. Otherwise the two-government system established by the Framers would give way to a system that vests power in one central government, and individual liberty would suffer.

That insight has led this Court to strike down federal legislation that commandeers a State's legislative or administrative apparatus for federal purposes. See, *e.g., Printz; New York*. It has also led us to scrutinize Spending Clause legislation to ensure that Congress is not using financial inducements to exert a "power akin to undue influence." *Steward Machine Co. v. Davis*, 301 U.S. 548 (1937). Congress may use its spending power to create incentives for States to act in accordance with federal policies. But when "pressure turns into compulsion," *ibid.*, the legislation runs contrary to our system of federalism. "[T]he Constitution simply does not give Congress the authority to require the States to regulate." *New York*. That is true whether Congress directly commands a State to regulate or indirectly coerces a State to adopt a federal regulatory system as its own.

Permitting the Federal Government to force the States to implement a federal program would threaten the political accountability key to our federal system. " [W]here the Federal Government directs the States to regulate, it may be state officials who will bear the brunt of public disapproval, while the federal officials who devised the regulatory program may remain insulated from the electoral ramifications of their decision." [*New York.*] Spending Clause programs do not pose this danger when a State has a legitimate choice whether to accept the federal conditions in exchange for federal funds. In such a situation, state officials can fairly be held politically accountable for choosing to accept or refuse the federal offer. But when the State has no choice, the Federal Government can achieve its objectives without accountability, just as in *New York* and *Printz.* Indeed, this danger is heightened when Congress acts under the Spending Clause, because Congress can use that power to implement federal policy it could not impose directly under its enumerated powers.

We addressed such concerns in *Steward Machine.* That case involved a federal tax on employers that was abated if the businesses paid into a state unemployment plan that met certain federally specified conditions. An employer sued, alleging that the tax was impermissibly "driv[ing] the state legislatures under the whip of economic pressure into the enactment of unemployment compensation laws at the bidding of the central government." We acknowledged the danger that the Federal Government might employ its taxing power to exert a "power akin to undue influence" upon the States. But we observed that Congress adopted the challenged tax and abatement program to channel money to the States that would otherwise have gone into the Federal Treasury for use in providing national unemployment services. Congress was willing to direct businesses to instead pay the money into state programs only on the condition that the money be used for the same purposes. Predicating tax abatement on a State's adoption of a particular type of unemployment legislation was therefore a means to "safeguard [the Federal Government's] own treasury." We held that "[i]n such circumstances, if in no others, inducement or persuasion does not go beyond the bounds of power."

In rejecting the argument that the federal law was a "weapon[ ] of coercion, destroying or impairing the autonomy of the states," the Court noted that there was no reason to suppose that the State in that case acted other than through "her unfettered will." Indeed, the State itself did "not offer a suggestion that in passing the unemployment law she was affected by duress."

As our decision in *Steward Machine* confirms, Congress may attach appropriate conditions to federal taxing and spending programs to preserve its control over the use of federal funds. In the typical case we look to the States to defend their prerogatives by adopting "the simple expedient of not yielding" to federal blandishments when they do not want to embrace the federal policies as their own. The States are separate and independent sovereigns. Sometimes they have to act like it.

A   The States, however, argue that the Medicaid expansion is far from the typical case. They object that Congress has "crossed the line distinguishing encouragement from coercion," *New York*, in the way it has structured the funding: Instead of simply refusing to grant the new funds to States that will not accept the new conditions, Congress has also threatened to withhold those States' existing Medicaid funds. The States claim that this threat serves no purpose other than to force unwilling States to sign up for the dramatic expansion in health care coverage effected by the Act.

Given the nature of the threat and the programs at issue here, we must agree. We have upheld Congress's authority to condition the receipt of funds on the States' complying with restrictions on the use of those funds, because that is the means by which Congress ensures that the funds are spent according to its view of the "general Welfare." Conditions that do not here govern the use of the funds, however, cannot be justified on that basis. When, for example, such conditions take the form of threats to terminate other significant independent grants, the conditions are properly viewed as a means of pressuring the States to accept policy changes.

In *South Dakota v. Dole,* we considered a challenge to a federal law that threatened to withhold five percent of a State's federal highway funds if the State did not raise its drinking age to 21. The Court found that the condition was "directly related to one of the main purposes for which highway funds are expended—safe interstate travel." At the same time, the condition was not a restriction on how the highway funds—set aside for specific highway improvement and maintenance efforts—were to be used.

We accordingly asked whether "the financial inducement offered by Congress" was "so coercive as to pass the point at which 'pressure turns into compulsion.'" By "financial inducement" the Court meant the threat of losing five percent of highway funds; no new money was offered to the States to raise their drinking ages. We found that the inducement was not impermissibly coercive, because Congress was offering only "relatively mild encouragement to the States." We observed that "all South Dakota would lose if she adheres to her chosen course as to a suitable minimum drinking age is 5%" of her highway funds. In fact, the federal funds at stake constituted less than half of one percent of South Dakota's budget at the time. In consequence, "we conclude[d] that [the] encouragement to state action [was] a valid use of the spending power." Whether to accept the drinking age change "remain[ed] the prerogative of the States not merely in theory but in fact."

In this case, the financial "inducement" Congress has chosen is much more than "relatively mild encouragement"—it is a gun to the head. Section 1396c of the Medicaid Act provides that if a State's Medicaid plan does not comply with the Act's requirements, the Secretary of Health and Human Services may declare that "further payments will not be made to the State." 42 U.S.C. § 1396c. A State that opts out of the Affordable Care Act's expansion in health care coverage thus stands to lose not merely "a relatively small percentage" of its existing Medicaid funding, but *all* of it. Medicaid spending accounts for over

20 percent of the average State's total budget, with federal funds covering 50 to 83 percent of those costs. The Federal Government estimates that it will pay out approximately $3.3 trillion between 2010 and 2019 in order to cover the costs of *pre*expansion Medicaid. In addition, the States have developed intricate statutory and administrative regimes over the course of many decades to implement their objectives under existing Medicaid. It is easy to see how the *Dole* Court could conclude that the threatened loss of less than half of one percent of South Dakota's budget left that State with a "prerogative" to reject Congress's desired policy, "not merely in theory but in fact." The threatened loss of over 10 percent of a State's overall budget, in contrast, is economic dragooning that leaves the States with no real option but to acquiesce in the Medicaid expansion.[g]

Justice Ginsburg claims that *Dole* is distinguishable because here "Congress has not threatened to withhold funds earmarked for any other program." But that begs the question: The States contend that the expansion is in reality a new program and that Congress is forcing them to accept it by threatening the funds for the existing Medicaid program. We cannot agree that existing Medicaid and — the expansion dictated by the Affordable Care Act are all one program simply because "Congress styled" them as such. If the expansion is not properly viewed as a modification of the existing Medicaid program, Congress's decision to so title it is irrelevant.[h]

Here, the Government claims that the Medicaid expansion is properly viewed merely as a modification of the existing program because the States agreed that Congress could change the terms of Medicaid when they signed on in the first place. The Government observes that the Social Security Act, which includes the original Medicaid provisions, contains a clause expressly reserving "[t]he right to alter, amend, or repeal any provision" of that statute. 42 U.S.C. §1304. So it does. But "if Congress intends to impose a condition on the grant of federal moneys, it must do so unambiguously." *Pennhurst*. A State confronted with statutory language reserving the right to "alter" or "amend" the pertinent provisions of the Social Security Act might reasonably assume that Congress

g. Justice Ginsburg observes that state Medicaid spending will increase by only 0.8 percent after the expansion. That not only ignores increased state administrative expenses, but also assumes that the Federal Government will continue to fund the expansion at the current statutorily specified levels. It is not unheard of, however, for the Federal Government to increase requirements in such a manner as to impose unfunded mandates on the States. More importantly, the size of the new financial burden imposed on a State is irrelevant in analyzing whether the State has been coerced into accepting that burden. "Your money or your life" is a coercive proposition, whether you have a single dollar in your pocket or $500.

h. Nor, of course, can the number of pages the amendment occupies, or the extent to which the change preserves and works within the existing program, be dispositive. Take, for example, the following hypothetical amendment: "All of a State's citizens are now eligible for Medicaid." That change would take up a single line and would not alter any "operational aspect[ ] of the program" beyond the eligibility requirements. Yet it could hardly be argued that such an amendment was a permissible modification of Medicaid, rather than an attempt to foist an entirely new health care system upon the States.

was entitled to make adjustments to the Medicaid program as it developed. Congress has in fact done so, sometimes conditioning only the new funding, other times both old and new.

The Medicaid expansion, however, accomplishes a shift in kind, not merely degree. The original program was designed to cover medical services for four particular categories of the needy: the disabled, the blind, the elderly, and needy families with dependent children. Previous amendments to Medicaid eligibility merely altered and expanded the boundaries of these categories. Under the Affordable Care Act, Medicaid is transformed into a program to meet the health care needs of the entire nonelderly population with income below 133 percent of the poverty level. It is no longer a program to care for the neediest among us, but rather an element of a comprehensive national plan to provide universal health insurance coverage.[i]

Indeed, the manner in which the expansion is structured indicates that while Congress may have styled the expansion a mere alteration of existing Medicaid, it recognized it was enlisting the States in a new health care program. Congress created a separate funding provision to cover the costs of providing services to any person made newly eligible by the expansion. While Congress pays 50 to 83 percent of the costs of covering individuals currently enrolled in Medicaid, once the expansion is fully implemented Congress will pay 90 percent of the costs for newly eligible persons. The conditions on use of the different funds are also distinct. Congress mandated that newly eligible persons receive a level of coverage that is less comprehensive than the traditional Medicaid benefit package.

As we have explained, "[t]hough Congress' power to legislate under the spending power is broad, it does not include surprising participating States with postacceptance or 'retroactive' conditions." *Pennhurst.* A State could hardly anticipate that Congress's reservation of the right to "alter" or "amend" the Medicaid program included the power to transform it so dramatically.

Justice Ginsburg claims that in fact this expansion is no different from the previous changes to Medicaid, such that "a State would be hard put to complain that it lacked fair notice." But the prior change she discusses—presumably the most dramatic alteration she could find—does not come close to working the transformation the expansion accomplishes. She highlights an amendment requiring States to cover pregnant women and increasing the number of eligible children. But this modification can hardly be described as a major change in a

---

i. Justice Ginsburg suggests that the States can have no objection to the Medicaid expansion, because "Congress could have repealed Medicaid [and,] [t]hereafter, . . . could have enacted Medicaid II, a new program combining the pre-2010 coverage with the expanded coverage required by the ACA." But it would certainly not be that easy. Practical constraints would plainly inhibit, if not preclude, the Federal Government from repealing the existing program and putting every feature of Medicaid on the table for political reconsideration. Such a massive undertaking would hardly be "ritualistic." The same is true of Justice Ginsburg's suggestion that Congress could establish Medicaid as an exclusively federal program.

program that—from its inception—provided health care for "families with dependent children." Previous Medicaid amendments simply do not fall into the same category as the one at stake here.

The Court in *Steward Machine* did not attempt to "fix the outermost line" where persuasion gives way to coercion. The Court found it "[e]nough for present purposes that wherever the line may be, this statute is within it." We have no need to fix a line either. It is enough for today that wherever that line may be, this statute is surely beyond it. Congress may not simply "conscript state [agencies] into the national bureaucratic army," and that is what it is attempting to do with the Medicaid expansion.

B

Nothing in our opinion precludes Congress from offering funds under the Affordable Care Act to expand the availability of health care, and requiring that States accepting such funds comply with the conditions on their use. What Congress is not free to do is to penalize States that choose not to participate in that new program by taking away their existing Medicaid funding. Section 1396c gives the Secretary of Health and Human Services the authority to do just that. It allows her to withhold *all* "further [Medicaid] payments . . . to the State" if she determines that the State is out of compliance with any Medicaid requirement, including those contained in the expansion. In light of the Court's holding, the Secretary cannot apply §1396c to withdraw existing Medicaid funds for failure to comply with the requirements set out in the expansion.

That fully remedies the constitutional violation we have identified. The chapter of the United States Code that contains §1396c includes a severability clause confirming that we need go no further. That clause specifies that "[i]f any provision of this chapter, or the application thereof to any person or circumstance, is held invalid, the remainder of the chapter, and the application of such provision to other persons or circumstances shall not be affected thereby." Today's holding does not affect the continued application of §1396c to the existing Medicaid program. Nor does it affect the Secretary's ability to withdraw funds provided under the Affordable Care Act if a State that has chosen to participate in the expansion fails to comply with the requirements of that Act.

This is not to say, as the joint dissent suggests, that we are "rewriting the Medicaid Expansion." Instead, we determine, first, that §1396c is unconstitutional when applied to withdraw existing Medicaid funds from States that decline to comply with the expansion. We then follow Congress's explicit textual instruction to leave unaffected "the remainder of the chapter, and the application of [the challenged] provision to other persons or circumstances." When we invalidate an application of a statute because that application is unconstitutional, we are not "rewriting" the statute; we are merely enforcing the Constitution.

The question remains whether today's holding affects other provisions of the Affordable Care Act. In considering that question, "[w]e seek to determine what Congress would have intended in light of the Court's constitutional holding." Our "touchstone for any decision about remedy is legislative intent, for a court cannot use its remedial powers to circumvent the intent of the legislature." The question here is whether Congress would have wanted the rest of the Act to stand, had it known that States would have a genuine choice whether to participate in the new Medicaid expansion. Unless it is "evident" that the answer is no, we must leave the rest of the Act intact.

We are confident that Congress would have wanted to preserve the rest of the Act. It is fair to say that Congress assumed that every State would participate in the Medicaid expansion, given that States had no real choice but to do so. The States contend that Congress enacted the rest of the Act with such full participation in mind; they point out that Congress made Medicaid a means for satisfying the mandate, and enacted no other plan for providing coverage to many low-income individuals. According to the States, this means that the entire Act must fall.

We disagree. The Court today limits the financial pressure the Secretary may apply to induce States to accept the terms of the Medicaid expansion. As a practical matter, that means States may now choose to reject the expansion; that is the whole point. But that does not mean all or even any will. Some States may indeed decline to participate, either because they are unsure they will be able to afford their share of the new funding obligations, or because they are unwilling to commit the administrative resources necessary to support the expansion. Other States, however, may voluntarily sign up, finding the idea of expanding Medicaid coverage attractive, particularly given the level of federal funding the Act offers at the outset.

We have no way of knowing how many States will accept the terms of the expansion, but we do not believe Congress would have wanted the whole Act to fall, simply because some may choose not to participate. The other reforms Congress enacted, after all, will remain "fully operative as a law," and will still function in a way "consistent with Congress' basic objectives in enacting the statute[.]" Confident that Congress would not have intended anything different, we conclude that the rest of the Act need not fall in light of our constitutional holding.

* * *

The Affordable Care Act is constitutional in part and unconstitutional in part. The individual mandate cannot be upheld as an exercise of Congress's power under the Commerce Clause. That Clause authorizes Congress to regulate interstate commerce, not to order individuals to engage in it. In this case, however, it is reasonable to construe what Congress has done as increasing taxes on those who have a certain amount of income, but choose to go without health insurance. Such legislation is within Congress's power to tax.

As for the Medicaid expansion, that portion of the Affordable Care Act violates the Constitution by threatening existing Medicaid funding. Congress has no authority to order the States to regulate according to its instructions. Congress may offer the States grants and require the States to comply with accompanying conditions, but the States must have a genuine choice whether to accept the offer. The States are given no such choice in this case: They must either accept a basic change in the nature of Medicaid, or risk losing all Medicaid funding. The remedy for that constitutional violation is to preclude the Federal Government from imposing such a sanction. That remedy does not require striking down other portions of the Affordable Care Act.

The Framers created a Federal Government of limited powers, and assigned to this Court the duty of enforcing those limits. The Court does so today. But the Court does not express any opinion on the wisdom of the Affordable Care Act. Under the Constitution, that judgment is reserved to the people.

The judgment of the Court of Appeals for the Eleventh Circuit is affirmed in part and reversed in part.

It is so ordered.

Justice GINSBURG, with whom Justice SOTOMAYOR joins, and with whom Justice BREYER and Justice KAGAN join as to Parts I, II, III, and IV, concurring in part, concurring in the judgment in part, and dissenting in part.

I agree with The Chief Justice that the Anti-Injunction Act does not bar the Court's consideration of this case, and that the minimum coverage provision is a proper exercise of Congress' taxing power. I therefore join Parts I, II, and III-C of The Chief Justice's opinion. Unlike The Chief Justice, however, I would hold, alternatively, that the Commerce Clause authorizes Congress to enact the minimum coverage provision. I would also hold that the Spending Clause permits the Medicaid expansion exactly as Congress enacted it.

I

. . .

A

In enacting the Patient Protection and Affordable Care Act (ACA), Congress comprehensively reformed the national market for health-care products and services. By any measure, that market is immense. Collectively, Americans spent $2.5 trillion on health care in 2009, accounting for 17.6% of our Nation's economy. Within the next decade, it is anticipated, spending on health care will nearly double.

The health-care market's size is not its only distinctive feature. Unlike the market for almost any other product or service, the market for medical care is one in which all individuals inevitably participate. Virtually every person residing in the United States, sooner or later, will visit a doctor or other health-care professional. See Dept. of Health and Human Services, National Center for Health Statistics, Summary Health Statistics for U.S. Adults: National Health Interview Survey 2009 (Dec. 2010) (Over 99.5% of adults above 65 have visited a health-care professional.). Most people will do so repeatedly. See *id.* (In 2009 alone, 64% of adults made two or more visits to a doctor's office.).

When individuals make those visits, they face another reality of the current market for medical care: its high cost. In 2010, on average, an individual in the United States incurred over $7,000 in health-care expenses. Over a lifetime, costs mount to hundreds of thousands of dollars. When a person requires nonroutine care, the cost will generally exceed what he or she can afford to pay. A single hospital stay, for instance, typically costs upwards of $10,000. Treatments for many serious, though not uncommon, conditions similarly cost a substantial sum.

Although every U.S. domiciliary will incur significant medical expenses during his or her lifetime, the time when care will be needed is often unpredictable. An accident, a heart attack, or a cancer diagnosis commonly occurs without warning. Inescapably, we are all at peril of needing medical care without a moment's notice.

To manage the risks associated with medical care—its high cost, its unpredictability, and its inevitability—most people in the United States obtain health insurance. Many (approximately 170 million in 2009) are insured by private insurance companies. Others, including those over 65 and certain poor and disabled persons, rely on government-funded insurance programs, notably Medicare and Medicaid. Combined, private health insurers and State and Federal Governments finance almost 85% of the medical care administered to U.S. residents.

Not all U.S. residents, however, have health insurance. In 2009, approximately 50 million people were uninsured, either by choice or, more likely, because they could not afford private insurance and did not qualify for government aid. As a group, uninsured individuals annually consume more than $100 billion in healthcare services, nearly 5% of the Nation's total. Over 60% of those without insurance visit a doctor's office or emergency room in a given year.

B

The large number of individuals without health insurance, Congress found, heavily burdens the national health-care market. As just noted, the cost of emergency care or treatment for a serious illness generally exceeds what an individual can afford to pay on her own. Unlike markets for most products, however, the inability to pay for care does not mean that an uninsured individual will receive no care. Federal and state law, as well as professional obligations and embedded social norms, require hospitals and physicians to provide care when it is most needed, regardless of the patient's ability to pay.

As a consequence, medical-care providers deliver significant amounts of care to the uninsured for which the providers receive no payment. In 2008, for example, hospitals, physicians, and other health-care professionals received no compensation for $43 billion worth of the $116 billion in care they administered to those without insurance.

Health-care providers do not absorb these bad debts. Instead, they raise their prices, passing along the cost of uncompensated care to those who do pay reliably: the government and private insurance companies. In response, private insurers increase their premiums, shifting the cost of the elevated bills from providers onto those who carry insurance. The net result: Those with health insurance subsidize the medical care of those without it. As economists would describe what happens, the uninsured "free ride" on those who pay for health insurance.

The size of this subsidy is considerable. Congress found that the cost-shifting — just described "increases family [insurance] premiums by on average over $1,000 a year." Higher premiums, in turn, render health insurance less afford-able, forcing more people to go without insurance and leading to further costshifting.

And it is hardly just the currently sick or injured among the uninsured who prompt elevation of the price of health care and health insurance. Insurance — companies and health-care providers know that some percentage of healthy, uninsured people will suffer sickness or injury each year and will receive medical care despite their inability to pay. In anticipation of this uncompensated care, health-care companies raise their prices, and insurers their premiums. In other words, because any uninsured person may need medical care at any moment and because health-care companies must account for that risk, every uninsured person impacts the market price of medical care and medical insurance.

The failure of individuals to acquire insurance has other deleterious effects on the health-care market. Because those without insurance generally lack access to preventative care, they do not receive treatment for conditions—like hypertension and diabetes—that can be successfully and affordably treated if diagnosed early on. When sickness finally drives the uninsured to seek care, once treatable conditions have escalated into grave health problems, requiring more costly and extensive intervention. The extra time and resources providers spend serving the uninsured lessens the providers' ability to care for those who do have insurance.

C

States cannot resolve the problem of the uninsured on their own. Like Social — Security benefits, a universal health-care system, if adopted by an individual State, would be "bait to the needy and dependent elsewhere, encouraging them to migrate and seek a haven of repose." *Helvering v. Davis.* An influx of unhealthy individuals into a State with universal health care would result in increased spending on medical services. To cover the increased costs, a State would have to raise taxes, and private health-insurance companies would have to increase premiums. Higher taxes and increased insurance costs would, in turn, encourage businesses and healthy individuals to leave the State.

States that undertake health-care reforms on their own thus risk "placing themselves in a position of economic disadvantage as compared with neighbors or competitors." *Davis*. See also Brief for Health Care for All, Inc., et al. as *Amici Curiae* in No. 11-398, p. 4 ("[O]utofstate residents continue to seek and receive millions of dollars in uncompensated care in Massachusetts hospitals, limiting the State's efforts to improve its health care system through the elimination of uncompensated care."). Facing that risk, individual States are unlikely to take the initiative in addressing the problem of the uninsured, even though solving that problem is in all States' best interests. Congress' intervention was needed to overcome this collective action impasse.

D

Aware that a national solution was required, Congress could have taken over the health-insurance market by establishing a tax-and-spend federal program like Social Security. Such a program, commonly referred to as a single-payer system (where the sole payer is the Federal Government), would have left little, if any, room for private enterprise or the States. Instead of going this route, Congress enacted the ACA, a solution that retains a robust role for private insurers and state governments. To make its chosen approach work, however, Congress had to use some new tools, including a requirement that most individuals obtain private health insurance coverage. . . .

The minimum coverage provision serves a further purpose vital to Congress' plan to reduce the number of uninsured. Congress knew that encouraging individuals to purchase insurance would not suffice to solve the problem, because most of the uninsured are not uninsured by choice. Of particular concern to Congress were people who, though desperately in need of insurance, often cannot acquire it: persons who suffer from preexisting medical conditions.

Before the ACA's enactment, private insurance companies took an applicant's medical history into account when setting insurance rates or deciding whether to insure an individual. Because individuals with preexisting medical conditions cost insurance companies significantly more than those without such conditions, insurers routinely refused to insure these individuals, charged them substantially higher premiums, or offered only limited coverage that did not include the preexisting illness.

To ensure that individuals with medical histories have access to affordable insurance, Congress devised a three-part solution. First, Congress imposed a "guaranteed issue" requirement, which bars insurers from denying coverage to any person on account of that person's medical condition or history. Second, Congress required insurers to use "community rating" to price their insurance policies. See §300gg. Community rating, in effect, bars insurance companies from charging higher premiums to those with preexisting conditions.

But these two provisions, Congress comprehended, could not work effec- —
tively unless individuals were given a powerful incentive to obtain insurance.

In the 1990's, several States—including New York, New Jersey, Washington, Kentucky, Maine, New Hampshire, and Vermont—enacted guaranteed-issue and community-rating laws without requiring universal acquisition of insurance coverage. The results were disastrous. "All seven states suffered from skyrocketing insurance premium costs, reductions in individuals with coverage, and reductions in insurance products and providers." Brief for American Association of People with Disabilities et al. as *Amici Curiae* in No. 11-398, p. 9 (hereinafter AAPD Brief). See also Brief for Governor of Washington Christine Gregoire as *Amicus Curiae* in No. 11-398, pp. 11-14 (describing the "death spiral" in the insurance market Washington experienced when the State passed a law requiring coverage for preexisting conditions).

Congress comprehended that guaranteed-issue and community-rating laws alone will not work. When insurance companies are required to insure the sick at affordable prices, individuals can wait until they become ill to buy insurance. Pretty soon, those in need of immediate medical care—*i.e.,* those who cost insurers the most—become the insurance companies' main customers. This "adverse selection" problem leaves insurers with two choices: They can either raise premiums dramatically to cover their everincreasing costs or they can exit the market. In the seven States that tried guaranteedissue and community-rating requirements without a minimum coverage provision, that is precisely what insurance companies did. See, *e.g.,* AAPD Brief 10 ("[In Maine,] [m]any insurance providers doubled their premiums in just three years or less."); *id.,* at 12 ("Like New York, Vermont saw substantial increases in premiums after its . . . insurance reform measures took effect in 1993."); Hall, An Evaluation of New York's Reform Law, 25 J. Health Pol. Pol'y & L. 71, 91-92 (2000) (Guaranteed-issue and community-rating laws resulted in a "dramatic exodus of indemnity insurers from New York's individual [insurance] market."); Brief for Barry Friedman et al. as *Amici Curiae* in No. 11-398, p. 17 ("In Kentucky, all but two insurers (one State-run) abandoned the State.").

Massachusetts, Congress was told, cracked the adverse selection problem. By requiring most residents to obtain insurance, the Commonwealth ensured that insurers would not be left with only the sick as customers. As a result, federal lawmakers observed, Massachusetts succeeded where other States had failed. In coupling the minimum coverage provision with guaranteed-issue and community-rating prescriptions, Congress followed Massachusetts' lead. . . .

II

A

The Commerce Clause, it is widely acknowledged, "was the Framers' response to the central problem that gave rise to the Constitution itself." Under the Articles of Confederation, the Constitution's precursor, the regulation of commerce was left to the States. This scheme proved unworkable, because the individual States, understandably focused on their own economic interests, often failed to take actions critical to the success of the Nation as a whole.

What was needed was a "national Government . . . armed with a positive & compleat authority in all cases where uniform measures are necessary." See Letter from James Madison to Edmund Randolph (Apr. 8, 1787), in 9 Papers of James Madison 368, 370 (R. Rutland ed. 1975). See also Letter from George Washington to James Madison (Nov. 30, 1785), in 8 *id.,* at 428, 429 ("We are either a United people, or we are not. If the former, let us, in all matters of general concern act as a nation, which ha[s] national objects to promote, and a national character to support."). The Framers' solution was the Commerce Clause, which, as they perceived it, granted Congress the authority to enact economic legislation "in all Cases for the general Interests of the Union, and also in those Cases to which the States are separately incompetent." 2 Records of the Federal Convention of 1787, pp. 131-132, 8 (M. Farrand rev.1966).

The Framers understood that the "general Interests of the Union" would change over time, in ways they could not anticipate. Accordingly, they recognized that the Constitution was of necessity a "great outlin[e]," not a detailed blueprint, see *McCulloch v. Maryland,* and that its provisions included broad concepts, to be "explained by the context or by the facts of the case," Letter from James Madison to N.P. Trist (Dec. 1831), in 9 Writings of James Madison 471, 475 (G. Hunt ed. 1910). . . .

B

[W]e owe a large measure of respect to Congress when it frames and enacts economic and social legislation. . . . When appraising such legislation, we ask only (1) whether Congress had a "rational basis" for concluding that the regulated activity substantially affects interstate commerce, and (2) whether there is a "reasonable connection between the regulatory means selected and the asserted ends." In answering these questions, we presume the statute under review is constitutional and may strike it down only on a "plain showing" that Congress acted irrationally.

C

Straightforward application of these principles would require the Court to hold that the minimum coverage provision is proper Commerce Clause legislation. Beyond dispute, Congress had a rational basis for concluding that the uninsured, as a class, substantially affect interstate commerce. Those without insurance consume billions of dollars of health-care products and services each year. Those goods are produced, sold, and delivered largely by national and regional companies who routinely transact business across state lines. The uninsured also cross state lines to receive care. Some have medical emergencies while away from home. Others, when sick, go to a neighboring State that provides better care for those who have not prepaid for care.

Not only do those without insurance consume a large amount of health care each year; critically, as earlier explained, their inability to pay for a significant portion of that consumption drives up market prices, foists costs on other consumers, and reduces market efficiency and stability. Given these farreaching effects on interstate commerce, the decision to forgo insurance is hardly inconsequential or equivalent to "doing nothing," . . . ; it is, instead, an economic decision Congress has the authority to address under the Commerce Clause. See also *Wickard* ("It is well established by decisions of this Court that the power to regulate commerce includes the power to regulate the prices at which commodities in that commerce are dealt in and *practices affecting such prices.*" (emphasis added)).

The minimum coverage provision, furthermore, bears a "reasonable connection" to Congress' goal of protecting the health-care market from the disruption caused by individuals who fail to obtain insurance. By requiring those who do not carry insurance to pay a toll, the minimum coverage provision gives individuals a strong incentive to insure. This incentive, Congress had good reason to believe, would reduce the number of uninsured and, correspondingly, mitigate the adverse impact the uninsured have on the national health-care market.

Congress also acted reasonably in requiring uninsured individuals, whether sick or healthy, either to obtain insurance or to pay the specified penalty. As earlier observed, because every person is at risk of needing care at any moment, all those who lack insurance, regardless of their current health status, adversely affect the price of health care and health insurance. Moreover, an insurance-purchase requirement limited to those in need of immediate care simply could not work. Insurance companies would either charge these individuals prohibitively expensive premiums, or, if communityrating regulations were in place, close up shop.

"[W]here we find that the legislators . . . have a rational basis for finding a chosen regulatory scheme necessary to the protection of commerce, our investigation is at an end." Congress' enactment of the minimum coverage provision, which addresses a specific interstate problem in a practical, experience-informed manner, easily meets this criterion.

D

Rather than evaluating the constitutionality of the minimum coverage provision in the manner established by our precedents, The Chief Justice relies on a newly minted constitutional doctrine. The commerce power does not, The Chief Justice announces, permit Congress to "compe[l] individuals to become active in commerce by purchasing a product."

1

a

[E]veryone will, at some point, consume health-care products and services. See *supra,* at 3. Thus, if The Chief Justice is correct that an insurance-purchase requirement can be applied only to those who "actively" consume health care, the minimum coverage provision fits the bill.

The Chief Justice does not dispute that all U.S. residents participate in the market for health services over the course of their lives. But, The Chief Justice insists, the uninsured cannot be considered active in the market for health care, because "[t]he proximity and degree of connection between the [uninsured today] and [their] subsequent commercial activity is too lacking."

This argument has multiple flaws. First, more than 60% of those without insurance visit a hospital or doctor's office each year. Nearly 90% will within five years. An uninsured's consumption of health care is thus quite proximate: It is virtually certain to occur in the next five years and more likely than not to occur this year.

Equally evident, Congress has no way of separating those uninsured individuals who will need emergency medical care today (surely their consumption of medical care is sufficiently imminent) from those who will not need medical services for years to come. No one knows when an emergency will occur, yet emergencies involving the uninsured arise daily. To capture individuals who unexpectedly will obtain medical care in the very near future, then, Congress needed to include individuals who will not go to a doctor anytime soon. Congress, our decisions instruct, has authority to cast its net that wide.

✗   Second, it is Congress' role, not the Court's, to delineate the boundaries of the market the Legislature seeks to regulate. The Chief Justice defines the health-care market as including only those transactions that will occur either in the next instant or within some (unspecified) proximity to the next instant. But Congress could reasonably have viewed the market from a long-term perspective, encompassing all transactions virtually certain to occur over the next decade, not just those occurring here and now.

–   Third, contrary to The Chief Justice's contention, our precedent does indeed support "[t]he proposition that Congress may dictate the conduct of an individual today because of prophesied future activity." In *Wickard,* the Court upheld a penalty the Federal Government imposed on a farmer who grew more wheat than he was permitted to grow under the Agricultural Adjustment Act of 1938 (AAA). He could not be penalized, the farmer argued, as he was growing the wheat for home consumption, not for sale on the open market. The Court rejected this argument. Wheat intended for home consumption, the Court noted, "overhangs the market, and if induced by rising prices, tends to flow into the market and check price increases [intended by the AAA]."

Similar reasoning supported the Court's judgment in *Raich,* which upheld Congress' authority to regulate marijuana grown for personal use. Homegrown marijuana substantially affects the interstate market for marijuana, we observed, for "the high demand in the interstate market will [likely] draw such marijuana into that market."

Our decisions thus acknowledge Congress' authority, under the Commerce Clause, to direct the conduct of an individual today (the farmer in *Wickard,* stopped from growing excess wheat; the plaintiff in *Raich,* ordered to cease cultivating marijuana) because of a prophesied future transaction (the eventual sale of that wheat or marijuana in the interstate market). Congress' actions are even more rational in this case, where the future activity (the consumption of medical care) is certain to occur, the sole uncertainty being the time the activity will take place.

Maintaining that the uninsured are not active in the health-care market, The Chief Justice draws an analogy to the car market. An individual "is not 'active in the car market,'" The Chief Justice observes, simply because he or she may someday buy a car. The analogy is inapt. The inevitable yet unpredictable need for medical care and the guarantee that emergency care will be provided when required are conditions nonexistent in other markets. That is so of the market for cars, and of the market for broccoli as well. Although an individual *might* buy a car or a crown of broccoli one day, there is no certainty she will ever do so. And if she eventually wants a car or has a craving for broccoli, she will be obliged to pay at the counter before receiving the vehicle or nourishment. She will get no free ride or food, at the expense of another consumer forced to pay an inflated price. Upholding the minimum coverage provision on the ground that all are participants or will be participants in the health-care market would therefore carry no implication that Congress may justify under the Commerce Clause a mandate to buy other products and services.

Nor is it accurate to say that the minimum coverage provision "compel[s] individuals . . . to purchase an unwanted product," or "suite of products." If unwanted today, medical service secured by insurance may be desperately needed tomorrow. Virtually everyone, I reiterate, consumes health care at some point in his or her life. Health insurance is a means of paying for this care, nothing more. In requiring individuals to obtain insurance, Congress is therefore not mandating the purchase of a discrete, unwanted product. Rather, Congress is merely defining the terms on which individuals pay for an interstate good they consume: Persons subject to the mandate must now pay for medical care in advance (instead of at the point of service) and through insurance (instead of out of pocket). Establishing payment terms for goods in or affecting interstate commerce is quintessential economic regulation well within Congress' domain.

The Chief Justice also calls the minimum coverage provision an illegitimate effort to make young, healthy individuals subsidize insurance premiums paid by the less hale and hardy. This complaint, too, is spurious. Under the current health-care system, healthy persons who lack insurance receive a benefit for which they do not pay: They are assured that, if they need it, emergency medical care will be available, although they cannot afford it. Those who have insurance bear the cost of this guarantee. By requiring the healthy unin-sured to obtain insurance or pay a penalty structured as a tax, the minimum coverage provision ends the free ride these individuals currently enjoy.

In the fullness of time, moreover, today's young and healthy will become society's old and infirm. Viewed over a lifespan, the costs and benefits even out: The young who pay more than their fair share currently will pay less than their fair share when they become senior citizens. And even if, as undoubtedly will be the case, some individuals, over their lifespans, will pay more for health insurance than they receive in health services, they have little to complain about, for that is how insurance works. Every insured person receives protection against a catastrophic loss, even though only a subset of the covered class will ultimately need that protection.

b

[A]rticle I, §8, of the Constitution grants Congress the power "[t]o regulate Commerce . . . among the several States." Nothing in this language implies that Congress' commerce power is limited to regulating those actively engaged in commercial transactions. Indeed, as the D.C. Circuit observed, "[a]t the time the Constitution was [framed], to 'regulate' meant," among other things, "to require action." See *Seven-Sky v. Holder,* 661 F.3d 1, 16 (2011).

Arguing to the contrary, The Chief Justice notes that "the Constitution gives Congress the power to 'coin Money,' in addition to the power to 'regulate the Value thereof,'" and similarly "gives Congress the power to 'raise and support Armies' and to 'provide and maintain a Navy,' in addition to the power to 'make Rules for the Government and Regulation of the land and naval Forces.'" In separating the power to regulate from the power to bring the subject of the regulation into existence, The Chief Justice asserts, "[t]he language of the Constitution reflects the natural understanding that the power to regulate assumes there is already something to be regulated."

This argument is difficult to fathom. Requiring individuals to obtain insur-ance unquestionably regulates the interstate health-insurance and health-care markets, both of them in existence well before the enactment of the ACA. See *Wickard,* 317 U.S., at 128 ("The stimulation of commerce is a use of the regulatory function quite as definitely as prohibitions or restrictions thereon."). Thus, the "something to be regulated" was surely there when Congress created the minimum coverage provision.[a]

---

a. The Chief Justice's reliance on the quoted passages of the Constitution . . . is also dubious on other grounds. The power to "regulate the Value" of the national currency presumably includes the power to increase the currency's worth—*i.e.,* to create value where none previously existed. And if the power to "[r]egulat[e] . . . the land and naval Forces" presupposes "there is already [in existence] something to be regulated," *i.e.,* an Army and a Navy, does Congress lack authority to create an Air Force?

Nor does our case law toe the activity versus inactivity line. In *Wickard*, for example, we upheld the penalty imposed on a farmer who grew too much wheat, even though the regulation had the effect of compelling farmers to — purchase wheat in the open market. "[F]orcing some farmers into the market to buy what they could provide for themselves" was, the Court held, a valid means of regulating commerce. In another context, this Court similarly upheld — Congress' authority under the commerce power to compel an "inactive" landholder to submit to an unwanted sale. See *Monongahela Nav. Co. v. United States,* 148 U.S. 312 (1893) ("[U]pon *the [great] power to regulate commerce*[,]" Congress has the authority to mandate the sale of real property to the Government, where the sale is essential to the improvement of a navigable waterway (emphasis added)); *Cherokee Nation v. Southern Kansas R. Co.,* 135 U.S. 641 (1890) (similar reliance on the commerce power regarding mandated sale of private property for railroad construction).

[T]his Court's former endeavors to impose categorical limits on the commerce power have not fared well. In several pre-New Deal cases, the Court attempted to cabin Congress' Commerce Clause authority by distinguishing "commerce" from activity once conceived to be noncommercial, notably, "production," "mining," and "manufacturing." See, *e.g., United States v. E.C. Knight Co.,* 156 U.S. 1 (1895) ("Commerce succeeds to manufacture, and is not a part of it."); *Carter v. Carter Coal Co.,* 298 U.S. 238 (1936) ("Mining brings the subject matter of commerce into existence. Commerce disposes of it."). The Court also sought to distinguish activities having a "direct" effect on interstate commerce, and for that reason, subject to federal regulation, from those having only an "indirect" effect, and therefore not amenable to federal control. See, *e.g., A.L.A. Schechter Poultry Corp. v. United States,* 295 U.S. 495 (1935) ("[T]he distinction between direct and indirect effects of intrastate transactions upon interstate commerce must be recognized as a fundamental one.").

These line-drawing exercises were untenable, and the Court long ago abandoned them. "[Q]uestions of the power of Congress [under the Commerce Clause]," we held in *Wickard*, "are not to be decided by reference to any formula which would give controlling force to nomenclature such as 'production' and 'indirect' and foreclose consideration of the actual effects of the activity in question upon interstate commerce." Failing to learn from this history, The Chief Justice plows ahead with his formalistic distinction between those who are "active in commerce," and those who are not.

It is not hard to show the difficulty courts (and Congress) would encounter in distinguishing statutes that regulate "activity" from those that regulate "inactivity." As Judge Easterbrook noted, "it is possible to restate most actions as corresponding inactions with the same effect." *Archie v. Racine,* 847 F.2d 1211, 1213 (C.A.7 1988) (en banc). Take this case as an example. An individual who opts not to purchase insurance from a private insurer can be seen as actively selecting another form of insurance: selfinsurance. The minimum coverage provision could therefore be described as regulating activists in the self-insurance market.[b] *Wickard* is another example. Did the statute there at issue target activity (the growing of too much wheat) or inactivity (the farmer's failure to purchase wheat in the marketplace)? If anything, the Court's analysis suggested the latter.

At bottom, The Chief Justice's and the joint dissenters' "view that an individual cannot be subject to Commerce Clause regulation absent voluntary, affirmative acts that enter him or her into, or affect, the interstate market expresses a concern for individual liberty that [is] more redolent of Due Process Clause arguments." Plaintiffs have abandoned any argument pinned to substantive due process, however, and now concede that the provisions here at issue do not offend the Due Process Clause.

[The concern that without the activity/inactivity distinction] the commerce power would otherwise know no limits . . . is unfounded.

First, The Chief Justice could certainly uphold the individual mandate without giving Congress *carte blanche* to enact any and all purchase mandates. As several times noted, the unique attributes of the healthcare market render everyone active in that market and give rise to a significant freeriding problem that does not occur in other markets. . . .

Congress would remain unable to regulate noneconomic conduct that has only an attenuated effect on interstate commerce and is traditionally left to state law. See *Lopez*; *Morrison*. . . . [But] [a]n individual's decision to selfinsure . . . is an economic act with the requisite connection to interstate commerce. Other choices individuals make are unlikely to fit the same or similar description. . . . The Chief Justice cites a Government mandate to purchase green vegetables. One could call this concern "the broccoli horrible." Congress, The Chief Justice posits, might adopt such a mandate, reasoning that an individual's failure to eat a healthy diet, like the failure to purchase health insurance, imposes costs on others.

Consider the chain of inferences the Court would have to accept to conclude that a vegetablepurchase mandate was likely to have a substantial effect on the healthcare costs borne by lithe Americans. The Court would have to believe that individuals forced to buy vegetables would then eat them (instead of throwing or giving them away), would prepare the vegetables in a healthy way (steamed or raw, not deepfried), would cut back on unhealthy foods, and would not allow other factors (such as lack of exercise or little sleep) to trump the improved diet.[c]

---

b. The Chief Justice's characterization of individuals who choose not to purchase private insurance as "doing nothing[]" is similarly questionable. A person who self-insures opts against prepayment for a product the person will in time consume. When aggregated, exercise of that option has a substantial impact on the healthcare market.

c. The failure to purchase vegetables in The Chief Justice's hypothetical, then, is *not* what leads to higher healthcare costs for others; rather, it is the failure of individuals to maintain a healthy diet, and the resulting obesity, that creates the costshifting problem. Requiring individuals to purchase vegetables is thus several steps removed from solving the problem. The failure to obtain health insurance, by contrast, is the *immediate cause* of the costshifting Congress sought to address through the ACA. Requiring individuals to obtain insurance attacks the source of the problem directly, in a single step.

Such "pil[ing of] inference upon inference" is just what the Court refused to do in *Lopez* and *Morrison*.

Other provisions of the Constitution also check congressional overreaching. A mandate to purchase a particular product would be unconstitutional if, for example, the edict impermissibly abridged the freedom of speech, interfered with the free exercise of religion, or infringed on a liberty interest protected by the Due Process Clause.

Supplementing these legal restraints is a formidable check on congressional power: the democratic process. As the controversy surrounding the passage of the Affordable Care Act attests, purchase mandates are likely to engender political resistance. This prospect is borne out by the behavior of state legislators. Despite their possession of unquestioned authority to impose mandates, state governments have rarely done so.

When contemplated in its extreme, almost any power looks dangerous. The commerce power, hypothetically, would enable Congress to prohibit the purchase and home production of all meat, fish, and dairy goods, effectively compelling Americans to eat only vegetables. Yet no one would offer the "hypothetical and unreal possibilit[y][]" of a vegetarian state as a credible reason to deny Congress the authority ever to ban the possession and sale of goods. The Chief Justice accepts just such specious logic when he cites the broccoli horrible as a reason to deny Congress the power to pass the individual mandate. Cf. R. Bork, The Tempting of America 169 (1990) ("Judges and lawyers live on the slippery slope of analogies; they are not supposed to ski it to the bottom."). . . .

III

A

[T]he Necessary and Proper Clause "empowers Congress to enact laws in effectuation of its [commerce] powe[r] that are not within its authority to enact in isolation." *Raich,* 545 U.S., at 39 (Scalia, J., concurring in judgment). Hence, "[a] complex regulatory program . . . can survive a Commerce Clause challenge without a showing that every single facet of the program is independently and directly related to a valid congressional goal." "It is enough that the challenged provisions are an integral part of the regulatory program and that the regulatory scheme when considered as a whole satisfies this test." See also *Raich,* 545 U.S., at 24-25 (A challenged statutory provision fits within Congress' commerce authority if it is an "essential par[t] of a larger regulation of economic activity," such that, in the absence of the provision, "the regulatory scheme could be undercut." (quoting *Lopez,* 514 U.S., at 561)); *Raich,* 545 U.S., at 37 (Scalia, J., concurring in judgment) ("Congress may regulate even noneconomic local activity if that regulation is a necessary part of a more general regulation of interstate commerce. The relevant question is simply whether the means chosen are 'reasonably adapted' to the attainment of a legitimate end under the commerce power."). . . .

Congress knew . . . that simply barring insurance companies from relying on an applicant's medical history would not work in practice. Without the individual mandate, Congress learned, guaranteedissue and communityrating requirements would trigger an adverseselection deathspiral in the healthinsurance market: Insurance premiums would skyrocket, the number of uninsured would increase, and insurance companies would exit the market. When complemented by an insurance mandate, on the other hand, guaranteed issue and community rating would work as intended, increasing access to insurance and reducing uncompensated care. The minimum coverage provision is thus an "essential par[t] of a larger regulation of economic activity"; without the provision, "the regulatory scheme [w]ould be undercut." *Raich*. Put differently, the minimum coverage provision, together with the guaranteedissue and communityrating requirements, is "'reasonably adapted' to the attainment of a legitimate end under the commerce power": the elimination of pricing and sales practices that take an applicant's medical history into account.

B

[The Chief Justice contends that] [a] mandate to purchase health insurance is not "proper" legislation, . . . because the command "undermine[s] the structure of government established by the Constitution." [relying on *Printz* and *New York v. United States*.] The statutes at issue in both cases, however, compelled *state officials* to act on the Federal Government's behalf. . . . The minimum coverage provision, in contrast, acts "directly upon individuals, without employing the States as intermediaries." The provision is thus entirely consistent with the Constitution's design. See *Printz*, 521 U.S., at 920 ("[T]he Framers explicitly chose a Constitution that confers upon Congress the power to regulate individuals, not States."). . . .

The Chief Justice [does not] pause to explain *why* the power to direct either the purchase of health insurance or, alternatively, the payment of a penalty collectible as a tax is more farreaching than other implied powers this Court has found meet under the Necessary and Proper Clause. These powers include the power to enact criminal laws; the power to imprison, including civil imprisonment, see, *e.g., Comstock*; and the power to create a national bank, see *McCulloch*.[d]

[H]ow is a judge to decide, when ruling on the constitutionality of a federal statute, whether Congress employed an "independent power," or merely a "derivative" one, [w]hether the power used is "substantive," or just "inciden-

---

d. Indeed, Congress regularly and uncontroversially requires individuals who are "doing nothing," to take action. Examples include federal requirements to report for jury duty; to register for selective service; to purchase firearms and gear in anticipation of service in the Militia ([as it did in the] Uniform Militia Act of 1792); to turn gold currency over to the Federal Government in exchange for paper currency; and to file a tax return.

tal"? The instruction The Chief Justice, in effect, provides lower courts: You will know it when you see it.

It is more than exaggeration to suggest that the minimum coverage provision improperly intrudes on "essential attributes of state sovereignty." First, the Affordable Care Act does not operate "in [an] are[a] such as criminal law enforcement or education where States historically have been sovereign." *Lopez.* As evidenced by Medicare, Medicaid, the Employee Retirement Income Security Act of 1974 (ERISA), and the Health Insurance Portability and Accountability Act of 1996 (HIPAA), the Federal Government plays a lead role in the healthcare sector, both as a direct payer and as a regulator.

Second, and perhaps most important, the minimum coverage provision, along with other provisions of the ACA, addresses the very sort of interstate problem that made the commerce power essential in our federal system. The crisis created by the large number of U.S. residents who lack health insurance is one of national dimension that States are "separately incompetent" to handle. See also Maryland Brief 15-26 (describing "the impediments to effective state policymaking that flow from the interconnectedness of each state's healthcare economy" and emphasizing that "statelevel reforms cannot fully address the problems associated with uncompensated care"). Far from trampling on States' sovereignty, the ACA attempts a federal solution for the very reason that the States, acting separately, cannot meet the need. Notably, the ACA serves the general welfare of the people of the United States while retaining a prominent role for the States.[e]

. . .

V

[T]he spending power conferred by the Constitution, the Court has never doubted, permits Congress to define the contours of programs financed with federal funds. And to expand coverage, Congress could have recalled the existing legislation, and replaced it with a new law making Medicaid as embracive of the poor as Congress chose.

The question posed by the 2010 Medicaid expansion, then, is essentially this: To cover a notably larger population, must Congress take the repeal/reenact route, or may it achieve the same result by amending existing law? The answer should be that Congress may expand by amendment the classes of needy persons entitled to Medicaid benefits. A ritualistic requirement that Congress

---

e. [T]he joint dissenters contend that the minimum coverage provision is not necessary and proper because it was not the "only . . . way" Congress could have made the guaranteedissue and communityrating reforms work. . . . [E]ven assuming there were "practicable" alternatives to the minimum coverage provision, "we long ago rejected the view that the Necessary and Proper Clause demands that an Act of Congress be '*absolutely* necessary' to the exercise of an enumerated power." Rather, the statutory provision at issue need only be "conducive" and "[reasonably] adapted" to the goal Congress seeks to achieve.

repeal and reenact spending legislation in order to enlarge the population served by a federally funded program would advance no constitutional principle and would scarcely serve the interests of federalism. To the contrary, such a requirement would rigidify Congress' efforts to empower States by partnering with them in the implementation of federal programs.

Medicaid is a prototypical example of federalstate cooperation in serving the Nation's general welfare. Rather than authorizing a federal agency to administer a uniform national healthcare system for the poor, Congress offered States the opportunity to tailor Medicaid grants to their particular needs, so long as they remain within bounds set by federal law. In shaping Medicaid, Congress did not endeavor to fix permanently the terms participating states must meet; instead, — Congress reserved the "right to alter, amend, or repeal" any provision of the Medicaid Act. States, for their part, agreed to amend their own Medicaid plans consistent with changes from time to time made in the federal law. And from 1965 to the present, States have regularly conformed to Congress' alterations of the Medicaid Act.

The Chief Justice['s argument] that the 2010 expansion is unduly coercive . . . rests on three premises, each of them essential to his theory. First, the Medicaid expansion is . . . a new grant program, not an addition to the Medicaid program existing before the ACA's enactment. Congress . . . has threatened States with the loss of funds from an old program in an effort to get them to adopt a new one. Second, the expansion was unforeseeable by the States when they first signed on to Medicaid. Third, the threatened loss of funding is so large that the States have no real choice but to participate in the Medicaid expansion. The Chief Justice therefore—*for the first time ever*—finds an exercise of Congress' spending power unconstitutionally coercive.

Medicaid, as amended by the ACA, however, is not two spending programs; it is a single program with a constant aim—to enable poor persons to receive basic health care when they need it. Given past expansions, plus express statutory warning that Congress may change the requirements participating States must meet, there can be no tenable claim that the ACA fails for lack of notice. Moreover, States have no entitlement to receive any Medicaid funds; they enjoy only the opportunity to accept funds on Congress' terms. Future Congresses are not bound by their predecessors' dispositions; they have authority to spend federal revenue as they see fit. The Federal Government, therefore, is not, as The Chief Justice charges, threatening States with the loss of "existing" funds from one spending program in order to induce them to opt into another program. Congress is simply requiring States to do what States have long been required to do to receive Medicaid funding: comply with the conditions Congress prescribes for participation.

A majority of the Court, however, buys the argument that prospective withholding of funds formerly available exceeds Congress' spending power. Given that holding, I entirely agree with The Chief Justice as to the appropriate remedy. It is to bar the withholding found impermissible—not, as the joint dissenters would have it, to scrap the expansion altogether. The dissenters' view that the ACA must fall in its entirety is a radical departure from the Court's normal course. When a constitutional infirmity mars a statute, the Court ordinarily removes the infirmity. It undertakes a salvage operation; it does not demolish the legislation. See, *e.g., Brockett v. Spokane Arcades, Inc.,* 472 U.S. 491 (1985) (Court's normal course is to declare a statute invalid "to the extent that it reaches too far, but otherwise [to leave the statute] intact"). That course is plainly in order where, as in this case, Congress has expressly instructed courts to leave untouched every provision not found invalid. See 42 U.S.C. §1303. Because The Chief Justice finds the withholding—not the granting—of federal funds incompatible with the Spending Clause, Congress' extension of Medicaid remains available to any State that affirms its willingness to participate.

A

[S]ince 1965, Congress has amended the Medicaid program on more than 50 occasions, sometimes quite sizably. Most relevant here, between 1988 and 1990, Congress required participating States to include among their beneficiaries pregnant women with family incomes up to 133% of the federal poverty level, children up to age 6 at the same income levels, and children ages 6 to 18 with family incomes up to 100% of the poverty level. These amendments added millions to the Medicaideligible population.

Between 1966 and 1990, annual federal Medicaid spending grew from $631.6 million to $42.6 billion; state spending rose to $31 billion over the same period. And between 1990 and 2010, federal spending increased to $269.5 billion. Enlargement of the population and services covered by Medicaid, in short, has been the trend.

Compared to past alterations, the ACA is notable for the extent to which the Federal Government will pick up the tab. Medicaid's 2010 expansion is financed largely by federal outlays. In 2014, federal funds will cover 100% of the costs for newly eligible beneficiaries; that rate will gradually decrease before settling at 90% in 2020. By comparison, federal contributions toward the care of beneficiaries eligible preACA range from 50% to 83%, and averaged 57% between 2005 and 2008.

Nor will the expansion exorbitantly increase state Medicaid spending. The Congressional Budget Office (CBO) projects that States will spend 0.8% more than they would have, absent the ACA.[f] . . .

---

f. Even the study on which the plaintiffs rely, see Brief for Petitioners 10, concludes that "[w]hile most states will experience some increase in spending, this is quite small relative to the federal matching payments and low relative to the costs of uncompensated care that [the states] would bear if the[re] were no health reform." Thus there can be no objection to the ACA's expansion of Medicaid as an "unfunded mandate." Quite the contrary, the program is impressively well funded.

[T]he alternative to conditional federal spending, it bears emphasis, is not state autonomy but state marginalization. In 1965, Congress elected to nationalize health coverage for seniors through Medicare. It could similarly have established Medicaid as an exclusively federal program. Instead, Congress gave the States the opportunity to partner in the program's administration and development. Absent from the nationalized model, of course, is the state-level policy discretion and experimentation that is Medicaid's hallmark; undoubtedly the interests of federalism are better served when States retain a meaningful role in the implementation of a program of such importance. See Caminker, State Sovereignty and Subordinacy, 95 Colum. L. Rev. 1001, 1002-1003 (1995) (cooperative federalism can preserve "a significant role for state discretion in achieving specified federal goals, where the alternative is complete federal preemption of any state regulatory role"); Rose-Ackerman, Cooperative Federalism and Co-optation, 92 Yale L.J. 1344, 1346 (1983) ("If the federal government begins to take full responsibility for social welfare spending and preempts the states, the result is likely to be weaker . . . state governments.").[g] . . .

B

[T]here are federalism-based limits on the use of Congress' conditional spending power. In the leading decision in this area, *South Dakota v. Dole,* the Court identified four criteria. The conditions placed on federal grants to States must (a) promote the "general welfare," (b) "unambiguously" inform States what is demanded of them, (c) be germane "to the federal interest in particular national projects or programs," and (d) not "induce the States to engage in activities that would themselves be unconstitutional."

The Court in *Dole* mentioned, but did not adopt, a further limitation, one hypothetically raised a half-century earlier: In "some circumstances," Congress might be prohibited from offering a "financial inducement . . . so coercive as to pass the point at which 'pressure turns into compulsion.'" (quoting *Steward Machine Co. v. Davis*). Prior to today's decision, however, the Court has never ruled that the terms of any grant crossed the indistinct line between temptation and coercion. . . . The small percentage of highway-construction funds South Dakota stood to lose by adhering to 19 as the age of eligibility to purchase 3.2% beer, however, was not enough to qualify as coercion, the Court concluded.

---

g. The Chief Justice and the joint dissenters perceive in cooperative federalism a "threa[t]" to "political accountability." By that, they mean voter confusion: Citizens upset by unpopular government action, they posit, may ascribe to state officials blame more appropriately laid at Congress' door. But no such confusion is apparent in this case: Medicaid's status as a federally funded, state-administered program is hardly hidden from view.

This case does not present the concerns that led the Court in *Dole* even to consider the prospect of coercion. In *Dole,* the condition—set 21 as the minimum drinking age—did not tell the States how to use funds Congress provided for highway construction. Further, in view of the Twenty-First Amendment, it was an open question whether Congress could directly impose a national minimum drinking age.   *Dist. Dole*

The ACA, in contrast, relates solely to the federally funded Medicaid program; if States choose not to comply, Congress has not threatened to withhold funds earmarked for any other program. Nor does the ACA use Medicaid funding to induce States to take action Congress itself could not undertake. The Federal Government undoubtedly could operate its own health-care program for poor persons, just as it operates Medicare for seniors' health care.

That is what makes this such a simple case, and the Court's decision so unsettling. Congress, aiming to assist the needy, has appropriated federal money to subsidize state health-insurance programs that meet federal standards. The principal standard the ACA sets is that the state program cover adults earning no more than 133% of the federal poverty line. Enforcing that prescription ensures that federal funds will be spent on health care for the poor in furtherance of Congress' present perception of the general welfare.

C

1

... The Chief Justice calls the ACA new, but in truth, it simply reaches more of America's poor than Congress originally covered.

Medicaid was created to enable States to provide medical assistance to — "needy persons." By bringing health care within the reach of a larger population of Americans unable to afford it, the Medicaid expansion is an extension of that basic aim.

The Medicaid Act contains hundreds of provisions governing operation of the program. . . . The Medicaid expansion leaves unchanged the vast majority of these provisions; it adds beneficiaries to the existing program and specifies the rate at which States will be reimbursed for services provided to the added beneficiaries. The ACA does not describe operational aspects of the program for these newly eligible persons; for that information, one must read the existing Medicaid Act.

Congress styled and clearly viewed the Medicaid expansion as an amendment to the Medicaid Act, not as a "new" health-care program. . . .

Endeavoring to show that Congress created a new program, The Chief Justice cites three aspects of the expansion. First, he asserts that, in covering those earning no more than 133% of the federal poverty line, the Medicaid expansion, unlike pre-ACA Medicaid, does not "care for the neediest among us." What makes that so? Single adults earning no more than $14,856 per year—133% of the current federal poverty level—surely rank among the Nation's poor.

Second, according to The Chief Justice, "Congress mandated that newly eligible persons receive a level of coverage that is less comprehensive than the traditional Medicaid benefit package." That less comprehensive benefit package, however, is not an innovation introduced by the ACA; since 2006, States have been free to use it for many of their Medicaid beneficiaries. The level of benefits offered therefore does not set apart post-ACA Medicaid recipients from all those entitled to benefits pre-ACA.

Third, The Chief Justice correctly notes that the reimbursement rate for participating States is different regarding individuals who became Medicaid-eligible through the ACA. *Ibid.* But the rate differs only in its generosity to participating States. Under pre-ACA Medicaid, the Federal Government pays up to 83% of the costs of coverage for current enrollees. Even if one agreed that a change of as little as 7 percentage points carries constitutional significance, is it not passing strange to suggest that the purported incursion on state sovereignty might have been averted, or at least mitigated, had Congress offered States *less* money to carry out the same obligations?

Consider also that Congress could have repealed Medicaid. Thereafter, Congress could have enacted Medicaid II, a new program combining the pre-2010 coverage with the expanded coverage required by the ACA. By what right does a court stop Congress from building up without first tearing down?

2

The Chief Justice finds the Medicaid expansion vulnerable because it took participating States by surprise. [He relies on] *Pennhurst*[, which] instructs that "if Congress intends to impose a condition on the grant of federal moneys, it must do so unambiguously." That requirement is met in this case. Section 2001 does not take effect until 2014. The ACA makes perfectly clear what will be required of States that accept Medicaid funding after that date: They must extend eligibility to adults with incomes no more than 133% of the federal poverty line.

The Chief Justice appears to find in *Pennhurst* a requirement that, when spending legislation is first passed, or when States first enlist in the federal program, Congress must provide clear notice of conditions it might later impose. If I understand his point correctly, it was incumbent on Congress, in 1965, to warn the States clearly of the size and shape potential changes to Medicaid might take. And absent such notice, sizable changes could not be made mandatory. Our decisions do not support such a requirement.[h]

---

h. The Chief Justice observes that "Spending Clause legislation [i]s much in the nature of a *contract.*" But the Court previously has recognized that "[u]nlike normal contractual undertakings, federal grant programs originate in and remain governed by statutory provisions expressing the judgment of Congress concerning desirable public policy." *Bennett v. Kentucky Dept. of Ed.,* 470 U.S. 656 (1985).

In *Bennett v. New Jersey,* 470 U.S. 632 (1985), . . . we rejected the Secretary [of Education]'s attempt to recover funds based on the States' alleged violation of a rule that did not exist when the State accepted and spent the funds. . . . [But] [w]hen amendment of an existing grant program has no such retroactive effect, however, we have upheld Congress' instruction. . . . *Pennhurst's* rule demands that conditions on federal funds be unambiguously clear at the time a State receives and uses the money—not at the time, perhaps years earlier, when Congress passed the law establishing the program.

In any event, from the start, the Medicaid Act put States on notice that the program could be changed: "The right to alter, amend, or repeal any − provision of [Medicaid]," the statute has read since 1965, "is hereby reserved to the Congress." The "effect of these few simple words" has long been settled. See *National Railroad Passenger Corporation v. Atchison, T. & S.F.R. Co.,* 470 U.S. 451 (1985) (citing *Sinking Fund Cases,* 99 U.S. 700, 720, 25 L. Ed. 496 (1879)). By reserving the right to "alter, amend, [or] repeal" a spending program, Congress "has given special notice of its intention to retain . . . full and complete power to make such alterations and amendments . . . as come within the just scope of legislative power." . . .

The Chief Justice insists that the most recent expansion, in contrast to its predecessors, "accomplishes a shift in kind, not merely degree." But why was Medicaid altered only in degree, not in kind, when Congress required States to cover millions of children and pregnant women? In short, given § 1304, this Court's construction of §1304's language in [previous decisions], and the enlargement of Medicaid in the years since 1965, a State would be hard put to complain that it lacked fair notice when, in 2010, Congress altered Medicaid to embrace a larger portion of the Nation's poor.

3

The Chief Justice sees no need to "fix the outermost line," *Steward Machine,* "where persuasion gives way to coercion[.]" Neither do the joint dissenters. Notably, the decision on which they rely, *Steward Machine,* found the statute at issue inside the line, "wherever the line may be."

When future Spending Clause challenges arrive, as they likely will in the − wake of today's decision, how will litigants and judges assess whether "a State has a legitimate choice whether to accept the federal conditions in exchange for federal funds"? Are courts to measure the number of dollars the Federal Government might withhold for noncompliance? The portion of the State's budget at stake? And which State's—or States'—budget is determinative: the lead plaintiff, all challenging States (26 in this case, many with quite different fiscal situations), or some national median? Does it matter that Florida, unlike most States, imposes no state income tax, and therefore might be able to replace foregone federal funds with new state revenue?[i] Or that the coercion state officials in fact fear is punishment at the ballot box for turning down a politically popular federal grant?

The coercion inquiry, therefore, appears to involve political judgments that defy judicial calculation. See *Baker v. Carr,* 369 U.S. 186 (1962). Even commentators sympathetic to robust enforcement of *Dole*'s limitations . . . have concluded that conceptions of "impermissible coercion" premised on States' perceived inability to decline federal funds "are just too amorphous to be judicially administrable."

At bottom, my colleagues' position is that the States' reliance on federal funds limits Congress' authority to alter its spending programs. This gets things backwards: Congress, not the States, is tasked with spending federal money in service of the general welfare. And each successive Congress is empowered to appropriate funds as it sees fit. When the 110th Congress reached a conclusion about Medicaid funds that differed from its predecessors' view, it abridged no State's right to "existing," or "pre-existing," funds. For, in fact, there are no such funds. There is only money States *anticipate* receiving from future Congresses.

D

[T]he Court does not strike down any provision of the ACA. It prohibits only the "application" of the Secretary's authority to withhold Medicaid funds from States that decline to conform their Medicaid plans to the ACA's requirements. Thus the ACA's authorization of funds to finance the expansion remains intact, and the Secretary's authority to withhold funds for reasons other than noncompliance with the expansion remains unaffected. . . . The Chief Justice is undoubtedly right to conclude that Congress may offer States funds "to expand the availability of health care, and requir[e] that States accepting such funds comply with the conditions on their use." I therefore concur in the judgment with respect to Part IV-B of The Chief Justice's opinion. . . .

Justice SCALIA, Justice KENNEDY, Justice THOMAS, and Justice ALITO, dissenting.

---

i. Federal taxation of a State's citizens, according to the joint dissenters, may diminish a State's ability to raise new revenue. This, in turn, could limit a State's capacity to replace a federal program with an "equivalent" state-funded analog. But it cannot be true that "the amount of the federal taxes extracted from the taxpayers of a State to pay for the program in question is relevant in determining whether there is impermissible coercion." When the United States Government taxes United States citizens, it taxes them "in their individual capacities" as "the people of America"—not as residents of a particular State. . . . A State therefore has no claim on the money its residents pay in federal taxes, and federal "spending programs need not help people in all states in the same measure." In 2004, for example, New Jersey received 55 cents in federal spending for every dollar its residents paid to the Federal Government in taxes, while Mississippi received $1.77 per tax dollar paid. Thus no constitutional problem was created when Arizona declined for 16 years to participate in Medicaid, even though its residents' tax dollars financed Medicaid programs in every other State.

[T]here are structural limits upon federal power—upon what it can prescribe with respect to private conduct, and upon what it can impose upon the sovereign States. Whatever may be the conceptual limits upon the Commerce Clause and — upon the power to tax and spend, they cannot be such as will enable the Federal Government to regulate all private conduct and to compel the States to function as administrators of federal programs.

[T]he Act before us here exceeds federal power both in mandating the purchase of health insurance and in denying nonconsenting States all Medicaid funding. These parts of the Act are central to its design and operation, and all the Act's other provisions would not have been enacted without them. In our view it must follow that the entire statute is inoperative.

I

The Individual Mandate

Article I, §8, of the Constitution gives Congress the power to "regulate Commerce . . . among the several States." The Individual Mandate in the Act commands that every "applicable individual shall for each month beginning after 2013 ensure that the individual, and any dependent of the individual who is an applicable individual, is covered under minimum essential coverage." 26 U.S.C. §5000A(a) (2006 ed., Supp. IV). If this provision "regulates" anything, it is the *failure* to maintain minimum essential coverage. One might argue that it regulates that failure by requiring it to be accompanied by payment of a penalty. But that failure—that abstention from commerce—is not "Commerce." To be sure, *purchasing* insurance *is* "Commerce"; but one does not regulate commerce that does not exist by compelling its existence.

In *Gibbons v. Ogden*, Chief Justice Marshall wrote that the power to regulate commerce is the power "to prescribe the rule by which commerce is to be governed." That understanding is consistent with the original meaning of "regulate" at the time of the Constitution's ratification, when "to regulate" meant "[t]o adjust by rule, method or established mode," 2 N. Webster, An American Dictionary of the English Language (1828); "[t]o adjust by rule or method," 2 S. Johnson, A Dictionary of the English Language (7th ed. 1785); "[t]o adjust, to direct according to rule," 2 J. Ash, New and Complete Dictionary of the English Language (1775); "to put in order, set to rights, govern or keep in order," T. Dyche & W. Pardon, A New General English Dictionary (16th ed. 1777). It can mean to direct the manner of something but not to direct that something come into being. There is no instance in which this Court or Congress (or anyone else, to our knowledge) has used "regulate" in that peculiar fashion. If the word bore that meaning, Congress' authority "[t]o make Rules for the Government and Regulation of the land and naval Forces," U.S. Const., Art. I, §8, cl. 14, would have made superfluous the later provision for authority "[t]o raise and support Armies," *id.,* §8, cl. 12, and "[t]o provide and maintain a Navy," *id.,* §8, cl. 13.

We do not doubt that the buying and selling of health insurance contracts is commerce generally subject to federal regulation. But when Congress provides that (nearly) all citizens must buy an insurance contract, it goes beyond "adjust [ing] by rule or method," or "direct[ing] according to rule," it directs the creation of commerce.

A

[T]he Government presents the Individual Mandate as a unique feature of a complicated regulatory scheme governing many parties with countervailing incentives that must be carefully balanced. [The problem of adverse selection] is not a dilemma unique to regulation of the health-insurance industry. Government regulation typically imposes costs on the regulated industry—especially regulation that prohibits economic behavior in which most market participants are already engaging, such as "piecing out" the market by selling the product to different classes of people at different prices (in the present context, providing much lower insurance rates to young and healthy buyers). And many industries so regulated face the reality that, without an artificial increase in demand, they cannot continue on. When Congress is regulating these industries directly, it enjoys the broad power to enact "'all appropriate legislation'" to "'protec[t]'" and "'advanc[e]'" commerce, *NLRB v. Jones & Laughlin Steel Corp.* Thus, Congress might protect the imperiled industry by prohibiting low-cost competition, or by according it preferential tax treatment, or even by granting it a direct subsidy.

Here, however, Congress has impressed into service third parties, healthy individuals who could be but are not customers of the relevant industry, to offset the undesirable consequences of the regulation. Congress' desire to force these individuals to purchase insurance is motivated by the fact that they are further removed from the market than unhealthy individuals with pre-existing conditions, because they are less likely to need extensive care in the near future. If Congress can reach out and command even those furthest removed from an interstate market to participate in the market, then the Commerce Clause becomes a font of unlimited power, or in Hamilton's words, "the hideous monster whose devouring jaws . . . spare neither sex nor age, nor high nor low, nor sacred nor profane." The Federalist No. 33, p. 202 (C. Rossiter ed. 1961). . . .

Raich is no precedent for what Congress has done here. That case's prohibition of growing (cf. *Wickard*), and of possession (cf. innumerable federal statutes) did not represent the expansion of the federal power to direct into a broad new field. The mandating of economic activity does, and since it is a field so limitless that it converts the Commerce Clause into a general authority to direct the economy, that mandating is not "consist[ent] with the letter and spirit of the constitution." *McCulloch v. Maryland.*

Moreover, . . . [t]he Court's opinion in *Raich* pointed out that the growing and possession prohibitions were the only practicable way of enabling the prohibition of interstate traffic in marijuana to be effectively enforced. [But]

[t]here are many ways other than this unprecedented Individual Mandate by which the regulatory scheme's goals of reducing insurance premiums and ensuring the profitability of insurers could be achieved. For instance, those who did not purchase insurance could be subjected to a surcharge when they do enter the health insurance system. Or they could be denied a full income tax credit given to those who do purchase the insurance.

The Government was invited, at oral argument, to suggest what federal controls over private conduct (other than those explicitly prohibited by the Bill of Rights or other constitutional controls) could *not* be justified as necessary and proper for the carrying out of a general regulatory scheme. It was unable to name any. As we said at the outset, whereas the precise scope of the Commerce Clause and the Necessary and Proper Clause is uncertain, the proposition that the Federal Government cannot do everything is a fundamental precept. Section 5000A is defeated by that proposition.

B

The Government [also argues that the mandate] directs the manner in which individuals purchase health care services and related goods (directing that they be purchased through insurance) and is therefore a straightforward exercise of the commerce power.

The primary problem with this argument is that §5000A does not apply only to persons who purchase all, or most, or even any, of the health care services or goods that the mandated insurance covers. Indeed, the main objection many have to the Mandate is that they have no intention of purchasing most or even any of such goods or services and thus no need to buy insurance for those purchases. The Government responds that the health-care market involves "essentially universal participation[.]" [This is] not true. It is true enough that ─ everyone consumes "health care," if the term is taken to include the purchase of a bottle of aspirin. But the health care "market" that is the object of the Individual Mandate not only includes but principally consists of goods and services that the young people primarily affected by the Mandate *do not purchase.* They are quite simply not participants in that market, and cannot be made so (and thereby subjected to regulation) by the simple device of defining participants to include all those who will, later in their lifetime, probably purchase the goods or services covered by the mandated insurance. Such a definition of market participants is unprecedented, and were it to be a premise for the exercise of national power, it would have no principled limits.

[T]he Government [argues] that Congress . . . has purported to regulate "economic and financial decision[s] to forego *[sic]* health insurance coverage and [to] attempt to self-insure," since those decisions have "a substantial and deleterious effect on interstate commerce[.]" But . . . the decision to forgo participation in an interstate market is not itself commercial activity (or indeed any activity at all) within Congress' power to regulate. It is true that, at the end of the day, it is inevitable that each American will affect commerce and become a part of it, even if not by choice. But if every person comes within the Commerce Clause power of Congress to regulate by the simple reason that he will one day engage in commerce, the idea of a limited Government power is at an end. . . .

[Both] *Wickard v. Filburn* [and] *Perez v. United States* . . . involved commercial *activity.* To go beyond that, and to say that the failure to grow wheat or the refusal to make loans affects commerce, so that growing and lending can be federally compelled, is to extend federal power to virtually everything. All of us consume food, and when we do so the Federal Government can prescribe what its quality must be and even how much we must pay. But the mere fact that we all consume food and are thus, sooner or later, participants in the "market" for food, does not empower the Government to say when and what we will buy. That is essentially what this Act seeks to do with respect to the purchase of health care. It exceeds federal power.

C

[I]t is true enough that Congress needs only a "'rational basis' for concluding that the *regulated activity* substantially affects interstate commerce[.]" But it must be *activity* affecting commerce that is regulated, and not merely the failure to engage in commerce. And one is not now purchasing the health care covered by the insurance mandate simply because one is likely to be purchasing it in the future. Our test's premise of regulated activity is not invented out of whole cloth, but rests upon the Constitution's requirement that it be commerce which is regulated. If all inactivity affecting commerce is commerce, commerce is everything. Ultimately [Justice Ginsburg's] dissent is driven to saying that there is really no difference between action and inaction, a proposition that has never recommended itself, neither to the law nor to common sense. To say, for example, that the inaction here consists of activity in "the self-insurance market[]" seems to us wordplay. By parity of reasoning the failure to buy a car can be called participation in the non-private-car-transportation market. Commerce becomes everything.

[T]he individual mandate threatens our constitutional order . . . because it gives such an expansive meaning to the Commerce Clause that *all* private conduct (including failure to act) becomes subject to federal control, effectively destroying the Constitution's division of governmental powers. Thus the dissent, on the theories proposed for the validity of the Mandate, would alter the accepted constitutional relation between the individual and the National Government. The dissent protests that the Necessary and Proper Clause has been held to include "the power to enact criminal laws, . . . the power to imprison, . . . and the power to create a national bank[.]" Is not the power to compel purchase of health insurance much lesser? No, not if (unlike those other dispositions) its application rests upon a theory that everything is within federal control simply because it exists.

The dissent's exposition of the wonderful things the Federal Government has achieved through exercise of its assigned powers, such as "the provision of old-age and survivors' benefits" in the Social Security Act, is quite beside the point. The issue here is whether the federal government can impose the Individual Mandate through the Commerce Clause. And the relevant history is not that Congress has achieved wide and wonderful results through the proper exercise of its assigned powers in the past, but that it has never before used the Commerce Clause to compel entry into commerce. The dissent treats the Constitution as though it is an enumeration of those problems that the Federal Government can address—among which, it finds, is "the Nation's course in the economic and social welfare realm," and more specifically "the problem of the uninsured." The Constitution is not that. It enumerates not federally soluble — *problems,* but federally available *powers.* The Federal Government can address whatever problems it wants but can bring to their solution only those powers that the Constitution confers, among which is the power to regulate commerce. None of our cases say anything else. Article I contains no whatever-it-takes-to-solve-a-national-problem power.

The dissent dismisses the conclusion that the power to compel entry into the healthinsurance market would include the power to compel entry into the new-car or broccoli markets. The latter purchasers, it says, "will be obliged to pay at the counter before receiving the vehicle or nourishment," whereas those refusing to purchase healthinsurance will ultimately get treated anyway, at others' expense. "[T]he unique attributes of the health-care market . . . give rise to a significant free-riding problem that does not occur in other markets." And "a vegetable-purchase mandate" (or a carpurchase mandate) is not "likely to have a substantial effect on the health-care costs" borne by other Americans. Those differences make a very good argument by the dissent's own lights, since they show that the failure to purchase health insurance, unlike the failure to purchase cars or broccoli, creates a national, social-welfare problem that is (in the dissent's view) included among the unenumerated "problems" that the Constitution authorizes the Federal Government to solve. But those differences do not show that the failure to enter the health-insurance market, unlike the failure to buy cars and broccoli, is an *activity* that Congress can "regulate." (Of course one day the failure of some of the public to purchase American cars may endanger the existence of domestic automobile manufacturers; or the failure of some to eat broccoli may be found to deprive them of a newly discovered cancerfighting chemical which only that food contains, producing health-care costs that are a burden on the rest of us—in which case, under the theory of Justice Ginsburg's dissent, moving against those inactivities will also come within the Federal Government's unenumerated problem-solving powers.)

II

The Taxing Power

[T]he Government contends, however, as expressed in the caption to Part II of its brief, that "THE MINIMUM COVERAGE PROVISION IS INDEPEN-

DENTLY AUTHORIZED BY CONGRESS'S TAXING POWER." [This] suggests the existence of a creature never hitherto seen in the United States Reports: A penalty for constitutional purposes that is *also* a tax for constitutional purposes. In all our cases the two are mutually exclusive. The provision challenged under the Constitution is either a penalty or else a tax. Of course in many cases what was a regulatory mandate enforced by a penalty *could have been* imposed as a tax upon permissible action; or what was imposed as a tax upon permissible action *could have been* a regulatory mandate enforced by a penalty. But we know of no case, and the Government cites none, in which the imposition was, for constitutional purposes, both. The issue is not whether Congress had the *power* to frame the minimum-coverage provision as a tax, but whether it *did* so.[a]

In answering that question we must, if "fairly possible," construe the provision to be a tax rather than a mandate-with-penalty, since that would render it constitutional rather than unconstitutional (*ut res magis valeat quam pereat*). But we cannot rewrite the statute to be what it is not. [T]here is simply no way, "without doing violence to the fair meaning of the words used," to escape what Congress enacted: a mandate that individuals maintain minimum essential coverage, enforced by a penalty.

Our cases establish a clear line between a tax and a penalty: "'[A] tax is an enforced contribution to provide for the support of government; a penalty . . . is an exaction imposed by statute as punishment for an unlawful act.'" In a few cases, this Court has held that a "tax" imposed upon private conduct was so onerous as to be in effect a penalty. But we have never held—*never*—that a penalty imposed for violation of the law was so trivial as to be in effect a tax. We have never held that *any* exaction imposed for violation of the law is an exercise of Congress' taxing power—even when the statute *calls* it a tax, much less when (as here) the statute repeatedly calls it a penalty. When an act "adopt[s] the criteria of wrongdoing" and then imposes a monetary penalty as the "principal consequence on those who transgress its standard," it creates a regulatory penalty, not a tax. *Child Labor Tax Case* [Bailey v. Drexel Furniture Co.], 259 U.S. 20 (1922).

So the question is, quite simply, whether the exaction here is imposed for violation of the law. It unquestionably is. The minimum-coverage provision is found in 26 U.S.C. §5000A, entitled "*Requirement* to maintain minimum essential coverage." (Emphasis added.) It commands that every "applicable individual *shall* . . . ensure that the individual . . . is covered under minimum essential coverage." *Ibid.* (emphasis added). And the immediately following provision states that, "[i]f . . . an applicable individual . . . fails to meet the *requirement* of subsection (a) . . . there is hereby imposed . . . a *penalty*." § 5000A(b) (emphasis added). And several of Congress' legislative "findings"

---

a. No one seriously contends that any of Congress' other enumerated powers gives it the authority to enact § 5000A *as a regulation*. [relocated footnote] with regard to §5000A confirm that it sets forth a legal requirement and constitutes the assertion of regulatory power, not mere taxing power. See 42 U.S.C. §18091(2)(A) ("The requirement regulates activity . . . "); §18091(2)(C) ("The requirement . . . will add millions of new consumers to the health insurance market . . . "); §18091(2)(D) ("The requirement achieves near-universal coverage"); §18091(2)(H) ("The requirement is an essential part of this larger regulation of economic activity, and the absence of the requirement would undercut Federal regulation of the health insurance market"); §18091(3) ("[T]he Supreme Court of the United States ruled that insurance is interstate commerce subject to Federal regulation"). . . .

Quite separately, the fact that Congress (in its own words) "imposed . . . a penalty," 26 U.S.C. §5000A(b)(1), for failure to buy insurance is alone sufficient to render that failure unlawful. It is one of the canons of interpretation that a statute that penalizes an act makes it unlawful. . . .

We never have classified as a tax an exaction imposed for violation of the law, and so too, we never have classified as a tax an exaction described in the legislation itself as a penalty. To be sure, we have sometimes treated as a tax a statutory exaction (imposed for something other than a violation of law) which bore an agnostic label that does not entail the significant constitutional consequences of a penalty—such as "license" or "surcharge[.]" But we have never—*never*—treated as a tax an exaction which faces up to the critical difference between a tax and a penalty, and explicitly denominates the exaction a "penalty." Eighteen times in §5000A itself and elsewhere throughout the Act, Congress called the exaction in §5000A(b) a "penalty."

That §5000A imposes not a simple tax but a mandate to which a penalty is attached is demonstrated by the fact that some are exempt from the tax who are not exempt from the mandate—a distinction that would make no sense if the mandate were not a mandate. Section 5000A(d) exempts three classes of people from the definition of "applicable individual" subject to the minimum coverage requirement: Those with religious objections or who participate in a "health care sharing ministry," those who are "not lawfully present" in the United States, and those who are incarcerated. Section 5000A(e) then creates a separate set of exemptions, excusing from liability for the penalty certain individuals who are subject to the minimum coverage requirement: Those who cannot afford coverage, who earn too little income to require filing a tax return, who are members of an Indian tribe, who experience only short gaps in coverage, and who, in the judgment of the Secretary of Health and Human Services, "have suffered a hardship with respect to the capability to obtain coverage[.]" If §5000A were a tax, these two classes of exemption would make no sense; there being no requirement, *all* the exemptions would attach to the penalty (renamed tax) alone.

In the face of all these indications of a regulatory requirement accompanied by a penalty, the Solicitor General assures us that "neither the Treasury Department nor the Department of Health and Human Services interprets Section 5000A as imposing a legal obligation," and that "[i]f [those subject to the

Act] pay the tax penalty, they're in compliance with the law[.]" These self-serving litigating positions are entitled to no weight. What counts is what the statute says, and that is entirely clear. . . .

Against the mountain of evidence that the minimum coverage requirement is what the statute calls it—a requirement—and that the penalty for its violation is what the statute calls it—a penalty—the Government brings forward the flimsiest of indications to the contrary. It notes that "[t]he minimum coverage provision amends the Internal Revenue Code to provide that a non-exempted individual . . . will owe a monetary penalty, in addition to the income tax itself," and that "[t]he [Internal Revenue Service (IRS)] will assess and collect the penalty in the same manner as assessable penalties under the Internal Revenue Code." The manner of collection could perhaps suggest a tax if IRS penalty-collection were unheard-of or rare. It is not. In *Reorganized CF & I Fabricators of Utah, Inc.,* 518 U.S. 213, we held that an exaction not only *enforced* by the Commissioner of Internal Revenue but even *called* a "tax" was in fact a penalty. "[I]f the concept of penalty means anything," we said, "it means punishment for an unlawful act or omission." Moreover, while the penalty is assessed and collected by the IRS, §5000A is administered both by that agency and by the Department of Health and Human Services (and also the Secretary of Veteran Affairs), which is responsible for defining its substantive scope—a feature that would be quite extraordinary for taxes.

The Government points out that "[t]he amount of the penalty will be calculated as a percentage of household income for federal income tax purposes, subject to a floor and [a] ca[p]," and that individuals who earn so little money that they "are not required to file income tax returns for the taxable year are not subject to the penalty" (though they are, as we discussed earlier, subject to the mandate). But varying a penalty according to ability to pay is an utterly familiar practice.

The last of the feeble arguments in favor of petitioners that we will address is the contention that what this statute repeatedly calls a penalty is in fact a tax because it contains no scienter requirement. The *presence* of such a requirement suggests a penalty—though one can imagine a tax imposed only on willful action; but the *absence* of such a requirement does not suggest a tax. Penalties for absolute-liability offenses are commonplace. And where a statute is silent as to scienter, we traditionally presume a *mens rea* requirement if the statute imposes a "severe penalty." Since we have an entire jurisprudence addressing when it is that a scienter requirement should be inferred from a penalty, it is quite illogical to suggest that a penalty is not a penalty for want of an express scienter requirement.

And the nail in the coffin is that the mandate and penalty are located in Title I of the Act, its operative core, rather than where a tax would be found—in Title IX, containing the Act's "Revenue Provisions." In sum, "the terms of [the] act rende[r] it unavoidable[]" that Congress imposed a regulatory penalty, not a tax.

For all these reasons, to say that the Individual Mandate merely imposes a tax is not to interpret the statute but to rewrite it. Judicial tax-writing is particularly troubling. Taxes have never been popular, see, *e.g.,* Stamp Act of 1765, and in part for that reason, the Constitution requires tax increases to originate in the House of Representatives. See Art. I, §7, cl. 1. That is to say, they must originate in the legislative body most accountable to the people, where legislators must weigh the need for the tax against the terrible price they might pay at their next election, which is never more than two years off. The Federalist No. 58 "defend [ed] the decision to give the origination power to the House on the ground that the Chamber that is more accountable to the people should have the primary role in raising revenue." We have no doubt that Congress knew precisely what it was doing when it rejected [the House] version of this legislation that imposed a tax instead of a requirement-with-penalty. Imposing a tax through judicial legislation inverts the constitutional scheme, and places the power to tax in the branch of government least accountable to the citizenry.

Finally, we must observe that rewriting §5000A as a tax in order to sustain its constitutionality would force us to confront a difficult constitutional question: whether this is a direct tax that must be apportioned among the States according to their population. Art. I, §9, cl. 4. Perhaps it is not (we have no need to address — the point); but the meaning of the Direct Tax Clause is famously unclear, and its application here is a question of first impression that deserves more thoughtful consideration than the lick-and-a-promise accorded by the Government and its supporters. . . . One would expect this Court to demand more than fly-by-night briefing and argument before deciding a difficult constitutional question of first impression.

. . .

IV

The Medicaid Expansion

[I]n light of the ACA's goal of near-universal coverage, petitioners argue, if Congress had thought that anything less than 100% state participation was a realistic possibility, Congress would have provided a backup scheme. But no such scheme is to be found anywhere in the more than 900 pages of the Act. This shows, they maintain, that Congress was certain that the ACA's Medicaid offer was one that no State could refuse. [T]he Government contends that any congressional assumption about uniform state participation was based on the simple fact that the offer of federal funds associated with the expanded coverage is such a generous gift that no State would want to turn it down. . . .

C

This practice of attaching conditions to federal funds greatly increases federal power. "[O]bjectives not thought to be within Article I's enumerated legislative fields, may nevertheless be attained through the use of the spending power and the conditional grant of federal funds." *Dole.*

This formidable power, if not checked in any way, would present a grave threat to the system of federalism created by our Constitution. . . . When federal legislation gives the States a real choice whether to accept or decline a federal aid package, the federal-state relationship is in the nature of a contractual relationship. And just as a contract is voidable if coerced, "[t]he legitimacy of Congress' power to legislate under the spending power . . . rests on whether the State *voluntarily* and knowingly accepts the terms of the 'contract.'" If a federal spending program coerces participation the States have not "exercise[d] their choice"—let alone made an "informed choice."

Fed.

Coercing States to accept conditions risks the destruction of the "unique role of the States in our system." "[T]he Constitution has never been understood to confer upon Congress the ability to require the States to govern according to Congress' instructions." *New York.* Congress may not "simply commandeer the legislative processes of the States by directly compelling them to enact and enforce a federal regulatory program." Congress effectively engages in this impermissible compulsion when state participation in a federal spending program is coerced, so that the States' choice whether to enact or administer a federal regulatory program is rendered illusory.

Where all Congress has done is to "encourag[e] state regulation rather than compe[l] it, state governments remain responsive to the local electorate's preferences; state officials remain accountable to the people. [But] where the Federal Government compels States to regulate, the accountability of both state and federal officials is diminished." *New York.*

Amici who support the Government argue that forcing state employees to implement a federal program is more respectful of federalism than using federal workers to implement that program. They note that Congress, instead of expanding Medicaid, could have established an entirely federal program to provide coverage for the same group of people. By choosing to structure Medicaid as a cooperative federal-state program, they contend, Congress allows for more state control.

This argument reflects a view of federalism that our cases have rejected—and with good reason. When Congress compels the States to do its bidding, it blurs the lines of political accountability. If the Federal Government makes a controversial decision while acting on its own, "it is the Federal Government that makes the decision in full view of the public, and it will be federal officials that suffer the consequences if the decision turns out to be detrimental or unpopular." *New York.* But when the Federal Government compels the States to take unpopular actions, "it may be state officials who will bear the brunt of public disapproval, while the federal officials who devised the regulatory program may remain insulated from the electoral ramifications of their decision." For this reason, federal officeholders may view this "departur[e] from the federal structure to be in their personal interests . . . as a means of shifting responsibility for the eventual decision." *New York.* And even state officials may favor such a "departure from the constitutional plan," since uncertainty concerning responsibility may also permit them to escape accountability. If a program is popular, state officials may claim credit; if it is unpopular, they may protest that they were merely responding to a federal directive.

. . . .

D

[I]f States really have no choice other than to accept the package, the offer is coercive, and the conditions cannot be sustained under the spending power. And as our decision in *South Dakota* v. *Dole* makes clear, theoretical voluntariness is not enough. . . .

The Federal Government suggests that it is sufficient if States are "free, *as a matter of law,* to turn down" federal funds. According to the Federal Government, neither the amount of the offered federal funds nor the amount of the federal taxes extracted from the taxpayers of a State to pay for the program in question is relevant in determining whether there is impermissible coercion.

This argument ignores reality. When a heavy federal tax is levied to support a federal program that offers large grants to the States, States may, as a practical matter, be unable to refuse to participate in the federal program and to substitute a state alternative. Even if a State believes that the federal program is ineffective and inefficient, withdrawal would likely force the State to impose a huge tax increase on its residents, and this new state tax would come on top of the federal taxes already paid by residents to support subsidies to participating States.[b]

Acceptance of the Federal Government's interpretation of the anticoercion rule would permit Congress to dictate policy in areas traditionally governed primarily at the state or local level. Suppose, for example, that Congress enacted legislation offering each State a grant equal to the State's entire annual expenditures for primary and secondary education. Suppose also that this funding came with conditions governing such things as school curriculum, the hiring and tenure of teachers, the drawing of school districts, the length and hours of the school day, the school calendar, a dress code for students, and rules for student discipline. *As a matter of law,* a State could turn down that offer, but if it did so, its residents would not only be required to pay the federal taxes needed to support this expensive new program, but they would also be forced to pay an equivalent amount in state taxes. And if the State gave in to the federal law, the State and its subdivisions would surrender their traditional authority in the field of education. Asked at oral argument whether such a law would be allowed under the spending power, the Solicitor General responded that it would.

b. Justice Ginsburg argues that "[a] State . . . has no claim on the money its residents pay in federal taxes." This is true as a formal matter. "When the United States Government taxes United States citizens, it taxes them 'in their individual capacities' as 'the people of America'—not as residents of a particular State." But unless Justice Ginsburg thinks that there is no limit to the amount of money that can be squeezed out of taxpayers, heavy federal taxation diminishes the practical ability of States to collect their own taxes.

E

Whether federal spending legislation crosses the line from enticement to coercion is often difficult to determine, and courts should not conclude that legislation is unconstitutional on this ground unless the coercive nature of an offer is unmistakably clear. In this case, however, there can be no doubt. In structuring the ACA, Congress unambiguously signaled its belief that every — State would have no real choice but to go along with the Medicaid Expansion. If the anticoercion rule does not apply in this case, then there is no such rule.

1

[M]edicaid has long been the largest federal program of grants to the States. In 2010, the Federal Government directed more than $552 billion in federal funds to the States. *This amount equals nearly 22% of all state expenditures combined.*

The Court of Appeals concluded that the States failed to establish coercion in this case in part because the "states have the power to tax and raise revenue, and therefore can create and fund programs of their own if they do not like Congress's terms." But the sheer size of this federal spending program in relation to state expenditures means that a State would be very hard pressed to compensate for the loss of federal funds by cutting other spending or raising additional revenue. Arizona, for example, commits 12% of its state expenditures to Medicaid, and relies on the Federal Government to provide the rest: $5.6 billion, equaling roughly one-third of Arizona's annual state expenditures of $17 billion. Therefore, if Arizona lost federal Medicaid funding, the State would have to commit an additional 33% of all its state expenditures to fund an equivalent state program along the lines of pre-expansion Medicaid. This means that the State would have to allocate 45% of its annual expenditures for that one purpose.

The States are far less reliant on federal funding for any other program. After Medicaid, the next biggest federal funding item is aid to support elementary and secondary education, which amounts to 12.8% of total federal outlays to the States, and equals only 6.6% of all state expenditures combined.

A State forced out of the Medicaid program would face burdens in addition to the loss of federal Medicaid funding. For example, a nonparticipating State might be found to be ineligible for other major federal funding sources, such as Temporary Assistance for Needy Families (TANF), which is premised on the expectation that States will participate in Medicaid. And withdrawal or expulsion from the Medicaid program would not relieve a State's hospitals of their obligation under federal law to provide care for patients who are unable to pay for medical services. The Emergency Medical Treatment and Active Labor Act requires hospitals that receive any federal funding to provide stabilization care for indigent patients but does not offer federal funding to assist facilities in carrying out its mandate. Many of these patients are now covered by Medicaid.

If providers could not look to the Medicaid program to pay for this care, they would find it exceedingly difficult to comply with federal law unless they were given substantial state support.

For these reasons, the offer that the ACA makes to the States—go along with a dramatic expansion of Medicaid or potentially lose all federal Medicaid funding—is quite unlike anything that we have seen in a prior spending-power case. In *South Dakota v. Dole,* the total amount that the States would have lost if every single State had refused to comply with the 21-year-old drinking age was approximately $614.7 million—or about 0.19% of all state expenditures combined. South Dakota stood to lose, at most, funding that amounted to less than 1% of its annual state expenditures. Under the ACA, by contrast, the Federal Government has threatened to withhold 42.3% of all federal outlays to the states, or approximately $233 billion. South Dakota stands to lose federal funding equaling 28.9% of its annual state expenditures. Withholding $614.7 million, equaling only 0.19% of all state expenditures combined, is aptly characterized as "relatively mild encouragement," but threatening to withhold $233 billion, equaling 21.86% of all state expenditures combined, is a different matter.

2

[I]n crafting the ACA, Congress clearly expressed its informed view that no State could possibly refuse the offer that the ACA extends.

The stated goal of the ACA is near-universal health care coverage. . . . [F]or lowincome individuals who are simply not able to obtain insurance, Congress expanded Medicaid, transforming it from a program covering only members of a limited list of vulnerable groups into a program that provides at least the requisite minimum level of coverage for the poor. This design was intended to provide at least a specified minimum level of coverage for all Americans, but the achievement of that goal obviously depends on participation by every single State. If any State—not to mention all of the 26 States that brought this suit—chose to decline the federal offer, there would be a gaping hole in the ACA's coverage.

It is true that some persons who are eligible for Medicaid coverage under the ACA may be able to secure private insurance, either through their employers or by obtaining subsidized insurance through an exchange. But the new federal subsidies are not available to those whose income is below the federal poverty level, and the ACA provides no means, other than Medicaid, for these individuals to obtain coverage and comply with the Mandate. The Government counters that these people will not have to pay the penalty, but that argument misses the point: Without Medicaid, these individuals will not have coverage – and the ACA's goal of near-universal coverage will be severely frustrated.

If Congress had thought that States might actually refuse to go along with the expansion of Medicaid, Congress would surely have devised a backup scheme so that the most vulnerable groups in our society, those previously eligible for

Medicaid, would not be left out in the cold. But nowhere in the over 900-page Act is such a scheme to be found. By contrast, because Congress thought that some States might decline federal funding for the operation of a "health benefit exchange," Congress provided a backup scheme; if a State declines to participate in the operation of an exchange, the Federal Government will step in and operate an exchange in that State. Likewise, knowing that States would not necessarily provide affordable health insurance for aliens lawfully present in the United States—because Medicaid does not require States to provide such coverage—Congress extended the availability of the new federal insurance subsidies to all aliens. Congress did not make these subsidies available for citizens with incomes below the poverty level because Congress obviously assumed that they would be covered by Medicaid. . . .

The Federal Government does not dispute the inference that Congress anticipated 100% state participation, but it argues that this assumption was based on the fact that ACA's offer was an "exceedingly generous" gift. . . . [But] [i]f that offer is "exceedingly generous," as the Federal Government maintains, why have more than half the States brought this lawsuit, contending that the offer is coercive? And why did Congress find it necessary to threaten that any State refusing to accept this "exceedingly generous" gift would risk losing all Medicaid funds? Congress could have made just the *new* funding provided under the ACA contingent on acceptance of the terms of the Medicaid Expansion. Congress took such an approach in some earlier amendments to Medicaid, separating new coverage requirements and funding from the rest of the program so that only new funding was conditioned on new eligibility extensions. See, *e.g.,* Social Security Amendments of 1972, 86 Stat. 1465.

Congress' decision to do otherwise here reflects its understanding that the ACA offer is not an "exceedingly generous" gift that no State in its right mind would decline. Instead, acceptance of the offer will impose very substantial costs on participating States. It is true that the Federal Government will bear most of the initial costs associated with the Medicaid Expansion, first paying 100% of the costs of covering newly eligible individuals between 2014 and 2016. But that is just part of the picture. Participating States will be forced to shoulder substantial costs as well, because after 2019 the Federal Government will cover only 90% of the costs associated with the Expansion, with state spending projected to increase by at least $20 billion by 2020 as a consequence. After 2019, state spending is expected to increase at a faster rate; the CBO estimates new state spending at $60 billion through 2021. And these costs may increase in the future because of the very real possibility that the Federal Government will change funding terms and reduce the percentage of funds it will cover. This would leave the States to bear an increasingly large percentage of the bill. Finally, after 2015, the States will have to pick up the tab for 50% of all administrative costs associated with implementing the new program, costs that could approach $12 billion between fiscal years 2014 and 2020.

In sum, it is perfectly clear from the goal and structure of the ACA that the offer of the Medicaid Expansion was one that Congress understood no State could refuse. The Medicaid Expansion therefore exceeds Congress' spending power and cannot be implemented.

F

Seven Members of the Court agree that the Medicaid Expansion, as enacted by Congress, is unconstitutional. Because the Medicaid Expansion is unconstitutional, the question of remedy arises. The most natural remedy would be to invalidate the Medicaid Expansion. However, the Government proposes—in two cursory sentences at the very end of its brief—preserving the Expansion. Under its proposal, States would receive the additional Medicaid funds if they expand eligibility, but States would keep their preexisting Medicaid funds if they do not expand eligibility. We cannot accept the Government's suggestion. [T]he ACA depends on States' having no choice, because its Mandate requires low-income individuals to obtain insurance many of them can afford only through the Medicaid Expansion. Furthermore, a State's withdrawal might subject everyone in the State to much higher insurance premiums. That is because the Medicaid Expansion will no longer offset the cost to the insurance industry imposed by the ACA's insurance regulations and taxes. . . . To make the Medicaid Expansion optional despite the ACA's structure and design "'would be to make a new law, not to enforce an old one. This is no part of our duty.'"

Worse, the Government's proposed remedy introduces a new dynamic: States must choose between expanding Medicaid or paying huge tax sums to the federal fisc for the sole benefit of expanding Medicaid in other States. If this divisive dynamic between and among States can be introduced at all, it should be by conscious congressional choice, not by Court-invented interpretation. We do not doubt that States are capable of making decisions when put in a tight spot. We do doubt the authority of this Court to put them there.

The Government cites a severability clause codified with Medicaid . . . [b]ut that clause tells us only that other provisions in Chapter 7 should not be invalidated if §1396c, the authorization for the cut-off of all Medicaid funds, is unconstitutional. It does not tell us that §1396c can be judicially revised, to say what it does not say. . . . The Court today opts for permitting the cut-off of only incremental Medicaid funding, but it might just as well have permitted, say, the cut-off of funds that represent no more than x percent of the State's budget. The Court severs nothing, but simply revises §1396c to read as the Court would desire.

We should not accept the Government's invitation to attempt to solve a constitutional problem by rewriting the Medicaid Expansion so as to allow States that reject it to retain their pre-existing Medicaid funds. Worse, the Government's remedy, now adopted by the Court, takes the ACA and this Nation in a new direction and charts a course for federalism that the Court, not the Congress, has chosen; but under the Constitution, that power and authority do not rest with this Court.

V

Severability

[T]he two pillars of the [Affordable Care] Act are the Individual Mandate and the expansion of coverage under Medicaid. In our view, both these central provisions of the Act . . . are invalid. It follows . . . that all other provisions of the Act must fall as well.

— [A]n automatic or too cursory severance of statutory provisions risks "rewrit[ing] a statute and giv[ing] it an effect altogether different from that sought by the measure viewed as a whole." The Judiciary, if it orders uncritical severance, then assumes the legislative function; for it imposes on the Nation, by the Court's decree, its own new statutory regime, consisting of policies, risks, and duties that Congress did not enact. That can be a more extreme exercise of the judicial power than striking the whole statute and allowing Congress to address the conditions that pertained when the statute was considered at the outset.

The Court has applied a two-part guide as the framework for severability analysis. The test has been deemed "well established." First, if the Court holds a statutory provision unconstitutional, it then determines whether the now truncated statute will operate in the manner Congress intended. If not, the remaining provisions must be invalidated. . . . Second, even if the remaining provisions can operate as Congress designed them to operate, the Court must determine if Congress would have enacted them standing alone and without the unconstitutional portion. If Congress would not, those provisions, too, must be invalidated. . . .

— Major provisions of the Affordable Care Act—*i.e.,* the insurance regulations and taxes, the reductions in federal reimbursements to hospitals and other Medicare spending reductions, the exchanges and their federal subsidies, and the employer responsibility assessment—cannot remain once the Individual Mandate and Medicaid Expansion are invalid. That result follows from the undoubted inability of the other major provisions to operate as Congress intended without the Individual Mandate and Medicaid Expansion. . . . Without the Individual Mandate and Medicaid Expansion, the Affordable Care Act's insurance regulations and insurance taxes impose risks on insurance companies and their customers that this Court cannot measure. Those risks would undermine Congress' scheme of "shared responsibility." . . . Higher costs may mean higher premiums for consumers, despite the Act's goal of "lower[ing] health insurance premiums." Higher costs also could threaten the survival of health-insurance companies, despite the Act's goal of "effective health insurance markets."

The actual cost of the regulations and taxes may be more or less than predicted. What is known, however, is that severing other provisions from the Individual Mandate and Medicaid Expansion necessarily would impose significant risks and real uncertainties on insurance companies, their customers, all other major actors in the system, and the government treasury. And what also is known is this: Unnecessary risks and avoidable uncertainties are hostile to economic progress and fiscal stability and thus to the safety and welfare of the Nation and the Nation's freedom. If those risks and uncertainties are to be imposed, it must not be by the Judiciary.

[T]he Affordable Care Act reduces payments by the Federal Government to hospitals by more than $200 billion over 10 years [because] [n]ear-universal coverage will reduce uncompensated care, which will increase hospitals' revenues, which will offset the government's reductions in Medicare and Medicaid reimbursements to hospitals. Responsibility will be shared, as burdens and benefits balance each other. This is typical of the whole dynamic of the Act.

Invalidating the key mechanisms for expanding insurance coverage, such as community rating and the Medicaid Expansion, without invalidating the reductions in Medicare and Medicaid, distorts the ACA's design of "shared responsibility." Some hospitals may be forced to raise the cost of care in order to offset the reductions in reimbursements, which could raise the cost of insurance premiums, in contravention of the Act's goal of "lower[ing] health insurance premiums." Other hospitals, particularly safety-net hospitals that serve a large number of uninsured patients, may be forced to shut down. Like the effect of preserving the insurance regulations and taxes, the precise degree of risk to hospitals is unknowable. It is not the proper role of the Court, by severing part of a statute and allowing the rest to stand, to impose unknowable risks that Congress could neither measure nor predict. And Congress could not have intended that result in any event.

[Second,] Congress chose to offset new federal expenditures with budget cuts — and tax increases. . . . If the Medicare and Medicaid reductions would no longer be needed to offset the costs of the Medicaid Expansion, the reductions would no longer operate in the manner Congress intended. They would lose their justification and foundation. In addition, to preserve them would be "to eliminate a significant *quid pro quo* of the legislative compromise" and create a statute Congress did not enact. It is no secret that cutting Medicare is unpopular; and it is most improbable Congress would have done so without at least the assurance that it would render the ACA deficit-neutral. . . .

The ACA requires each State to establish a health-insurance "exchange." Each exchange is a one-stop marketplace for individuals and small businesses to compare community-rated health insurance and purchase the policy of their choice. The exchanges cannot operate in the manner Congress intended if the Individual Mandate, Medicaid Expansion, and insurance regulations cannot remain in force.

The Act's design is to allocate billions of federal dollars to subsidize individuals' purchases on the exchanges. . . . Without the community-rating insurance regulation, however, the average federal subsidy could be much higher; for community rating greatly lowers the enormous premiums unhealthy individuals would otherwise pay. Federal subsidies would make up much of the difference.

The result would be an unintended boon to insurance companies, an unintended harm to the federal fisc, and a corresponding breakdown of the "shared responsibility" between the industry and the federal budget that Congress intended. Thus, the federal subsidies must be invalidated.

In the absence of federal subsidies to purchasers, insurance companies will have little incentive to sell insurance on the exchanges. . . . Without the federal subsidies, individuals would lose the main incentive to purchase insurance inside the exchanges, and some insurers may be unwilling to offer insurance inside of exchanges. With fewer buyers and even fewer sellers, the exchanges would not operate as Congress intended and may not operate at all.

[In addition,] Congress designed the exchanges so the shopper can compare benefits and prices. But the comparison cannot be made in the way Congress designed if the prices depend on the shopper's pre-existing health conditions. The prices would vary from person to person. So without community rating— which prohibits insurers from basing the price of insurance on pre-existing conditions—the exchanges cannot operate in the manner Congress intended.

[T]he employer responsibility assessment provides an incentive for employers with at least 50 employees to provide their employees with health insurance options that meet minimum criteria. Unlike the Individual Mandate, the employer-responsibility assessment does not require employers to provide an insurance option. Instead, it requires them to make a payment to the Federal Government if they do not offer insurance to employees and if insurance is bought on an exchange by an employee who qualifies for the exchange's federal subsidies.

For two reasons, the employer-responsibility assessment must be invalidated. First, the ACA makes a direct link between the employer-responsibility assessment and the exchanges. The financial assessment against employers occurs only under certain conditions. One of them is the purchase of insurance by an employee on an exchange. With no exchanges, there are no purchases on the exchanges; and with no purchases on the exchanges, there is nothing to trigger the employer-responsibility assessment.

Second, after the invalidation of burdens on individuals (the Individual Mandate), insurers (the insurance regulations and taxes), States (the Medicaid Expansion), the Federal Government (the federal subsidies for exchanges and for the Medicaid Expansion), and hospitals (the reductions in reimbursements), the preservation of the employer-responsibility assessment would upset the ACA's design of "shared responsibility." It would leave employers as the only parties bearing any significant responsibility. That was not the congressional intent.

[T]he ACA is over 900 pages long. Its regulations include requirements ranging from a break time and secluded place at work for nursing mothers, to displays of nutritional content at chain restaurants. The Act raises billions of dollars in taxes and fees, including exactions imposed on high-income taxpayers, and tanning booths. It spends government money on, among other things, the study of how to spend less government money. And it includes a number of provisions that provide benefits to the State of a particular legislator. For example, §10323 . . . extends Medicare coverage to individuals exposed to asbestos from a mine in Libby, Montana. Another provision, §2006, increases Medicaid payments only in Louisiana.

Such provisions validate the Senate Majority Leader's statement, "'I don't know if there is a senator that doesn't have something in this bill that was important to them. . . . [And] if they don't have something in it important to them, then it doesn't speak well of them. That's what this legislation is all about: It's the art of compromise.'" Often, a minor provision will be the price paid for support of a major provision. So, if the major provision were unconstitutional, Congress would not have passed the minor one.

Without the ACA's major provisions, many of these minor provisions will not operate in the manner Congress intended. . . . Some provisions, such as requiring chain restaurants to display nutritional content, appear likely to operate as Congress intended, but they fail the second test for severability. There is no reason to believe that Congress would have enacted them independently. The Court has not previously had occasion to consider severability in the context of an omnibus enactment like the ACA, which includes not only many provisions that are ancillary to its central provisions but also many that are entirely unrelated— hitched on because it was a quick way to get them passed despite opposition, or because their proponents could exact their enactment as the *quid pro quo* for their needed support. When we are confronted with such a socalled "Christmas tree," a law to which many nongermane ornaments have been attached, we think the proper rule must be that when the tree no longer exists the ornaments are superfluous. We have no reliable basis for knowing which pieces of the Act would have passed on their own. It is certain that many of them would not have, and it is not a proper function of this Court to guess which. . . .

This Court must not impose risks unintended by Congress or produce legislation Congress may have lacked the support to enact. For those reasons, the unconstitutionality of both the Individual Mandate and the Medicaid Expansion requires the invalidation of the Affordable Care Act's other provisions.

* * *

The Court today decides to save a statute Congress did not write. It rules that what the statute declares to be a requirement with a penalty is instead an option subject to a tax. And it changes the intentionally coercive sanction of a total cutoff of Medicaid funds to a supposedly noncoercive cut-off of only the incremental funds that the Act makes available.

The Court regards its strained statutory interpretation as judicial modesty. It is not. It amounts instead to a vast judicial overreaching. It creates a debilitated, inoperable version of health-care regulation that Congress did not enact and the public does not expect. It makes enactment of sensible health-care regulation more difficult, since Congress cannot start afresh but must take as its point of departure a jumble of now senseless provisions, provisions that certain interests favored under the Court's new design will struggle to retain. And it leaves the public and the States to expend vast sums of money on requirements that may or may not survive the necessary congressional revision.

The Court's disposition, invented and atextual as it is, does not even have the merit of avoiding constitutional difficulties. It creates them. The holding that the Individual Mandate is a tax raises a difficult constitutional question (what is a direct tax?) that the Court resolves with inadequate deliberation. And the judgment on the Medicaid Expansion issue ushers in new federalism concerns and places an unaccustomed strain upon the Union. Those States that decline the Medicaid Expansion must subsidize, by the federal tax dollars taken from their citizens, vast grants to the States that accept the Medicaid Expansion. If that destabilizing political dynamic, so antagonistic to a harmonious Union, is to be introduced at all, it should be by Congress, not by the Judiciary.

The values that should have determined our course today are caution, minimalism, and the understanding that the Federal Government is one of limited powers. But the Court's ruling undermines those values at every turn. In the name of restraint, it overreaches. In the name of constitutional avoidance, it creates new constitutional questions. In the name of cooperative federalism, it undermines state sovereignty.

The Constitution, though it dates from the founding of the Republic, has powerful meaning and vital relevance to our own times. The constitutional protections that this case involves are protections of structure. Structural protections—notably, the restraints imposed by federalism and separation of powers—are less romantic and have less obvious a connection to personal freedom than the provisions of the Bill of Rights or the Civil War Amendments. Hence they tend to be undervalued or even forgotten by our citizens. It should be the responsibility of the Court to teach otherwise, to remind our people that the Framers considered structural protections of freedom the most important ones, for which reason they alone were embodied in the original Constitution and not left to later amendment. The fragmentation of power produced by the structure of our Government is central to liberty, and when we destroy it, we place liberty at peril. Today's decision should have vindicated, should have taught, this truth; instead, our judgment today has disregarded it.

For the reasons here stated, we would find the Act invalid in its entirety. We respectfully dissent.

Justice THOMAS, dissenting.

I dissent for the reasons stated in our joint opinion, but I write separately to say a word about the Commerce Clause. The joint dissent and The Chief Justice correctly apply our precedents to conclude that the Individual Mandate is beyond the power granted to Congress under the Commerce Clause and the Necessary and Proper Clause. Under those precedents, Congress may regulate "economic activity [that] substantially affects interstate commerce." I adhere to my view that "the very notion of a 'substantial effects' test under the Commerce Clause is inconsistent with the original understanding of Congress' powers and with this Court's early Commerce Clause cases." As I have explained, the Court's continued use of that test "has encouraged the Federal Government to persist in its view that the Commerce Clause has virtually no limits." The Government's unprecedented claim in this suit that it may regulate not only economic activity but also *inactivity* that substantially affects interstate commerce is a case in point.

Discussion

1. *The* Health Care Cases *and the Constitution outside the courts.* The *Health Care Cases* offer an excellent example of how constitutional ideas in politics eventually influence judicial decisions. The debate over the Affordable Care Act in 2009 and 2010 was extremely contentious, with opponents arguing that the Act would involve a government takeover of health care, and former vice presidential candidate Sarah Palin (among others) darkly warning about "death panels" hidden in the Act. The individual mandate had originally been a Republican idea, developed at the Heritage Foundation as a conservative alternative to the Clinton health care proposal in the 1990s. However, after President Obama and the Democrats made it a key element of their proposal, Congressional Republicans began to oppose it, first on policy grounds, and later, on constitutional grounds. The Act passed along party lines in March 2010. Several lawsuits were quickly filed around the country, targeting the individual mandate and the Medicaid extension. The hope was that if either or both of these elements were struck down, the courts might invalidate the entire Act.

When the litigation began, most constitutional scholars, relying on existing precedents, believed that the odds that either provision would be held unconstitutional were fairly small. Nevertheless, the rise of the Tea Party and the Republican landslide of 2010 gave hope to mandate opponents. The unconstitutionality of the mandate became virtually the official position of the Republican Party, which put its considerable resources behind promoting constitutional arguments against the mandate, not only in the courts but also in the public sphere. As a result, constitutional arguments against the mandate quickly moved from "off the wall" to "on the wall," and, by the conclusion of the oral arguments at the Supreme Court in March 2012, many observers expected that the individual mandate would be held unconstitutional. For a discussion of the role of different actors in altering public understandings of the challenge, see Jack M. Balkin, From Off the Wall to On the Wall: How the Mandate Challenge Went Mainstream, Atlantic, June 4, 2012, at *http://www.theatlantic.com/national/archive/2012/06/from-off-the-wall-to-on-the-wall-how-the-mandate-challenge-went-mainstream/258040/.*

What do these events tell us about the relationship between political change and constitutional change? Can you think of other examples in the cases we have studied in which powerful political mobilizations changed the plausibility of constitutional arguments? What are the similarities to and differences from the health care litigation?

2. *The Commerce Clause and individual liberty.* Mandate opponents argued that it was unprecedented for the government to force individuals to purchase goods and services from private parties. If the mandate was upheld, Congress could force individuals to do all sorts of things, thus undermining personal

liberty, and working a fundamental change in the relationship between the federal government and its citizens. See Randy E. Barnett, Commandeering the People: Why the Individual Health Insurance Mandate Is Unconstitutional, 5 N.Y.U. J. L. & Liberty 581 (2010). Although the arguments against the mandate technically concerned the limits to Congress's commerce power (and the Necessary and Proper Clause), they sounded in notions of individual liberty, including, in particular, economic liberty.

In the post–New Deal era, mandate opponents were unlikely to argue for protecting freedom of contract as a matter of substantive due process. (And nothing in Chief Justice Roberts's opinion or the joint dissent would prevent *states* from imposing mandates identical to the ACA's.) Nevertheless, the idea of protecting economic liberty through limitations on federal power has a long history in debates in American constitutional law. Can you think of examples?

3. *The* Health Care Cases *and the future of constitutional development.* One remarkable feature of the *Health Care Cases* is that the Supreme Court gave its blessing to the most important change to the social contract since the Great Society in the 1960s. Yet, at the same time, five Justices argued for a more limited understanding of the Commerce Clause and the Necessary and Proper Clause, while seven Justices argued—for the first time since the New Deal—for significant limits on the spending power.

Which result turns out to be more important in the long run—the change in the role of government or the change in constitutional doctrine—will likely depend on who wins the next several presidential elections and thus gets to appoint most of the federal judiciary. A Republican-dominated judiciary will likely expand on the decision's innovations, while a Democrat-dominated judiciary may read them quite narrowly. In the meantime, the doctrinal puzzles created by the *Health Care Cases* will keep lawyers busy for many years to come.

4. *The constitutional avoidance canon.* Was Roberts's Commerce Clause argument necessary to his tax power holding? If it was not, then presumably the discussion is merely dicta. At issue is the constitutional avoidance canon, which counsels that courts should avoid interpreting statutes in ways that render them unconstitutional if reasonably possible. What theory of judicial review justifies this canon?

Roberts argued that "[t]he most straightforward reading of the mandate is that it commands individuals to purchase insurance" because it imposes a "requirement" and says that the relevant individuals "shall" purchase insurance. Therefore, he argued that he had to consider the Commerce Clause/Necessary and Proper Clause issues before he could reach the taxing power argument, which was only a "fairly possible" reading. Do you agree? Does the answer depend on whether the tax interpretation is also a natural or obvious reading?

Here is the text of Section 5000A as it currently appears in the U.S. Code:

USC Title 26—Internal Revenue Code

Subtitle D: Miscellaneous Excise Taxes

CHAPTER 48—MAINTENANCE OF MINIMUM ESSENTIAL COVERAGE

§5000A. Requirement to maintain minimum essential coverage

(a) Requirement to maintain minimum essential coverage

An applicable individual shall for each month beginning after 2013 ensure that the individual, and any dependent of the individual who is an applicable individual, is covered under minimum essential coverage for such month.

(b) Shared responsibility payment

(1) In general

If a taxpayer who is an applicable individual, or an applicable individual for whom the taxpayer is liable under paragraph (3), fails to meet the requirement of subsection (a) for 1 or more months, then, except as provided in subsection (e), there is hereby imposed on the taxpayer a penalty with respect to such failures in the amount determined under subsection (c).

(2) Inclusion with return

Any penalty imposed by this section with respect to any month shall be included with a taxpayer's return under chapter 1 for the taxable year which includes such month.

(3) Payment of penalty

If an individual with respect to whom a penalty is imposed by this section for any month—

(A) is a dependent (as defined in section 152) of another taxpayer for the other taxpayer's taxable year including such month, such other taxpayer shall be liable for such penalty, or

(B) files a joint return for the taxable year including such month, such individual and the spouse of such individual shall be jointly liable for such penalty.

(c) Amount of penalty

(1) In general

The amount of the penalty imposed by this section on any taxpayer for any taxable year with respect to failures described in subsection (b)(1) shall be equal to the lesser of—

(A) the sum of the monthly penalty amounts determined under paragraph (2) for months in the taxable year during which 1 or more such failures occurred, or

(B) an amount equal to the national average premium for qualified health plans which have a bronze level of coverage, provide coverage for the applicable family size involved, and are offered through Exchanges for plan years beginning in the calendar year with or within which the taxable year ends.

Subsection (d) defines "applicable individual . . . as an individual other than an individual described in paragraph[s] (2), (3), or (4)"—which refer to people with religious objections, people operating "health care sharing ministries," aliens (lawfully or unlawfully present), and incarcerated persons. In addition, subsection (e) states that "[n]o penalty shall be imposed under subsection (a) with respect to . . . (1) Individuals who cannot afford coverage[;] (2) Taxpayers with income below [the income tax] filing threshold[;] (3) Members of Indian tribes; (4) [Persons who have] short coverage gaps [in insurance; and] (5) [Cases of] [h]ardship."

5. *The taxing power.* What are the limits of the taxing power after the *Health Care Cases*? Roberts points to four features that distinguish a lawful tax from an

unlawful penalty: First, "for most Americans the amount due will be far less than the price of insurance, and, by statute, it can never be more." This means "that [i]t may often be a reasonable financial decision to make the payment rather than purchase insurance, unlike the 'prohibitory' financial punishment in *Drexel Furniture*." Second, the tax was not structured like a criminal penalty—for example, it did not have a scienter requirement. Third, the tax was administered and collected by the IRS like other taxes. Fourth, failure to purchase insurance was not treated as an unlawful act, and there were no adverse consequences other than having to pay the tax. Which of these criteria is the most important?

Note that the upshot of Roberts's argument is that a constitutional tax creates *incentives* rather than *mandates* for behavior; that is, it always preserves the option to pay the tax, which is not so high that it effectively compels or coerces compliance with the government's preferred regulatory outcome. For a discussion of the constitutional limits on the tax power, see Robert D. Cooter & Neil Siegel, Not the Power to Destroy: A Theory of the Tax Power for a Court That Limits the Commerce Power, 99 Va. L. Rev. __ (forthcoming October 2012), available at *http://papers.ssrn.com/sol3/papers.cfm?abstract_id=1989537*.

Roberts could also have added a fifth criterion: the tax did not burden a fundamental right. Thus, a tax on people who refuse to attend church weekly would violate the Free Exercise Clause (and the Establishment Clause); a tax on people who refuse to eat broccoli might violate the Due Process Clause. Are all taxes that affect the exercise of fundamental rights unconstitutional? The federal income tax sometimes taxes married couples filing jointly more than two people filing separately. Is this constitutional?

6. *Using taxes rather than mandates.* The effect of Roberts's argument is that if Congress wishes to impose mandates on people who are not already engaged in an activity that could be regulated by the Commerce Clause, it must use the taxing power instead, always giving people the option to pay the tax. Are there structural reasons to prefer taxes to mandates in these circumstances? Does the doctrine promote federalism? Regardless of whether it promotes federalism, does it promote individual liberty?

7. *Holding or dicta?* What parts of Roberts's opinion constitute the holding of the Court? Parts III-A and III-B (which no other Justices join) purport to hold that Congress may not enact the individual mandate under the Commerce Clause, even assisted by the Necessary and Proper Clause, and Part IV (joined only by Breyer and Kagan) holds that the Medicaid extension goes beyond Congress's spending power. (Justice Ginsburg and Justice Sotomayor join only the remedy.)

In *Marks v. United States,* 430 U.S. 188, 193 (1977), the Court explained its test for determining the holding of a case when there is no majority opinion on a particular issue: "When a fragmented Court decides a case and no single rationale explaining the result enjoys the assent of five Justices, the holding of the Court may be viewed as that position taken by those Members who concurred in the judgments on the narrowest grounds."

The problem here is that the Justices who agree with Roberts on limiting the Commerce Clause and the Necessary and Proper Clause do not concur in the judgment; they dissent. The joint dissenters make arguments similar to and even more restrictive than Roberts' arguments, but they do not agree with the judgment of the Court and they do not join either Part III or Part IV of Roberts's opinion. Instead, they merely criticize his holding on the tax power, and the remedy with respect to the Medicaid extension.

Are Roberts's positions on these issues binding law? Note, interestingly, that Part III-C of his opinion, joined by five Justices, notes in passing that "[t]he Court today holds that our Constitution protects us from federal regulation under the Commerce Clause so long as we abstain from the regulated activity." Part IV-B, joined only by Roberts, Breyer, and Kagan, states that "[i]n light of the Court's holding, the Secretary cannot apply §1396c to withdraw existing Medicaid funds for failure to comply with the requirements set out in the expansion."

Even if you believe that Roberts's arguments (other than the tax power holding) are either dicta or a plurality opinion, do you expect that lower federal courts will treat them as law, given that lower courts know that five Justices now support doctrines that limit federal powers? How *should* lower courts interpret these opinions?

8. *The activity/inactivity distinction.* Both Roberts and the joint dissent argue that Congress can regulate activities under the Commerce Clause (and Necessary and Proper Clause), but not inactivity. If Congress could regulate inactivity, they argue, there would be no limit to the federal government's powers. However, such limits already exist, for example, in *Lopez* and *Morrison.* Is the activity/inactivity distinction necessary to preserve the rule of *Lopez* and *Morrison* or the principle that the federal government is one of limited and enumerated powers? Why? Does the distinction promote federalism, individual freedom, or both?

The activity/inactivity distinction is related to the act/omission distinction. Lawyers are sometimes able to manipulate this distinction by expanding or contracting the relevant time frame or by redescribing events in different ways. See Mark Kelman, Interpretive Construction in the Substantive Criminal Law, 33 Stan. L. Rev. 591 (1981); J.M. Balkin, The Rhetoric of Responsibility, 76 Va. L. Rev. 197 (1990).

Is the activity/inactivity distinction subject to manipulation in the same way? For example, people may be active or inactive in commerce depending on how broadly we describe the market in which they participate (health care, health insurance, purchase of over-the-counter remedies, etc.) and depending on how broadly we consider the relevant time frame (day, month, year, decade, lifetime). Another example: at the time Title II of the Civil Rights Act was passed in 1964, the proprietor of the Heart of Atlanta Motel was not serving black people—and the law required him to do so. However, the owner was operating a hotel that served white people. In *Wickard v. Filburn*, Justice Jackson described Filburn's conduct both as activity and inactivity: "The effect of the statute before us is to restrict the amount which may be produced for market and the extent, as well, to which one may forestall resort to the market by producing to meet his own needs." That is, the problem that Congress sought to address was that Filburn was failing to purchase wheat in the market. Mark Tushnet, The "Activity-Inactivity" Distinction, Balkinization, Dec. 13, 2010, at *http://balkin. blogspot.com/2010/12/activity-inactivity-distinction.html*.

Are there administrable ways for courts to fix the relevant description of events, the relevant market, and the relevant time frame in order to decide how to apply the activity/inactivity distinction? Can judges just rely on "common sense"? In her opinion in the *Health Care Cases*, Justice Ginsburg argued that it was obvious that almost everyone was engaged in the health care market, or soon would be; therefore requiring the purchase of health insurance was simply a way of regulating how people pay for commercial transactions in which they will inevitably engage. The joint dissent argued that this description of the situation was too broad—because it would suggest that since everyone is in the food market, or soon will be, they can be required to purchase broccoli—and that the relevant market was the market for health insurance. Is there a correct answer to this question?

9. *Workarounds.* Assuming that the activity/inactivity distinction is now part of Commerce Clause doctrine, could Congress get around the distinction by requiring that everyone who purchases more than $500 of health care related products or services in a calendar year must henceforth be subject to an insurance mandate or pay a $500 yearly penalty? Could Congress require that everyone who buys more than $500 worth of food in a given year must henceforth purchase $500 of broccoli each year or be subject to a $500 penalty?

Could Congress require purchase of health insurance if a person has ever been previously covered by health insurance? Has ever visited an emergency room and received subsidized treatment? Has ever crossed state lines in order to receive medical care? Has ever received medical care in more than one state? (Would such requirements be constitutional if applied retroactively? What if they were only applied prospectively?)

10. *Necessary but not proper?* Chief Justice Roberts and the joint dissent argue that the mandate was not necessary and proper to make the guaranteed issue and community ratings rules effective. Roberts claimed that even if the mandate was "necessary," it was not "proper." He argued that the mandate would "undermine the structure of government established by the Constitution" and was "not consist[ent] with the letter and spirit of the constitution." It would involve a "great substantive and independent power," and work "a substantial expansion of federal authority." How should judges apply these ideas in future cases? Did the vast expansion of Commerce Clause authority in *Darby* and *Wickard* (already) violate this test? Note that Roberts assumes that the statute challenged in *Wickard* is "proper." If so, is Roberts's argument just another way of saying that Congress cannot reach inactivity through the Necessary and Proper Clause if it cannot reach it through the Commerce Clause? To what extent is this consistent with the logic of *McCulloch*? With logic of *Comstock*?

The joint dissent reached the same conclusion a little differently. It argued that the mandate is not necessary and proper for two reasons. First, *Raich* involved a situation of true necessity, whereas in this case there were other ways to achieve the goals of the ACA other than using a mandate. (Is this consistent with *McCulloch*?) Second, the joint dissent argued that mandates greatly expand federal power into new fields. If mandates are necessary and proper to realize the statute's goals, there are no limits to federal power, and that cannot be proper. Again, does this assume that *Lopez* and *Morrison* would become effectively irrelevant?

Is it clear that there is no limiting principle that would allow the mandate but not give the federal government unlimited regulatory power? For example, what if the Court had held that only mandates to exchange money for goods or services—that is, to engage in commerce—were permitted under the Commerce Clause and Necessary and Proper Clause, but no other mandates? (Thus, a mandate to eat broccoli or to exercise once a day would not fall within the commerce power, even when assisted by the Necessary and Proper Clause). Is *this* distinction significantly less administrable than the activity/inactivity distinction?

11. *The spending power.* Note carefully the differences between Chief Justice Roberts's account of the spending power (joined by Justices Breyer and Kagan) and that of the joint dissent.

The joint dissent argues that because the size of the threatened withdrawal of − federal funding is so great, the Medicaid expansion is an offer the states cannot refuse, and therefore it is coercive. This might suggest that the federal government may not impose new conditions on (and thus threaten to withdraw funding from) *any* program that has become a sufficiently large percentage of a state's budget. Does the joint dissent's test allow the federal government to abolish existing programs that constitute a significant proportion of a state's budget?

The joint dissenters also argue that if the federal government offers the states − participation in a sufficiently large social welfare program, states may not be able to refuse and so the offer is coercive. First, the federal tax dollars paid by a state's citizens that the state forgoes will be given to the poor in other states. Second, the state will have to raise additional state taxes to provide comparable services. Does this mean that it was unconstitutional for Congress to offer the states Medicaid in the first place? Does it mean that there is a limit on how much money the federal government can offer to the states with conditions attached?

Roberts's argument is different. He distinguishes between two situations. In − the first, Congress places conditions on funds it gives to states for a particular program. For example, Congress gives highway funds to states in exchange for states' promise that the roads will be built with certain types of materials, and will have certain types of safety signs. These conditions, Roberts argues, are perfectly appropriate because they help ensure that Congress's distribution of money serves the general welfare, as required by the text of the General Welfare Clause.

The second situation is when Congress asks states to do something or else it will withdraw funds from an *unrelated* or *independent* program. Imagine, for example, that Congress requires states to spend highway funds on extra roadway signs; but if a state refuses, Congress will withdraw not only its highway funding but also all of its educational grants to the state. In this situation, Roberts argues, we must inquire into whether there is undue coercion.

In *South Dakota v. Dole*, for example, federal highway funding was made conditional on raising a state's drinking age. *Dole* held that the condition had to be—and was—germane to the purposes for which the funds were offered, in this case, highway safety. Nevertheless, Roberts pointed out, the condition did not concern how states should use the highway funds themselves.

In this sort of situation, when "conditions take the form of threats to terminate other significant independent grants," Roberts argues, courts must inquire whether the bargain is unduly coercive. In *Dole*, the amount of money that the state would lose was very small: about 5 percent of South Dakota's highway funds, and less than half of 1 percent of South Dakota's budget. Therefore, the Court concluded that the bargain was not coercive. In the case of the Medicaid extension, by contrast, "Medicaid spending accounts for over 20 percent of the average State's total budget, with federal funds covering 50 to 83 percent of those costs." Therefore, Roberts concludes, this bargain, which threatens to withdraw at least 10 percent of a state's budget, is coercive. (Note in particular Roberts's statement that although one half of 1 percent would not be coercive, 10 percent would be "dragooning").

There is an obvious rejoinder: in this case, Congress is not threatening to terminate *another* program. Its conditions are all conditions on states' use of Medicaid funds. The ACA simply expands Medicaid, and all the federal government has done is add new conditions. That is permissible because Congress had reserved the right to add new conditions to Medicaid by statute, and the states agreed to that bargain.

Roberts responds that if the changes to an existing program are sufficiently drastic, they are changes in kind rather than degree, and the resulting program is a "new" and independent program. In essence, Roberts says, Congress is threatening to withdraw funding from Old Medicaid if the states do not agree to participate in New Medicaid. It is true that Congress reserved the right to add new conditions to Medicaid in its original agreement with the states. However, "[a] State could hardly anticipate that Congress's reservation of the right to 'alter' or 'amend' the Medicaid program included the power to transform it so dramatically." Because there is no fair warning, courts should treat the new conditions as part of a new program separate from Old Medicaid. Therefore, we must ask whether the amount that Congress threatens to withdraw from the older program is so great as to be coercive.

How would this test apply to other federal statutes, for example, federal civil rights laws? Title IX of the Education Amendments of 1972 and Title VI of the Civil Rights Act of 1964 impose conditions on federal grants of funds to states and local governments and require nondiscrimination on the basis of sex, race, and other categories. The Civil Rights Restoration Act of 1988, 42 U.S.C. § 2000d4a, states that state agencies, school districts, and municipalities that receive federal funds must comply with these laws in all areas of their operations, not merely in the particular program or activity that has received federal funding. If Congress amended its civil rights laws to prohibit sexual orientation discrimination in entities that receive federal funds, could states refuse to accept the new conditions on the grounds that Congress had created a "new" program? On the grounds that they had become dependent on federal funding for many decades and could not realistically refuse any new conditions?

12. *More workarounds.* How easy will it be for Congress to work around Roberts's new test? For example, could Congress simply abolish Medicaid and create a new program in its place and invite the states to participate? Could Congress stipulate that a state may participate in Medicaid for only a year at a time and then must reapply each year to a new program in order to receive funding?

Congress can, if it wishes, simply convert Medicaid into a fully federal program like Medicare. But then it would have to increase the number of federal employees in order to administer the program. Are there good reasons for the federal government to ask states to administer federal-state cooperative programs like Medicaid? How does Roberts's new test affect the federal government's incentives?

Insert the following before Section III on p. 649:

COLEMAN v. COURT OF APPEALS OF MARYLAND, 132 S. Ct. 1327 (2012): 29 U.S.C. §2612(a)(1), part of the Family and Medical Leave Act, entitles an employee to take up to 12 workweeks of unpaid leave per year for the employee's own serious health condition when the condition interferes with the employee's ability to perform at work. Justice Kennedy, in a plurality ￢ opinion joined by Chief Justice Roberts, Justice Alito, and Justice Thomas, held that the logic of *Nevada Department of Human Resources v. Hibbs,* 538 U.S. 721 (2003), did not apply to the FMLA's "self-care provisions." Therefore, Congress lacked the power under section 5 of the Fourteenth Amendment to abrogate the states' immunity from damage lawsuits when state employers unlawfully refused to grant self-care leaves to their employees: "Without widespread evidence of sex discrimination or sex stereotyping in the administration of sick leave, it is apparent that the congressional purpose in enacting the self-care provision is unrelated to these supposed wrongs. The legislative history of the self-care provision reveals a concern for the economic burdens on the employee and the employee's family resulting from illnessrelated job loss and a concern for discrimination on the basis of illness, not sex." Justice Thomas ￢ concurred, adding that he believed *Hibbs* was wrongly decided. Justice Scalia ￢

concurred in the judgment, arguing that the Court should abandon its "congruence and proportionality" test: "I would limit Congress's §5 power to the regulation of conduct that *itself* violates the Fourteenth Amendment. Failing to grant state employees leave for the purpose of self-care—or any other purpose, for that matter—does not come close."

Justice Ginsburg, joined by Justice Breyer, Justice Sotomayor, and Justice Kagan, dissented. Justice Ginsburg argued that the FMLA was designed, among other things, to prevent discrimination against pregnant women. Accordingly, Justice Ginsburg would overrule *Geduldig v. Aiello* and hold that discrimination against pregnant women is a form of sex discrimination. "The self-care provision responds to . . . evidence [of discrimination against pregnant women] by requiring employers to allow leave for "ongoing pregnancy, miscarriages, . . . the need for prenatal care, childbirth, and recovery from childbirth." Justice Ginsburg quoted congressional reports explaining that it was better to require employers to provide self-care leave for *both* men and women—instead of providing leave only following pregnancy or due to pregnancy-related illness—because this would remove employers' incentives to discriminate against pregnant women and women of child-bearing age. Because a guarantee of self-care leave for both men and women alleviated employer incentives toward pregnancy discrimination, and because it was without pay and therefore not too burdensome to employers, Justice Ginsburg concluded that it was congruent and proportional to Congress's evidence of pregnancy discrimination in employment.

Even if pregnancy discrimination did not count as sex discrimination, Ginsburg argued, Congress understood that "[r]equiring States to provide gender-neutral parental and family-care leave alone [without self-care leave] . . . would promote precisely the type of workplace discrimination Congress sought to reduce. The 'pervasive sex-role stereotype that caring for family members is women's work,' [Congress believed], led employers to regard required parental and family-care leave as a woman's benefit" that few men would use. "Congress therefore had good reason to conclude that the self-care provision—which men no doubt would use—would counter employers' impressions that the FMLA would otherwise install female leave. Providing for self-care would thus reduce employers' corresponding incentive to discriminate against women in hiring and promotion."

NORTHWEST AUSTIN MUNICIPAL UTILITY DISTRICT NUMBER ONE v. HOLDER, 557 U.S. 193 (2009): [Section Five of the Voting Rights Act of 1965 requires that covered jurisdictions must preclear any changes to their voting systems with the Department of Justice (or with a three judge district court in Washington) to ensure that they do not "ha[ve] the purpose nor . . . the effect of denying or abridging the right to vote on account of race or color." 42 U.S.C. §1973c(a). Jurisdictions subject to §5 were originally determined by a test of those states that had used a forbidden test or device in

November 1964, and had less than 50 percent voter registration or turnout in the 1964 Presidential election. Today covered jurisdictions include most of the South, Arizona, and Alaska, along with various counties and townships throughout the United States.

Congress reauthorized the Act for five years in 1970, for seven years in 1975, and for 25 years in 1982. The coverage formula based on the use of voting-eligibility tests and the rate of registration and turnout among all voters, remained the same, but the measurements were based on 1968 and eventually 1972 levels. In 2006, Congress extended §5 for 25 more years, keeping 1972 as the baseline date for measuring which jurisdictions would be subject to pre-clearance requirements.

A Texas municipal utility district (NAMUDNO) challenged the constitution- A ality of Section Five, arguing that it had never discriminated against minority voters. It argued that the Voting Rights Act's preclearance provision in §5, passed under Congress's enforcement powers in section 2 of the Fifteenth Amendment, should be judged under the "congruence and proportionality" standard of *City of Boerne v. Flores*; the municipality argued that §5 failed the *Boerne* standard because the baseline for measuring whether jurisdictions should be covered were decades out of date. A three judge District Court in the *P* District of Columbia rejected the challenge, arguing that §5 met both the test of *Boerne* and the rational means test originally applied in *South Carolina v. Katzenbach*.

On appeal, the Supreme Court, in an 8-1 decision written by Chief Justice Roberts, did not reach the constitutional question. Instead, it reinterpreted the statute to allow NAMUDNO to make use of the Voting Right Act's "bailout" provision in §4(a). This allows a political subdivision to be released from the preclearance requirements if certain conditions are met. The Court held that although NAMUDNO did not register its own voters, it should be considered a "political subdivision" within the meaning of the Act.

This statutory interpretation, the Court explained, allowed it to avoid reaching whether the preclearance requirements unduly restricted the rights of states and local governments and were thus beyond Congress's powers. Nevertheless, Chief Justice Roberts strongly suggested that §5 of the Voting Rights Act might violate the Constitution:]

ROBERTS, C.J.:

Things have changed in the South. Voter turnout and registration rates now approach parity. Blatantly discriminatory evasions of federal decrees are rare. And minority candidates hold office at unprecedented levels. . . . It may be that these improvements are insufficient and that conditions continue to warrant preclearance under the Act. But the Act imposes current burdens and must be justified by current needs.

The Act also differentiates between the States, despite our historic tradition that all the States enjoy equal sovereignty. Distinctions can be justified in some cases. . . . But a departure from the fundamental principle of equal sovereignty requires a showing that a statute's disparate geographic coverage is sufficiently related to the problem that it targets.

These federalism concerns are underscored by the argument that the pre-clearance requirements in one State would be unconstitutional in another. See *Georgia v. Ashcroft*, 539 U.S. 461, 491-492 (2003) (Kennedy, J., concurring) (Race cannot be the predominant factor in redistricting under our decision in *Miller v. Johnson*, 515 U.S. 900 (1995). Yet considerations of race that would doom a redistricting plan under the Fourteenth Amendment or §2 [of the Voting Rights Act, which prohibits practices that abridge voting rights based on race] seem to be what save it under §5.) Additional constitutional concerns are raised in saying that this tension between §§2 and 5 must persist in covered jurisdictions and not elsewhere.

The evil that §5 is meant to address may no longer be concentrated in the jurisdictions singled out for preclearance. The statute's coverage formula is based on data that is now more than 35 years old, and there is considerable evidence that it fails to account for current political conditions. For example, the racial gap in voter registration and turnout is lower in the States originally covered by §5 than it is nationwide. Congress heard warnings from supporters of extending §5 that the evidence in the record did not address systematic differences between the covered and the non-covered areas of the United States[,] . . . and, in fact, the evidence that is in the record suggests that there is more similarity than difference. . . . [S]ee also Persily, The Promise and Pitfalls of the New Voting Rights Act, 117 Yale L.J. 174, 208 (2007) ("The most one can say in defense of the [coverage] formula is that it is the best of the politically feasible alternatives or that changing the formula would . . . disrupt settled expectations").

The parties do not agree on the standard to apply in deciding whether, in light of the foregoing concerns, Congress exceeded its Fifteenth Amendment enforcement power in extending the preclearance requirements. The district argues that "'[t]here must be a congruence and proportionality between the injury to be prevented or remedied and the means adopted to that end,'" quoting *City of Boerne v. Flores,* 521 U.S. 507 (1997); the Federal Government asserts that it is enough that the legislation be a "'rational means to effectuate the constitutional prohibition,'" quoting *Katzenbach.* . . . [W]e need not resolve [the question.] The Act's preclearance requirements and its coverage formula raise serious constitutional questions under either test.

THOMAS, J., concurring in the judgment in part and dissenting in part:

[T]he lack of current evidence of intentional discrimination with respect to voting renders §5 unconstitutional. The provision can no longer be justified as an appropriate mechanism for enforcement of the Fifteenth Amendment.

[B]y 1965, Congress had every reason to conclude that States with a history of disenfranchising voters based on race would continue to do all they could to evade the constitutional ban on voting discrimination. . . . In upholding §5 in *Katzenbach*, the Court nonetheless noted that the provision was an "uncommon exercise of congressional power" that would not have been "appropriate" absent the "exceptional conditions" and "unique circumstances" present in the targeted jurisdictions at that particular time. In reaching its decision, the Court thus refused to simply accept Congress' representation that the extreme measure was necessary to enforce the Fifteenth Amendment; rather, it closely reviewed the record compiled by Congress to ensure that §5 was "'appropriate'" antievasion legislation. [For example], the Court highlighted evidence showing that black voter registration rates ran approximately 50 percentage points lower than white voter registration in several States. . . . The statistical evidence confirmed Congress' judgment that "the extraordinary stratagem of contriving new rules of various kinds for the sole purpose of perpetuating voting discrimination in the face of adverse federal court decrees" was working and could not be defeated through case-by-case enforcement of the Fifteenth Amendment. This record also clearly supported Congress' predictive judgment that such "States might try similar maneuvers in the future in order to evade the remedies for voting discrimination contained in the Act itself." These stark statistics—in conjunction with the unrelenting use of discriminatory tests and practices that denied blacks the right to vote—constituted sufficient proof of "actual voting discrimination" to uphold the preclearance requirement imposed by §5 on the covered jurisdictions as an appropriate exercise of congressional power under the Fifteenth Amendment. It was only "[u]nder the compulsion of these unique circumstances [that] Congress responded in a permissibly decisive manner."

[Section] 5 is the quintessential prophylaxis; it "goes beyond the prohibition of the Fifteenth Amendment by suspending *all* changes to state election law—however innocuous—until they have been precleared by federal authorities in Washington, D.C." . . . [B]ecause it sweeps more broadly than the substantive command of the Fifteenth Amendment, §5 pushes the outer boundaries of Congress' Fifteenth Amendment enforcement authority. . . . Indeed, §5's preclearance requirement is "one of the most extraordinary remedial provisions in an Act noted for its broad remedies. Even the Department of Justice has described it as a 'substantial departure . . . from ordinary concepts of our federal system'; its encroachment on state sovereignty is significant and undeniable." This "encroachment is especially troubling because it destroys local control of the means of self-government, one of the central values of our polity." More than 40 years after its enactment, this intrusion has become increasingly difficult to justify. . . . [T]he constitutionality of §5 has always depended on the proven existence of intentional discrimination so extensive that elimination of it through case-by-case enforcement would be impossible. . . . Congress must establish a "history and pattern" of constitutional violations to establish the need for §5 by justifying a remedy that pushes the limits of its constitutional authority. As a result, for §5 to withstand renewed constitutional scrutiny, there must be a demonstrated connection between the "remedial measures" chosen and the "evil presented" in the record made by Congress when it renewed the Act. *City of Boerne v. Flores.*

[T]he extensive pattern of discrimination that led the Court to previously uphold §5 as enforcing the Fifteenth Amendment no longer exists. Covered jurisdictions are not now engaged in a systematic campaign to deny black citizens access to the ballot through intimidation and violence. . . . There is thus currently no concerted effort in these jurisdictions to engage in the "unremitting and ingenious defiance of the Constitution," that served as the constitutional basis for upholding the "uncommon exercise of congressional power" embodied in §5.

The lack of sufficient evidence that the covered jurisdictions currently engage in the type of discrimination that underlay the enactment of §5 undermines any basis for retaining it. Punishment for long past sins is not a legitimate basis for imposing a forward-looking preventative measure that has already served its purpose. Those supporting §5's reenactment argue that without it these jurisdictions would return to the racially discriminatory practices of 30 and 40 years ago. But there is no evidence that public officials stand ready, if given the chance, to again engage in concerted acts of violence, terror, and subterfuge in order to keep minorities from voting. Without such evidence, the charge can only be premised on outdated assumptions about racial attitudes in the covered jurisdictions. Admitting that a prophylactic law as broad as §5 is no longer constitutionally justified based on current evidence of discrimination is not a sign of defeat. It is an acknowledgment of victory. . . .

Indeed, when reenacting §5 in 2006, Congress evidently understood that the emergency conditions which prompted §5's original enactment no longer exist. . . . Instead of relying on the kind of evidence that the *Katzenbach* Court had found so persuasive, Congress instead based reenactment on evidence of what it termed "second generation barriers constructed to prevent minority voters from fully participating in the electoral process." But such evidence is not probative of the type of purposeful discrimination that prompted Congress to enact §5 in 1965. For example, Congress relied upon evidence of racially polarized voting within the covered jurisdictions. But racially polarized voting is not evidence of unconstitutional discrimination, is not state action, and is not a problem unique to the South. . . .

This is not to say that voter discrimination is extinct. Indeed, the District Court singled out a handful of examples of allegedly discriminatory voting practices from the record made by Congress. But the existence of discrete and isolated incidents of interference with the right to vote has never been sufficient justification for the imposition of §5's extraordinary requirements. From its inception, the statute was promoted as a measure needed to neutralize a coordinated and unrelenting campaign to deny an entire race access to the ballot. Perfect compliance with the Fifteenth Amendment's substantive command is not now—nor has it ever been—the yardstick for determining whether Congress has the power to employ broad prophylactic legislation to enforce that Amendment. The burden remains with Congress to prove that the extreme circumstances warranting §5's enactment persist today. A record of scattered infringement of the right to vote is not a constitutionally acceptable substitute.

* * *

In 1870, the Fifteenth Amendment was ratified in order to guarantee that no citizen would be denied the right to vote based on race, color, or previous condition of servitude. Congress passed §5 of the VRA in 1965 because that promise had remained unfulfilled for far too long. But now—more than 40 years later—the violence, intimidation, and subterfuge that led Congress to pass §5 and this Court to uphold it no longer remains. An acknowledgment of §5's unconstitutionality represents a fulfillment of the Fifteenth Amendment's promise of full enfranchisement and honors the success achieved by the VRA.

Discussion

1. *A stern warning or a punt?* Although Chief Justice Roberts's opinion, joined by eight Justices, points out problems with section five of the Voting Rights Act, the Court backed away from striking it down. Only Justice Thomas was willing to do so. Instead, the opinion reads more like a thinly disguised piece of advice to Congress to revise the evidentiary basis for section 5's preclearance requirements.

What explains the Court's reticence? One possibility is that the Chief Justice could not obtain the votes of five Justices (including Justice Kennedy) for striking down the Act. But this simply begs the question of why that was not possible. After all, during the Rehnquist Court's federalism revolution, discussed more fully in Chapter Five, a coalition of five conservative Justices (which included Justice Kennedy) struck down literally dozens of federal statutes, and even decided a Presidential election. The Court did not turn to the canon of constitutional avoidance as it did in this case.

One reason might be that the Voting Rights Act is not just any statute: Along with the Civil Rights Act of 1964, it is a symbol (and central accomplishment) of the American Civil Rights movement. Chief Justice Roberts speaks of the act's "historic accomplishments," and Justice Thomas emphasizes its importance to African-Americans even as he goes on to explain why it is now unnecessary and outmoded.

Statutes like the Voting Rights Act become important parts of our constitutional tradition and symbolize important values and cultural memories that Americans now associate with their Constitution. The Court's legitimacy as an institution comes in part from respecting the basic boundaries of the constitutional tradition as the public understands them. (By comparison, five members of the Court had few qualms in striking down the Violence Against Women Act in 2000 in *United States v. Morrison*. VAWA simply did not have the same symbolic significance as the Voting Rights Act.)

Put another way, the Voting Rights Act is part of the current constitutional regime. A constitutional regime consists of a set of basic assumptions and principles concerning government's power and authority, and a set of institutions and practices that form a background to politics. The current constitutional regime was shaped by the growth of the administrative and regulatory state that came with the New Deal, the national security state that arose after World War II, and the civil rights revolution of the 1960s. Key framework statutes, such as the Social Security Act, the Fair Labor Standards Act, the Civil Rights Act, and the Voting Rights Act, reflect these commitments and are part of the current constitutional regime. Congress can amend them at any time, and indeed all of these acts have been altered in various ways through the years. But they remain central to the current generation's expectations about the powers and obligations of government.

If the Court had struck down elements of a framework statute like the Voting Rights Act, one of the crown jewels of the civil rights era, and passed by democratic majorities, it would have had powerful symbolic significance. It might possibly have undermined the Justices' legitimacy, especially if the decision had been by a vote of 5-4, with the more conservative Justices voting to use the power of judicial review to hold a key civil rights provision unconstitutional. The path of least resistance, therefore, was to invite Congress to amend the Voting Rights Act, as Congress has done before. However, this analysis begs the obvious question of whether the Court will strike the VRA down in a later case if Congress fails to amend it in the next several years. That is to say, it is unclear whether *NAMUDNO* is a genuine threat to overturn section 5 or is a way for the Court to increase the number of individual jurisdictions that can escape preclearance (through the bailout provision) without striking down the statute in its entirety.

2. *Prophylactic statutes.* Justice Thomas identifies section 5 as a "quintessential" prophylactic statute. Generally speaking such measures are designed to prevent future violations of the Constitution when it is difficult or costly to police violations in individual cases. But section 5, which is over 40 years old, serves a somewhat different purpose: It prevents potential backsliding in jurisdictions that are now, at least by the standards of the 1960s, comparatively well behaved. In these circumstances, it may be difficult to tell whether section 5 is unnecessary because states and local governments have completely reformed and would never think of trying to violate minority rights, or whether section 5 has become an important part of the framework of expectations that maintains good behavior. Under the latter view, states and local governments do not even try many strategies to disenfranchise minorities or dilute their voting rights because these attempts will never get past preclearance. If so, the statute would be congruent and proportional even if there were very few voting act violations. Similarly, the preclearance provisions of section 5 prevent the evolution of novel forms of strategic vote dilution or denial of minority rights that people did not imagine in the 1960s because any such practices will require approval by the Justice Department. But if we do not see many new strategies in practice, how would we know whether this is the case? If Congress claims that this is how section 5 works, should the Court defer to that judgment?

Insert before section C on p. 795:

FREE ENTERPRISE FUND v. PUBLIC COMPANY ACCOUNTING OVERSIGHT BOARD, 130 S. Ct. 3138 (2010), 2010 WL 2555191: [Congress created the Public Company Accounting Oversight Board (PCAOB), as part of a series of accounting reforms in the Sarbanes-Oxley Act of 2002, which responded to corporate scandals in the early 2000s. The Board is modeled on private self-regulatory organizations in the securities industry—such as the New York Stock Exchange—that investigate and discipline their own members subject to Commission oversight. The PCAOB, however, is a Government-created entity with expansive powers to govern an entire industry. Every accounting firm that audits public companies under the securities laws must register with the Board, pay it an annual fee, and comply with its rules and oversight. The Board may inspect registered firms, initiate formal investigations, and issue severe sanctions in its disciplinary proceedings.

The Board inspected petitioner Beckstead and Watts, an accounting firm, released a report critical of its auditing procedures, and began a formal investigation. The firm and petitioner Free Enterprise Fund, a nonprofit trade organization of to which Beckstead and Watts belonged, sued the Board and its members, arguing that the Board was unconstitutional because, among other things, the President could not remove members of the Board directly.

The Board is composed of five members appointed by the Securities and Exchange Commission. While the SEC has oversight of the Board, it cannot remove Board members at will, but only "for good cause shown," and in accordance with specified procedures. For purposes of the litigation the parties agreed that the Board is part of the Government for constitutional purposes, that its members are "Officers of the United States," and that the SEC Commissioners cannot be removed by the President except for "inefficiency, neglect of duty, or malfeasance in office." *Humphrey's Executor v. United States.*]

ROBERTS, C.J.:

[W]e have previously upheld limited restrictions on the President's removal power. In those cases, however, only one level of protected tenure separated the President from an officer exercising executive power. It was the President—or a subordinate he could remove at will—who decided whether the officer's conduct merited removal under the good-cause standard.

The Act before us does something quite different. It not only protects Board members from removal except for good cause, but withdraws from the President any decision on whether that good cause exists. That decision is vested instead in other tenured officers—the Commissioners—none of whom is subject to the President's direct control. The result is a Board that is not accountable to the President, and a President who is not responsible for the Board.

[A] second level of tenure protection changes the nature of the President's review. Now the Commission cannot remove a Board member at will. The

President therefore cannot hold the Commission fully accountable for the Board's conduct, to the same extent that he may hold the Commission accountable for everything else that it does. The Commissioners are not responsible for the Board's actions. They are only responsible for their own determination of whether the Act's rigorous good-cause standard is met. And even if the President disagrees with their determination, he is powerless to intervene—unless that determination is so unreasonable as to constitute "inefficiency, neglect of duty, or malfeasance in office."

[N]either the President, nor anyone directly responsible to him, nor even an officer whose conduct he may review only for good cause, has full control over the Board. The President is stripped of the power our precedents have preserved, and his ability to execute the laws—by holding his subordinates accountable for their conduct—is impaired.

That arrangement is contrary to Article II's vesting of the executive power in the President. Without the ability to oversee the Board, or to attribute the Board's failings to those whom he can oversee, the President is no longer the judge of the Board's conduct. He is not the one who decides whether Board members are abusing their offices or neglecting their duties. He can neither ensure that the laws are faithfully executed, nor be held responsible for a Board member's breach of faith. This violates the basic principle that the President "cannot delegate ultimate responsibility or the active obligation to supervise that goes with it," because Article II "makes a single President responsible for the actions of the Executive Branch."

[I]f Congress can shelter the bureaucracy behind two layers of good-cause tenure, why not a third? . . . The officers of such an agency—safely encased within a Matryoshka doll of tenure protections—would be immune from Presidential oversight, even as they exercised power in the people's name.

Perhaps an individual President might find advantages in tying his own hands. But the separation of powers does not depend on the views of individual Presidents. The President can always choose to restrain himself in his dealings with subordinates. He cannot, however, choose to bind his successors by diminishing their powers, nor can he escape responsibility for his choices by pretending that they are not his own.

The diffusion of power carries with it a diffusion of accountability. The people do not vote for the "Officers of the United States." Art. II, §2, cl. 2. They instead look to the President to guide the "assistants or deputies . . . subject to his superintendence." The Federalist No. 72, p. 487 (J. Cooke ed. 1961) (A. Hamilton). Without a clear and effective chain of command, the public cannot "determine on whom the blame or the punishment of a pernicious measure, or series of pernicious measures ought really to fall." Id., No. 70, at 476 (same). . . . By granting the Board executive power without the Executive's oversight, this Act subverts the President's ability to ensure that the laws are faithfully executed—as well as the public's ability to pass judgment on his efforts. The Act's restrictions are incompatible with the Constitution's separation of powers. . . . [Moreover,] multilevel protection . . . "provides a blueprint for extensive expansion of the legislative power." . . . Congress has plenary control over the salary, duties, and even existence of executive offices. Only Presidential oversight can counter its influence. That is why the Constitution vests certain powers in the President that "the Legislature has no right to diminish or modify." 1 Annals of Cong., at 463 (J. Madison). . . .

[M]any civil servants within independent agencies would not qualify as "Officers of the United States," who [like members of the Board] "exercis[e] significant authority pursuant to the laws of the United States." . . . We do not decide the status of other Government employees, nor do we decide whether "lesser functionaries subordinate to officers of the United States" must be subject to the same sort of control as those who exercise "significant authority pursuant to the laws." . . . Nothing in our opinion . . . should be read to cast doubt on the use of what is colloquially known as the civil service system within independent agencies.

[F]or similar reasons, our holding also does not address that subset of independent agency employees who serve as administrative law judges. Whether administrative law judges are necessarily "Officers of the United States" is disputed. And unlike members of the Board, many administrative law judges of course perform adjudicative rather than enforcement or policymaking functions, or possess purely recommendatory powers. [relocated footnote—EDS.]

[Nor does] today's opinion . . . increase the President's authority to remove military officers. Without expressing any view whatever on the scope of that authority, it is enough to note that we see little analogy between our Nation's armed services and the Public Company Accounting Oversight Board. Military officers are broadly subject to Presidential control through the chain of command and through the President's powers as Commander in Chief. The President and his subordinates may also convene boards of inquiry or courts-martial to hear claims of misconduct or poor performance by those officers. Here, by contrast, the President has no authority to initiate a Board member's removal for cause. . . .

[The majority held that the for-cause provisions were severable and did not affect the constitutionality of the rest of the Sarbanes-Oxley Act. It also rejected other challenges to the act. It held that the Securities and Exchange Commission is a "Department" under the meaning of the Appointments Clause, that the members of the Commission collectively constitute the head of the department for purposes of the Constitution, and that the members of the PCAOB are inferior officers whose appointment Congress may permissibly vest in a "Hea[d] of Departmen[t]" under Article II, Section 2, Clause 2.]

BREYER, J., dissenting, joined by STEVENS, J., GINSBURG, J., and SOTOMAYOR, J.:

[T]he restriction [at issue] directly limits, not the President's power, but the power of an already independent agency. . . . According to the Court, the President "is powerless to intervene" if he has determined that the Board members' "conduct merit[s] removal" because "[t]hat decision is vested instead in other tenured officers—the Commissioners—none of whom is subject to the President's direct control." But so long as the President is legitimately foreclosed from removing the Commissioners except for cause (as the majority assumes), nullifying the Commission's power to remove Board members only for cause will not resolve the problem the Court has identified: The President will still be "powerless to intervene" by removing the Board members if the Commission reasonably decides not to do so.

In other words, the Court fails to show why two layers of "for cause" protection—Layer One insulating the Commissioners from the President, and Layer Two insulating the Board from the Commissioners—impose any more serious limitation upon the President's powers than one layer. Consider the four scenarios that might arise:

1. The President and the Commission both want to keep a Board member in office. Neither layer is relevant.

2. The President and the Commission both want to dismiss a Board member. Layer Two stops them both from doing so without cause. The President's ability to remove the Commission (Layer One) is irrelevant, for he and the Commission are in agreement.

3. The President wants to dismiss a Board member, but the Commission wants to keep the member. Layer One allows the Commission to make that determination notwithstanding the President's contrary view. Layer Two is irrelevant because the Commission does not seek to remove the Board member.

4. The President wants to keep a Board member, but the Commission wants to dismiss the Board member. Here, Layer Two helps the President, for it hinders the Commission's ability to dismiss a Board member whom the President wants to keep in place.

Thus, the majority's decision to eliminate only Layer Two accomplishes virtually nothing. [What really matters is] the real-world nature of the President's relationship with the Commission. If the President confronts a Commission that seeks to resist his policy preferences—a distinct possibility when, as here, a Commission's membership must reflect both political parties,—the restriction on the Commission's ability to remove a Board member is either irrelevant (as in scenario 3) or may actually help the President (as in scenario 4). And if the President faces a Commission that seeks to implement his policy preferences, Layer One is irrelevant, for the President and Commission see eye to eye.

[T]he Court creates two alternative scenarios. In the first, the Commission and the President both want to remove a Board member, but have varying judgments as to whether they have good "cause" to do so—i.e., the President and the Commission both conclude that a Board member should be removed, but disagree as to whether that conclusion (which they have both reached) is reasonable. In the second, the President wants to remove a Board member and the Commission disagrees; [but instead tells the President that its hands are tied by the "for-cause" provisions.]

Both of these circumstances seem unusual. I do not know if they have ever occurred. But I do not deny their logical possibility. I simply doubt their importance. And the fact that, with respect to the President's power, the double layer of for-cause removal sometimes might help, sometimes might hurt, leads me to conclude that its overall effect is at most indeterminate. . . .

[Perhaps more important,] the statute provides the Commission with full authority and virtually comprehensive control over all of the Board's functions.

[I]f the President's control over the Commission is sufficient [for purposes of the Constitution], and the Commission's control over the Board is virtually absolute, then, as a practical matter, the President's control over the Board should prove sufficient as well.

[C]ongress and the President had good reason for enacting the challenged "for cause" provision. First and foremost, the Board adjudicates cases. This Court has long recognized the appropriateness of using "for cause" provisions to protect the personal independence of those who even only sometimes engage in adjudicatory functions. Indeed, as early as 1789 James Madison stated that "there may be strong reasons why an" executive "officer" such as the Comptroller of the United States "should not hold his office at the pleasure of the Executive branch" if one of his "principal dut[ies]" "partakes strongly of the judicial character." 1 Annals of Congress 611-612. . . .

Moreover, . . . the Accounting Board members supervise, and are themselves, technical professional experts. This Court has recognized that the "difficulties involved in the preparation of" sound auditing reports require the application of "scientific accounting principles." And this Court has recognized the constitutional legitimacy of a justification that rests agency independence upon the need for technical expertise. See *Humphrey's Executor*. [H]ere, the justification for insulating the "technical experts" on the Board from fear of losing their jobs due to political influence is particularly strong [because] the Accounting Board was created in response to "a series of celebrated accounting debacles." And historically, this regulatory subject matter—financial regulation—has been thought to exhibit a particular need for independence. . . .

[B]y . . . providing the Board with a revenue stream independent of the congressional appropriations process, [Congress] helped insulate the Board from congressional, as well as other, political influences. . . . [I]n a world in which we count on the Federal Government to regulate matters as complex as, say, nuclear-power production, the Court's assertion that we should simply learn to get by "without being" regulated "by experts" is, at best, unrealistic—at worst, dangerously so.

[Our] "separation-of-powers jurisprudence generally focuses on the danger of one branch's *aggrandizing its power* at the expense of another branch." . . . Congress here has "drawn" no power to itself to remove the Board members. It has instead sought to *limit* its own power, by, for example, providing the Accounting Board with a revenue stream independent of the congressional appropriations process. . . .

[E]ven if I assume that the majority categorically excludes the competitive service from the scope of its new rule, the exclusion would be insufficient . . . because the Court's "double for-cause" rule applies to appointees who are "inferior officer[s]." And who are they? Courts and scholars have struggled for more than a century to define the constitutional term "inferior officers," without much success. . . . The problem is not simply that the term "inferior officer" is indefinite but also that efforts to define it inevitably conclude that the term's sweep is unusually broad. Consider the Court's definitions: Inferior officers are, *inter alia,* (1) those charged with "the administration and enforcement of the public law;" (2) those granted "significant authority;" (3) those with "responsibility for conducting civil litigation in the courts of the United States;" and (4) those "who can be said to hold an office," that has been created either by "regulations" or by "statute." . . .

I see no way to avoid sweeping hundreds, perhaps thousands of high level government officials within the scope of the Court's holding, putting their job security and their administrative actions and decisions constitutionally at risk. To make even a conservative estimate, one would have to begin by listing federal departments, offices, bureaus and other agencies whose heads are by statute removable only "for cause." I have found 48 such agencies, Then it would be necessary to identify the senior officials in those agencies (just below the top) who themselves are removable only "for cause." I have identified 573 such high-ranking officials. They include most of the leadership of the Nuclear Regulatory Commission (including that agency's executive director as well as the directors of its Office of Nuclear Reactor Regulation and Office of Enforcement), virtually all of the leadership of the Social Security Administration, the executive directors of the Federal Energy Regulatory Commission and the Federal Trade Commission, as well as the general counsels of the Chemical Safety Board, the Federal Mine Safety and Health Review Commission, and the National Mediation Board.

[T]he potential list of those whom today's decision affects is yet larger [because] administrative law judges (ALJs) "are all executive officers." And ALJs are each removable "only for good cause established and determined by the Merit Systems Protection Board," But the members of the Merit Systems Protection Board are themselves protected from removal by the President absent good cause.

My research reflects that the Federal Government relies on 1,584 ALJs to adjudicate administrative matters in over 25 agencies. These ALJs adjudicate Social Security benefits, employment disputes, and other matters highly important to individuals. Does every losing party before an ALJ now have grounds to appeal on the basis that the decision entered against him is unconstitutional?

And what about the military? Commissioned military officers "are 'inferior officers.'" There are over 210,000 active-duty commissioned officers currently serving in the armed forces. And such officers can generally be so removed only by *other* commissioned officers, who themselves enjoy the same career protections.

The majority might simply say that the military is different. But it will have to explain *how* it is different. It is difficult to see why the Constitution would provide a President who is the military's "commander-in-chief," Art. II, §2, cl. 1, with *less* authority to remove "inferior" military "officers" than to remove comparable civil officials.

The majority sees "no reason . . . to address whether" any of "these positions," "or any others," might be deemed unconstitutional under its new rule, preferring instead to leave these matters for a future case. But what is to happen in the meantime? Is the work of all these various officials to be put on hold while the courts of appeals determine whether today's ruling applies to them? Will Congress have to act to remove the "for cause" provisions? Can the President then restore them via executive order? And, still, what about the military? A clearer line would help avoid these practical difficulties.

The majority asserts that its opinion will not affect the Government's ability to function while these many questions are litigated in the lower courts because the Court's holding concerns only "the conditions under which th[e]se officers might some day be removed." But this case was not brought by federal officials challenging their potential removal. It was brought by private individuals who were *subject to regulation* "*'here-and-now'*" and who "object to the" very "existence" of the regulators themselves. And those private individuals have prevailed. Thus, any person similarly regulated by a federal official who is potentially subject to the Court's amorphous new rule will be able to bring an "implied private right of action directly under the Constitution" "seeking . . . a declaratory judgment that" the official's actions are "unconstitutional and an injunction preventing the" official "from exercising [his] powers." Such a plaintiff need not even first exhaust his administrative remedies.

Nor is it clear that courts will always be able to cure such a constitutional defect merely by severing an offending removal provision. . . . [C]ourts called upon to resolve the many questions the majority's opinion raises [may have to] determine that the only available remedy to certain double for-cause problems is to invalidate entire agencies.

Thus, notwithstanding the majority's assertions to the contrary, the potential consequences of today's holding are worrying. The upshot, I believe, is a legal dilemma. To interpret the Court's decision as applicable only in a few circumstances will make the rule less harmful but arbitrary. To interpret the rule more broadly will make the rule more rational, but destructive.

Discussion

1. *Taking a good thing too far?* Justice Breyer tries to show that the Court's principle of decision does not realistically engage with the way that the federal government is actually structured, putting at risk large swaths of the administrative state and basic military structure. What would be your prediction as to whether the Court will use *Free Enterprise Fund* to drastically reshape the federal government? What principle limits the scope of the decision in a way that would not also legitimate the for-cause provisions struck down in this case?

2. *The "unitary executive" and presidential control of the Administration.* Behind debates over the principle of a "unitary executive" is the sprawling

character of the executive branch and the fact that many persons within it are practically beyond the control of the President and the advisers closest to him. Will the Court's new rule outlawing double (or triple) good-cause provisions significantly assist the President's control over the executive branch? The Court also emphasizes the importance of political accountability. Will the new rule actually make the President and the actions of the executive branch more accountable to the public? Is increased presidential control over every facet of the executive branch the best way to make Presidents accountable to the public and ensure that Presidents are faithful to the law? Justice Breyer emphasizes that where expertise is important or where executive branch officials engage in adjudication, it may be better to isolate them from the President's political ambitions. Consider in this light the debate over the independence of the Office of Legal Counsel during the Bush Administration and the debate over the so-called "Torture Memos" discussed in the Casebook at pp. 878-881.

Insert after note 1 on p. 836:

1a. *Why didn't Truman use the Taft-Hartley Act?* Note that instead of seizing the steel mills, President Truman could have sought an injunction to stop a labor strike, a course of action available to him under the 1947 Taft-Hartley Act. See Maeva Marcus, Truman and the Steel Seizure Case: The Limits of Presidential Power 77-78 (1994).

Nevertheless, Truman rejected the use of Taft-Hartley to resolve the crisis for several reasons. First, Truman had long been a supporter of (and supported by) organized labor; the Taft-Hartley Act was strongly opposed by labor and in fact had been passed over Truman's veto. Second, Truman believed that seeking a labor injunction was unfair to workers because it would freeze their wages in place and give management little incentive to bargain, thus in effect taking management's side over labor's. Third, Truman argued that the Taft-Hartley procedure did not allow an immediate injunction, and that invoking it would only delay the ultimate resolution of the dispute between labor and management. See Harry S Truman, Special Message to the Congress on the Steel Strike, June 10th, 1952, The American Presidency Project, at *http://www. presidency.ucsb.edu/ws/index.php?pid=14152.*

As Neal Devins and Louis Fisher explain, "[a]gainst this backdrop, Truman had a hard time convincing the nation that the steel seizure represented a national emergency instead of a labor dispute. . . . *Time* magazine accused Truman of acting 'primarily as a politician, not as a President . . . Politician Harry Truman was obviously operating on the axiom of political arithmetic that there are more votes in Big Labor than in Big Steel.' And the *Nation* argued that 'a just settlement of a labor dispute' is not enough to excuse the president's 'arbitrary exercise of executive power.'" Neal Devins & Louis Fisher, The Steel Seizure Case: One of a Kind?, 19 Const. Comm. 63, 67 (2002) (citing Marcus at 89-90).

In addition, by this point in his Presidency Truman was a very unpopular President, in large part due to the deeply unpopular Korean War, which Truman had used to justify the seizure in the first place. Truman had sent troops into Korea without a formal declaration of war. Although the public initially supported his action, Truman took much of the blame as the war dragged on. Devins and Fisher speculate that "[h]ad the nation supported Truman and his war, there would have been no public outcry following the seizure and, consequently, the courts would not have been pressured to check a runaway president. For example, had Truman seized the steel mills in 1950 (when the public stood behind his Korean initiative), the Supreme Court might well have looked for a way to avoid ruling against the president." *Id.* at 74. Do you agree?

Insert after note 11 on p. 841:

Note: The Libya Intervention

In mid-February 2011 a popular uprising began against the autocratic government of Colonel Muammar Qaddafi of Libya. Qaddafi used military force to attempt to end the protests, and a civil war ensued, with Qaddafi losing control of much of the eastern half of the country, including the city of Benghazi.

The Libyan government was reported to have bombed and strafed protesters and deliberately targeted civilians. Many refugees fled to Egypt and other neighboring countries to escape the violence. In March, Qaddafi prepared for an assault on Benghazi, a city of approximately 700,000 people, and threatened "no mercy and no pity" to anyone who resisted.

On March 12, The Arab League called for a no-fly zone in Libya. On March 17, the United Nations Security Council adopted Resolution 1973, which imposed a no-fly zone and called for the use of military force to protect civilians. See S.C. Res. 1973, U.N. Doc. S/RES/1973 (Mar. 17, 2011).

In response, on March 19, the United States along with its NATO allies launched airstrikes against Libyan targets to enforce Resolution 1973. President Obama provided a report to Congress on March 21, stating that no ground troops would be deployed.

Sometime around April 4, NATO took over leadership in maintaining the no-fly zone in Libya, and the United States adopted a supporting role. According to the Obama Administration, the United States provided surveillance and refueling for allied warplanes. The United States continued to fire missiles from unmanned drones; it also engaged in a relatively small percentage of manned air missions (approximately 10 percent) in proportion to the manned air missions by NATO forces.

Treating the March 21, 2011, report as the starting date of the introduction of American forces into hostilities, and assuming that the clock was not tolled by intervening events, the War Power Resolution's 60-day clock would have run out on May 20, 2011, and the 30-day extension to withdraw forces would have run out around June 18.

On June 15, the Obama Administration provided an explanation to Congress. It argued that the President had constitutional authority to begin the Libya operation without congressional approval:

> Given the important U.S. interests served by U.S. military operations in Libya and the limited nature, scope and duration of the anticipated actions, the President had constitutional authority, as Commander in Chief and Chief Executive and pursuant to his foreign affairs powers, to direct such limited military operations abroad.

"United States Activities in Libya," June 15, 2011, at *http://www.foreignpolicy. com/files/fp_uploaded_documents/110615_United_States_Activities_in_Li-bya_-_6_15_11.pdf.*
The Administration also argued that the Libya operation was in full compliance with the War Powers Resolution because the 60-day clock had stopped in early April, when American forces took a supporting role:

> The President is of the view that the current U.S. military operations in Libya are consistent with the War Powers Resolution and do not under that law require further congressional authorization, because U.S. military operations are distinct from the kind of "hostilities" contemplated by the Resolution's 60 day termination provision. U.S. forces are playing a constrained and supporting role in a multinational coalition, whose operations are both legitimated by and limited to the terms of a United Nations Security Council Resolution that authorizes the use of force solely to protect civilians and civilian populated areas under attack or threat of attack and to enforce a no-fly zone and an arms embargo. U.S. operations do not involve sustained fighting or active exchanges of fire with hostile forces, nor do they involve the presence of U.S. ground troops, U.S. casualties or a serious threat thereof, or any significant chance of escalation into a conflict characterized by those factors.

Discussion
Fighting in Libya ended in October 2011 following the death of Muammar Qaddafi. Congress debated but ultimately never authorized the Libya operation. In June 2011, the House of Representatives passed two resolutions. The first protested the operation and stated that "[t]he President shall not deploy, establish, or maintain the presence of units and members of the United States Armed Forces on the ground in Libya unless the purpose of the presence is to rescue a member of the Armed Forces from imminent danger." The second, added to an appropriations bill funding military construction and the Department of Veterans Affairs, stated that none of the money in the bill could be spent "in contravention of the War Powers Act." The Senate never passed a similar resolution, and congressional interest in the controversy lapsed following the end of the operation.
The question addressed in this note is whether congressional authorization was required, either under the Constitution or because of the War Powers Resolution.

1. *The constitutional issues.* Under the Constitution, did the Libya intervention require congressional approval?

Consider three positions. One position is that the President can use military force at his complete discretion whenever he likes. The Declare War clause is irrelevant to this decision; it means only that Congress has power to declare that war exists for purposes of international law. (In addition, under the General Welfare Clause, Congress also has the power to appropriate or refuse to appropriate funds for military actions.)

A second view would maintain that "declare war" in Article I, section 8, means "make war" or "engage in war" and hence whenever the President uses military force he must obtain congressional consent. This position must make an exception for serious emergencies but would otherwise restrict most presidential uses of armed forces abroad. In addition, Congress could give the President continuing advance authorization for emergencies; an example of such a statute is the early Militia Acts discussed in the *Prize Cases.*

A third position is closer to actual practice since World War II. It holds that the President, even without prior congressional authorization, has discretion to use military force in furtherance of American interests in at least two situations: The first are comparatively "minor" actions of brief duration and involving limited military intervention. The second are emergency situations where important American interests are at stake and there is no time for Congress to deliberate and approve military action in advance. In other cases, Congress must offer some kind of authorization of military force, which may or may not also include a formal declaration of war. Under this third reading, some (but not all) military actions constitute "war" within the meaning of the Declare War clause and therefore require congressional authorization, even if they do not require a formal declaration of war for purposes of international law and no such declaration ever occurs.

This textual argument creates its own difficulties. As Martin Lederman has pointed out, the Constitution also uses the term "war" in Article I, section 10, which provides that "No state shall, without the consent of Congress, . . . engage in a war, unless actually invaded, or in such imminent danger as will not admit of delay." Does this mean that the President must obtain congressional approval in all cases in which a state would have to obtain congressional approval to engage in "war"?

The answer is almost certainly no. Quite apart from the differences between "declare war" and "engage in a war," there are important structural differences between these two provisions. Article I, section 10, is designed to prevent the states, as much as possible, from interfering with (and causing problems for) a single national foreign policy. By contrast, the President generally takes the lead in shaping American foreign policy, and strategic use of military force may be an important element in conducting an effective foreign policy. Thus, the balance of powers between the President and Congress is designed to ensure *democratic accountability* for significant military interventions rather than to prevent meddlesome states from creating foreign policy crises. Hence, the question of "war" for purposes of Article I, section 10, concerns state interventions that might interfere with a unitary U.S. foreign and military policy, while the question of "war" for purposes of the Declare War Clause concerns those interventions that, for reasons of democratic accountability, both President and Congress should have to commit to.

Is the Libya intervention the sort of military action that constitutes "war" for purposes of the Constitution and therefore requires Congressional authorization?

In answering this question, consider three different questions: The first is whether the President faces an emergency that requires quick action so that there is insufficient time to obtain prior approval from Congress. In such a situation the President may employ significant military force in order to repel attacks or prevent a situation from spinning out of control.

The second question is the nature of the interests at stake—i.e., whether the situation threatens sufficiently important American interests. The third question is whether the military intervention is sufficiently serious to constitute "war" for purposes of the Constitution; this concerns, among other things, the nature of the force being used, the scope of the operation, its likely duration, and the extent to which American soldiers have been placed in harm's way.

The need for quick action. As to the first question, President Obama argued that immediate action was necessary given Qaddafi's threats of civilian massacre. The Libyan situation had developed over a few months and calls for a no-fly zone had been circulating for some time. However, the Arab League and the UN did not vote until the middle of March, at which point President Obama acted quickly without consulting Congress. Were there good diplomatic reasons for the President not to seek congressional authorization until the Arab League and the UN weighed in? If so, he might argue that there was insufficient time for congressional deliberations at that point.

The existence of vital American interests. As to the second question, President Obama was not responding to an attack on American soil, to threats of danger to Americans living abroad, to threats to American property, or to an attack on American allies. Instead, the President intervened in Libya in order to avoid a humanitarian disaster. By imposing a no-fly zone, NATO sought to limit Qaddafi's forces and weaken his military power so that he could not threaten or harm innocent civilians.

At a press conference on March 18, President Obama argued that the intervention promoted important American interests:

> Now, here is why this matters to us. Left unchecked, we have every reason to believe that Qaddafi would commit atrocities against his people. Many thousands could die. A humanitarian crisis would ensue. The entire region could be destabilized, endangering many of our allies and partners. The calls of the Libyan people for help would go unanswered. The democratic values that we stand for would be overrun. Moreover, the words of the international community would be rendered hollow.

Remarks by the President on the Situation in Libya (Mar. 18, 2011), at *http://www.whitehouse.gov/the-press-office/2011/03/18/remarks-president-situation-libya.*

Are these interests sufficient to justify presidential military intervention without congressional authorization? When the President uses force for humanitarian reasons rather than to protect American citizens, troops, or material interests, is there a greater reason to require congressional authorization, either before or immediately after the intervention begins? In an OLC opinion dated April 1, 2011, the Administration also argued that supporting the United Nations Security Council's "credibility and effectiveness" was another national interest. Is this sufficient justification under the circumstances?

The extent and scope of the intervention. The third question is whether the Libya intervention was sufficiently serious to amount to "war" under the Constitution and therefore required congressional authorization. (Note this is a different question from whether authorization is required under the statutory terms of the War Powers Resolution.)

In an OLC opinion dated April 1, 2011, the Administration argued that congressional authorization was not required under the Constitution because the operation was limited in three ways. Authority to Use Military Force in Libya, April 1, 2011, at *http://www.justice.gov/olc/2011/authority-military-use-in-libya.pdf.*

First, the OLC argued that the Libyan intervention involves airpower, not ground troops. Compared to airpower, the use of ground troops makes withdrawal difficult and hence tends to restrict Congress's options once the operation begins. Moreover, airpower limits the number and degree of casualties that can be inflicted on American soldiers. Second, the goals of the intervention are limited to enforcing the no-fly zone and preventing humanitarian disaster; they do not involve conquest of territory. Third, the bombing does not prepare the way for a later ground invasion, which reduces the risk that it will result in a sustained commitment.

The OLC memo also notes that "although the [War Powers Resolution] does not itself provide affirmative statutory authority for military operations, the Resolution's 'structure . . . recognizes and presupposes the existence of unilateral presidential authority to deploy armed forces' into hostilities or circumstances presenting an imminent risk of hostilities." The WPR requirement of a report within 48 hours and termination within 60 days "makes sense only if the President may introduce troops into hostilities or potential hostilities without prior authorization by the Congress."

What do you make of these arguments? Why does the fact that America uses a technology that (mostly) shields troops from harm mean that "war" is not occurring and that Congress need not approve the action? Does this mean that presidents can use long-range missiles, unmanned drones, and various forms of military robotics without engaging in "war"? Even if American troops face no immediate threat of reprisal, does this mean that no reprisals will be forthcoming, especially in the form of terrorist attacks and other forms of asymmetrical warfare?

Indeed, one might worry that the development of long-distance technologies that are likely to risk harm only to people who are not Americans might mean that ordinary democratic processes are no longer sufficient to check presidential ambitions or presidential adventurism. Because Americans will not return home in body bags, the President will feel freer to employ these technologies and intervene militarily in other parts of the world. Could this change in technology create some of the same problems that originally led the framers to require consultation with Congress before the country goes to war?

The Administration argued that the Libyan intervention was designed to be short term. If an intervention goes on for several months, at what point is the threshold crossed when Congress must authorize the action? (The War Powers Resolution, of course, has its own standards on this question, as discussed below.).

2. *The constitutionality of the War Powers Resolution (again).* Although most Administrations have taken the position that Congress may not end presidential involvement through a joint resolution that is not subject to a presidential veto, this constitutional objection does not apply to the rest of the War Powers Resolution. The Obama Administration, relying on a 1980 Office of Legal Counsel opinion, has assumed that the 60-day requirement of the War Powers Act is constitutional. See *Presidential Power to Use the Armed Forces Abroad Without Statutory Authorization*, 4A Op. O.L.C. 185, 196 (1980), and has stated that it is committed "to acting consistently with both the Constitution and the War Powers Resolution" in testimony before Congress. Testimony by Legal Adviser Harold Hongju Koh, U.S. Department of State, on Libya and War Powers Before the Senate Foreign Relations Committee June 28, 2011, at *http:// foreign.senate.gov/imo/media/doc/Koh_Testimony.pdf.* Thus the Administration also considered whether the Libya intervention was consistent with the 60-day requirement.

3. *The interpretation of the War Powers Resolution.* Section 4(a)(1) of the WPR requires the President to report to Congress "in any case in which United States Armed Forces are introduced . . . into hostilities or into situations where imminent involvement in hostilities is clearly indicated by the circumstances." Section 5(b) states that "[w]ithin sixty calendar days after a report is submitted or is required to be submitted pursuant to section 4(a)(1), whichever is earlier, the President shall terminate any use of United States Armed Forces with respect to which such report was submitted (or required to be submitted)."

The Obama Administration's position is that this "use of United States Armed Forces" ended on April 4, because after that date the United States role was greatly reduced and essentially supported NATO operations.

Testifying before Congress, State Department Legal Adviser Harold Koh argued that "the operative term 'hostilities,' is an ambiguous standard" which must be developed case by case through inter-branch dialogue in light of changing circumstances that the drafters could not have foreseen. However, as a general matter, "the Executive Branch understands the term 'to mean a situation in which units of the U.S. armed forces are actively engaged in exchanges of fire with opposing units of hostile forces.'" Koh Testimony at 4-5.

Koh offered a four-part test to determine whether "hostilities" exist, looking to the nature of the mission, the degree of exposure of American armed forces, the risk of escalation, and the type of military means used. *Id.* at 7-10. He argued that the nature of the mission was limited because it was approved by the United Nations Security Council for limited goals, led by NATO, not the United States, and enjoyed broad international support. The exposure of U.S. forces was limited because since the handoff to NATO, U.S. do not "involve active exchanges of fire with hostile forces, and members of our military have not been involved in significant armed confrontations or sustained confrontations of any kind with hostile forces." The risk of escalation was limited because there are no ground troops or "any significant chance" that ground troops would be deployed in the future. The military means are limited because "the violence that U.S. armed forces have directly inflicted or facilitated after the handoff to NATO has been modest in terms of its frequency, intensity, and severity." Only a small percentage of strikes have been by Americans: "American strikes have been confined, on an as-needed basis, to the suppression of enemy air defenses to enforce the no-fly zone, and to limited strikes by Predator unmanned aerial vehicles against discrete targets in support of the civilian protection mission; since the handoff to NATO, the total number of U.S. munitions dropped has been a tiny fraction of the number dropped in Kosovo." *Id.* at 11.

Koh argued that the four factors, taken together, created an "unusual" situation that did not constitute "hostilities" within the meaning of the WPR: "Had any of these elements been absent in Libya, or present in different degrees, a different legal conclusion might have been drawn." *Id.*

In considering this balance of factors, why does the switch to unmanned drones increase the chances that "hostilities" have ended? One possible reason is that "hostilities" require more or less continuous exchanges of fire between combatants. As long as unmanned drones are doing most of the killing, and American troops are not being fired at, or only being attacked intermittently, there are no hostilities. The use of drones, moreover, means that American involvement can be ended easily, unlike the use of ground troops.

This statutory argument, however, recapitulates the constitutional issues discussed above: the fact that an aggressor is not vulnerable does not mean that there are no hostilities occurring. Such a reading would give presidents incentives to use remote-control weapons and make increased investments in missiles, unmanned drones and robotics in order to get around the 60-day limitation. Is this a good thing or a bad thing, given the purposes of the War Powers Resolution?

Note, however, that under Koh's "balancing" approach, if the amount, intensity, or duration of bombing was significantly different, there might well be "hostilities" within the meaning of the War Powers Resolution. In particular, the Administration stopped short of claiming that the use of remote-control weaponry could never constitute "hostilities" under the War Powers Resolution: it asserted only that it did not constitute "hostilities" in the circumstances presented. Does the proposed balancing test make it too difficult to tell whether the President is complying with the War Powers Resolution, or is the real problem the use of an open-ended term like "hostilities"?

The War Powers Resolution was drafted in light of the experience of the Vietnam War: a large commitment of ground troops that was difficult to extricate once operations had begun. Yet military technology and military strategy have changed in the interim. How should we interpret the War Powers Resolution in interventions that primarily involve long-distance warfare like drones or robotics? Consider the possibility that the War Powers Resolution, designed for Vietnam-style conflicts, is technologically outmoded and must be redrafted to take into account these changed realities.

Consider, for example, the problem of cyberattacks, where belligerents seek to use the Internet to destroy infrastructural capacities, or in the alternative, seek to exploit computers (and the resources these computers control) in other countries. Do cyberattacks count as "hostilities" under the WPR? How should the WPR be redrafted to account for them?

Another difficulty stems from the fact that the United States is working with NATO. Whether or not American activities constitute "hostilities," the collective actions of NATO—which include bombing raids by manned aircraft—surely do. NATO's supreme allied commander is an American admiral, and other members of the U.S. armed forces work in NATO. In addition, the United States is heavily funding the military effort. In short, the U.S. is doing a lot of what would ordinarily constitute "hostilities" in a coordinated multinational effort; but foreign troops are doing the shooting, and, as a consequence, are exposed to most of the enemy fire. Does this mean that the U.S. is no longer engaged in "hostilities," or rather, does it mean that the U.S. is enmeshed even more deeply into NATO's hostilities?

Two different parts of the War Powers Resolution seem to point in opposite directions on this question. On the one hand, Section 8(c) of the War Powers Resolution provides that "the term 'introduction of United States Armed Forces' includes the assignment of members of such armed forces to command, coordinate, participate in the movement of, or accompany the regular or irregular military forces of any foreign country or government when such military forces are engaged, or there exists an imminent threat that such forces will become engaged, in hostilities." Does the language of Section 8(c) mean that the introduction of American forces into hostilities did not cease on April 4 but continues as long as American officers are commanding, directing, coordinating, or accompanying part of the NATO effort? Ready broadly enough, 8(c) might invoke the WPR 60-day clock as long as a single American soldier is working for NATO. Is there a narrower way to read the statute?

By contrast, Section 8(b) seems to grandfather in certain types of operations. It provides that: "Nothing in this joint resolution shall be construed to require any further specific statutory authorization to permit members of United States Armed Forces to participate jointly with members of the armed forces of one or more foreign countries in the headquarters operations of high-level military commands which were established prior to the date of enactment of this joint resolution and pursuant to the United Nations Charter or any treaty ratified by the United States prior to such date." Which provision, 8(b) or 8(c), should control in the case of Libya?

4. *So what?* Even if the Libya intervention went beyond presidential power or violated the War Powers Resolution, it is not clear that these issues could be challenged in court. In *Raines v. Byrd*, 521 U.S. 811 (1997), the Supreme Court held that Congressmen and Senators did not have standing as legislators to challenge the constitutionality of a line-time-veto bill. In *Campbell v. Clinton*, 203 F.3d 19, 21 (D.C. Cir. 2000), cert. denied, 531 U.S. 815 (2000), which relied on *Raines v. Byrd*, the D.C. Circuit rejected the standing of congressmen to challenge President Clinton's intervention in Kosovo. (Note that, even if one gets past the standing question, one must also show that the constitutional and statutory questions are not political questions. Even if the constitutional question involves a political question, why would the application of a statute like the War Powers Resolution be non-justiciable?)

5. *Political remedies and collective action problems.* Even if members of Congress lack standing to challenge military operations like the Libya intervention, that does not mean that there is no constitutional or legal remedy. As the Court noted in *Raines*, the most likely remedy comes from the political process. Congress can attempt to pass legislation over the President's veto requiring that he end the intervention. Congress can refuse to appropriate funding for the intervention and it can refuse to allow existing funds to be used for the intervention. And, of course, if all else fails, Congress can threaten to impeach the President or threaten to hold up other legislation that the President wants passed.

It may not even be necessary for Congress to pass new legislation to have an effect. Pressure exercised through resolutions by one House or a joint resolution by both Houses may strongly signal to the President that the country is not behind him, that he is in violation of the law, and that he should end the intervention quickly. Congress can also use public debates and hearings to shape public opinion against an intervention, although usually not as effectively as the President can. (As noted above, the House passed two resolutions of disapproval in June 2011, which led to Legal Adviser Koh's testimony explaining the Administration's position.)

Nevertheless, political remedies face political obstacles. Congress as a whole has incentives to sit on its hands and wait to see whether a military mission is successful or not. That is because Congress as a whole is composed of individual Congressmen and Senators, who have various incentives to avoid responsibility. Congressmen and Senators, especially those who may consider running for President some day, do not want to guess wrong about military operations. If a candidate takes a strong stand against an intervention that goes well, this will be used against the candidate later. Conversely, as Hillary Clinton discovered in the 2008 presidential campaign, supporting a war that later becomes unpopular can undermine a candidate's political support.

As a result of these pressures, Congress may adopt a position of what we might call belligerent acquiescence: while individual members denounce the

Administration, measures designed either to approve or to hinder a presidential intervention are difficult to pass.

In addition, quite apart from its tendencies toward inertia, the Congress has incentives not to undermine organizations like NATO whose effectiveness serves the long-term interests of the United States. If Congress believes that defunding the intervention would destroy NATO's future credibility, or the credibility of the United States within NATO, it may do nothing.

These considerations help explain why Congress decided to create the decisional structure of the War Powers Resolution. If Congress does nothing, the President must end an intervention after 60 days. Does this shifting of the default rule better serve American interests?

Note that since the passage of the War Powers Act, Congress has authorized major operations in the Gulf and Iraq wars. Other military operations since 1973 have, for the most part, either been relatively brief (so that they fall within the 60-day period) or relatively inconsequential. The most interesting contrary example before the Libya intervention was President Clinton's decision to bomb Kosovo in 1999. The Kosovo intervention was also performed in conjunction with NATO, and it was also justified largely on humanitarian grounds. Ultimately, the Clinton Administration argued that Congress had retroactively authorized the intervention because of a subsequent appropriations measure. The Kosovo example shows why Congress is in a difficult situation; if Congress funds an ongoing mission to maintain the credibility of the United States or NATO, or to avoid a military disaster, the President may use this as evidence of implicit congressional approval.

Note, however, that many members of Congress might want to have it both ways. They might want to assert that the President has gone beyond the 60-day limit and is acting illegally but they might not want to force the President to end an intervention that has already begun. As a result, Congress does nothing, or, as in the Kosovo case, provides appropriations. Does this mean that the 60-day clock is a bad idea? Would another model make more sense?

Insert before section 3 at p. 871:

BOUMEDIENE v. BUSH
553 U.S. 723 (2008)

Justice KENNEDY delivered the opinion of the Court.

Petitioners are aliens designated as enemy combatants and detained at the United States Naval Station at Guantanamo Bay, Cuba. . . . After *Hamdi* [*v. Rumsfeld*], the Deputy Secretary of Defense established Combatant Status Review Tribunals (CSRTs) to determine whether individuals detained at Guantanamo were "enemy combatants," . . . . Some of these individuals were apprehended on the battlefield in Afghanistan, others in places as far away from there as Bosnia and Gambia. All are foreign nationals, but none is a citizen of a nation now at war with the United States. Each denies he is a member of the al Qaeda terrorist network that carried out the September 11 attacks or of the Taliban regime that provided sanctuary for al Qaeda.

Each petitioner appeared before a separate CSRT; was determined to be an enemy combatant; and has sought a writ of habeas corpus in the United States District Court for the District of Columbia. . . . While appeals were pending from the District Court decisions, Congress passed the DTA. Subsection (e) of §1005 of the DTA amended 28 U.S.C. §2241 to provide that no court, justice, or judge shall have jurisdiction to hear or consider . . . an application for a writ of habeas corpus filed by or on behalf of an alien detained by the Department of Defense at Guantanamo Bay, Cuba. 119 Stat. 2742. Section 1005 further provides that the Court of Appeals for the District of Columbia Circuit shall have "exclusive" jurisdiction to review decisions of the CSRTs.

In *Hamdan v. Rumsfeld,* 548 U.S. 557 (2006), the Court held this provision did not apply to cases (like petitioners') pending when the DTA was enacted. Congress responded by passing [section 7 of the Military Commissions Act (MCA)], which provides that:

> (1) No court, justice, or judge shall have jurisdiction to hear or consider an application for a writ of habeas corpus filed by or on behalf of an alien detained by the United States who has been determined by the United States to have been properly detained as an enemy combatant or is awaiting such determination.

> (2) Except as provided in [§§1005(e)(2) and (e)(3) of the DTA] no court, justice, or judge shall have jurisdiction to hear or consider any other action against the United States or its agents relating to any aspect of the detention, transfer, treatment, trial, or conditions of confinement of an alien who is or was detained by the United States and has been determined by the United States to have been properly detained as an enemy combatant or is awaiting such determination./EXT

[28 U.S.C.A. §2241(e) (Supp. 2007)]

Section 7(b) of the MCA provides [that it] "shall take effect on the date of the enactment of this Act, and shall apply to all cases, without exception, pending on or after the date of the enactment of this Act which relate to any aspect of the detention, transfer, treatment, trial, or conditions of detention of an alien detained by the United States since September 11, 2001."

[T]he MCA was a direct response to *Hamdan*'s holding that the DTA's jurisdiction-stripping provision had no application to pending cases. . . . [T]he MCA deprives the federal courts of jurisdiction to entertain the habeas corpus actions now before us [so that if the statute is valid, petitioners' cases must be dismissed.]

III

[P]rotection for the privilege of habeas corpus was one of the few safeguards of liberty specified in a Constitution that, at the outset, had no Bill of Rights. . . . The Framers viewed freedom from unlawful restraint as a fundamental precept of liberty, and they understood the writ of habeas corpus as a vital instrument to secure that freedom. Experience taught, however, that the common-law writ all too often had been insufficient to guard against the abuse of monarchial power. That history counseled the necessity for specific language in the Constitution to secure the writ and ensure its place in our legal system. . . . It no doubt confirmed their view that pendular swings to and away from individual liberty were endemic to undivided, uncontrolled power. The Framers' inherent distrust of governmental power was the driving force behind the constitutional plan that allocated powers among three independent branches. This design serves not only to make Government accountable but also to secure individual liberty. Because the Constitution's separation-of-powers structure, like the substantive guarantees of the Fifth and Fourteenth Amendments, see *Yick Wo v. Hopkins,* 118 U.S. 356 (1886), protects persons as well as citizens, foreign nationals who have the privilege of litigating in our courts can seek to enforce separation-of-powers principles, see, *e.g., INS v. Chadha,* 462 U.S. 919 (1983).

[I]n our own system the Suspension Clause is designed to protect against . . . cyclical abuses [of power]. The Clause protects the rights of the detained by a means consistent with the essential design of the Constitution. It ensures that, except during periods of formal suspension, the Judiciary will have a time-tested device, the writ, to maintain the "delicate balance of governance" that is itself the surest safeguard of liberty. The Clause protects the rights of the detained by affirming the duty and authority of the Judiciary to call the jailer to account. The separation-of-powers doctrine, and the history that influenced its design, therefore must inform the reach and purpose of the Suspension Clause.

[T]he specific question before us [is] whether foreign nationals, apprehended and detained in distant countries during a time of serious threats to our Nation's security, may assert the privilege of the writ and seek its protection. The Court has been careful not to foreclose the possibility that the protections of the Suspension Clause have expanded along with post-1789 developments that define the present scope of the writ. See *INS v. St. Cyr,* 533 U.S. 289 (2001). But . . . "at the absolute minimum" the Clause protects the writ as it existed when the Constitution was drafted and ratified.

[T]he Government argues the common-law writ ran only to those territories over which the Crown was sovereign. Petitioners argue that jurisdiction followed the King's officers. Diligent search by all parties reveals no certain conclusions [about whether] a common-law court would or would not have granted, or refused to hear for lack of jurisdiction, a petition for a writ of habeas corpus brought by a prisoner deemed an enemy combatant, under a standard like the one the Department of Defense has used in these cases, and when held in a territory, like Guantanamo, over which the Government has total military and civil control. . . . [E]vidence as to the geographic scope of the writ at common law informative, but, again, not dispositive. Petitioners argue the site of their detention is analogous to two territories outside of England to which the writ did run: the so-called "exempt jurisdictions," like the Channel Islands; and (in former times) India [but these are not precisely analogous.] The Government argues . . . that Guantanamo is more closely analogous to Scotland and Hanover, territories that were not part of England but nonetheless controlled by the English monarch (in his separate capacities as King of Scotland and Elector of Hanover). [However] the common-law courts' refusal to issue the writ to these places [may have been] motivated [by] "prudential concerns."

Each side . . . argues that the very lack of a precedent on point supports its position, [but this assumes] that the historical record is complete and that the common law, if properly understood, yields a definite answer to the questions before us. [G]iven the unique status of Guantanamo Bay and the particular dangers of terrorism in the modern age, the common-law courts simply may not have confronted cases with close parallels to this one. We decline, therefore, to infer too much, one way or the other, from the lack of historical evidence on point. Cf. *Brown v. Board of Education,* 347 U.S. 483, 489, 74 S. Ct. 686, 98 L. Ed. 873 (1954) (noting evidence concerning the circumstances surrounding the adoption of the Fourteenth Amendment, discussed in the parties' briefs and uncovered through the Court's own investigation, "convince us that, although these sources cast some light, it is not enough to resolve the problem with which we are faced. At best, they are inconclusive"); *Reid v. Covert,* 354 U.S. 1 (1957) (Frankfurter, J., concurring in result) (arguing constitutional adjudication should not be based upon evidence that is "too episodic, too meager, to form a solid basis in history, preceding and contemporaneous with the framing of the Constitution").

IV

[T]he Government says the Suspension Clause affords petitioners no rights because the United States does not claim sovereignty over the place of detention. [We] do not question the Government's position that Cuba, not the United States, maintains sovereignty, in the legal and technical sense of the term, over Guantanamo Bay. [But] it is not altogether uncommon for a territory to be under the *de jure* sovereignty of one nation, while under the plenary control, or practical sovereignty, of another. This condition can occur when the territory is seized during war, as Guantanamo was during the Spanish-American War. . . . Accordingly, for purposes of our analysis, we accept the Government's position that Cuba, and not the United States, retains *de jure* sovereignty over Guantanamo Bay. As we did in *Rasul,* however, we take notice of the obvious and uncontested fact that the United States, by virtue of its complete jurisdiction and control over the base, maintains *de facto* sovereignty over this territory.

[We do not] accept the Government's premise that *de jure* sovereignty is the touchstone of habeas corpus jurisdiction. . . . The Court has discussed the issue of the Constitution's extraterritorial application on many occasions. These decisions undermine the Government's argument that, at least as applied to noncitizens, the Constitution necessarily stops where *de jure* sovereignty ends.

[F]undamental questions regarding the Constitution's geographic scope first arose at the dawn of the 20th century when the Nation acquired noncontiguous Territories: Puerto Rico, Guam, and the Philippines—ceded to the United States by Spain at the conclusion of the Spanish-American War—and Hawaii—annexed by the United States in 1898. At this point Congress chose to discontinue its previous practice of extending constitutional rights to the territories by statute. In a series of opinions later known as the Insular Cases, the Court addressed whether the Constitution, by its own force, applies in any territory that is not a State. The Court held that the Constitution has independent force in these territories, a force not contingent upon acts of legislative grace. Yet it took note of the difficulties inherent in that position. [T]he former Spanish colonies operated under a civil-law system, without experience in the various aspects of the Anglo-American legal tradition, for instance the use of grand and petit juries. At least with regard to the Philippines, a complete transformation of the prevailing legal culture would have been not only disruptive but also unnecessary, as the United States intended to grant independence to that Territory. . . . These considerations resulted in the doctrine of territorial incorporation, under which the Constitution applies in full in incorporated Territories surely destined for statehood but only in part in unincorporated Territories.

Practical considerations likewise influenced the Court's analysis a half-century later in *Reid* [*v. Covert,* 354 U.S. 1 (1957)]. The petitioners there, spouses of American servicemen, lived on American military bases in England and Japan. They were charged with crimes committed in those countries and tried before military courts . . . Because the petitioners were not themselves military personnel, they argued they were entitled to trial by jury. [The] plurality[] conclu[ded] that the Fifth and Sixth Amendments apply to American civilians tried outside the United States. But practical considerations, related not to the petitioners' [U.S.] citizenship but to the place of their confinement and trial, were relevant to each Member of the *Reid* majority. And to Justices Harlan and Frankfurter (whose [concurring] votes were necessary to the Court's disposition) these considerations were the decisive factors in the case.

Practical considerations weighed heavily as well in *Johnson v. Eisentrager,* 339 U.S. 763 (1950), where the Court addressed whether habeas corpus jurisdiction extended to enemy aliens who had been convicted of violating the laws of war. The prisoners were detained at Landsberg Prison in Germany during the Allied Powers' postwar occupation. The Court stressed the difficulties of ordering the Government to produce the prisoners in a habeas corpus proceeding. . . . In considering these factors the Court sought to balance the constraints of military occupation with constitutional necessities.

True, the Court in *Eisentrager* denied access to the writ, and it noted the prisoners "at no relevant time were within any territory over which the United States is sovereign, and [that] the scenes of their offense, their capture, their trial and their punishment were all beyond the territorial jurisdiction of any court of the United States." The Government seizes upon this language as proof positive that the *Eisentrager* Court adopted a formalistic, sovereignty-based test for determining the reach of the Suspension Clause. [But] [w]e reject this reading [because] practical considerations were integral to [its holding], because the United States lacked both *de jure* sovereignty and plenary control over Landsberg Prison, [and because such a reading] would have marked not only a change in, but a complete repudiation of, the Insular Cases' (and later *Reid*'s) functional approach to questions of extraterritoriality. . . . Nothing in *Eisentrager* says that *de jure* sovereignty is or has ever been the only relevant consideration in determining the geographic reach of the Constitution or of habeas corpus. [W]e see . . . a common thread uniting the Insular Cases, *Eisentrager,* and *Reid:* the idea that questions of extraterritoriality turn on objective factors and practical concerns, not formalism.

B

The Government's formal sovereignty-based test raises troubling separation-of-powers concerns as well. The political history of Guantanamo illustrates the deficiencies of this approach. The United States has maintained complete and uninterrupted control of the bay for over 100 years. . . . Yet the Government's view is that the Constitution [has] had no effect there, at least as to noncitizens, because the United States disclaimed sovereignty in the formal sense of the term. The necessary implication of the argument is that by surrendering formal sovereignty over any unincorporated territory to a third party, while at the same time entering into a lease that grants total control over the territory back to the United States, it would be possible for the political branches to govern without legal constraint.

Our basic charter cannot be contracted away like this. The Constitution grants Congress and the President the power to acquire, dispose of, and govern territory, not the power to decide when and where its terms apply. Even when the United States acts outside its borders, its powers are not "absolute and unlimited" but are subject "to such restrictions as are expressed in the Constitution. [T]o hold the political branches have the power to switch the Constitution on or off at will . . . would permit a striking anomaly in our tripartite system of government, leading to a regime in which Congress and the President, not this Court, say "what the law is." *Marbury v. Madison,* 1 Cranch 137 (1803).

These concerns have particular bearing upon the Suspension Clause question in the cases now before us, for the writ of habeas corpus is itself an indispensable mechanism for monitoring the separation of powers. The test for determining the scope of this provision must not be subject to manipulation by those whose power it is designed to restrain.

C

Based on . . . *Eisentrager,* and the reasoning in our other extraterritoriality opinions, we conclude that at least three factors are relevant in determining the reach of the Suspension Clause: (1) the citizenship and status of the detainee and the adequacy of the process through which that status determination was made; (2) the nature of the sites where apprehension and then detention took place; and (3) the practical obstacles inherent in resolving the prisoner's entitlement to the writ.

Applying this framework, we note at the onset that the status of these detainees is a matter of dispute. The petitioners, like those in *Eisentrager,* are not American citizens. But the petitioners in *Eisentrager* did not contest, it seems, the Court's assertion that they were "enemy alien[s]." In the instant cases, by contrast, the detainees deny they are enemy combatants. They have been afforded some process in CSRT proceedings to determine their status; but, unlike in *Eisentrager,* there has been no trial by military commission for violations of the laws of war. In comparison the procedural protections afforded to the detainees in the CSRT hearings are far more limited, and, we conclude, fall well short of the procedures and adversarial mechanisms that would eliminate the need for habeas corpus review.

[S]econd, the detainees here are similarly situated to the *Eisentrager* petitioners in that the sites of their apprehension and detention are technically outside the sovereign territory of the United States. [But] [u]nlike its present control over the naval station, the United States' control over the prison in Germany was neither absolute nor indefinite. Like all parts of occupied Germany, the prison was under the jurisdiction of the combined Allied Forces. . . . The Allies had not planned a long-term occupation of Germany, nor did they intend to displace all German institutions even during the period of occupation. . . . Guantanamo Bay, on the other hand, is no transient possession. In every practical sense Guantanamo is not abroad; it is within the constant jurisdiction of the United States.

As to the third factor, we recognize, as the Court did in *Eisentrager,* that there are costs to holding the Suspension Clause applicable in a case of military detention abroad. Habeas corpus proceedings may require expenditure of funds by the Government and may divert the attention of military personnel from other pressing tasks. While we are sensitive to these concerns, we do not find them dispositive. Compliance with any judicial process requires some incremental expenditure of resources. Yet civilian courts and the Armed Forces have functioned along side each other at various points in our history. The Government presents no credible arguments that the military mission at Guantanamo would be compromised if habeas corpus courts had jurisdiction to hear the detainees' claims. And in light of the plenary control the United States asserts over the base, none are apparent to us. The situation in *Eisentrager* was far different, given the historical context and nature of the military's mission in post-War Germany. . . . In retrospect the post-War occupation may seem uneventful. But at the time *Eisentrager* was decided, the Court was right to be concerned about judicial interference with the military's efforts to contain "enemy elements, guerilla fighters, and 'were-wolves.'" Similar threats are not apparent here; nor does the Government argue that they are. The United States

Naval Station at Guantanamo Bay consists of 45 square miles of land and water. The base has been used, at various points, to house migrants and refugees temporarily. At present, however, other than the detainees themselves, the only long-term residents are American military personnel, their families, and a small number of workers. At present, dangerous as they may be if released, they are contained in a secure prison facility located on an isolated and heavily fortified military base.

[I]t is true that before today the Court has never held that noncitizens detained by our Government in territory over which another country maintains *de jure* sovereignty have any rights under our Constitution. But the cases before us lack any precise historical parallel. They involve individuals detained by executive order for the duration of a conflict that, if measured from September 11, 2001, to the present, is already among the longest wars in American history. See Oxford Companion to American Military History 849 (1999). The detainees, moreover, are held in a territory that, while technically not part of the United States, is under the complete and total control of our Government. Under these circumstances the lack of a precedent on point is no barrier to our holding.

We hold that Art. I, §9, cl. 2, of the Constitution has full effect at Guantanamo Bay. If the privilege of habeas corpus is to be denied to the detainees now before us, Congress must act in accordance with the requirements of the Suspension Clause. The MCA does not purport to be a formal suspension of the writ; and the Government, in its submissions to us, has not argued that it is. Petitioners, therefore, are entitled to the privilege of habeas corpus to challenge the legality of their detention.

V

[T]he Government submits there has been compliance with the Suspension Clause because the DTA review process in the Court of Appeals, see DTA §1005(e), provides an adequate substitute. [I]n the ordinary course we would remand to the Court of Appeals to consider this question in the first instance. [But] [t]he gravity of the separation-of-powers issues raised by these cases and the fact that these detainees have been denied meaningful access to a judicial forum for a period of years render these cases exceptional. . . . And, given there are few precedents addressing what features an adequate substitute for habeas corpus must contain, in all likelihood a remand simply would delay ultimate resolution of the issue by this Court.

A

Congress has taken [care] throughout our Nation's history to preserve the writ and its function. Indeed, most of the major legislative enactments pertaining to habeas corpus have acted not to contract the writ's protection but to expand it or to hasten resolution of prisoners' claims. . . . [T]he DTA and the MCA . . . were intended to circumscribe habeas review. Congress' purpose is evident . . . from the unequivocal nature of MCA §7's jurisdiction-stripping language. [T]he Court of Appeals has jurisdiction not to inquire into the legality of the detention generally but only to assess whether the CSRT complied with the "standards and procedures specified by the Secretary of Defense" and whether those standards and procedures are lawful. [M]oreover, there has been no effort to preserve habeas corpus review as an avenue of last resort.

No saving clause exists in either the MCA or the DTA. And MCA §7 eliminates habeas review for these petitioners.

[T]he DTA should be interpreted to accord some latitude to the Court of Appeals to fashion procedures necessary to make its review function a meaningful one, but, if congressional intent is to be respected, the procedures adopted cannot be as extensive or as protective of the rights of the detainees as they would be in a §2241 [habeas] proceeding. Otherwise there would have been no, or very little, purpose for enacting the DTA. [T]he legislative history confirms what the plain text strongly suggests: In passing the DTA Congress did not intend to create a process that differs from traditional habeas corpus process in name only. It intended to create a more limited procedure. See, e.g., 151 Cong. Rec. S14263 (Dec. 21, 2005) (statement of Sen. Graham) (noting that the DTA "extinguish[es] these habeas and other actions in order to effect a transfer of jurisdiction over these cases to the DC Circuit Court" and agreeing that the bill "create[s] in their place a very limited judicial review of certain military administrative decisions"); id., at S14268 (statement of Sen. Kyl) ("It is important to note that the limited judicial review authorized by paragraphs 2 and 3 of subsection (e) [of DTA §1005] are not habeas-corpus review. It is a limited judicial review of its own nature").

[W]e do not endeavor to offer a comprehensive summary of the requisites for an adequate substitute for habeas corpus. We do consider it uncontroversial, however, that the privilege of habeas corpus entitles the prisoner to a meaningful opportunity to demonstrate that he is being held pursuant to "the erroneous application or interpretation" of relevant law. And the habeas court must have the power to order the conditional release of an individual unlawfully detained—though release need not be the exclusive remedy and is not the appropriate one in every case in which the writ is granted. [D]epending on the circumstances, more may be required. . . .

Petitioners identify what they see as myriad deficiencies in the CSRTs. The most relevant for our purposes are the constraints upon the detainee's ability to rebut the factual basis for the Government's assertion that he is an enemy combatant. [A]t the CSRT stage the detainee has limited means to find or present evidence to challenge the Government's case against him. He does not have the assistance of counsel and may not be aware of the most critical allegations that the Government relied upon to order his detention. See App. to Pet. for Cert. in No. 06-1196, at 156, F(8) (noting that the detainee can access only the "unclassified portion of the Government Information). The detainee can confront witnesses that testify during the CSRT proceedings. But given that there are in effect no limits on the admission of hearsay evidence—the only requirement is that the tribunal deem the evidence "relevant and helpful,"—the detainee's opportunity to question witnesses is likely to be more theoretical than real.

The Government defends the CSRT process, arguing that it was designed to conform to the procedures suggested by the plurality in *Hamdi*. [But] [n]one of the parties in *Hamdi* argued there had been a suspension of the writ. [T]he Court had no occasion to define the necessary scope of habeas review, for Suspension Clause purposes, in the context of enemy combatant detentions. The closest the plurality came to doing so was in discussing whether, in light of separation-of-powers concerns, §2241 should be construed to forbid the District Court from inquiring beyond the affidavit Hamdi's custodian provided in answer to the detainee's habeas petition. The plurality answered this question with an emphatic "no."

[A]lthough we make no judgment as to whether the CSRTs, as currently constituted, satisfy due process standards, we agree with petitioners that, even when all the parties involved in this process act with diligence and in good faith, there is considerable risk of error in the tribunal's findings of fact. This is a risk inherent in any process that, in the words of the former Chief Judge of the Court of Appeals, is "closed and accusatorial." And given that the consequence of error may be detention of persons for the duration of hostilities that may last a generation or more, this is a risk too significant to ignore.

For the writ of habeas corpus, or its substitute, to function as an effective and proper remedy in this context, the court that conducts the habeas proceeding must have the means to correct errors that occurred during the CSRT proceedings. This includes some authority to assess the sufficiency of the Government's evidence against the detainee. It also must have the authority to admit and consider relevant exculpatory evidence that was not introduced during the earlier proceeding. . . . Consistent with the historic function and province of the writ, habeas corpus review may be more circumscribed if the underlying detention proceedings are more thorough than they were here. . . . The extent of the showing required of the Government in these cases is a matter to be determined. We need not explore it further at this stage. We do hold that when the judicial power to issue habeas corpus properly is invoked the judicial officer must have adequate authority to make a determination in light of the relevant law and facts and to formulate and issue appropriate orders for relief, including, if necessary, an order directing the prisoner's release.

The DTA does not explicitly empower the Court of Appeals to order the applicant in a DTA review proceeding released should the court find that the standards and procedures used at his CSRT hearing were insufficient to justify detention. [Nor is there specific language] allow[ing] the petitioners to assert . . . that the President has no authority under the AUMF to detain them indefinitely [by challenging] the Department's definition of enemy combatant. [Even if we construed the statute to fix these problems] [t]he more difficult question is whether the DTA permits the Court of Appeals to make requisite findings of fact. [Even] [a]ssuming the DTA can be construed to allow the

Court of Appeals to review or correct the CSRT's factual determinations, as opposed to merely certifying that the tribunal applied the correct standard of proof, we see no way to construe the statute to allow what is also constitutionally required in this context: an opportunity for the detainee to present relevant exculpatory evidence that was not made part of the record in the earlier proceedings.

[E]ven if it were possible, as a textual matter, to read into the statute each of the necessary procedures we have identified, we could not overlook the cumulative effect of our doing so. To hold that the detainees at Guantanamo may, under the DTA, challenge the President's legal authority to detain them, contest the CSRT's findings of fact, supplement the record on review with exculpatory evidence, and request an order of release would come close to reinstating the §2241 habeas corpus process Congress sought to deny them. The language of the statute, read in light of Congress' reasons for enacting it, cannot bear this interpretation. Petitioners have met their burden of establishing that the DTA review process is, on its face, an inadequate substitute for habeas corpus.

Although we do not hold that an adequate substitute must duplicate §2241 in all respects, it suffices that the Government has not established that the detainees' access to the statutory review provisions at issue is an adequate substitute for the writ of habeas corpus. MCA §7 thus effects an unconstitutional suspension of the writ. In view of our holding we need not discuss the reach of the writ with respect to claims of unlawful conditions of treatment or confinement.

VI

The Government argues petitioners must seek review of their CSRT determinations in the Court of Appeals before they can proceed with their habeas corpus actions in the District Court. . . . In cases involving foreign citizens detained abroad by the Executive, it likely would be both an impractical and unprecedented extension of judicial power to assume that habeas corpus would be available at the moment the prisoner is taken into custody. If and when habeas corpus jurisdiction applies, as it does in these cases, then proper deference can be accorded to reasonable procedures for screening and initial detention under lawful and proper conditions of confinement and treatment for a reasonable period of time. . . . The cases before us, however, do not involve detainees who have been held for a short period of time while awaiting their CSRT determinations. Were that the case, or were it probable that the Court of Appeals could complete a prompt review of their applications, the case for requiring temporary abstention or exhaustion of alternative remedies would be much stronger. These qualifications no longer pertain here. In some of these cases six years have elapsed without the judicial oversight that habeas corpus or an adequate substitute demands. And there has been no showing that the Executive faces such onerous burdens that it cannot respond to habeas corpus actions. To require these detainees to complete DTA review before proceeding with their habeas corpus actions would be to require additional months, if not years, of delay. The first

DTA review applications were filed over a year ago, but no decisions on the merits have been issued. While some delay in fashioning new procedures is unavoidable, the costs of delay can no longer be borne by those who are held in custody. The detainees in these cases are entitled to a prompt habeas corpus hearing. [B]oth the DTA and the CSRT process remain intact. Our holding with regard to exhaustion should not be read to imply that a habeas court should intervene the moment an enemy combatant steps foot in a territory where the writ runs. The Executive is entitled to a reasonable period of time to determine a detainee's status before a court entertains that detainee's habeas corpus petition. The CSRT process is the mechanism Congress and the President set up to deal with these issues. Except in cases of undue delay, federal courts should refrain from entertaining an enemy combatant's habeas corpus petition at least until after the Department, acting via the CSRT, has had a chance to review his status.

Although we hold that the DTA is not an adequate and effective substitute for habeas corpus, it does not follow that a habeas corpus court may disregard the dangers the detention in these cases was intended to prevent. . . . Certain accommodations can be made to reduce the burden habeas corpus proceedings will place on the military without impermissibly diluting the protections of the writ.

[Congress has sought] to avoid the widespread dissemination of classified information. . . . We make no attempt to anticipate all of the evidentiary and access-to-counsel issues that will arise during the course of the detainees' habeas corpus proceedings. We recognize, however, that the Government has a legitimate interest in protecting sources and methods of intelligence gathering; and we expect that the District Court will use its discretion to accommodate this interest to the greatest extent possible. . . .

It bears repeating that our opinion does not address the content of the law that governs petitioners' detention. That is a matter yet to be determined. We hold that petitioners may invoke the fundamental procedural protections of habeas corpus. The laws and Constitution are designed to survive, and remain in force, in extraordinary times. Liberty and security can be reconciled; and in our system they are reconciled within the framework of the law. The Framers decided that habeas corpus, a right of first importance, must be a part of that framework, a part of that law. . . .

Justice SOUTER, with whom Justice GINSBURG and Justice BREYER join, concurring.

[J]ustice Scalia is . . . correct that here, for the first time, this Court holds there is (he says "confers") constitutional habeas jurisdiction over aliens imprisoned by the military outside an area of *de jure* national sovereignty. But no one who reads the Court's opinion in *Rasul* could seriously doubt that the jurisdictional question must be answered the same way in purely constitutional cases, given the Court's reliance on the historical background of habeas generally in answering the statutory question. [W]hether one agrees or disagrees with today's decision, it is no bolt out of the blue.

[S]ome of the prisoners represented here today having been locked up for six years. Hence the hollow ring when the dissenters suggest that the Court is somehow precipitating the judiciary into reviewing claims that the military (subject to appeal to the Court of Appeals for the District of Columbia Circuit) could handle within some reasonable period of time. These suggestions of judicial haste are all the more out of place given the Court's realistic acknowledgment that in periods of exigency the tempo of any habeas review must reflect the immediate peril facing the country.

It is in fact the very lapse of four years from the time *Rasul* put everyone on notice that habeas process was available to Guantanamo prisoners, and the lapse of six years since some of these prisoners were captured and incarcerated, that stand at odds with the repeated suggestions of the dissenters that these cases should be seen as a judicial victory in a contest for power between the Court and the political branches. The several answers to the charge of triumphalism might start with a basic fact of Anglo-American constitutional history: that the power, first of the Crown and now of the Executive Branch of the United States, is necessarily limited by habeas corpus jurisdiction to enquire into the legality of executive detention. And one could explain that in this Court's exercise of responsibility to preserve habeas corpus something much more significant is involved than pulling and hauling between the judicial and political branches. Instead, though, it is enough to repeat that some of these petitioners have spent six years behind bars. After six years of sustained executive detentions in Guantanamo, subject to habeas jurisdiction but without any actual habeas scrutiny, today's decision is no judicial victory, but an act of perseverance in trying to make habeas review, and the obligation of the courts to provide it, mean something of value both to prisoners and to the Nation.

Chief Justice Roberts, with whom Justice Scalia, Justice Thomas, and Justice Alito join, dissenting.

Today the Court strikes down as inadequate the most generous set of procedural protections ever afforded aliens detained by this country as enemy combatants. The political branches crafted these procedures amidst an ongoing military conflict, after much careful investigation and thorough debate. The Court rejects them today out of hand, without bothering to say what due process rights the detainees possess, without explaining how the statute fails to vindicate those rights, and before a single petitioner has even attempted to avail himself of the law's operation. And to what effect? The majority merely replaces a review system designed by the people's representatives with a set of shapeless procedures to be defined by federal courts at some future date. One cannot help but think, after surveying the modest practical results of the majority's ambitious opinion, that this decision is not really about the detainees at all, but about control of federal policy regarding enemy combatants.

[T]he Court should have resolved these cases on other grounds. Habeas is most fundamentally a procedural right, a mechanism for contesting the legality of executive detention. The critical threshold question in these cases, prior to any inquiry about the writ's scope, is whether the system the political branches designed protects whatever rights the detainees may possess. If so, there is no need for any additional process, whether called "habeas" or something else.

[The Court's] opinion fails to determine what rights the detainees possess and whether the DTA system satisfies them. The majority instead compares the undefined DTA process to an equally undefined habeas right—one that is to be given shape only in the future by district courts on a case-by-case basis. This whole approach is misguided.

It is also fruitless. How the detainees' claims will be decided now that the DTA is gone is anybody's guess. But the habeas process the Court mandates will most likely end up looking a lot like the DTA system it replaces, as the district court judges shaping it will have to reconcile review of the prisoners' detention with the undoubted need to protect the American people from the terrorist threat-precisely the challenge Congress undertook in drafting the DTA. All that today's opinion has done is shift responsibility for those sensitive foreign policy and national security decisions from the elected branches to the Federal Judiciary. . . .

There is no reason to suppose that review according to procedures the Federal Judiciary will design, case by case, will proceed any faster than the DTA process petitioners disdained. On the contrary, the system the Court has launched (and directs lower courts to elaborate) promises to take longer. The Court assures us that before bringing their habeas petitions, detainees must usually complete the CSRT process. Then they may seek review in federal district court. Either success or failure there will surely result in an appeal to the D.C. Circuit—exactly where judicial review *starts* under Congress's system. The effect of the Court's decision is to add additional layers of quite possibly redundant review. And because nobody knows how these new layers of "habeas" review will operate, or what new procedures they will require, their contours will undoubtedly be subject to fresh bouts of litigation. If the majority were truly concerned about delay, it would have required petitioners to use the DTA process that has been available to them for 2 1/2 years, with its Article III review in the D.C. Circuit. That system might well have provided petitioners all the relief to which they are entitled long before the Court's newly installed habeas review could hope to do so.

[T]he majority strikes down the statute because it is not an "adequate substitute" for habeas review, but fails to show what rights the detainees have that cannot be vindicated by the DTA system.

[A]fter much hemming and hawing, the majority appears to concede that the DTA provides an Article III court competent to order release. The only issue in dispute is the process the Guantanamo prisoners are entitled to use to test the legality of their detention. *Hamdi* concluded that American citizens detained as enemy combatants are entitled to only limited process, and that much of that process could be supplied by a military tribunal, with review to follow in an Article III court. That is precisely the system we have here. It is adequate to vindicate whatever due process rights petitioners may have. [T]he *Hamdi* plurality concluded that this type of review would be enough to satisfy due process, even for citizens. Congress followed the Court's lead, only to find itself the victim of a constitutional bait and switch. . . .

For my part, I will assume that any due process rights petitioners may possess are no greater than those of American citizens detained as enemy combatants. It is worth noting again that the *Hamdi* controlling opinion said the Constitution guarantees citizen detainees only "basic" procedural rights, and that the process for securing those rights can "be tailored to alleviate [the] uncommon potential to burden the Executive at a time of ongoing military conflict." The majority, however, objects that "the procedural protections afforded to the detainees in the CSRT hearings are . . . limited." But the evidentiary and other limitations the Court complains of reflect the nature of the issue in contest, namely, the status of aliens captured by our Armed Forces abroad and alleged to be enemy combatants. Contrary to the repeated suggestions of the majority, DTA review need not parallel the habeas privileges enjoyed by noncombatant American citizens. . . . It need only provide process adequate for noncitizens detained as alleged combatants.

To what basic process are these detainees due as habeas petitioners? We have said that "at the absolute minimum," the Suspension Clause protects the writ as it existed in 1789. The majority admits that a number of historical authorities suggest that at the time of the Constitution's ratification, "common-law courts abstained altogether from matters involving prisoners of war." If this is accurate, the process provided prisoners under the DTA is plainly more than sufficient—it allows alleged combatants to challenge both the factual and legal bases of their detentions.

Assuming the constitutional baseline is more robust, the DTA still provides adequate process, and by the majority's own standards. Today's Court opines that the Suspension Clause guarantees prisoners such as the detainees "a meaningful opportunity to demonstrate that [they are] being held pursuant to the erroneous application or interpretation of relevant law." Further, the Court holds that to be an adequate substitute, any tribunal reviewing the detainees' cases "must have the power to order the conditional release of an individual unlawfully detained." The DTA system-CSRT review of the Executive's determination followed by D.C. Circuit review for sufficiency of the evidence and the constitutionality of the CSRT process—meets these criteria.

. . .

Detainees not only have the opportunity to confront any witness who appears before the tribunal, they may call witnesses of their own. The Implementation Memo requires only that detainees' witnesses be "reasonably available,". . . . The dangerous mission assigned to our forces abroad is to fight terrorists, not serve subpoenas. The Court is correct that some forms of hearsay evidence are admissible before the CSRT, but *Hamdi* expressly approved this use of hearsay by habeas courts.

As to classified information, while detainees are not permitted access to it themselves, the Implementation Memo provides each detainee with a "Personal

Representative" who may review classified documents at the CSRT stage and summarize them for the detainee. The prisoner's counsel enjoys the same privilege on appeal before the D.C. Circuit. That is more access to classified material for alleged alien enemy combatants than ever before provided. I am not aware of a single instance—and certainly the majority cites none—in which detainees such as petitioners have been provided access to classified material in *any* form. Indeed, prisoners of war who challenge their status determinations under the Geneva Convention are afforded no such access. . . .

What alternative does the Court propose? Allow free access to classified information and ignore the risk the prisoner may eventually convey what he learns to parties hostile to this country, with deadly consequences for those who helped apprehend the detainee? If the Court can design a better system for communicating to detainees the substance of any classified information relevant to their cases, without fatally compromising national security interests and sources, the majority should come forward with it. Instead, the majority fobs that vexing question off on district courts to answer down the road.

. . .

For all its eloquence about the detainees' right to the writ, the Court makes no effort to elaborate how exactly the remedy it prescribes will differ from the procedural protections detainees enjoy under the DTA. The Court objects to the detainees' limited access to witnesses and classified material, but proposes no alternatives of its own. Indeed, it simply ignores the many difficult questions its holding presents. What, for example, will become of the CSRT process? The majority says federal courts should *generally* refrain from entertaining detainee challenges until after the petitioner's CSRT proceeding has finished. But to what deference, if any, is that CSRT determination entitled?

There are other problems. Take witness availability. What makes the majority think witnesses will become magically available when the review procedure is labeled "habeas"? Will the location of most of these witnesses change—will they suddenly become easily susceptible to service of process? Or will subpoenas issued by American habeas courts run to Basra? And if they did, how would they be enforced? Speaking of witnesses, will detainees be able to call active-duty military officers as witnesses? If not, why not?

The majority has no answers for these difficulties. What it does say leaves open the distinct possibility that its "habeas" remedy will, when all is said and done, end up looking a great deal like the DTA review it rejects. . . .

The majority rests its decision on abstract and hypothetical concerns. Step back and consider what, in the real world, Congress and the Executive have actually granted aliens captured by our Armed Forces overseas and found to be enemy combatants:

- The right to hear the bases of the charges against them, including a summary of any classified evidence.
- The ability to challenge the bases of their detention before military tribunals modeled after Geneva Convention procedures. Some 38

detainees have been released as a result of this process. Brief for Federal Respondents 57, 60.

- The right, before the CSRT, to testify, introduce evidence, call witnesses, question those the Government calls, and secure release, if and when appropriate.
- The right to the aid of a personal representative in arranging and presenting their cases before a CSRT.
- Before the D.C. Circuit, the right to employ counsel, challenge the factual record, contest the lower tribunal's legal determinations, ensure compliance with the Constitution and laws, and secure release, if any errors below establish their entitlement to such relief./BL

In sum, the DTA satisfies the majority's own criteria for assessing adequacy. This statutory scheme provides the combatants held at Guantanamo greater procedural protections than have ever been afforded alleged enemy detainees—whether citizens or aliens—in our national history.

$$* \quad * \quad *$$

So who has won? Not the detainees. The Court's analysis leaves them with only the prospect of further litigation to determine the content of their new habeas right, followed by further litigation to resolve their particular cases, followed by further litigation before the D.C. Circuit—where they could have started had they invoked the DTA procedure. Not Congress, whose attempt to "determine—through democratic means—how best" to balance the security of the American people with the detainees' liberty interests, see *Hamdan v. Rumsfeld* (BREYER, J., concurring), has been unceremoniously brushed aside. Not the Great Writ, whose majesty is hardly enhanced by its extension to a jurisdictionally quirky outpost, with no tangible benefit to anyone. Not the rule of law, unless by that is meant the rule of lawyers, who will now arguably have a greater role than military and intelligence officials in shaping policy for alien enemy combatants. And certainly not the American people, who today lose a bit more control over the conduct of this Nation's foreign policy to unelected, politically unaccountable judges.

I respectfully dissent.

Justice SCALIA, with whom The CHIEF JUSTICE, Justice THOMAS, and Justice ALITO join, dissenting.

Today, for the first time in our Nation's history, the Court confers a constitutional right to habeas corpus on alien enemies detained abroad by our military forces in the course of an ongoing war. . . . The writ of habeas corpus does not, and never has, run in favor of aliens abroad; the Suspension Clause thus has no application, and the Court's intervention in this military matter is entirely *ultra vires*. . . .

America is at war with radical Islamists. The enemy began by killing Americans and American allies abroad: 241 at the Marine barracks in Lebanon,

19 at the Khobar Towers in Dhahran, 224 at our embassies in Dar es Salaam and Nairobi, and 17 on the USS Cole in Yemen. On September 11, 2001, the enemy brought the battle to American soil, killing 2,749 at the Twin Towers in New York City, 184 at the Pentagon in Washington, D.C., and 40 in Pennsylvania. It has threatened further attacks against our homeland; one need only walk about buttressed and barricaded Washington, or board a plane anywhere in the country, to know that the threat is a serious one. Our Armed Forces are now in the field against the enemy, in Afghanistan and Iraq. Last week, 13 of our countrymen in arms were killed.

The game of bait-and-switch that today's opinion plays upon the Nation's Commander in Chief will make the war harder on us. It will almost certainly cause more Americans to be killed. That consequence would be tolerable if necessary to preserve a time-honored legal principle vital to our constitutional Republic. But it is this Court's blatant *abandonment* of such a principle that produces the decision today. The President relied on our settled precedent in *Johnson v. Eisentrager* when he established the prison at Guantanamo Bay for enemy aliens. Citing that case, the President's Office of Legal Counsel advised him "that the great weight of legal authority indicates that a federal district court could not properly exercise habeas jurisdiction over an alien detained at [Guantanamo Bay]." Memorandum from Patrick F. Philbin and John C. Yoo, Deputy Assistant Attorneys General, Office of Legal Counsel, to William J. Haynes II, General Counsel, Dept. of Defense (Dec. 28, 2001). Had the law been otherwise, the military surely would not have transported prisoners there, but would have kept them in Afghanistan, transferred them to another of our foreign military bases, or turned them over to allies for detention. Those other facilities might well have been worse for the detainees themselves.

In the long term, then, the Court's decision today accomplishes little, except perhaps to reduce the well-being of enemy combatants that the Court ostensibly seeks to protect. In the short term, however, the decision is devastating. At least 30 of those prisoners hitherto released from Guantanamo Bay have returned to the battlefield. Some have been captured or killed. But others have succeeded in carrying on their atrocities against innocent civilians. . . . These, mind you, were detainees whom *the military* had concluded were not enemy combatants. Their return to the kill illustrates the incredible difficulty of assessing who is and who is not an enemy combatant in a foreign theater of operations where the environment does not lend itself to rigorous evidence collection. Astoundingly, the Court today raises the bar, requiring military officials to appear before civilian courts and defend their decisions under procedural and evidentiary rules that go beyond what Congress has specified. As The Chief Justice's dissent makes clear, we have no idea what those procedural and evidentiary rules are, but they will be determined by civil courts and (in the Court's contemplation at least) will be more detainee-friendly than those now applied, since otherwise there would no reason to hold the congressionally prescribed procedures unconstitutional. If they impose a higher standard of proof (from foreign battlefields) than the current procedures require, the number of the enemy returned to combat will obviously increase.

But even when the military has evidence that it can bring forward, it is often foolhardy to release that evidence to the attorneys representing our enemies. And one escalation of procedures that the Court *is* clear about is affording the detainees increased access to witnesses (perhaps troops serving in Afghanistan?) and to classified information. During the 1995 prosecution of Omar Abdel Rahman, federal prosecutors gave the names of 200 unindicted co-conspirators to the "Blind Sheik's" defense lawyers; that information was in the hands of Osama Bin Laden within two weeks. In another case, trial testimony revealed to the enemy that the United States had been monitoring their cellular network, whereupon they promptly stopped using it, enabling more of them to evade capture and continue their atrocities.

And today it is not just the military that the Court elbows aside. A mere two Terms ago in *Hamdan v. Rumsfeld*, when the Court held (quite amazingly) that the Detainee Treatment Act of 2005 had not stripped habeas jurisdiction over Guantanamo petitioners' claims, four Members of today's five-Justice majority joined an opinion saying [that] "[n]othing prevents the President from returning to Congress to seek the authority [for trial by military commission] he believes necessary. . . . Where, as here, no emergency prevents consultation with Congress, judicial insistence upon that consultation does not weaken our Nation's ability to deal with danger. To the contrary, that insistence strengthens the Nation's ability to determine-through democratic means—how best to do so. The Constitution places its faith in those democratic means." *Id.,* at 636 (Breyer, J., concurring).

Turns out they were just kidding. For in response, Congress, at the President's request, quickly enacted the Military Commissions Act, emphatically reasserting that it did not want these prisoners filing habeas petitions. It is therefore clear that Congress and the Executive—*both* political branches— have determined that limiting the role of civilian courts in adjudicating whether prisoners captured abroad are properly detained is important to success in the war that some 190,000 of our men and women are now fighting. As the Solicitor General argued, "the Military Commissions Act and the Detainee Treatment Act . . . represent an effort by the political branches to strike an appropriate balance between the need to preserve liberty and the need to accommodate the weighty and sensitive governmental interests in ensuring that those who have in fact fought with the enemy during a war do not return to battle against the United States."

But it does not matter. The Court today decrees that no good reason to accept the judgment of the other two branches is "apparent." "The Government," it declares, "presents no credible arguments that the military mission at Guantanamo would be compromised if habeas corpus courts had jurisdiction to hear the detainees' claims." What competence does the Court have to second-guess the judgment of Congress and the President on such a point? None whatever. But the Court blunders in nonetheless. Henceforth, as today's opinion makes unnervingly clear, how to handle enemy prisoners in this war will ultimately lie with the branch that knows least about the national security concerns that the subject entails. . . .

What drives today's decision is neither the meaning of the Suspension Clause, nor the principles of our precedents, but rather an inflated notion of judicial supremacy. The Court says that if the extraterritorial applicability of the Suspension Clause turned on formal notions of sovereignty, "it would be possible for the political branches to govern without legal constraint" in areas beyond the sovereign territory of the United States. That cannot be, the Court says, because it is the duty of this Court to say what the law is. It would be difficult to imagine a more question-begging analysis. . . . Our power "to say what the law is" is circumscribed by the limits of our statutorily and constitutionally conferred jurisdiction. And that is precisely the question in these cases: whether the Constitution confers habeas jurisdiction on federal courts to decide petitioners' claims. It is both irrational and arrogant to say that the answer must be yes, because otherwise we would not be supreme.

But so long as there are *some* places to which habeas does not run—so long as the Court's new "functional" test will not be satisfied *in every case*—then there will be circumstances in which "it would be possible for the political branches to govern without legal constraint." Or, to put it more impartially, areas in which the legal determinations of the *other* branches will be (shudder!) *supreme*. In other words, judicial supremacy is not really assured by the constitutional rule that the Court creates. The gap between rationale and rule leads me to conclude that the Court's ultimate, unexpressed goal is to preserve the power to review the confinement of enemy prisoners held by the Executive anywhere in the world. The "functional" test usefully evades the precedential landmine of *Eisentrager* but is so inherently subjective that it clears a wide path for the Court to traverse in the years to come. . . .

[A]ll available historical evidence points to the conclusion that the writ would not have been available at common law for aliens captured and held outside the sovereign territory of the Crown. . . . The Court finds it significant that there is no recorded case *denying* jurisdiction to such prisoners either. But a case standing for the remarkable proposition that the writ could issue to a foreign land would surely have been reported, whereas a case denying such a writ for lack of jurisdiction would likely not. At a minimum, the absence of a reported case either way leaves unrefuted the voluminous commentary stating that habeas was confined to the dominions of the Crown.

What history teaches is confirmed by the nature of the limitations that the Constitution places upon suspension of the common-law writ. It can be suspended only "in Cases of Rebellion or Invasion." Art. I, §9, cl. 2. The latter case (invasion) is plainly limited to the territory of the United States; and while it is conceivable that a rebellion could be mounted by American citizens abroad, surely the overwhelming majority of its occurrences would be domestic. If the extraterritorial scope of habeas turned on flexible, "functional" considerations, as the Court holds, why would the Constitution limit its suspension almost entirely to instances of domestic crisis? Surely there is an even greater justification for suspension in foreign lands where the United States might hold prisoners of war during an ongoing conflict. And correspondingly, there is less threat to liberty when the Government suspends the writ's (supposed) application in foreign lands, where even on the most extreme view prisoners are entitled to fewer constitutional rights. It makes no sense, therefore, for the Constitution generally to forbid suspension of the writ abroad if indeed the writ has application there.

It may be objected that the foregoing analysis proves too much, since this Court has already suggested that the writ of habeas corpus *does* run abroad for the benefit of United States citizens. "[T]he position that United States citizens throughout the world may be entitled to habeas corpus rights . . . is precisely the position that this Court adopted in *Eisentrager,* even while holding that aliens abroad did not have habeas corpus rights." The reason for that divergence is not difficult to discern. The common-law writ, as received into the law of the new constitutional Republic, took on such changes as were demanded by a system in which rule is derived from the consent of the governed, and in which citizens (not "subjects") are afforded defined protections against the Government. . . . It accords with that principle to say, as the plurality opinion said in *Reid:* When the Government reaches out to punish a citizen who is abroad, the shield which the Bill of Rights and other parts of the Constitution provide to protect his life and liberty should not be stripped away just because he happens to be in another land. On that analysis, "[t]he distinction between citizens and aliens follows from the undoubted proposition that the Constitution does not create, nor do general principles of law create, any juridical relation between our country and some undefined, limitless class of noncitizens who are beyond our territory."

In sum, because I conclude that the text and history of the Suspension Clause provide no basis for our jurisdiction, I would affirm the Court of Appeals even if *Eisentrager* did not govern these cases.

* * *

Today the Court warps our Constitution in a way that goes beyond the narrow issue of the reach of the Suspension Clause, invoking judicially brainstormed separation-of-powers principles to establish a manipulable "functional" test for the extraterritorial reach of habeas corpus (and, no doubt, for the extraterritorial reach of other constitutional protections as well). It blatantly misdescribes important precedents, most conspicuously Justice Jackson's opinion for the Court in *Johnson v. Eisentrager.* It breaks a chain of precedent as old as the common law that prohibits judicial inquiry into detentions of aliens abroad absent statutory authorization. And, most tragically, it sets our military commanders the impossible task of proving to a civilian court, under whatever standards this Court devises in the future, that evidence supports the confinement of each and every enemy prisoner.

The Nation will live to regret what the Court has done today. I dissent.

Discussion

1. *The Court pushes back. Boumediene* is the third in a series of cases involving the Court's jurisdiction to hear appeals from the Guantanamo detainees. *Rasul v. Bush* (textbook at pp. 868-869) and *Hamdan* (described infra) were nominally statutory cases, in which Court restricted what the President could do and invited the President and Congress to respond if they liked. Congress and the President did so twice. First, in response to *Rasul*, they attempted to keep the federal courts from hearing habeas petitions from Guantanamo detainees in the Detainee Treatment Act of 2005. In *Hamdan* the Court construed the DTA to allow it to hear habeas petitions in the cases before it and then held that the President's military commissions were illegal. In response to *Hamdan*, the President and Congress passed the Military Commissions Act of 2006, reinstating the commissions. Section 7 of the MCA once again sought to eliminate habeas and federal question jurisdiction for the Guantanamo detainees. In *Boumediene*, the Court struck down section 7, making clear that the Suspension Clause applies to detainees held at Guantanamo Bay. In theory, the President and Congress could respond once again by officially suspending the writ of habeas corpus, but it is very unlikely that they will so do.

In one sense, the sequence of cases from *Hamdi v. Rumsfeld* to *Rasul* to *Hamdan* to *Boumediene* is remarkable: They are among a very small number of decisions in which the Supreme Court rejects a claim made by the President in wartime, *Youngstown* being the most obvious example.

In *Youngstown*, the Court believed that Congress had not gone along with the President's decision to seize the steel mills. Hence, it treated the case as falling into "box three" of Justice Jackson's theory, where the President's power was at its lowest ebb.

In *Hamdi* and *Hamdan*, the Court construed Congress as giving its authority (under the AUMF and the UCMJ) for some presidential actions but not for others. The President could do only what (the Court said) Congress had authorized; the President could not do what (the Court said) Congress had not authorized. (The Court also artfully read the Detainee Treatment Act as giving it permission to hear the cases before it.) Likewise, in *Rasul*, the Court interpreted the existing habeas statute as covering the Guantanamo detainees.

In *Boumediene*, by contrast, the President and Congress explicitly agreed to strip jurisdiction in habeas cases. Why then, isn't this a case in "box one" of *Youngstown* where the full war powers of the national government are being asserted, and why didn't the Court defer?

Why do you think the Court was willing to deny the President what he wanted under these circumstances? One answer might be the political situation in the country: an unpopular war in Iraq coupled with continuing reports of torture and abuse at Guantanamo Bay, Abu Ghraib, Bagram, and the CIA "black sites."

Note that President Truman was weakened by the Korean War and had lost much of his popularity when *Youngstown* was decided in 1952. Given President Bush's record-setting levels of unpopularity, and the fact that the Democrats took control of Congress following the 2006 elections (after the passage of the Military Commissions Act), the Court risked very little by refusing to defer to the President. Is it particularly inappropriate for courts to intervene in matters of war when Presidents are politically weakened; or on the contrary, is it only when Presidents are weakened politically that courts feel able to insist that Presidents abide by constitutional guarantees?

A second possible reason why the Court intervened in *Boumediene* is that the majority no longer believed that the separation of powers between Congress and the White House acted as a realistic check on the President, especially when one party controlled the political branches. As Justice Jackson explained in *Youngstown*: "[The] rise of the party system has made a significant extraconstitutional supplement to real executive power. No appraisal of his necessities is realistic which overlooks that he heads a political system as well as a legal system. Party loyalties and interests, sometimes more binding than law, extend his effective control into branches of government other than his own and he often may win, as a political leader, what he cannot command under the Constitution." In this context, note that members of Congress might have been unwilling to cross a President of their own party but perfectly happy to let the courts take the political heat. Senator Arlen Specter, head of the Senate Judiciary Committee, denounced the Military Commissions Act for unconstitutionally suspending habeas corpus but voted for it anyway, presumably hoping that the courts would strike it down. See Charles Babington & Jonathan Weisman, Senate Approves Detainee Bill Backed by Bush: Constitutional Challenges Predicted, Washington Post, Sept. 29, 2006 at A01, available at *http://www.washington-post.com/wp-dyn/content/article/2006/09/28/AR2006092800824.html* (quoting Specter as supporting the bill because "the court will clean it up."). Does this mean that courts *should* be less deferential to national security laws passed under periods of one-party rule?

A third possible explanation of *Boumediene* was that the MCA was not simply a dispute about the relative powers of Congress vis-à-vis the President, but involved an attempt to strip the Court of its own jurisdiction. Hence the Court was far more likely to be protective of its own turf and far more willing to push back at the President. This, however, begs the question of what the Court's power should have been in the first place. According to Justice Scalia and the dissenters, the Court had no authority to hear the cases in the first place, so it lost nothing by the passage of Section 7.

2. *You've come a long way, baby.* Justice Kennedy, without a trace of irony, cites to *Marbury v. Madison* as a justification for the Court's jurisdiction to hear these cases and subject the actions of the political branches to the rule of law. In *Marbury,* the Supreme Court went out of its way to hold that it did not have jurisdiction to hear *Marbury*'s case in order to avoid provoking a confrontation with a Republican President and Congress. (And in *Stuart v. Laird,* decided a

week later, the Court meekly refused to stand up to the Republicans' elimination of circuit judgeships despite the Constitution's guarantee of life tenure.). Clearly the Court feels it is more powerful today than it was in Jefferson's time. Is it fair to say that *Boumediene* could only have occurred in a world after *Cooper v. Aaron* and *Bush v. Gore*?

3. *Could Congress respond by suspending the writ?* In theory, at least, Congress and the President could respond by repassing section 7 of the MCA with a clear statement that they intended to suspend the writ of habeas corpus under Article I, section 9. However, as noted above, it is very unlikely that the current Congress would do this.

Suspensions under the habeas corpus clause are permitted only if the United States is currently in a state of rebellion or invasion, and the public safety requires suspension. Is this test satisfied under current conditions? Note that section 7 of the MCA is permanent legislation that is not limited to a temporary state of emergency—it has no sunset provision, and it applies to detainees captured and held anywhere in the world.

One argument for the constitutionality of a suspension would be that the judgment whether these tests have been satisfied and a state of emergency exists rests solely with Congress and is a political question that cannot be reviewed by the courts. So if Congress declares that the United States is under an emergency of indefinite or even permanent duration, the Court should defer to its decision. Does this prove too much?

4. *The scope of habeas corpus.* Although Congress may not suspend habeas within an undefined constitutional core unless there is rebellion or invasion, the Suspension Clause does not protect purely statutory grants of habeas outside of the constitutional core. Hence, Congress may eliminate purely statutory grants of habeas permanently even without a showing of emergency. In *Rasul v. Bush*, the Supreme Court held that the Guantanamo detainees had a statutory right to habeas without deciding whether their right was part of the constitutional core. In *Boumediene*, the Court explained that the detainees were also covered by the constitutional core of habeas corpus protected by the Suspension Clause.

The Suspension Clause preserved, "at the absolute minimum," the common law right to habeas corpus as it existed in 1789, *INS v. St. Cyr*, 533 U.S. 289, 301 (2001). However, the Constitution left it to Congress to create a statutory framework to provide for the right in the new system of federal courts. Thus, in *Ex Parte Bollman*, 8 U.S. 75, 94-95 (1807), Chief Justice Marshall explained that "for the meaning of the term habeas corpus, resort may unquestionably be had to the common law; but the power to award the writ by any of the courts of the United States, must be given by written law." This makes it difficult to determine whether a particular application of habeas is merely statutory and left to Congress's discretion or is constitutionally protected from alteration by the Suspension Clause. Moreover, if the right of habeas corpus is truly a common law right, its scope might not be limited to circumstances as they existed in 1789 but might evolve in common law fashion.

One additional complication is that if Congress had never created any lower federal courts, the right to habeas would have rested primarily in state courts. However, Congress did create both a lower system of federal courts and a federal habeas statute. Moreover, during Reconstruction, the Supreme Court, anxious to limit meddling by Southern state courts, held in *Tarble's Case,* 80 U.S. 397 (1872), that state courts do not generally have the power to issue writs of habeas corpus to federal officials acting under claim of or color of federal authority. Hence the right to habeas against the President would exist, if at all, in the federal courts.

How does the Court deal with the historical question in *Boumediene*? Note Justice Kennedy's claim that the historical evidence of habeas may be incomplete. Note also his citation to *Brown v. Board of Education,* in which Chief Justice Warren surveyed the historical evidence at the time of the Fourteenth Amendment and then stated that, because it was inconclusive, the Court would ask what the equal protection clause meant in 1954. Is Justice Kennedy saying that if the record were complete it would be determinative, or is he saying that the Court is not bound by the historical record and may expand the scope of the writ in contemporary circumstances?

In fact, Justice Kennedy's argument for the scope of habeas is primarily structural rather than historical. It prevents the Executive from shuttling detainees to places where the judiciary cannot reach them. Does this principle prove too much? Justice Kennedy's multifactor test and his focus on practical circumstances suggest that there might be at least some places where detainees might be held without access to habeas. For example, how would Justice Kennedy's test apply to Bagram Air Base in Afghanistan, or to the secret CIA black sites in undisclosed locations around the world?

Why can't the President simply find places where habeas hearings would be genuinely impractical under Kennedy's multifactor test and stash detainees there? If the President did so, would this fall afoul of Kennedy's assertion that "[t]he test for determining the scope of [habeas] must not be subject to manipulation by those whose power it is designed to restrain." If it would be permissible for the President to avoid habeas review in this way, then what exactly did Kennedy mean by his statement?

5. *Habeas corpus and the separation of powers.* Justice Kennedy argues that habeas serves important separation of powers values. What precisely are those values and why does extension of habeas corpus serve them in the context of this case? As Justice Scalia points out, the separation of powers argument cuts both ways. Why isn't the judiciary overreaching its proper authority by trenching on the joint determinations of Congress and the President that the President needs special procedures for dealing with terrorist suspects apprehended overseas?

6. *What process is due?* How does the majority answer Chief Justice Roberts's argument that the detainees were given rights based on the *Hamdi* decision? How does it answer the charge that habeas hearings will face all of the same problems (protecting classified evidence, the difficulty of producing

witnesses, the need for the use of hearsay evidence) that the Bush Administration faced in its construction of the CSRTs?

Originally the Supreme Court decided not to hear the appeal of the Guantanamo detainees, but it reversed itself dramatically near the end of the October 2006 Term, on June 29, 2007. Shortly before the Court agreed to hear *Boumediene*, stories appeared in the press suggesting that the tribunals used faulty evidence, were rigged to produce a foreordained outcome, and that military officers were pressured to find that detainees were enemy combatants. See William Glauberson, Unlikely Adversary Arises to Criticize Detainee Hearings, N.Y. Times, July 23, 2007, at *http://www.nytimes.com/2007/07/23/us/23gitmo. html.* The Court says nothing about these reports. Instead of suggesting that the procedures may have been abused in practice, it simply holds that the procedures themselves are defective. Why did the Court do this?

7. *Who do you trust?* One possible reason for the Court's decision is that it trusted hearings by judges more than hearings by military officers. Doesn't this cut both ways? Will judges be at a disadvantage in making determinations of dangerousness and enemy combatant status given the necessarily limited factual records that the military will be able to produce? Why wouldn't military officers be better suited to make these determinations? Does *Boumediene* contemplate that all future detainees will receive a judicial hearing on their combatant status?

Consider in this respect Justice Scalia's claim that even without judicial intervention the military had mistakenly released detainees who were enemy combatants: "Their return to the kill illustrates the incredible difficulty of assessing who is and who is not an enemy combatant in a foreign theater of operations where the environment does not lend itself to rigorous evidence collection."

In the recent past, most prisoners of war have been uniformed, and captured in battlefield conditions, so that identifying them as enemy combatants is not particularly difficult. By contrast, the United States has embarked on a policy of rounding up detainees from all parts of the world, often far from battlefields, and often based on hearsay and classified information whose reliability cannot easily be proven or disproven. As a result, some detainees might not be dangerous at all, much less members of a terrorist organization. Moreover, unlike traditional prisoners of war who would only be held for the duration of hostilities, or fairly quickly exchanged or repatriated, these new detainees might be held indefinitely. (This was an issue that the Court dodged in *Hamdi*.) While traditional prisoners of war could not be interrogated or coerced consistent with the laws of war, a key purpose of rounding up a wide swath of detainees—even if they were not particularly dangerous—was to interrogate them to gain intelligence about terrorist networks and potential terrorist threats.

Given changed conditions, the reasons for detention, and the formidable difficulties of proof, Justice Scalia's suggestion appears to be that courts should defer to the military's decision to hold indefinitely anyone it regards as potentially dangerous.[1] What, precisely, is wrong with this solution from the majority's standpoint?

Note: After **Boumediene**

Following its decisions in *Hamdi*, *Hamdan*, and *Boumediene*, the Supreme Court has largely delegated the task of developing the law of executive detention to the District of Columbia Circuit Court of Appeals. In a series of decisions following *Boumediene*, the D.C. Circuit has interpreted the Supreme Court's decisions mostly in favor of executive power and against the claims of detainees.

1. *The reach of* Boumediene. In *Maqaleh v. Gates*, 605 F.3d 84 (D.C. Cir. 2010), the D.C. Circuit held that *Boumediene*'s reading of the Suspension Clause was premised on the special conditions at Guantanamo Bay, Cuba: "The United States has maintained its total control of Guantanamo Bay for over a century, even in the face of a hostile government maintaining *de jure* sovereignty over the property." In addition, there were relatively few practical obstacles to allowing habeas proceedings there. These considerations did not apply to non-citizens detained in the Afghan theater of war at Bagram Air Field. The United States operates Bagram through a lease with the Afghan government and it does not enjoy *de facto* sovereignty there. In addition, practical obstacles existed at Bagram because it was in a theater of war, and "all of the attributes of a facility exposed to the vagaries of war are present." Therefore, the court held, "the jurisdiction of the courts to afford the right to habeas relief and the protection of the Suspension Clause does not extend to aliens held in Executive detention in the Bagram detention facility in the Afghan theater of war."

2. *The power to detain*. In *Hamdi*, the Supreme Court used the laws of war to limit the scope of the President's power to detain enemy combatants. In *Al-Bihani v. Obama*, 590 F.3d 866 (D.C. Cir. 2010), cert denied, 131 S. Ct. 1814 (2011), however, Judge Janice Rodgers Brown's opinion argued that reference to the laws of war was not constitutionally required: "while the international laws of war are helpful to courts when identifying the general set of war powers to which the AUMF speaks, their lack of controlling legal force and firm definition render their use both inapposite and inadvisable when courts seek to determine the limits of the President's war powers." *Id.* at 871. Looking instead to the Military Commissions Act of 2006, Judge Brown held that the President may detain persons "who are part of forces associated with Al Qaeda or the Taliban or those who purposefully and materially support such forces in hostilities against U.S. Coalition partners." Read most expansively, this formula would allow the President to detain indefinitely anyone that he believed had

---

1. See Marty Lederman, The Strangest (and Perhaps Most Revealing) Sentence in Justice Scalia's Boumediene Dissent, Balkinization, June 23, 2008, at *http://balkin.blogspot.com/2008/06/strange-stand-perhaps-most-revealing.html*.

violated the material support provisions of federal criminal law, a very broad category that might include people who gave charitable contributions or legal advice to an organization associated with Al Qaeda or the Taliban. See *Holder v. Humanitarian Law Project*, 130 S. Ct. 2705 (2010). Indeed, the position taken by the panel was much broader than the Obama Administration had asked for. The D.C. Circuit ultimately denied rehearing en banc on the grounds that "the panel's discussion of [the role of international law in interpreting the President's powers under the AUMF] is not necessary to the disposition of the merits." *Al-Bihani v. Obama*, 619 F.3d 1 (D.C. Cir. 2010) (mem.)

3. *The burden of proof and procedural protections in habeas proceedings.* In *Al-Bihani*, the D.C. Circuit also held that a preponderance of the evidence standard, while not constitutionally required, is appropriate in habeas cases challenging executive detention, and that hearsay evidence is generally admissible. 590 F.3d 866, at 877-79. Later decisions confirmed these rules and held that district courts should not "weigh each piece of evidence in isolation, but consider all of the evidence taken as a whole." *Awad v. Obama*, 608 F.3d 1, 6-7 (D.C. Cir. 2010), cert denied, 131 S. Ct. 1814 (2011). See also *Al-Adahi v. Obama*, 613 F.3d 1102, 1105 (D.C. Cir. 2010), cert denied, 131 S. Ct. 1001 (2011) (accepting preponderance of the evidence standard *arguendo*, but expressing doubts that a preponderance of the evidence is constitutionally required to justify detention and implicitly criticizing the government for failing to argue for a lesser standard).

Concurring in *Esmail v. Obama*, 639 F.3d 1075 (D.C. Cir. 2011), Judge Silberman reflected on "the unusual incentives and disincentives that bear on judges on the D.C. Circuit courts—particularly the Court of Appeals—charged with deciding these detainee habeas cases." He criticized the Supreme Court and argued that his colleagues should always err on the side of denying habeas petitions brought by Guantanamo inmates:

> In the typical criminal case, a good judge will vote to overturn a conviction if the prosecutor lacked sufficient evidence, even when the judge is virtually certain that the defendant committed the crime. That can mean that a thoroughly bad person is released onto our streets, but I need not explain why our criminal justice system treats that risk as one we all believe, or should believe, is justified.
>
> When we are dealing with detainees, candor obliges me to admit that one can not help but be conscious of the infinitely greater downside risk to our country, and its people, of an order releasing a detainee who is likely to return to terrorism. . . . That means that there are powerful reasons for the government to rely on our opinion in *Al-Adahi v. Obama*, 613 F.3d 1102 (D.C. Cir. 2010), which persuasively explains that in a habeas corpus proceeding the preponderance of evidence standard that the government assumes binds it, is unnecessary—and moreover, unrealistic. *Id.* at 1104-05. I doubt any of my colleagues will vote to grant a petition if he or she believes that it is somewhat likely that the petitioner is an al Qaeda adherent or an active supporter. Unless, of course, the Supreme Court were to adopt the preponderance of the evidence standard (which it is unlikely to do—taking a case might obligate it to assume direct responsibility for the consequences of *Boumediene v. Bush*). But I, like my

colleagues, certainly would release a petitioner against whom the government could not muster even "some evidence."

Of course, if it turns out that regardless of our decisions the executive branch does not release winning petitioners because no other country will accept them and they will not be released into the United States, see *Kiyemba v. Obama*, 605 F.3d 1046, 1048 (D.C. Cir. 2010); Kiyemba v. Obama, 561 F.3d 509, 516 (D.C. Cir. 2009), then the whole process leads to virtual advisory opinions. It becomes a charade prompted by the Supreme Court's defiant—if only theoretical—assertion of judicial supremacy, see *Boumediene*, sustained by posturing on the part of the Justice Department, and providing litigation exercise for the detainee bar.

Note that in *Hamdi* the Supreme Court rejected the view that the executive could detain merely on the basis of "some evidence" when it was offered by the Bush Administration. See 542 U.S. at 537 (plurality opinion).

What do you make of Judge Silberman's remarkably candid opinion? Given that the D.C. Circuit has been given the responsibility for developing the law of executive detention, do its members have good reason to read the Supreme Court's decisions as narrowly as possible in favor of the executive and, in some cases, even beyond what the executive itself asks for?

Insert the following after note 5 on p. 878:

HAMDAN v. RUMSFELD
548 U.S. 557 (2006)

[During the war against the Taliban in Afghanistan following the September 11, 2001 attacks, militia forces captured Salim Ahmed Hamdan, a Yemeni national, in November 2001, and turned him over to the U.S. military. In June 2002, the military transported him to the detention facility at Guantanamo Bay, Cuba. Over a year later, the President deemed Hamdan eligible for trial by military commission for then-unspecified crimes. After another year, he was charged with conspiracy "to commit . . . offenses triable by military commission." He filed petitions for habeas corpus and mandamus, challenging the legality of the military tribunals under military and international law, and arguing that the charge of conspiracy was not a violation of the law of war. A panel of the D.C. Circuit, which included then Judge John Roberts, rejected his challenge. On appeal to the Supreme Court, Justice Stevens, speaking for five Justices, held that "the military commission convened to try Hamdan lacks power to proceed because its structure and procedures violate both the UCMJ [Uniform Code of Military Justice] and the Geneva Conventions." Justice Stevens, joined by Justices Souter, Ginsburg, and Breyer, also concluded "that the offense with which Hamdan has been charged is not an 'offens[e] that by . . . the law of war may be tried by military commissions.'"]

Justice STEVENS announced the judgment of the Court and delivered the opinion of the Court with respect to Parts I through IV, Parts VI through VI-D-iii, Part

VI-D-v, and Part VII, and an opinion with respect to Parts V and VI-D-iv, in which Justice SOUTER, Justice GINSBURG, and Justice BREYER join.

I.

. . .

On November 13, 2001, while the United States was still engaged in active combat with the Taliban, the President issued a comprehensive military order intended to govern the "Detention, Treatment, and Trial of Certain Non-Citizens in the War Against Terrorism," 66 Fed. Reg. 57833 (hereinafter November 13 Order or Order). Those subject to the November 13 Order include any noncitizen for whom the President determines "there is reason to believe" that he or she (1) "is or was" a member of al Qaeda or (2) has engaged or participated in terrorist activities aimed at or harmful to the United States. Any such individual "shall, when tried, be tried by military commission for any and all offenses triable by military commission that such individual is alleged to have committed, and may be punished in accordance with the penalties provided under applicable law, including imprisonment or death." . . .

On July 3, 2003, the President announced his determination that Hamdan and five other detainees at Guantanamo Bay were subject to the November 13 Order and thus triable by military commission. In December 2003, military counsel was appointed to represent Hamdan. Two months later, counsel filed demands for charges and for a speedy trial pursuant to Article 10 of the UCMJ, 10 U.S.C. §810. On February 23, 2004, the legal adviser to the Appointing Authority denied the applications, ruling that Hamdan was not entitled to any of the protections of the UCMJ. Not until July 13, 2004, after Hamdan had commenced this action in the United States District Court for the Western District of Washington, did the Government finally charge him with the offense for which, a year earlier, he had been deemed eligible for trial by military commission. . . . Meanwhile, a Combatant Status Review Tribunal (CSRT) convened pursuant to a military order issued on July 7, 2004, decided that Hamdan's continued detention at Guantanamo Bay was warranted because he was an "enemy combatant."[a] Separately, proceedings before the military commission commenced.

[Justice Stevens held that Hamdan's lawsuit was not barred by the Detainee Treatment Act of 2005 (DTA), signed into law on December 30, 2005. Section 1005(e)(1) of the act stripped jurisdiction of the courts to hear habeas petitions from aliens detained at Guantanamo Bay or "any other action against the

---

a. An "enemy combatant" is defined by the military order as "an individual who was part of or supporting Taliban or al Qaeda forces, or associated forces that are engaged in hostilities against the United States or its coalition partners." Memorandum from Deputy Secretary of Defense Paul Wolfowitz re: Order Establishing Combatant Status Review Tribunal §a (July 7, 2004), available at *http://www.defenselink.mil/news/Jul2004/d20040707review.pdf* (all Internet materials as visited June 26, 2006, and available in Clerk of Court's case file).

United States or its agents relating to any aspect of the detention by the Department of Defense of an alien at Guantanamo Bay, Cuba" who either "is currently in military custody" or has been determined to be an enemy combatant. Sections 1005(e)(2) and (3) placed exclusive jurisdiction to hear appeals from CSRTs or military commissions in the Circuit Court for the District of Columbia. Section 1005(h) stated that "[p]aragraphs (2) and (3) of subsection (e) shall apply with respect to any claim . . . pending on or after the date of the enactment of this Act" but said nothing about §1005(e)(1). As a result, Justice Stevens held that Hamdan's case, which was pending at the time of passage of the Detainee Treatment Act, was not barred by §1005(e)(1).

Justice Stevens also rejected the Government's argument based on Schlesinger v. Councilman, 420 U.S. 738 (1975), that civilian courts should abstain from intervening in pending courts-martial out of respect for "military discipline" and the "integrated system of military courts." The abstention rule did not apply because Hamdan was not a serviceman and the military commissions in question were not part of the integrated system.]

IV.

[E]xigency alone. . . . will not justify the establishment and use of penal tribunals not contemplated by Article I, §8 and Article III, §1 of the Constitution unless some other part of that document authorizes a response to the felt need. And that authority, if it exists, can derive only from the powers granted jointly to the President and Congress in time of war.

The Constitution makes the President the "Commander in Chief" of the Armed Forces, Art. II, §2, cl. 1, but vests in Congress the powers to "declare War . . . and make Rules concerning Captures on Land and Water," Art. I, §8, cl. 11, to "raise and support Armies," *id.*, cl. 12, to "define and punish . . . Offences against the Law of Nations," *id.*, cl. 10, and "To make Rules for the Government and Regulation of the land and naval Forces," id., cl. 14. The interplay between these powers was described by Chief Justice Chase in the seminal case of Ex parte Milligan:

> The power to make the necessary laws is in Congress; the power to execute in the President. Both powers imply many subordinate and auxiliary powers. Each includes all authorities essential to its due exercise. But neither can the President, in war more than in peace, intrude upon the proper authority of Congress, nor Congress upon the proper authority of the President. . . . Congress cannot direct the conduct of campaigns, nor can the President, or any commander under him, without the sanction of Congress, institute tribunals for the trial and punishment of offences, either of soldiers or civilians, unless in cases of a controlling necessity, which justifies what it compels, or at least insures acts of indemnity from the justice of the legislature.

Whether Chief Justice Chase was correct in suggesting that the President may constitutionally convene military commissions "without the sanction of Congress" in cases of "controlling necessity" is a question this Court has not answered definitively, and need not answer today. For we held in *Quirin* that Congress had, through Article of War 15, sanctioned the use of military commissions in such circumstances. Article 21 of the UCMJ, the language of which is substantially identical to the old Article 15 and was preserved by Congress after World War II, reads as follows:

> *Jurisdiction of courts-martial not exclusive.*
>
> The provisions of this code conferring jurisdiction upon courts-martial shall not be construed as depriving military commissions, provost courts, or other military tribunals of concurrent jurisdiction in respect of offenders or offenses that by statute or by the law of war may be tried by such military commissions, provost courts, or other military tribunals. 64 Stat. 115.

We have no occasion to revisit *Quirin's* controversial characterization of Article of War 15 as congressional authorization for military commissions. Contrary to the Government's assertion, however, even *Quirin* did not view the authorization as a sweeping mandate for the President to "invoke military commissions when he deems them necessary." Rather, the *Quirin* Court recognized that Congress had simply preserved what power, under the Constitution and the common law of war, the President had had before 1916 to convene military commissions—with the express condition that the President and those under his command comply with the law of war.[b] . . .

. . . Neither [the September 18, 2001 Authorization of the Use of Military Force (AUMF) or the Detainee Treatment Act (DTA)] expands the President's authority to convene military commissions. First, while we assume that the AUMF activated the President's war powers, and that those powers include the authority to convene military commissions in appropriate circumstances, there is nothing in the text or legislative history of the AUMF even hinting that Congress intended to expand or alter the authorization set forth in Article 21 of the UCMJ. Cf. [Ex Parte] Yerger, [8 Wall. 85, 105 (1869)] ("Repeals by implication are not favored")[c] . . . Although the DTA, unlike either Article 21 or the AUMF, was enacted after the President had convened Hamdan's commission, it contains no language authorizing that tribunal or any other at Guantanamo Bay. The DTA obviously "recognize[s]" the existence of the Guantanamo Bay commissions in the weakest sense, because it references some of the military orders governing them and creates limited judicial review of their "final decision[s]," DTA §1005(e)(3). But the statute also pointedly

---

b. Whether or not the President has independent power, absent congressional authorization, to convene military commissions, he may not disregard limitations that Congress has, in proper exercise of its own war powers, placed on his powers. See Youngstown Sheet & Tube Co. v. Sawyer, 343 U.S. 579, 637 (1952) (Jackson, J., concurring). The Government does not argue otherwise.

c. On this point, it is noteworthy that the Court in *Ex parte Quirin*, 317 U.S. 1 (1942), looked beyond Congress" declaration of war and accompanying authorization for use of force during World War II, and relied instead on Article of War 15 to find that Congress had authorized the use of military commissions in some circumstances.

reserves judgment on whether "the Constitution and laws of the United States are applicable" in reviewing such decisions and whether, if they are, the "standards and procedures" used to try Hamdan and other detainees actually violate the "Constitution and laws."

Together, the UCMJ, the AUMF, and the DTA at most acknowledge a general Presidential authority to convene military commissions in circumstances where justified under the "Constitution and laws," including the law of war. Absent a more specific congressional authorization, the task of this Court is, as it was in *Quirin*, to decide whether Hamdan's military commission is so justified. . . .

V.

[Justice Stevens, speaking for four Justices, held that charging Hamdan with a "conspiracy extending over a number of years, from 1996 to November 2001" was not consistent with the laws of war. First, most of this period fell before Congress passed the AUMF, which the President relied on as the source of his war powers to try detainees under the laws of war. Second, Congress had not specifically defined such a crime under its powers to "define and punish . . . Offences against the Law of Nations," U.S. Const., Art. I, §8, cl. 10. Third, the crime Hamdan was charged with was not a recognized crime under the laws of war.]

   . . .

VI.

Whether or not the Government has charged Hamdan with an offense against the law of war cognizable by military commission, the commission lacks power to proceed. The UCMJ conditions the President's use of military commissions on compliance not only with the American common law of war, but also with the rest of the UCMJ itself, insofar as applicable, and with the "rules and precepts of the law of nations," including, inter alia, the four Geneva Conventions signed in 1949. The procedures that the Government has decreed will govern Hamdan's trial by commission violate these laws.

A

[T]he accused and his civilian counsel may be excluded from, and precluded from ever learning what evidence was presented during, any part of the proceeding that either the Appointing Authority or the presiding officer decides to "close." Grounds for such closure "include the protection of information classified or classifiable . . . ; information protected by law or rule from unauthorized disclosure; the physical safety of participants in Commission proceedings, including prospective witnesses; intelligence and law enforcement sources, methods, or activities; and other national security interests." §6(B)(3). Appointed military defense counsel must be privy to these closed sessions, but may, at the presiding officer's discretion, be forbidden to reveal to his or her client what took place therein.

Another striking feature of the rules governing Hamdan's commission is that they permit the admission of *any* evidence that, in the opinion of the presiding officer, "would have probative value to a reasonable person." §6(D)(1). Under this test, not only is testimonial hearsay and evidence obtained through coercion fully admissible, but neither live testimony nor witnesses' written statements need be sworn. See §§6(D)(2)(b), (3). Moreover, the accused and his civilian counsel may be denied access to evidence in the form of "protected information" (which includes classified information as well as "information protected by law or rule from unauthorized disclosure" and "information concerning other national security interests," §§6(B)(3), 6(D)(5)(a)(v)), so long as the presiding officer concludes that the evidence is "probative" under §6(D)(1) and that its admission without the accused's knowledge would not "result in the denial of a full and fair trial." §6(D)(5)(b). Finally, a presiding officer's determination that evidence "would not have probative value to a reasonable person" may be overridden by a majority of the other commission members. §6(D)(1). . . .

B

Hamdan [objects] that he may, under the Commission Order, be convicted based on evidence he has not seen or heard, and that any evidence admitted against him need not comply with the admissibility or relevance rules typically applicable in criminal trials and court-martial proceedings.

The Government [responds that] Hamdan will be able to raise any such challenge following a "final decision" under the DTA, and [that] "there is . . . no basis to presume, before the trial has even commenced, that the trial will not be conducted in good faith and according to law." [However,] because Hamdan apparently is not subject to the death penalty (at least as matters now stand) and may receive a sentence shorter than 10 years' imprisonment, he has no automatic right to review of the commission's "final decision" before a federal court under the DTA. See §1005(e)(3), 119 Stat. 2743. [Moreover], contrary to the Government's assertion, there is a "basis to presume" that the procedures employed during Hamdan's trial will violate the law: The procedures are described with particularity in Commission Order No. 1, and implementation of some of them has already occurred. One of Hamdan's complaints is that he will be, and *indeed already has been*, excluded from his own trial. Under these circumstances, review of the procedures in advance of a "final decision"—the timing of which is left entirely to the discretion of the President under the DTA—is appropriate. . . .

C

[T]he procedures governing trials by military commission historically have been the same as those governing courts-martial. . . . The uniformity principle is not an inflexible one; it does not preclude all departures from the procedures dictated for use by courts-martial. But any departure must be tailored to the exigency that necessitates it. That understanding is reflected in Article 36 of the UCMJ, which provides:

> (a) The procedure, including modes of proof, in cases before courts-martial, courts of inquiry, military commissions, and other military tribunals may be prescribed by the President by regulations which shall, so far as he considers practicable, apply the principles of law and the rules of evidence generally recognized in the trial of criminal cases in the United States district courts, but which may not be contrary to or inconsistent with this chapter.

> (b) All rules and regulations made under this article shall be uniform insofar as practicable and shall be reported to Congress. 70A Stat. 50.

Article 36 places two restrictions on the President's power to promulgate rules of procedure for courts-martial and military commissions alike. First, no procedural rule he adopts may be "contrary to or inconsistent with" the UCMJ—however practical it may seem. Second, the rules adopted must be "uniform insofar as practicable." That is, the rules applied to military commissions must be the same as those applied to courts-martial unless such uniformity proves impracticable.

Hamdan . . . maintains that the procedures described in the Commission Order are inconsistent with the UCMJ and that the Government has offered no explanation for their deviation from the procedures governing courts-martial. . . . [T]he Government contends [that] military commissions would be of no use if the President were hamstrung by those provisions of the UCMJ that govern courts-martial. [It also points to] the President's determination [in the November 13th Order setting up the military commissions] that "the danger to the safety of the United States and the nature of international terrorism" renders it impracticable "to apply in military commissions . . . the principles of law and rules of evidence generally recognized in the trial of criminal cases in the United States district courts."

Hamdan has the better of this argument. Without reaching the question whether any provision of Commission Order No. 1 is strictly "contrary to or inconsistent with" other provisions of the UCMJ, we conclude that the "practicability" determination the President has made is insufficient to justify variances from the procedures governing courts-martial. Subsection (b) of Article 36 was added after World War II, and requires a different showing of impracticability from the one required by subsection (a). Subsection (a) requires that the rules the President promulgates for courts-martial, provost courts, and military commissions alike conform to those that govern procedures in *Article III courts*, "so far *as he considers* practicable." 10 U.S.C. §836(a) (emphasis added). Subsection (b), by contrast, demands that the rules applied in courts-martial, provost courts, and military commissions—whether or not they conform with the Federal Rules of Evidence—be "uniform *insofar as practicable.*" §836(b) (emphasis added). Under the latter provision, then, the rules set forth in the Manual for Courts-Martial must apply to military commissions unless impracticable.

The President here has determined, pursuant to subsection (a), that it is impracticable to apply the rules and principles of law that govern "the trial of criminal cases in the United States district courts," §836(a), to Hamdan's commission. We assume that complete deference is owed that determination. The President has not, however, made a similar official determination that it is impracticable to apply the rules for courts-martial.[d] And even if subsection (b)'s requirements may be satisfied without such an official determination, the requirements of that subsection are not satisfied here. Nothing in the record before us demonstrates that it would be impracticable to apply court-martial rules in this case. [T]he only reason offered in support of that determination is the danger posed by international terrorism.[e] Without for one moment under-estimating that danger, it is not evident to us why it should require, in the case of Hamdan's trial, any variance from the rules that govern courts-martial. . . . Under the circumstances, then, the rules applicable in courts-martial must apply. Since it is undisputed that Commission Order No. 1 deviates in many significant respects from those rules, it necessarily violates Article 36(b).

[T]he military commission was not born of a desire to dispense a more summary form of justice than is afforded by courts-martial; it developed, rather, as a tribunal of necessity to be employed when courts-martial lacked jurisdiction over either the accused or the subject matter. Exigency lent the commission its legitimacy, but did not further justify the wholesale jettisoning of procedural protections. That history explains why the military commission's procedures typically have been the ones used by courts-martial. . . . Article 36, confirming as much, strikes a careful balance between uniform procedure and the need to accommodate exigencies that may sometimes arise in a theater of war. That Article not having been complied with here, the rules specified for Hamdan's trial are illegal.

D

The procedures adopted to try Hamdan also violate the Geneva Conventions. . . . The Court of Appeals [rejected Hamdan's argument based] on

---

d. We may assume that such a determination would be entitled to a measure of deference. For the reasons given by Justice Kennedy, however, the level of deference accorded to a determination made under subsection (b) presumably would not be as high as that accorded to a determination under subsection (a).

e. Justice Thomas looks not to the President's official Article 36(a) determination, but instead to press statements made by the Secretary of Defense and the Under Secretary of Defense for Policy. We have not heretofore, in evaluating the legality of Executive action, deferred to comments made by such officials to the media. Moreover, the only additional reason the comments provide—aside from the general danger posed by international terrorism—for departures from court-martial procedures is the need to protect classified information. As we explain in the text, and as Justice Kennedy elaborates in his separate opinion, the structural and procedural defects of Hamdan's commission extend far beyond rules preventing access to classified information.

[a footnote in] Johnson v. Eisentrager, 339 U.S. 763 (1950), [which] involved a challenge by 21 German nationals to their 1945 convictions for war crimes by a military tribunal convened in Nanking, China, and to their subsequent imprisonment in occupied Germany. [Referring to the protections afforded by the 1929 Geneva Conventions the Court said:] "These prisoners claim to be and are entitled to its protection. It is, however, the obvious scheme of the Agreement that responsibility for observance and enforcement of these rights is upon political and military authorities. Rights of alien enemies are vindicated under it only through protests and intervention of protecting powers as the rights of our citizens against foreign governments are vindicated only by Presidential intervention."

[T]he *Eisentrager* footnote . . . does not control this case. We may assume that . . . absent some other provision of law . . . Hamdan [may not invoke] the Convention's provisions as an independent source of law binding the Government's actions and furnishing petitioner with any enforceable right. [But] regardless of the nature of the rights conferred on Hamdan, they are, as the Government does not dispute, part of the law of war. And compliance with the law of war is the condition upon which the authority set forth in Article 21 is granted.

ii

[T]he Court of Appeals [also] concluded that the Conventions did not in any event apply to the armed conflict during which Hamdan was captured . . . [because] Hamdan was captured and detained incident to the conflict with al Qaeda and not the conflict with the Taliban, and . . . al Qaeda, unlike Afghanistan, is not a "High Contracting Party"—i.e., a signatory of the Conventions. . . .

We need not decide the merits of this argument because there is at least one provision of the Geneva Conventions that applies here even if the relevant conflict is not one between signatories. Article 3, often referred to as Common Article 3 because, like Article 2, it appears in all four Geneva Conventions, provides that in a "conflict not of an international character occurring in the territory of one of the High Contracting Parties, each Party to the conflict shall be bound to apply, as a minimum," certain provisions protecting "[p]ersons taking no active part in the hostilities, including members of armed forces who have laid down their arms and those placed *hors de combat* by . . . detention." One such provision prohibits "the passing of sentences and the carrying out of executions without previous judgment pronounced by a regularly constituted court affording all the judicial guarantees which are recognized as indispensable by civilized peoples."

The Court of Appeals thought, and the Government asserts, that Common Article 3 does not apply to Hamdan because the conflict with al Qaeda, being "'international in scope,'" does not qualify as a "'conflict not of an international character.'" [But] [t]he term "conflict not of an international character" is used here in contradistinction to a conflict between nations. . . . Common Article 3 . . . affords some minimal protection, falling short of full protection under the Conventions, to individuals associated with neither a signatory nor even a nonsignatory "Power" who are involved in a conflict "in the territory of" a signatory. . . . Commentary on the Additional Protocols to the Geneva Conventions of 12 August 1949, p. 1351 (1987) ("[A] non-international armed conflict is distinct from an international armed conflict because of the legal status of the entities opposing each other").

iii

Common Article 3, then, is applicable here and, as indicated above, requires that Hamdan be tried by a "regularly constituted court affording all the judicial guarantees which are recognized as indispensable by civilized peoples." . . .

The commentary accompanying a provision of the Fourth Geneva Convention . . . defines "'regularly constituted'" tribunals to include "ordinary military courts" and "definitely exclud[e] all special tribunals." . . . And one of the Red Cross' own treatises defines "regularly constituted court" as used in Common Article 3 to mean "established and organized in accordance with the laws and procedures already in force in a country." Int'l Comm. of Red Cross, 1 Customary International Humanitarian Law 355 (2005). . . . As Justice Kennedy explains, . . . "[t]he regular military courts in our system are the courts-martial established by congressional statutes." At a minimum, a military commission "can be 'regularly constituted' by the standards of our military justice system only if some practical need explains deviations from court-martial practice." As we have explained . . . no such need has been demonstrated here.[f]

iv

Inextricably intertwined with the question of regular constitution is the evaluation of the procedures governing the tribunal and whether they afford "all the judicial guarantees which are recognized as indispensable by civilized peoples." Like the phrase "regularly constituted court," this phrase is not defined in the text of the Geneva Conventions. But it must be understood to incorporate at least the barest of those trial protections that have been recognized by customary international law. Many of these are described in Article 75 of Protocol I to the Geneva Conventions of 1949, adopted in 1977 (Protocol I). Although the United States declined to ratify Protocol I, its objections were not to Article 75 thereof. Indeed, it appears that the Government "regard[s] the provisions of Article 75 as an articulation of safeguards to which all persons in

---

f. Further evidence of this tribunal's irregular constitution is the fact that its rules and procedures are subject to change midtrial, at the whim of the Executive. See Commission Order No. 1, §11 (providing that the Secretary of Defense may change the governing rules "from time to time").

the hands of an enemy are entitled." Among the rights set forth in Article 75 is the "right to be tried in [one's] presence." Protocol I, Art. 75(4)(e). . . .

That the Government has a compelling interest in denying Hamdan access to certain sensitive information is not doubted. But, at least absent express statutory provision to the contrary, information used to convict a person of a crime must be disclosed to him. . . . Common Article 3 obviously tolerates a great degree of flexibility in trying individuals captured during armed conflict; its requirements are general ones, crafted to accommodate a wide variety of legal systems. But *requirements* they are nonetheless. The commission that the President has convened to try Hamdan does not meet those requirements.

VII.

We have assumed, as we must, that the allegations made in the Government's charge against Hamdan are true. We have assumed, moreover, the truth of the message implicit in that charge—viz., that Hamdan is a dangerous individual whose beliefs, if acted upon, would cause great harm and even death to innocent civilians, and who would act upon those beliefs if given the opportunity. It bears emphasizing that Hamdan does not challenge, and we do not today address, the Government's power to detain him for the duration of active hostilities in order to prevent such harm. But in undertaking to try Hamdan and subject him to criminal punishment, the Executive is bound to comply with the Rule of Law that prevails in this jurisdiction.

The judgment of the Court of Appeals is reversed, and the case is remanded for further proceedings.

It is so ordered.

THE CHIEF JUSTICE took no part in the consideration or decision of this case.

Justice BREYER, with whom Justice KENNEDY, Justice SOUTER, and Justice GINSBURG join, concurring.

. . . The Court's conclusion ultimately rests upon a single ground: Congress has not issued the Executive a "blank check." Cf. Hamdi v. Rumsfeld, 542 U.S. 507, 536 (2004) (plurality opinion). Indeed, Congress has denied the President the legislative authority to create military commissions of the kind at issue here. Nothing prevents the President from returning to Congress to seek the authority he believes necessary.

Where, as here, no emergency prevents consultation with Congress, judicial insistence upon that consultation does not weaken our Nation's ability to deal with danger. To the contrary, that insistence strengthens the Nation's ability to determine—through democratic means—how best to do so. The Constitution places its faith in those democratic means. Our Court today simply does the same.

Justice KENNEDY, with whom Justice SOUTER, Justice GINSBURG, and Justice BREYER join as to Parts I and II, concurring in part.

Military Commission Order No. 1, which governs the military commission established to try petitioner Salim Hamdan for war crimes, exceeds limits that certain statutes, duly enacted by Congress, have placed on the President's authority to convene military courts. This is not a case, then, where the Executive can assert some unilateral authority to fill a void left by congressional inaction. It is a case where Congress, in the proper exercise of its powers as an independent branch of government, and as part of a long tradition of legislative involvement in matters of military justice, has considered the subject of military tribunals and set limits on the President's authority. Where a statute provides the conditions for the exercise of governmental power, its requirements are the result of a deliberative and reflective process engaging both of the political branches. Respect for laws derived from the customary operation of the Executive and Legislative Branches gives some assurance of stability in time of crisis. The Constitution is best preserved by reliance on standards tested over time and insulated from the pressures of the moment.

[T]he requirement of the Geneva Conventions of 1949 that military tribunals be "regularly constituted" . . . controls here, if for no other reason, because Congress requires that military commissions like the ones at issue conform to the "law of war," 10 U.S.C. §821. Whatever the substance and content of the term "regularly constituted" as interpreted in this and any later cases, there seems little doubt that it relies upon the importance of standards deliberated upon and chosen in advance of crisis, under a system where the single power of the Executive is checked by other constitutional mechanisms. . . . [D]omestic statutes control this case. If Congress, after due consideration, deems it appropriate to change the controlling statutes, in conformance with the Constitution and other laws, it has the power and prerogative to do so. . . .

I.

Trial by military commission raises separation-of-powers concerns of the highest order. Located within a single branch, these courts carry the risk that offenses will be defined, prosecuted, and adjudicated by executive officials without independent review. Concentration of power puts personal liberty in peril of arbitrary action by officials, an incursion the Constitution's three-part system is designed to avoid. It is imperative, then, that when military tribunals are established, full and proper authority exists for the Presidential directive.

The proper framework for assessing whether Executive actions are authorized is the three-part scheme used by Justice Jackson in his opinion in Youngstown Sheet & Tube Co. v. Sawyer, 343 U.S. 579 (1952). "When the President acts pursuant to an express or implied authorization of Congress, his authority is at its maximum, for it includes all that he possesses in his own right plus all that Congress can delegate." "When the President acts in absence of either a congressional grant or denial of authority, he can only rely upon his own independent powers, but there is a zone of twilight in which he and Congress may have concurrent authority, or in which its distribution is uncertain." And "[w]hen the President takes measures incompatible with the expressed or implied will of Congress, his power is at its lowest ebb."

In this case, as the Court observes, the President has acted in a field with a history of congressional participation and regulation. In the Uniform Code of Military Justice (UCMJ), . . . Congress has set forth governing principles for military courts. . . . The UCMJ . . . provide[s] authority for certain forms of military courts, [but] also impose[s] limitations, at least two of which control this case. If the President has exceeded these limits, this becomes a case of conflict between Presidential and congressional action—a case within Justice Jackson's third category, not the second or first.

[Section 836 of the UCMJ] allows the President to implement and build on the UCMJ's framework by adopting procedural regulations, subject to three requirements: (1) Procedures for military courts must conform to district-court rules insofar as the President "considers practicable"; (2) the procedures may not be contrary to or inconsistent with the provisions of the UCMJ; and (3) [according to 836(b)] "insofar as practicable" all rules and regulations under §836 must be uniform, a requirement, as the Court points out, that indicates the rules must be the same for military commissions as for courts-martial unless such uniformity is impracticable.

[Section 836(b)] requires us to compare the military-commission procedures with those for courts-martial and determine, to the extent there are deviations, whether greater uniformity would be practicable. Although we can assume the President's practicability judgments are entitled to some deference, the Court observes that Congress' choice of language in the uniformity provision of 10 U.S.C. §836(b) contrasts with the language of §836(a). This difference suggests, at the least, a lower degree of deference for §836(b) determinations. The rules for military courts may depart from federal-court rules whenever the President "considers" conformity impracticable, §836(a); but the statute requires procedural uniformity across different military courts "insofar as [uniformity is] practicable," §836(b), not insofar as the President considers it to be so. [T]he Court is also correct [that] the term "practicable" cannot be construed to permit deviations based on mere convenience or expedience. "Practicable" means "feasible," that is, "possible to practice or perform" or "capable of being put into practice, done, or accomplished." Webster's Third New International Dictionary 1780 (1961). Congress' chosen language, then, is best understood to allow the selection of procedures based on logistical constraints, the accommodation of witnesses, the security of the proceedings, and the like. Insofar as the "[p]retrial, trial, and post-trial procedures" for the military commissions at issue deviate from court-martial practice, the deviations must be explained by some such practical need. . . .

In §821 [of the UCMJ] Congress has addressed the possibility that special military commissions—criminal courts other than courts-martial—may at times be convened. At the same time, however, the President's authority to convene military commissions is limited: It extends only to "offenders or offenses" that "by statute or by the law of war may be tried by" such military commissions.

The Government does not claim to base the charges against Hamdan on a statute; instead it invokes the law of war. That law, as the Court explained in Ex parte Quirin, 317 U.S. 1 (1942), derives from "rules and precepts of the law of nations"; it is the body of international law governing armed conflict. If the military commission at issue is illegal under the law of war, then an offender cannot be tried "by the law of war" before that commission.

[C]ommon Article 3 of the four Geneva Conventions of 1949 . . . prohibits . . . "[t]he passing of sentences and the carrying out of executions without previous judgment pronounced by a regularly constituted court affording all the judicial guarantees which are recognized as indispensable by civilized peoples."

The provision is part of a treaty the United States has ratified and thus accepted as binding law. By Act of Congress, moreover, violations of Common Article 3 are considered "war crimes," punishable as federal offenses, when committed by or against United States nationals and military personnel. See 18 U.S.C. §2441. There should be no doubt, then, that Common Article 3 is part of the law of war as that term is used in §821.

The dissent by Justice Thomas argues that Common Article 3 nonetheless is irrelevant to this case because in Johnson v. Eisentrager, 339 U.S. 763 (1950), it was said to be the "obvious scheme" of the 1929 Geneva Convention that "[r]ights of alien enemies are vindicated under it only through protests and intervention of protecting powers," i.e., signatory states. As the Court explains, this language from *Eisentrager* is not controlling here. Even assuming the *Eisentrager* analysis has some bearing upon the analysis of the broader 1949 Conventions and that, in consequence, rights are vindicated "under [those Conventions]" only through protests and intervention, Common Article 3 is nonetheless relevant to the question of authorization under §821. Common Article 3 is part of the law of war that Congress has directed the President to follow in establishing military commissions. Consistent with that view, the *Eisentrager* Court itself considered on the merits claims that "procedural irregularities" under the 1929 Convention "deprive[d] the Military Commission of jurisdiction."

In another military commission case, In re Yamashita, 327 U.S. 1 (1946), the Court likewise considered on the merits—without any caveat about remedies under the Convention—a claim that an alleged violation of the 1929 Convention "establish[ed] want of authority in the commission to proceed with the trial." That is the precise inquiry we are asked to perform here.

Assuming the President has authority to establish a special military commission to try Hamdan, the commission must satisfy Common Article 3's requirement of a "regularly constituted court affording all the judicial guarantees which are recognized as indispensable by civilized peoples." The terms of this general standard are yet to be elaborated and further defined, but Congress has required compliance with it by referring to the "law of war" in §821. The Court correctly concludes that the military commission here does not comply with this provision.

Common Article 3's standard ... of a "regularly constituted court affording all the judicial guarantees which are recognized as indispensable by civilized peoples," supports, at the least, a uniformity principle similar to that codified in §836(b). . . .

In addition, whether or not the possibility, contemplated by the regulations here, of midtrial procedural changes could by itself render a military commission impermissibly irregular, an acceptable degree of independence from the Executive is necessary to render a commission "regularly constituted" by the standards of our Nation's system of justice. And any suggestion of Executive power to interfere with an ongoing judicial process raises concerns about the proceedings' fairness.

[T]he standard of Common Article 3, applied here in conformity with §821, parallels the practicability standard of §836(b). Section 836, however, is limited by its terms to matters properly characterized as procedural—that is, "[p]retrial, trial, and post-trial procedures"—while Common Article 3 permits broader consideration of matters of structure, organization, and mechanisms to promote the tribunal's insulation from command influence. Thus the combined effect of the two statutes discussed here—§§836 and 821—is that considerations of practicability must support departures from court-martial practice. Relevant concerns, as noted earlier, relate to logistical constraints, accommodation of witnesses, security of the proceedings, and the like, not mere expedience or convenience. . . . .

II.

[T]he allegations against Hamdan are undoubtedly serious. Captured in Afghanistan during our Nation's armed conflict with the Taliban and al Qaeda—a conflict that continues as we speak—Hamdan stands accused of overt acts in furtherance of a conspiracy to commit terrorism: delivering weapons and ammunition to al Qaeda, acquiring trucks for use by Osama bin Laden's bodyguards, providing security services to bin Laden, and receiving weapons training at a terrorist camp. Nevertheless, the circumstances of Hamdan's trial present no exigency requiring special speed or precluding careful consideration of evidence. For roughly four years, Hamdan has been detained at a permanent United States military base in Guantanamo Bay, Cuba. And regardless of the outcome of the criminal proceedings at issue, the Government claims authority to continue to detain him based on his status as an enemy combatant.

Against this background, the Court is correct to conclude that the military commission the President has convened to try Hamdan is unauthorized. . . . It is no answer that, at the end of the day, the Detainee Treatment Act of 2005 (DTA) affords military-commission defendants the opportunity for judicial review in federal court. As the Court is correct to observe, the scope of that review is limited, and the review is not automatic if the defendant's sentence is under 10 years. Also, provisions for review of legal issues after trial cannot correct for structural defects, such as the role of the Appointing Authority, that can cast doubt on the factfinding process and the presiding judge's exercise of discretion during trial. Before military-commission defendants may obtain judicial review, furthermore, they must navigate a military review process that again raises fairness concerns . . . [and] lacks structural protections designed to help ensure impartiality.

[S]tructural differences between the military commissions and courts-martial—the concentration of functions, including legal decisionmaking, in a single executive official; the less rigorous standards for composition of the tribunal; and the creation of special review procedures in place of institutions created and regulated by Congress—remove safeguards that are important to the fairness of the proceedings and the independence of the court. Congress has prescribed these guarantees for courts-martial; and no evident practical need explains the departures here. For these reasons the commission cannot be considered regularly constituted under United States law and thus does not satisfy Congress' requirement that military commissions conform to the law of war.

Apart from these structural issues, moreover, the basic procedures for the commissions deviate from procedures for courts-martial, in violation of §836(b) [and] the Military Commission Order abandons the detailed Military Rules of Evidence, which are modeled on the Federal Rules of Evidence in conformity with §836(a)'s requirement of presumptive compliance with district-court rules. Instead, the order imposes just one evidentiary rule: "Evidence shall be admitted if . . . the evidence would have probative value to a reasonable person." . . . The rule here could permit admission of multiple hearsay and other forms of evidence generally prohibited on grounds of unreliability. Indeed, the commission regulations specifically contemplate admission of unsworn written statements, and they make no provision for exclusion of coerced declarations save those "established to have been made as a result of torture"; cf. Military Rule Evid. 304(c)(3) (generally barring use of statements obtained "through the use of coercion, unlawful influence, or unlawful inducement"); 10 U.S.C. §831 (d) (same). Besides, even if evidence is deemed nonprobative by the presiding officer at Hamdan's trial, the military-commission members still may view it. In another departure from court-martial practice the military commission members may object to the presiding officer's evidence rulings and determine themselves, by majority vote, whether to admit the evidence.

As the Court explains, the Government has made no demonstration of practical need for these special rules and procedures, either in this particular case or as to the military commissions in general, nor is any such need self-evident. For all the Government's regulations and submissions reveal, it would be feasible for most, if not all, of the conventional military evidence rules and procedures to be followed.

In sum, as presently structured, Hamdan's military commission exceeds the bounds Congress has placed on the President's authority in §§836 and 821 of the UCMJ. Because Congress has prescribed these limits, Congress can change them, requiring a new analysis consistent with the Constitution and other governing laws. . . .

Justice SCALIA, with whom Justice THOMAS and Justice ALITO join, dissenting.

On December 30, 2005, Congress enacted the Detainee Treatment Act (DTA). . . . The DTA provides: "[N]o court, justice, or judge shall have jurisdiction to hear or consider an application for a writ of habeas corpus filed by or on behalf of an alien detained by the Department of Defense at Guantanamo Bay, Cuba." §1005(e)(1), 119 Stat. 2742 (internal division omitted). This provision "t[ook] effect on the date of the enactment of this Act," §1005(h)(1), id., at 2743, which was December 30, 2005. As of that date, then, *no* court had jurisdiction to "hear or consider" the merits of petitioner's habeas application.

This repeal of jurisdiction is simply not ambiguous as between pending and future cases. It prohibits *any* exercise of jurisdiction, and it became effective as to *all* cases last December 30. It is also perfectly clear that the phrase "no court, *justice*, or judge" includes this Court and its Members, and that by exercising our appellate jurisdiction in this case we are "hear[ing] or consider[ing] . . . an application for a writ of habeas corpus."

. . .

Because I would hold that §1005(e)(1) unambiguously terminates the jurisdiction of all courts to "hear or consider" pending habeas applications, I must confront petitioner's arguments that the provision, so interpreted, violates the Suspension Clause. This claim is easily dispatched. We stated in Johnson v. Eisentrager, 339 U.S. 763, 768 (1950):

> We are cited to no instance where a court, in this or any other country where the writ is known, has issued it on behalf of an alien enemy who, at no relevant time and in no stage of his captivity, has been within its territorial jurisdiction. Nothing in the text of the Constitution extends such a right, nor does anything in our statutes.

Notwithstanding the ill-considered dicta in the Court's opinion in *Rasul,* it is clear that Guantanamo Bay, Cuba, is outside the sovereign "territorial jurisdiction" of the United States. Petitioner, an enemy alien detained abroad, has no rights under the Suspension Clause. . . .

Justice THOMAS, with whom Justice SCALIA joins, and with whom Justice ALITO joins in all but Parts I, II-C-1, and III-B-2, dissenting.

[T]he Court's resolution of the merits of petitioner's claims . . . openly flouts our well-established duty to respect the Executive's judgment in matters of military operations and foreign affairs. The Court's evident belief that it is qualified to pass on the "[m]ilitary necessity," of the Commander in Chief's decision to employ a particular form of force against our enemies is so antithetical to our constitutional structure that it simply cannot go unanswered. I respectfully dissent.

I.

Our review of petitioner's claims arises in the context of the President's wartime exercise of his commander-in-chief authority in conjunction with the complete support of Congress. Accordingly, it is important to take measure of the respective roles the Constitution assigns to the three branches of our Government in the conduct of war.

As I explained in Hamdi v. Rumsfeld, 542 U.S. 507 (2004), the structural advantages attendant to the Executive Branch—namely, the decisiveness, "'activity, secrecy, and dispatch'" that flow from the Executive's "'unity[]'"—led the Founders to conclude that the "President ha[s] primary responsibility—along with the necessary power—to protect the national security and to conduct the Nation's foreign relations." Consistent with this conclusion, the Constitution vests in the President "[t]he executive Power," Art. II, §1, provides that he "shall be Commander in Chief" of the Armed Forces, §2, and places in him the power to recognize foreign governments, §3. This Court has observed that these provisions confer upon the President broad constitutional authority to protect the Nation's security in the manner he deems fit. See, e.g., Prize Cases, 2 Black 635, 668 (1863) ("If a war be made by invasion of a foreign nation, the President is not only authorized but bound to resist force by force . . . without waiting for any special legislative authority"); Fleming v. Page, 9 How. 603, 615 (1850) (acknowledging that the President has the authority to "employ [the Nation's Armed Forces] in the manner he may deem most effectual to harass and conquer and subdue the enemy").

Congress, to be sure, has a substantial and essential role in both foreign affairs and national security. But "Congress cannot anticipate and legislate with regard to every possible action the President may find it necessary to take or every possible situation in which he might act," and "[s]uch failure of Congress . . . does not, 'especially . . . in the areas of foreign policy and national security,' imply 'congressional disapproval' of action taken by the Executive." Dames & Moore v. Regan, 453 U.S. 654, 678 (1981) (quoting Haig v. Agee, 453 U.S. 280, 291 (1981)). Rather, in these domains, the fact that Congress has provided the President with broad authorities does not imply—and the Judicial Branch should not infer—that Congress intended to deprive him of particular powers not specifically enumerated.

When "the President acts pursuant to an express or implied authorization from Congress," his actions are "'supported by the strongest of presumptions and the widest latitude of judicial interpretation, and the burden of persuasion . . . rest[s] heavily upon any who might attack it.'" [Dames & Moore] at 668 (quoting Youngstown Sheet & Tube Co. v. Sawyer, 343 U.S. 579, 637 (1952) (Jackson, J., concurring)). Accordingly, in the very context that we address today, this Court has concluded that "the detention and trial of petitioners—ordered by the President in the declared exercise of his powers as Commander in Chief of the Army in time of war and of grave public danger—are not to be set aside by the courts without the clear conviction that they are in conflict with the Constitution or laws of Congress constitutionally enacted." Ex parte Quirin, 317 U.S. 1, 25 (1942).

Under this framework, the President's decision to try Hamdan before a military commission for his involvement with al Qaeda is entitled to a heavy measure of deference. In the present conflict, Congress has authorized the

President "to use all necessary and appropriate force against those nations, organizations, or persons *he determines* planned, authorized, committed, or aided the terrorist attacks that occurred on September 11, 2001 . . . in order to prevent any future acts of international terrorism against the United States by such nations, organizations or persons." Authorization for Use of Military Force (AUMF) 115 Stat. 224 (emphasis added). As a plurality of the Court observed in *Hamdi*, the "capture, detention, and *trial* of unlawful combatants, by 'universal agreement and practice,' are 'important incident[s] of war,'" and are therefore "an exercise of the 'necessary and appropriate force' Congress has authorized the President to use." *Hamdi's* observation that military commissions are included within the AUMF's authorization is supported by this Court's previous recognition that "[a]n important incident to the conduct of war is the adoption of measures by the military commander, not only to repel and defeat the enemy, but to seize and subject to disciplinary measures those enemies who, in their attempt to thwart or impede our military effort, have violated the law of war." In re Yamashita, 327 U.S. 1, 11 (1946).

Although the Court concedes the legitimacy of the President's use of military commissions in certain circumstances, it suggests that the AUMF has no bearing on the scope of the President's power to utilize military commissions in the present conflict. Instead, the Court determines the scope of this power based exclusively on Article 21 of the Uniform Code of Military Justice (UCMJ), 10 U.S.C. §821, the successor to Article 15 of the Articles of War . . . Article 21 alone supports the use of commissions here. Nothing in the language of Article 21, however, suggests that it outlines the entire reach of congressional authorization of military commissions in all conflicts—quite the contrary, the language of Article 21 presupposes the existence of military commissions under an independent basis of authorization. Indeed, consistent with *Hamdi's* conclusion that the AUMF itself authorizes the trial of unlawful combatants, the original sanction for military commissions historically derived from congressional authorization of "the initiation of war" with its attendant authorization of "the employment of all necessary and proper agencies for its due prosecution." Accordingly, congressional authorization for military commissions pertaining to the instant conflict derives not only from Article 21 of the UCMJ, but also from the more recent, and broader, authorization contained in the AUMF.[a]

I note the Court's error respecting the AUMF . . . to emphasize the complete congressional sanction of the President's exercise of his commander-in-chief authority to conduct the present war. In such circumstances, as previously noted, our duty to defer to the Executive's military and foreign policy judgment is at its zenith; it does not countenance the kind of second-guessing the Court repeatedly engages in today. Military and foreign policy judgments "'are and

---

a. Although the President very well may have inherent authority to try unlawful combatants for violations of the law of war before military commissions, we need not decide that question because Congress has authorized the President to do so.

should be undertaken only by those directly responsible to the people whose welfare they advance or imperil. They are decisions of a kind for which the Judiciary has neither aptitude, facilities nor responsibility and which has long been held to belong in the domain of political power not subject to judicial intrusion or inquiry.'" . . .

III.

A

[T]he Court . . . concludes that Hamdan's commission is unlawful because the President has not explained why it is not practicable to apply the same rules and procedures to Hamdan's commission as would be applied in a trial by court martial. . . . [T]he Court's conclusion is flatly contrary to its duty not to set aside Hamdan's commission "without the *clear* conviction that [it is] in conflict with the . . . laws of Congress constitutionally enacted." *Quirin* (emphasis added).

[A]rticle 36(b) [requires] nothing more than uniformity across the separate branches of the armed services. There is no indication that the UCMJ was intended to require uniformity in procedure between courts-martial and military commissions, tribunals that the UCMJ itself recognizes are different. . . . Thus, Article 36(b) is best understood as establishing that, so far as practicable, the rules and regulations governing tribunals convened by the Navy must be uniform with the rules and regulations governing tribunals convened by the Army.

[I]t cannot be understood to require the President to conform the procedures employed by military commissions to those employed by courts-martial.

[Moreover,] [u]nder the Court's reading, the President is entitled to prescribe different rules for military commissions than for courts-martial when he determines that it is not "practicable" to prescribe uniform rules. The Court [asserts that] "[t]he President has not . . . [determined] that it is impracticable to apply the rules for courts-martial." This is simply not the case. On the same day that the President issued Military Commission Order No. 1, the Secretary of Defense explained that "the president decided to establish military commissions because he wanted the option of a process that is different from those processes which we already have, namely the federal court system . . . and the military court system," Dept. of Defense News Briefing on Military Commissions (Mar. 21, 2002) (remarks of Donald Rumsfeld), available at *http://www.dod.gov/transcrips/2002/ t03212002__t0321sd.html* (as visited June 26, 2006, and available in Clerk of Court's case file) (hereinafter News Briefing), and that "[t]he commissions are intended to be different . . . because the [P]resident recognized that there had to be differences to deal with the unusual situation we face and that a different approach was needed." Ibid. The President reached this conclusion because

we're in the middle of a war, and . . . had to design a procedure that would allow us to pursue justice for these individuals while at the same time prosecuting the war most effectively. And that means setting rules that would allow us to preserve our intelligence secrets, develop more information about terrorist activities that might be planned for the future so that we can take action to prevent terrorist attacks against the United States. . . . [T]here was a constant balancing of the requirements of our war policy and the importance of providing justice for individuals . . . and *each* deviation from the standard kinds of rules that we have in our criminal courts was motivated by the desire to strike the balance between individual justice and the broader war policy. Ibid. (remarks of Douglas J. Feith, Under Secretary of Defense for Policy (emphasis added)).

The Court provides no explanation why the President's determination that employing court-martial procedures in the military commissions established pursuant to Military Commission Order No. 1 would hamper our war effort is in any way inadequate to satisfy its newly minted "practicability" requirement. On the contrary, this determination is precisely the kind for which the "Judiciary has neither aptitude, facilities nor responsibility and which has long been held to belong in the domain of political power not subject to judicial intrusion or inquiry." And, in the context of the present conflict, it is exactly the kind of determination Congress countenanced when it authorized the President to use all necessary and appropriate force against our enemies. Accordingly, the President's determination is sufficient to satisfy any practicability requirement imposed by Article 36(b). . . .

B

The Court contends that Hamdan's military commission is also unlawful because it violates Common Article 3 of the Geneva Conventions. Furthermore, Hamdan contends that his commission is unlawful because it violates various provisions of the Third Geneva Convention. These contentions are untenable.

1

[B]oth of Hamdan's Geneva Convention claims are foreclosed by Johnson v. Eisentrager, 339 U.S. 763 (1950), [which stated] held, in the alternative, that the respondents could "not assert . . . that anything in the Geneva Convention makes them immune from prosecution or punishment for war crimes," [because] "the obvious scheme of the Agreement [is] that responsibility for observance and enforcement of these rights is upon political and military authorities. Rights of alien enemies are vindicated under it only through protests and intervention of protecting powers as the rights of our citizens against foreign governments are vindicated only by Presidential intervention." . . . [T]he Court concludes that petitioner may seek judicial enforcement of the provisions of the Geneva Conventions because "they are . . . part of the law of war. And compliance with the law of war is the condition upon which the authority set forth in Article 21 is granted." But Article 21 authorizes the use of military commissions; it does not purport to render judicially enforceable aspects of the law of war that are not so enforceable of their own accord. . . . *Eisentrager* [itself] involved a challenge to the legality of a World War II military commission, which, like all such commissions, found its authorization in Article 15 of the Articles of War, the predecessor to Article 21 of the UCMJ. Thus, the Court's interpretation of Article 21 is foreclosed by *Eisentrager*.

In any event, the Court's argument is too clever by half. The judicial nonenforceability of the Geneva Conventions derives from the fact that those Conventions have exclusive enforcement mechanisms, and this, too, is part of the law of war. . . .

2

In addition to being foreclosed by *Eisentrager*, Hamdan's claim under Common Article 3 of the Geneva Conventions is meritless. Common Article 3 applies to "armed conflict not of an international character occurring in the territory of one of the High Contracting Parties." "Pursuant to [his] authority as Commander in Chief and Chief Executive of the United States," the President has "accept[ed] the legal conclusion of the Department of Justice . . . that Common Article 3 of Geneva does not apply to . . . al Qaeda . . . detainees, because, among other reasons, the relevant conflicts are international in scope and Common Article 3 applies only to 'armed conflict not of an international character.'" Under this Court's precedents, "the meaning attributed to treaty provisions by the Government agencies charged with their negotiation and enforcement is entitled to great weight." Our duty to defer to the President's understanding of the provision at issue here is only heightened by the fact that he is acting pursuant to his constitutional authority as Commander in Chief and by the fact that the subject matter of Common Article 3 calls for a judgment about the nature and character of an armed conflict. See generally United States v. Curtiss-Wright Export Corp., 299 U.S. 304, 320 (1936). The President's interpretation of Common Article 3 is reasonable and should be sustained. The conflict with al Qaeda is international in character in the sense that it is occurring in various nations around the globe. Thus, it is also "occurring in the territory of" more than "one of the High Contracting Parties." The Court does not dispute the President's judgments respecting the nature of our conflict with al Qaeda, nor does it suggest that the President's interpretation of Common Article 3 is implausible or foreclosed by the text of the treaty. . . . But where, as here, an ambiguous treaty provision ("not of an international character") is susceptible of two plausible, and reasonable, interpretations, our precedents require us to defer to the Executive's interpretation.

3

[T]he Court concludes Hamdan's commission fails to satisfy the requirements of Common Article 3 . . . because it "deviate[s] from [the procedures] governing courts-martial." But there is neither a statutory nor historical requirement that military commissions conform to the structure and practice of courts-martial. A military commission is a different tribunal, serving a different function, and thus operates pursuant to different procedures. The 150-year pedigree of the military commission is itself sufficient to establish that such tribunals are "regularly constituted court[s]."

Similarly, the procedures to be employed by Hamdan's commission afford "all the judicial guarantees which are recognized as indispensable by civilized peoples." . . . "Petitioner is entitled to appointed military legal counsel, and may retain a civilian attorney (which he has done). Petitioner is entitled to the presumption of innocence, proof beyond a reasonable doubt, and the right to remain silent. He may confront witnesses against him, and may subpoena his own witnesses, if reasonably available. Petitioner may personally be present at every stage of the trial unless he engages in disruptive conduct or the prosecution introduces classified or otherwise protected information for which no adequate substitute is available and whose admission will not deprive him of a full and fair trial. If petitioner is found guilty, the judgment will be reviewed by a review panel, the Secretary of Defense, and the President, if he does not designate the Secretary as the final decisionmaker. The final judgment is subject to review in the Court of Appeals for the District of Columbia Circuit and ultimately in this Court."

[T]he plurality concludes that Hamdan's commission is unlawful because of the possibility that Hamdan will be barred from proceedings and denied access to evidence that may be used to convict him. But, under the commissions' rules, the Government may not impose such bar or denial on Hamdan if it would render his trial unfair, a question that is clearly within the scope of the appellate review contemplated by regulation and statute.

Moreover, while the Executive is surely not required to offer a particularized defense of these procedures prior to their application, the procedures themselves make clear that Hamdan would only be excluded (other than for disruption) if it were necessary to protect classified (or classifiable) intelligence, including the sources and methods for gathering such intelligence. The Government has explained that "we want to make sure that these proceedings, which are going on in the middle of the war, do not interfere with our war effort and . . . because of the way we would be able to handle interrogations and intelligence information, may actually assist us in promoting our war aims." News Briefing (remarks of Douglas J. Feith, Under Secretary of Defense for Policy). And this Court has concluded, in the very context of a threat to reveal our Nation's intelligence gathering sources and methods, that "[i]t is 'obvious and unarguable' that no governmental interest is more compelling than the security of the Nation," and that "[m]easures to protect the secrecy of our Government's foreign intelligence operations plainly serve these interests." This interest is surely compelling here. According to the Government, "[b]ecause al Qaeda operates as a clandestine force relying on sleeper agents to mount surprise attacks, one of the most critical fronts in the current war involves gathering intelligence about future terrorist attacks and how the terrorist network operates—identifying where its operatives are, how it plans attacks, who directs operations, and how they communicate." We should not rule out the possibility that this compelling interest can be protected, while at the same time affording Hamdan (and others like him) a fair trial.

In these circumstances, "civilized peoples" would take into account the context of military commission trials against unlawful combatants in the war on terrorism, including the need to keep certain information secret in the interest of preventing future attacks on our Nation and its foreign installations so long as it did not deprive the accused of a fair trial. Accordingly, the President's understanding of the requirements of Common Article 3 is entitled to "great weight." . . . For these reasons, I would affirm the judgment of the Court of Appeals.

[Justice ALITO, joined by Justices SCALIA and THOMAS, dissented on the grounds that the military commissions complied with the standards of section 836(b) and Common Article 3 of the Geneva Conventions].

Discussion

1. *Constitutional issues underground.* On its surface, *Hamdan* seems to be mostly about statutory interpretation; Justice Kennedy's concurrence says much more about separation of powers than the majority does. But behind the statutory issues are important constitutional questions. For example, when the Court insists that the President is bound by the laws of war because these are incorporated into Article 21 of the UCMJ, it is also saying that Congress has the right to conform the President's conduct to the requirements of the UCMJ, notwithstanding the President's Article II powers as Commander-in-Chief. When the Court interprets section 36(b) of the UCMJ to require uniformity between courts-martial and military commissions unless the President demonstrates that this would be impractical, it is also saying that it will not automatically accept any reasons the President gives; and therefore that courts have the right to subject his decisionmaking in this area to some degree of judicial scrutiny. When the Court holds that the Geneva Conventions, as part of the laws of war, are binding on the President, it is asserting that these treaties— and, equally important, the Court's interpretation of them—limit the President's discretion in conducting war, including, most importantly, how he holds, interrogates, and treats detainees. Indeed, the key constitutional principle of *Hamdan,* which is mentioned only in footnote b of Stevens's opinion, seems to be that the Executive must follow valid laws passed by Congress (and elements of the laws of war that have been incorporated by reference into domestic law) even if these laws constrain how he conducts warfare and foreign policy.

Justice Thomas and the dissenters, by contrast, are concerned that the President will be hamstrung by too many legal restraints and therefore seek to provide statutory constructions that give the President a far wider freedom of action and a much more relaxed degree of judicial scrutiny. In their view, what Presidents need above all in conducting war is flexibility, discretion, and secrecy. Interpreting laws to create statutory limits policed by the judiciary will hamper effective military decisionmaking in favor of courts who have very little expertise or understanding of the larger strategic issues.

Thus, the disagreements about statutory issues are actually shadow boxing over larger constitutional themes. Note as well that while Justice Stevens and Justice Kennedy interpret this case as falling within box three of *Youngstown*, where the executive's power is at its lowest ebb, Justice Thomas and the dissenters characterize the case as falling into box one, in which the President is supported by the AUMF, the DTA, and the UCMJ, and therefore is owed the greatest deference. Who has the better of the argument?

2. Hamdan *and the inherent powers of the executive.* Does *Hamdan* undermine the argument, made in the OLC "torture memo" that the President has inherent power to regulate the capture and treatment of enemy soldiers and that Congressional statutes that limit his discretion violate Article II? Why shouldn't the courts defer to the President's construction of the UCMJ and the Geneva Conventions to avoid a possible constitutional conflict? Why shouldn't the courts defer to the President's construction because the President is charged with interpreting and implementing the UCMJ and the Geneva Conventions? What might we infer about the Court's view about presidential power from the fact that it refuses to do either of these things?

3. *Common Article 3, detainee treatment, and the War Crimes Act.* The vast majority of guarantees of the Geneva Conventions apply only to regimes that have signed them and agreed to abide by them. Common Article 3, by contrast, offers only a small sliver of guarantees that apply to all human beings who have been captured in war. It provides:

> In the case of armed conflict not of an international character occurring in the territory of one of the High Contracting Parties, each Party to the conflict shall be bound to apply, as a minimum, the following provisions:
>
> (1) Persons taking no active part in the hostilities, including members of armed forces who have laid down their arms and those placed "hors de combat" by sickness, wounds, detention, or any other cause, shall in all circumstances be treated humanely, without any adverse distinction founded on race, colour, religion or faith, sex, birth or wealth, or any other similar criteria.
>
> To this end, the following acts are and shall remain prohibited at any time and in any place whatsoever with respect to the above-mentioned persons:
>
> > (a) violence to life and person, in particular murder of all kinds, mutilation, cruel treatment and torture;
> > (b) taking of hostages;
> > (c) outrages upon personal dignity, in particular humiliating and degrading treatment;
> > (d) the passing of sentences and the carrying out of executions without previous judgment pronounced by a regularly constituted court, affording all the judicial guarantees which are recognized as indispensable by civilized peoples.

(2) The wounded and sick shall be collected and cared for.

An impartial humanitarian body, such as the International Committee of the Red Cross, may offer its services to the Parties to the conflict.

The Parties to the conflict should further endeavour to bring into force, by means of special agreements, all or part of the other provisions of the present Convention.

The application of the preceding provisions shall not affect the legal status of the Parties to the conflict.

Hamdan holds that Common Article 3 is incorporated into the UCMJ as part of the laws of war. As Justice Kennedy's concurrence points out, it is also already incorporated into the War Crimes statute, 18 U.S.C. §2441, which makes it illegal for U.S. nationals or members of the U.S. Armed forces to commit war crimes "whether inside or outside the United States." War crimes are defined in 2441(c)(3) to include "any conduct . . . which constitutes a violation of common Article 3 of the international conventions signed at Geneva, 12 August 1949, or any protocol to such convention to which the United States is a party and which deals with non-international armed conflict."

On its face, Common Article 3 prohibits "mutilation, cruel treatment . . . outrages upon personal dignity, [and] in particular humiliating and degrading treatment" even if they do not rise to the level of torture. The Bush Administration denied that the Geneva Conventions, including Common Article 3, applied to the war against al Qaeda and therefore the administration was not legally bound by Common Article 3's limitations on detention and interrogation methods.[1] The Supreme Court has now held that this is not the case. Why does the Supreme Court's interpretation of the application of Common Article 3 trump the President's? Why shouldn't the Court at least offer great deference to the Executive in treaty interpretations? Cf. Kolovrat v. Oregon, 366 U.S. 187, 194 (1961) ("While courts interpret treaties for themselves, the meaning given them by the departments of government particularly charged with their negotiation and enforcement is given great weight."). Should CIA officials and U.S. servicemen be able to rely on the President's previous declaration that Common Article 3 did not apply as a defense to any prosecutions under the War Crimes Act? Note finally that, in response to *Hamdan*, Congress may insulate U.S. servicemen and U.S. officials from liability under the War Crimes Act by passing new legislation.

4. Hamdan *as a democracy-forcing decision.* Note that the Court did not tell President Bush that he could under no circumstances create military tribunals with limited procedural guarantees. Rather, the Court told the President that under Article 36 of the Uniform Code of Military Justice (UCMJ) and Common

1. At the same time, President Bush ordered "that the detainees be treated humanely and to the extent appropriate and consistent with military necessity, in a manner consistent with the principles of Geneva." See Memorandum, Humane Treatment of al Qaeda and Taliban Detainees, February 7, 2002, available at *http://www.humanrightsfirst.org/us_law/etn/gonzales/memos_dir/dir_20020207_Bush_Det.pdf.*

Article 3 of the Geneva Conventions, he could not do so. That is because Article 36 of the UCMJ requires that the rules for military commissions be roughly the same as those for courts-martial (which generally are used for offenses committed by our own soldiers). The UCMJ also requires that military commissions comport with the laws of war, which include the Geneva Conventions. Article 3 of the Geneva Conventions, in turn, requires that people like Hamdan be tried by "regularly constituted court[s] affording all the judicial guarantees ... recognized as indispensable by civilized peoples." As Justice Kennedy's concurrence points out, the latter requirement dovetails to some degree with the UCMJ's requirement of uniformity between what we do for our own soldiers and what we do for people like Hamdan. The courts have to be regularly constituted; they can't be special-purpose "fly-by-night" courts with their own made-up procedures, or with procedures that can be changed in the middle of the trial; in addition the procedures have to comport with basic guarantees of fairness.

Note, however, that if Congress decides to alter the UCMJ or override the Geneva Conventions, the President can have military tribunals with whatever procedures he likes. To do that, however, would require that Congress publicly decide either (1) that it no longer wanted to abide by the principle of uniformity announced in the UCMJ, (2) that it no longer would require that military commissions abide by the laws of war (as the Court interpreted them), or, finally, (3) that Congress no longer considered the Geneva Conventions binding on the United States. Taking any of those steps is possible—particularly the first two—but doing so would require that Congress make a public statement to that effect by passing new legislation. (The President could also withdraw the United States from the Geneva Conventions, but for political and military reasons alike, there is almost no chance that he would do so.)

Hence, what the Court did in *Hamdan* is not so much countermajoritarian as *democracy forcing*. It limits the President by making him to go back to Congress to ask for more authority than he already has; and if Congress gives it to him, then the Court will not stand in his way.

By forcing the President to ask for authorization, the Court does several things. First, it insists that both branches agree with what the President wants to do. Second, it requires the President to ask for authority when passions have cooled somewhat, as opposed to right after 9/11, when Congress would likely have given him almost anything he wanted. Third, it gives Congress an opportunity and an excuse for oversight. Thus, nothing in *Hamdan* means that the President is constitutionally forbidden from doing what he wants to do. What the Court has done, rather, is use the democratic process as a lever to discipline and constrain the President's unilateral decisionmaking and possible overreaching, recognizing that the President can still do what he likes if he can get Congress to go along. What are the advantages and disadvantages of this approach? Taking up the Court's challenge, President Bush persuaded Congress—which at that point was still controlled by his party—to overturn significant aspects of *Hamdan* in the Military Commissions Act of 2006, discussed below.

Note: The Military Commissions Act of 2006

In response to the *Hamdan* decision Congress passed the Military Commissions Act of 2006, Pub. L. No. 109-366, 120 Stat. 2600. The Act authorizes the President to create new military commissions to try "alien unlawful enemy combatants." It specifically excludes certain procedures in the UCMJ from applying to the new tribunals, including provisions concerning speedy trial, rights against self-incrimination and procedures for pretrial investigation. It also provides that rulings, interpretations and precedents applicable to ordinary military proceedings under the UCMJ will not apply to the new military commissions and vice versa.

1. *The reach of the new military commissions.* Section 3 of the MCA adds new sections to the U.S. Code detailing procedures for the new military commissions and to whom the commissions apply. New section 948a(1) defines "unlawful enemy combatant" to mean "(i) a person who has engaged in hostilities or who has purposefully and materially supported hostilities against the United States or its co-belligerents who is not a lawful enemy combatant (including a person who is part of the Taliban, al Qaeda, or associated forces);" or "(ii) a person who, before, on, or after the date of the enactment of the Military Commissions Act of 2006, has been determined to be an unlawful enemy combatant by a Combatant Status Review Tribunal or another competent tribunal established under the authority of the President or the Secretary of Defense." Section 948d(c) states that such a determination is "dispositive" for purposes of a military commission's jurisdiction to try the person as an unlawful enemy combatant.

2. *Prisoner interrogation rules.* Section 948r sets out rules regarding pretrial interrogation. Under 948r(b) statements obtained by use of torture are not admissible. However, under section 948r(c) statements obtained through interrogation before passage of the Detainee Treatment Act on December 30, 2005 (when Congress specifically banned the use of cruel, inhumane, and degrading treatment by the U.S. government overseas), are admissible where the degree of coercion is "disputed" and where the military judge finds the statement "reliable and possessing sufficient probative value" and "the interests of justice would best be served." Statements obtained through interrogation after December 30, 2005, are treated similarly except that the interrogation methods used to obtain the statement must not be "cruel, inhuman, or degrading" in violation of the Detainee Treatment Act.

In this context, note that Section 8 of the MCA exempts U.S. personnel from criminal prosecution under the War Crimes Act for any acts of "detention and interrogation of aliens" "occurring between September 11, 2001, and December 30, 2005," the date of the Detainee Treatment Act.

3. *Secret and hearsay evidence.* The MCA also responded to *Hamdan* with new rules permitting the introduction of secret and hearsay evidence. Section 949j(c) allows the military judge, on motion of trial counsel, to "delet[e] specified items of classified information from documents to be made available

to the accused" and to substitute summaries of the classified information or "a statement admitting relevant facts that the classified information would tend to prove." The provision also allows the military judge "to protect from disclosure the sources, methods, or activities by which the United States acquired evidence if the military judge finds that the sources, methods, or activities by which the United States acquired such evidence are classified." The judge may, where practical, allow the accused unclassified summaries of how the evidence was obtained.

Section 949a(b)(2)(E) allows the introduction of "hearsay evidence not otherwise admissible under the rules of evidence applicable in trial by general courts-martial" if the proponent discloses to the other side in advance "the particulars of the evidence (including information on the general circumstances under which the evidence was obtained)." However the requirement of disclosure may be modified or waived under section 949j(c) if the hearsay evidence (or how it was obtained) is classified.

4. *Limiting the legal applicability of the Geneva Conventions.* Several sections of the MCA respond to the *Hamdan* Court's use of the Geneva Conventions as a source of law to limit what the President could do. These provisions do not withdraw the U.S. from the Geneva Conventions but simply declare that what the United States does is in compliance with Geneva, block the use of the Geneva Conventions in judicial proceedings, and, in effect, state that only the President may enforce the Geneva Conventions.

Section 948b(f) declares that "A military commission established under this chapter is a regularly constituted court, affording all the necessary 'judicial guarantees which are recognized as indispensable by civilized peoples' for purposes of common Article 3 of the Geneva Conventions." Section 948b(g) attempts to further limit *Hamdan* by stating that "No alien unlawful enemy combatant subject to trial by military commission under this chapter may invoke the Geneva Conventions as a source of rights."

Section 5 of the act states that no person may invoke the Geneva Conventions as a source of legal rights in habeas corpus or civil actions against the United States, current or former officers, employees, agents, military personnel, in any U.S. or state court.

Violations of Geneva might be criminally prosecutable under the War Crimes Act. However, section 6 of the MCA amends the War Crimes Act to criminalize only "grave breaches" of Common Article 3 of the Geneva Conventions. These are defined as (1) torture, (2) cruel or inhuman treatment (acts "intended to inflict severe or serious physical or mental pain or suffering" . . . "including serious physical abuse[]") (3) performing biological experiments, (4) murder of persons not taking an active part in hostilities, (5) mutilation or maiming, (6) intentionally causing serious bodily injury, (7) rape, (8) sexual assault or abuse, or (9) taking hostages. The MCA adds that "No foreign or international source of law shall supply a basis for a rule of decision in the courts of the United States in interpreting" what constitutes a grave breach of Article 3 of the Geneva Conventions.

Violations of Geneva that are not "grave breaches" are not criminally punishable under the amended War Crimes Act, although they are still violations of international law. However, section 6(a)(3) states that "the President has the authority for the United States to interpret the meaning and application" of nongrave breaches, and that "[a]ny Executive Order" interpreting such breaches "shall be authoritative (except as to grave breaches of common Article 3) as a matter of United States law, in the same manner as other administrative regulations." In effect, the MCA declares that it is up to the President to determine whether to prosecute U.S. personnel for grave breaches of the Geneva Conventions under the War Crimes Act. It is also up to the President to determine what constitute nongrave breaches and what, if anything, to do about them. That becomes important because section 6 defines torture and cruel or inhuman treatment fairly narrowly, so that some interrogation methods may fall outside of them.[1]

5. *Limiting habeas corpus. Hamdan* interpreted the Detainee Treatment Act to allow a limited set of habeas appeals. Section 7 of the MCA responds to that interpretation. Section 7(a) eliminates habeas corpus jurisdiction to hear habeas petitions by aliens that the President has designated as enemy combatants. It amends the habeas statute (28 U.S.C. §2241) to read

> (e)(1) No court, justice, or judge shall have jurisdiction to hear or consider an application for a writ of habeas corpus filed by or on behalf of an alien detained by the United States who has been determined by the United States to have been properly detained as an enemy combatant or is awaiting such determination.

> (2) Except [for appeals of Combatant Status Review Tribunals and military commissions under] the Detainee Treatment Act of 2005 . . . no court, justice, or judge shall have jurisdiction to hear or consider any other action against the United States or its agents relating to any aspect of the detention, transfer, treatment, trial, or conditions of confinement of an alien who is or was detained by the United States and has been determined by the United States to have been properly detained as an enemy combatant or is awaiting such determination.

Section 7(b) states that the Act is effective immediately "and shall apply to all cases, without exception, pending on or after the date of the enactment of this Act which relate to any aspect of the detention, transfer, treatment, trial, or conditions of detention of an alien detained by the United States since September 11, 2001."

Detainee access to the federal courts is governed by Section 950g, which allows appeals of judgments of military commissions to the Circuit Court for the District of Columbia. Judicial review of military commissions is limited to "whether the final decision was consistent with the standards and procedures"

---

1. See Marty Lederman, Three of the Most Significant Problems with the "Compromise," Balkinization, Sept. 22, 2006, at *http://balkin.blogspot.com/2006/09/three-of-most-significantproblems.html.*

in the MCA and "to the extent applicable, the Constitution and the laws of the United States." The Supreme Court may review the D.C. Circuit by writ of certiorari.

Discussion

1. Consider the constitutional issues raised by the various provisions of the MCA. For convenience, we might divide them into three categories. One category creates the new tribunals and specifies their procedures. Both Congress and the President have agreed that the President has authority to create the tribunals and agreed how they should operate. This would seem to place the constitution of the new tribunals within box one of the Youngstown analysis. If the commissions are otherwise consistent with the separation of powers, the next question would be whether the commissions comport with due process under *Hamdi,* assuming that detainees at Guantanamo Bay and elsewhere have any due process rights.

2. A second category of the MCA's provisions attempts to shape the exercise of judicial review by the federal courts. One section limits the ability of courts to use foreign or international sources of law to interpret grave breaches of Geneva in the War Crimes Act. Another section of the MCA makes the Geneva Conventions unenforceable in civil and habeas proceedings against the United States (although apparently this limitation does not apply to civil proceedings against other nations or their agents.). Does either of these provisions raise separation of powers issues?

3. Finally, section 7 of the MCA strips federal courts of the ability to hear habeas petitions (not to mention cases under federal question jurisdiction) from persons the President determines are lawfully detained as alien enemy combatants. The Court struck down this feature of the MCA in *Boumediene v. Bush.*

Insert the following after note 5 on p. 881:

Note: Domestic Surveillance and Presidential Power

In December 2005, the New York Times and other news organizations revealed that President Bush, shortly after the September 11, 2001, attacks, had authorized a new secret surveillance program operated by the National Security Agency (NSA),[2] which intercepted communications involving U.S. citizens and other persons residing in the United States. As described by Attorney General Gonzales, "[t]he President has authorized a program to

---

2. James Risen & Eric Licthblau, Bush Lets U.S. Spy on Callers Without Courts, N.Y. Times, Dec. 15, 2005, at *http://www.nytimes.com/2005/12/16/politics/16program.html.*

engage in electronic surveillance [involving] intercepts of contents of communications where . . . one party to the communication is outside the United States," and there is "a reasonable basis to conclude that one party to the communication is a member of al Qaeda, affiliated with al Qaeda, or a member of an organization affiliated with al Qaeda, or working in support of al Qaeda."[3] Details of the program were not revealed, although it appeared to involve a combination of interception of e-mail and phone conversations and various data mining operations.[4] The Bush Administration did not seek warrants or court orders for the program. However, it engaged in an internal review of the NSA's activities every 45 days.

In United States v. United States District Court, 407 U.S. 297 (1972) (sometimes called the *Keith* case) the Supreme Court held that the Fourth Amendment's warrant requirement applied to investigations of wholly domestic threats to security, including domestic political violence and other crimes. But it said nothing about the Fourth Amendment's application to "the scope of the President's surveillance power with respect to the activities of foreign powers, within or without this country." Id. at 308. Although the Supreme Court has never definitively settled the question, several lower courts have subsequently held that the President does not violate the Fourth Amendment when he engages in warrantless surveillance of potential threats to national security coming from foreign governments or their agents. See, e.g., United States v. Truong, 629 F.2d 908 (4th Cir. 1980); United States v. Buck, 548 F.2d 871 (9th Cir. 1977); United States v. Butenko, 494 F.2d 593 (3d Cir. 1974) (en banc); United States v. Brown, 484 F.2d 418 (5th Cir. 1973); but see Zweibon v. Mitchell, 516 F.2d 594 (D.C. Cir. 1975). Instead, Congress has addressed the problem of foreign intelligence oversight through a comprehensive statutory scheme. (Note, however, that Fourth Amendment issues may still arise where the government seeks to target communications by U.S. citizens who are *not* agents of a foreign power. It remains unclear to what extent the NSA program targets any such individuals.)[5]

In 1978, Congress passed the Foreign Intelligence Surveillance Act (FISA) to regulate electronic surveillance within the United States for foreign intelligence purposes. FISA was passed after disclosures that the Nixon Administration had engaged in domestic surveillance of U.S. citizens, including members of the

---

3. Press Briefing by Attorney General Alberto Gonzales and General Michael Hayden, Principal Deputy Director for National Intelligence, Dec. 19, 2005, available at *http://www.whitehouse.gov/news/releases/2005/12/20051219-1.html.*

4. In May 2006, USA Today reported that the NSA had also been secretly working in conjunction with various phone companies to collect the phone records of all calls by U.S. citizens for the purposes of data mining and analysis of contact information. NSA Has Massive Database of Americans' Phone Calls, USA Today, May 10, 2006, at *http://www.usatoday.com/news/washington/2006-05-10-nsa_x. htm.*

5. The NSA program compiling lists of phone records, for example, includes calls by persons who are not associated with any foreign power, but the question here is the interception of the *contents* of phone calls and e-mails.

press who had reported stories embarrassing to the administration. Findings by a special Senate committee on intelligence chaired by Senator Frank Church of Idaho revealed significant abuses by and misuses of the nation's intelligence agencies both domestically and overseas over many years.

Generally speaking, FISA authorizes electronic foreign intelligence surveillance of persons within the United States only upon warrants (or ex parte court orders as FISA calls them) issued by a court. 50 U.S.C. §1805. It set up a special court, the Foreign Intelligence Surveillance Court (FISC) to handle secret requests for surveillance, composed of federal judges picked by the Chief Justice of the Supreme Court. 50 U.S.C. §1803. To obtain an order for electronic surveillance the President must demonstrate probable cause that "the target of the electronic surveillance is a foreign power or an agent of a foreign power" and that "each of the facilities or places at which the electronic surveillance is directed is being used, or is about to be used, by a foreign power or an agent of a foreign power." 50 U.S.C. §1805(a)(3). Notwithstanding these requirements, FISA allows for warrantless domestic surveillance during wartime for the first 15 days following a declaration of war. 50 U.S.C. §1811.

The purpose of this provision is to give the President time to request additional authorization from Congress if necessary. Finally, FISA makes it a crime to "engage[] in electronic surveillance under color of law except as authorized by statute," 18 U.S.C. §1809(a), and it establishes that the provisions of FISA and other provisions of the federal criminal code that deal with wiretaps for criminal investigations are "the exclusive means by which electronic surveillance . . . may be conducted." 18 U.S.C. §2511(2)(f).

Discussion

1. Given that the President does not appear to have made use of the procedural requirements of FISA or sought court orders from the FISC, does the NSA program exceed presidential powers or otherwise violate the law?

Consider two possible theories. The first is that the AUMF authorizes the program and makes it consistent with FISA. The second is that notwithstanding FISA, the President's inherent authority to conduct foreign intelligence in time of war gives him constitutional authority and makes the program legal.

2. *The AUMF argument.* According to the first theory, the September 18, 2001, Authorization for the Use of Military Force (AUMF) is a statute under the meaning of FISA that authorizes warrantless electronic surveillance of U.S. citizens and other persons within the country. It gives the President power "to use all necessary and appropriate force" against al Qaeda and associated organizations. The *Hamdi* Court held that although detention of enemy combatants during wartime was not specifically mentioned by the AUMF, it "is so fundamental and accepted an incident to war as to be an exercise of the 'necessary and appropriate force' Congress has authorized the President to use." The military traditionally engages in communications intelligence directed at the enemy during wartime and therefore intercepting enemy

communications is a traditional function of the President as Commander-in-Chief. According to the same logic, by authorizing war against al Qaeda, Congress has authorized the interception of foreign intelligence, which is at least as traditional and accepted a military function as detention according to the laws of war. The AUMF is specifically directed to the conflict against al Qaeda and it is later in time. Whenever possible, statutes that seem to conflict should be read together in a way that harmonizes them and avoids unnecessary constitutional conflicts. Therefore the best interpretation is that the AUMF provides statutory authorization for going outside of the ordinary requirements of FISA. Because Congress has approved the President's actions under the AUMF, the President acts at the zenith of his powers under *Youngstown*, and any doubts about illegality or unconstitutionality should be resolved in favor of the President.

Consider the response: The AUMF says nothing about authorizing electronic surveillance of persons within the United States during wartime. FISA, by contrast, is a comprehensive statute specifically addressed to the subject of foreign intelligence surveillance, and it is designed to facilitate surveillance under legal restraints and to limit executive overreaching based on assertions of national security. Far from being silent about the exigencies of wartime, it limits authorization for warrantless wartime surveillance to the first 15 days after war has been declared. Whether or not the AUMF is equivalent to a declaration of war, one cannot read it to provide authority for something far more—unlimited and indefinite authority for warrantless wiretapping. The purpose of §1811's 15-day requirement was to give the President time to request additional authority from Congress. Although President Bush asked for considerable new powers in the PATRIOT Act, he did not ask for new powers to engage in warrantless surveillance of electronic communications within the United States because the administration did not believe that it could obtain such authorization. As Attorney General Gonzales explained at his December 19, 2005, press briefing, "[w]e have had discussions with Congress in the past—certain members of Congress—as to whether or not FISA could be amended to allow us to adequately deal with this kind of threat, and we were advised that that would be difficult, if not impossible." Because the President is acting contrary to a Congressional scheme regulating warrantless wiretapping and foreign intelligence surveillance, his constitutional authority is at its lowest ebb under *Youngstown*.

In his opinion in *Hamdan v. Rumsfeld,* Justice Stevens stated that the Court would not interpret the AUMF implicitly to repeal or modify the Uniform Code of Military Justice (much less the U.S. assent to the Geneva Conventions), and that the AUMF at best acknowledged "Presidential authority to convene military commissions in circumstances where justified under the 'Constitution and laws,' including the law of war." Justice Kennedy's concurrence stated that the President's decision to create a military tribunal program inconsistent with the UCMJ placed it into *Youngstown's* third category, in which the President's power was at its lowest ebb. How does the reasoning of *Hamdan* affect the arguments for and against the legality of the NSA program based on the AUMF?

3. *The Article II argument.* According to the second theory, the AUMF should be held to supplement (or repeal) FISA in order to avoid potential constitutional difficulties. Under Article II of the Constitution, the President has inherent authority as Commander-in-Chief to engage in surveillance of foreign operatives in time of war. Congressional laws that unduly inhibit his powers are unconstitutional. Note that this is different from the argument that, absent Congressional action, the President would have inherent authority to engage in electronic surveillance for foreign intelligence purposes. Rather, it is the claim that Congressional action that regulates executive conduct of foreign intelligence surveillance—even to prevent overreaching or to protect privacy rights—cannot limit the President's inherent powers. Therefore, if Congress were to insist that the President had to abide by FISA's warrant requirements, the President would be free to disregard these requirements because FISA is unconstitutional. This argument is reminiscent of the OLC argument in the "torture memo" quoted in the Casebook at pp. 879-880. How strong is the Article II argument after *Hamdan?*

4. *Technological change and emergency power.* Another defense of the NSA program is that FISA is premised on particular forms of electronic eavesdropping that target only a small number of persons at a time. The war on terror, by contrast, necessitates a wide range of new surveillance techniques that may touch many different people; these techniques aren't well suited to individualized requests before a judge. (Because details of the program are still kept secret, it is hard to know exactly what features, if any, cause the problem). But if FISA is not well suited to today's surveillance technologies (or technologies used to defeat them), which way does this fact cut? Does it cut in favor of allowing the President to disregard FISA because of wartime emergency? Or, on the contrary, does it counsel even more urgently that President Bush should have gone to Congress to amend FISA to make it more practical given technological change and strategic necessity? One argument against approaching Congress was that even to reveal the details of the program (or proposed programs) would have jeopardized its success. If so, what does this mean for the possibility of democratic oversight of surveillance programs in the future?

5. *Resolution or Ratification?* In August 2007 Congress Passed the Protect America Act, under which surveillance directed at targets reasonably believed to be outside the United States could proceed outside of the requirements of FISA; it expired in February 2008. In July 2008, Congress passed a series of amendments to FISA. Title I of the new bill allows the President to engage in a broad range of electronic surveillance without seeking warrants against particular individual targets of surveillance. It thus allows the President to do much of what he sought to do in the disputed NSA program. Title II effectively immunizes telecommunications companies who complied with Presidential requests to cooperate in the President's NSA program. Does the new legislation in effect ratify the President's actions? How are these events similar to or different from

Lincoln's suspension of habeas corpus in April 1861 (casebook at pp. 276-279) and Congress's subsequent approval of Lincoln's actions in August of 1861?

Note: Presidential Signing Statements

Following passage of the McCain Amendment to the Detainee Treatment Act of 2005, which prohibited cruel, inhuman, and degrading treatment of detainees in the custody of the United States, the President issued the following statement accompanying his signature:

> The executive branch shall construe Title X in Division A of the Act, relating to detainees, in a manner consistent with the constitutional authority of the President to supervise the unitary executive branch and as Commander in Chief and consistent with the constitutional limitations on the judicial power, which will assist in achieving the shared objective of the Congress and the President, evidenced in Title X, of protecting the American people from further terrorist attacks.[6]

In the renewal of the PATRIOT Act in March 2005, Congress included two sections, 106A and 119, which required the Justice Department to perform audits looking for possible improper or illegal uses of two types of investigative tools that had come under criticism: national security letters—which are requests for records that lack the usual forms of judicial oversight because they do not require a warrant or court order—and FBI wiretapping requests under the Foreign Intelligence Surveillance Act. The bill required that the results of the audit were to be reported to Congress to assist with Congressional oversight of the PATRIOT Act. President Bush's March 9, 2006, signing statement stated that

> [t]he executive branch shall construe the provisions of H.R. 3199 that call for furnishing information to entities outside the executive branch, such as sections 106A and 119, in a manner consistent with the President's constitutional authority to supervise the unitary executive branch and to withhold information the disclosure of which could impair foreign relations, national security, the deliberative processes of the Executive, or the performance of the Executive's constitutional duties.[7]

George W. Bush is not the first president to issue statements accompanying signing of a bill. Many of these statements, however, have been celebratory, or offered political rhetoric explaining how the bill would help various causes or

---

6. President's Statement on Signing of H.R. 2863, the Department of Defense, Emergency Supplemental Appropriations to Address Hurricanes in the Gulf of Mexico, and Pandemic Influenza Act, 2006, Dec. 30, 2005, available at *http://www.whitehouse.gov/news/releases/2005/12/20051230-8.html* and *http://www.presidency.ucsb.edu/ws/index.php?pid=65259&st=&st1=*.

7. President's Statement on Signing the USA PATRIOT Improvement and Reauthorization Act of 2005, Mar. 9, 2006, available at *http://www.whitehouse.gov/news/releases/2006/03/20060309-8. html* and *http://www.presidency.ucsb.edu/ws/index.php?pid=65326*.

favored constituencies. Another purpose of signing statements has been to signal how the President intends to interpret and implement the statute in practice. A final category of presidential signing statements—actually a subset of the last group—involves the President's statement that a feature of a bill he signs is unconstitutional or has potentially unconstitutional applications. In the signing statement the President announces that he will not enforce the purportedly unconstitutional elements of a law or will enforce them only in limited ways to avoid problems of constitutionality. For purposes of this discussion we shall refer to this type of document as a "constitutional signing statement."

Although constitutional signing statements have occurred in previous administrations—the earliest versions occurred in the administrations of James Monroe and Andrew Jackson—the number of such statements suggesting non-acquiescence with legislation the President signs increased markedly with the Reagan Administration, which began to promote the practice aggressively, based on work by a young Justice Department lawyer named Samuel A. Alito, Jr.[8] The practice of issuing constitutional signing statements has skyrocketed during the George W. Bush Administration. A recent *Boston Globe* article estimated that while Bill Clinton issued 105 statements challenging 140 laws in eight years in office, and George H.W. Bush issued 146 statements challenging 232 laws in four years in office, George W. Bush had issued 130 constitutional signing statements challenging 750 laws in five years in office.[9] Although President George W. Bush has made ample use of constitutional signing statements during his tenure in office, he did not veto a single piece of legislation until July 2006. One reason for this, of course, is that the President's party was in control of both houses of Congress during almost all of this period.

Do constitutional signing statements pose any constitutional difficulties? Consider the following arguments:

1. Constitutional signing statements pose no significant constitutional problems. They are not binding on the judiciary, which is always free to decide any issues of constitutionality for itself. Given that the President heads a co-equal branch of government, and is sworn to uphold the Constitution, he presumably has not only the right, but also the duty to refuse to execute laws that he believes in good faith to be unconstitutional, at least until such time as courts make a definitive determination of a statute's constitutionality. Just as courts should

---

8. Christopher Lee, Alito Once Made Case For Presidential Power, Wash. Post, Monday, Jan. 2, 2006, at A11, at *http://www.washingtonpost.com/wp-dyn/content/article/2006/01/01/AR2006010100788.html.*

9. Charlie Savage, Bush Challenges Hundreds of Laws, Boston Globe, Apr. 30, 2006, at *http://www.boston.com/news/nation/articles/2006/04/30/bush_challenges_hundreds_of_laws;* Christopher Kelley, Number of New Statutes Challenged, Boston Globe, Apr. 30, 2006, at *http://www. boston. com/news/nation/washington/articles/2006/04/30/statutes_challenged.* See also Christopher S. Kelley, A Comparative Look at the Constitutional Signing Statement 18 (2003), at *http://mpsa. indiana.edu/conf2003papers/1031858822.pdf.* Kelley found that President Reagan had issued 71 constitutional signing statements but did not list the number of laws challenged.

interpret statutes to avoid constitutional conflicts where possible, Presidents, who are also sworn to uphold the Constitution, should endeavor to interpret the law so as to avoid possible constitutional difficulties in implementation. Although the President may veto legislation he deems unconstitutional, it is often impractical to veto large appropriations measures or other complex legislation because a few isolated elements raise constitutional problems. For example, Congress may add legislative veto provisions as boilerplate to bills, even though the Supreme Court held in *INS v. Chada,* 462 U.S. 919 (1983), that these provisions are unconstitutional. By signaling that the President regards a few features of legislation that he signs as constitutionally dubious, the President is able to salvage legislation that often requires considerable amounts of time, effort, and political compromise by both houses of Congress and the President.

Moreover, signing statements—both constitutional and otherwise—help inform members of the executive branch what the President's positions are so as to ensure consistent application and enforcement of law. They help coordinate executive functions and help maintain a unitary executive in practice as well as in theory. They also signal the President's positions on legislation to the public so that Congress and the courts can take whatever steps they feel are necessary in response.

Finally, constitutional signing statements are not an unconstitutional power grab from Congress because Congress has no power to pass unconstitutional laws in the first place. They are not an unconstitutional exertion of presidential power because the President has a duty to follow the Constitution, not Congress.

The constitutional duties to "preserve, protect and defend the Constitution of the United States," Article II, §1, cl. 8, and to "take care that the laws be faithfully executed," Article II, §3, require that the President must resolve any conflicts between statutory law and the Constitution—the supreme law of the land—in favor of the Constitution.

2. Constitutional signing statements are problematic because they allow Presidents to cherry-pick parts of a bill that they will enforce or unilaterally redefine the meaning of legislation in ways that they could not achieve through the regular legislative process. They allow a President to get what he wants from legislation without having to expend the political capital of threatening or executing a presidential veto. As such, they give the President far more power to shape legislation than the constitutional system provides for. In order to avoid using veto threats for very minor elements of significant legislation, it may sometimes be permissible for Presidents to issue constitutional signing statements. That is why earlier examples of constitutional signing statements are far less troublesome. However, when the constitutional signing statement becomes a regular practice for an administration, as it has in recent years, it is no longer simply a method of promoting legislative efficiency, but represents a deliberate attempt to shift power from Congress to the Presidency. Although the President has obligations to follow the Constitution, problems arise when the President's interpretations are idiosyncratic, and when Presidents selectively declare unconstitutional laws that limit or regulate the President's own powers or that require

any degree of oversight over executive functions. Presidents may be using signing statements to avoid political accountability and forestall appropriate inquiries into executive mismanagement, corruption, or illegality.

Although one might defend constitutional signing statements on grounds that they clarify the President's positions to the public, to the other branches and to subordinate officials in the Executive branch, the real problem is that signing statements—such as the ones involving the Detainee Treatment Act and the PATRIOT Act renewal—are often quite vague. They simply announce that the President feels free at some point in the future to disregard elements of the legislation without announcing exactly what he plans to do or what standards he will use. The problem then becomes one of accountability and oversight. Congress has no way of knowing what parts of the legislation it passes are actually being enforced and what rights are being denied or what procedures are being flouted. As the example of the Detainee Treatment Act suggests, many laws rely on good faith implementation by executive officials and are not easily subject to direct oversight by Congress. When the President announces that executive officials need not follow laws that the President deems (or later will deem) unconstitutional, it becomes difficult to know what the effects of laws are in practice, particularly if—as in the case of the PATRIOT Act renewal—the President also refuses to provide information about executive branch practices. Thus, the problem with constitutional signing statements (and interpretive signing statements more generally) is that they enable the President to direct his subordinates to refuse to enforce federal law routinely and without any consequences. When the President selectively refuses to enforce laws and refuses to provide sufficient information about which laws he is not enforcing and why, Congress has no way to investigate abuses or push back at executive overreaching. Thus, the proliferation of signing statements is not important in itself, but rather as a symptom of a significant shift in how the President treats the other branches. The concern is that the President is pushing the limits of his power systematically to create a new status quo where he is effectively free from oversight in a wide range of situations both outside the United States and within it.

Discussion

If constitutional signing statements raise separation of powers concerns, what remedies are available?

1. Could Congress require that if the President determines that he will not carry out part of any law he signs, he must submit a report to Congress within a reasonable period of time (say, ten days) offering detailed reasons for his determination and specifying the conditions and situations under which he will refuse to enforce the law? (Reasons that involve classified information could be addressed to congressional intelligence committees.)

2. Could Congress pass a law that required federal courts and federal executive officials to disregard or give no legal effect to presidential signing

statements? Would this law itself violate the separation of powers with respect to the judiciary? With respect to the executive?

3. Could Congress pass a law stating that no funds it appropriates may be used by the Executive branch for producing and publishing signing statements?

4. Could Congress pass a law that prohibits the expenditure of funds to enforce any bill signed by the President if he has declared in a signing statement that he will refuse to enforce any part of it? Note that the practical effect of this bill would be to make a signing statement into a de facto veto. If the President wanted funding for parts of the bill, he would have to accept all of it.

5. Finally, if you believe that some or all of these funding conditions are constitutional, can Congress condition funds on the President's disavowal of his previous signing statements, or the signing statements of previous administrations?

Chapter 6

The Burdens of History: The Constitutional Treatment of Race

Insert the following after discussion note 2 on p. 950:

PARENTS INVOLVED IN COMMUNITY SCHOOLS v.
SEATTLE SCHOOL DISTRICT NO. 1
551 U.S. 701 (2007)

Chief Justice ROBERTS announced the judgment of the Court, and delivered the opinion of the Court with respect to Parts I, II, III-A, and III-C, and an opinion with respect to Parts III-B and IV, in which Justices SCALIA, THOMAS, and ALITO join.

[The Seattle School District No. 1 and Jefferson County Public Schools in Louisville voluntarily adopted plans to promote racial diversity. Seattle has never been subject to court-ordered desegregation for operating segregated schools, but adopted its plan to correct for the effects of racially identifiable housing patterns on school assignments.

Seattle allocated slots in oversubscribed high schools by using tiebreakers. The first selects for students who have a sibling enrolled at the chosen school. The second selects for students whose race will help balance the oversubscribed school. Approximately 41 percent of enrolled students in the district's public schools are white; 59 percent are nonwhite. If an oversubscribed school is not within 10 percentage points of the district's overall white/nonwhite racial balance, the tiebreaker selects for the student who would bring the school closer into balance. The third tiebreaker selects for students who are closest in geographic proximity to the oversubscribed school.

The Louisville school district had been subject to a court-ordered desegregation decree since 1975. It was dissolved in 2000 when the district was declared unitary, having eliminated "[t]o the greatest extent practicable" the vestiges of its prior policy of segregation.

In 2001, after the decree was dissolved, Jefferson County adopted its voluntary student assignment plan. Schools that are not magnet schools must maintain a minimum black enrollment of 15 percent, and a maximum black enrollment of 50 percent. Approximately 34 percent of the district's 97,000 students are black; most of the remaining 66 percent are white.

Parents of kindergartners, first-graders, and students new to the district may select first and second choices among schools within their geographical area for initial assignment. Students are assigned based on available space, but once a school has reached less than 15 percent or more than 50 percent black, it will take only students who will keep the racial balance within these guidelines. Students initially assigned may also transfer to other schools in the district, subject to availability of space and the same requirements of racial balance. Petitioner Crystal Meredith, who sought to transfer her son Joshua for kindergarten from a school ten miles away to one a mile away was refused because she was told it would adversely impact the racial balance of the school to which he had been assigned.]

. . .

III.

A *(maj)*

It is well established that when the government distributes burdens or benefits on the basis of individual racial classifications, that action is reviewed under strict scrutiny. In order to satisfy this searching standard of review, the school districts must demonstrate that the use of individual racial classifications in the assignment plans here under review is "narrowly tailored" to achieve a "compelling" government interest.

[O]ur prior cases, in evaluating the use of racial classifications in the school context, have recognized two interests that qualify as compelling. The first is the compelling interest of remedying the effects of past intentional discrimina-tion. Yet the Seattle public schools have not shown that they were ever segregated by law, and were not subject to court-ordered desegregation decrees. The Jefferson County public schools were previously segregated by law [but] [i]n 2000, the District Court that entered that decree dissolved it, finding that Jefferson County had "eliminated the vestiges associated with the former policy of segregation and its pernicious effects," and thus had achieved "unitary" status. . . . We have emphasized that the harm being remedied by mandatory desegregation plans is the harm that is traceable to segregation, and that "the Constitution is not violated by racial imbalance in the schools, without more." *Milliken v. Bradley.* Once Jefferson County achieved unitary status, it had remedied the constitutional wrong that allowed race-based assignments. Any continued use of race must be justified on some other basis.[a]

---

a. The districts point to dicta in a prior opinion in which the Court suggested that, while not constitutionally mandated, it would be constitutionally permissible for a school district to seek racially balanced schools as a matter of "educational policy." See Swann v. Charlotte-Mecklenburg Bd. of Ed., 402 U.S. 1, 16 (1971). . . . *Swann,* evaluating a school district engaged in court-ordered desegregation, had no occasion to consider whether a district's voluntary adoption of race-based assignments in the absence of a finding of prior *de jure* segregation was constitutionally permissible, an issue that was again expressly reserved in Washington v. Seattle School Dist. No. 1, 458 U.S. 457, 472, n. 15 (1982). . . .

The second government interest we have recognized as compelling for purposes of strict scrutiny is the interest in diversity in higher education upheld in *Grutter* [v. Bollinger, 539 U.S. 306, 326 (2003)]. . . . The diversity interest was not focused on race alone but encompassed "all factors that may contribute to student body diversity." [including] "admittees who have lived or traveled widely abroad, are fluent in several languages, have overcome personal adversity and family hardship, have exceptional records of extensive community service, and have had successful careers in other fields." [*Grutter* quoted] Justice Powell's opinion in Regents of the University of California v. Bakke, 438 U.S. 265 (1978), noting that "it is not an interest in simple ethnic diversity, in which a specified percentage of the student body is in effect guaranteed to be members of selected ethnic groups, that can justify the use of race." Instead, what was upheld in *Grutter* was consideration of "a far broader array of qualifications and characteristics of which racial or ethnic origin is but a single though important element." . . . [T]he admissions program at issue [in *Grutter*] focused on each applicant as an individual, and not simply as a member of a particular racial group. The classification of applicants by race upheld in *Grutter* was only as part of a "highly individualized, holistic review." As the Court explained, "[t]he importance of this individualized consideration in the context of a race-conscious admissions program is paramount." The point of the narrow tailoring analysis in which the *Grutter* Court engaged was to ensure that the use of racial classifications was indeed part of a broader assessment of diversity, and not simply an effort to achieve racial balance, which the Court explained would be "patently unconstitutional."

In the present cases, by contrast, race is not considered as part of a broader effort to achieve "exposure to widely diverse people, cultures, ideas, and viewpoints"; race, for some students, is determinative standing alone. The districts argue that other factors, such as student preferences, affect assignment decisions under their plans, but under each plan when race comes into play, it is decisive by itself. It is not simply one factor weighed with others in reaching a decision, as in *Grutter*; it is *the* factor. Like the University of Michigan undergraduate plan struck down in *Gratz* [v. Bollinger], the plans here "do not provide for a meaningful individualized review of applicants" but instead rely on racial classifications in a "nonindividualized, mechanical" way.

Even when it comes to race, the plans here employ only a limited notion of diversity, viewing race exclusively in white/nonwhite terms in Seattle and black/"other" terms in Jefferson County.[b] The Seattle "Board Statement Reaffirming Diversity Rationale" speaks of the "inherent educational value" in "[p]roviding students the opportunity to attend schools with diverse student

---

b. The way Seattle classifies its students bears this out. Upon enrolling their child with the district, parents are required to identify their child as a member of a particular racial group. If a parent identifies more than one race on the form, "[t]he application will not be accepted and, if necessary, the enrollment service person taking the application will indicate one box."

enrollment." But under the Seattle plan, a school with 50 percent Asian-American students and 50 percent white students but no African-American, Native American, or Latino students would qualify as balanced, while a school with 30 percent Asian-American, 25 percent African-American, 25 percent Latino, and 20 percent white students would not. It is hard to understand how a plan that could allow these results can be viewed as being concerned with achieving enrollment that is "'broadly diverse,'" *Grutter.*

. . . In upholding the admissions plan in *Grutter*, [moreover] . . . this Court relied upon considerations unique to institutions of higher education, noting that in light of "the expansive freedoms of speech and thought associated with the university environment, universities occupy a special niche in our constitutional tradition." . . . The present cases are not governed by *Grutter.*

B (no K)

Perhaps recognizing that reliance on *Grutter* cannot sustain their plans, both school districts assert additional interests. . . . Seattle contends that its use of race helps to reduce racial concentration in schools and to ensure that racially concentrated housing patterns do not prevent nonwhite students from having access to the most desirable schools. Jefferson County has articulated a similar goal, phrasing its interest in terms of educating its students "in a racially integrated environment." Each school district argues that educational and broader socialization benefits flow from a racially diverse learning environment, and each contends that because the diversity they seek is racial diversity—not the broader diversity at issue in *Grutter*—it makes sense to promote that interest directly by relying on race alone.

The parties and their *amici* dispute whether racial diversity in schools in fact has a marked impact on test scores and other objective yardsticks or achieves intangible socialization benefits. The debate is not one we need to resolve, however, because it is clear that the racial classifications employed by the districts are not narrowly tailored to the goal of achieving the educational and social benefits asserted to flow from racial diversity. In design and operation, the plans are directed only to racial balance, pure and simple, an objective this Court has repeatedly condemned as illegitimate.

The plans are tied to each district's specific racial demographics, rather than to any pedagogic concept of the level of diversity needed to obtain the asserted educational benefits. In Seattle, the district seeks white enrollment of between 31 and 51 percent (within 10 percent of "the district white average" of 41 percent), and nonwhite enrollment of between 49 and 69 percent (within 10 percent of "the district minority average" of 59 percent). In Jefferson County, by contrast, the district seeks black enrollment of no less than 15 or more than 50 percent, a range designed to be "equally above and below Black student enrollment systemwide," based on the objective of achieving at "all schools . . . an African-American enrollment equivalent to the average district wide African-American enrollment" of 34 percent. In Seattle, then, the benefits of racial diversity require enrollment of at least 31 percent white students; in Jefferson County, at least 50 percent. There must be at least 15 percent nonwhite students under Jefferson County's plan; in Seattle, more than three times that figure. This comparison makes clear that the racial demographics in each district—whatever they happen to be—drive the required "diversity" numbers. The plans here are not tailored to achieving a degree of diversity necessary to realize the asserted educational benefits; instead the plans are tailored, in the words of Seattle's Manager of Enrollment Planning, Technical Support, and Demographics, to "the goal established by the school board of attaining a level of diversity within the schools that approximates the district's overall demographics."

The districts offer no evidence that the level of racial diversity necessary to achieve the asserted educational benefits happens to coincide with the racial demographics of the respective school districts—or rather the white/nonwhite or black/"other" balance of the districts, since that is the only diversity addressed by the plans. . . .

Jefferson County's expert referred to the importance of having "at least 20 percent" minority group representation for the group "to be visible enough to make a difference," and noted that "small isolated minority groups in a school are not likely to have a strong effect on the overall school." The Jefferson County plan, however, is based on a goal of replicating at each school "an African-American enrollment equivalent to the average district-wide African American enrollment." Joshua McDonald's requested transfer was denied because his race was listed as "other" rather than black, and allowing the transfer would have had an adverse effect on the racial guideline compliance of Young Elementary, the school he sought to leave. At the time, however, Young Elementary was 46.8 percent black. The transfer might have had an adverse effect on the effort to approach district-wide racial proportionality at Young, but it had nothing to do with preventing either the black or "other" group from becoming "small" or "isolated" at Young.

. . .

In *Grutter*, the number of minority students the school sought to admit was an undefined "meaningful number" necessary to achieve a genuinely diverse student body. [T]he majority concluded that the law school did not count back from its applicant pool to arrive at the "meaningful number" it regarded as necessary to diversify its student body. Here the racial balance the districts seek is a defined range set solely by reference to the demographics of the respective school districts.

This working backward to achieve a particular type of racial balance, rather than working forward from some demonstration of the level of diversity that provides the purported benefits, is a fatal flaw under our existing precedent. We have many times over reaffirmed that "[r]acial balance is not to be achieved for its own sake." *Grutter* itself reiterated that "outright racial balancing" is "patently unconstitutional."

Accepting racial balancing as a compelling state interest would justify the imposition of racial proportionality throughout American society, contrary to our repeated recognition that "[a]t the heart of the Constitution's guarantee of equal protection lies the simple command that the Government must treat citizens as individuals, not as simply components of a racial, religious, sexual or national class." Miller v. Johnson, 515 U.S. 900, 911 (1995). Allowing racial balancing as a compelling end in itself would "effectively assur[e] that race will always be relevant in American life, and that the 'ultimate goal' of 'eliminating entirely from governmental decisionmaking such irrelevant factors as a human being's race' will never be achieved." Croson. An interest "linked to nothing other than proportional representation of various races . . . would support indefinite use of racial classifications, employed first to obtain the appropriate mixture of racial views and then to ensure that the [program] continues to reflect that mixture."

— The validity of our concern that racial balancing has "no logical stopping point," Croson, is demonstrated here by the degree to which the districts tie their racial guidelines to their demographics. As the districts' demographics shift, so too will their definition of racial diversity.

[I]n Seattle the plans are defended as necessary to address the consequences of racially identifiable housing patterns. The sweep of the mandate claimed by the district is contrary to our rulings that remedying past societal discrimination does not justify race-conscious government action. See, e.g., Shaw v. Hunt, 517 U.S. 899, 909-910 (1996) ("[A]n effort to alleviate the effects of societal discrimination is not a compelling interest"); Croson.

The principle that racial balancing is not permitted is one of substance, not semantics. Racial balancing is not transformed from "patently unconstitutional" to a compelling state interest simply by relabeling it "racial diversity." While the school districts use various verbal formulations to describe the interest they seek to promote—racial diversity, avoidance of racial isolation, racial integration—they offer no definition of the interest that suggests it differs from racial balance.

Jefferson County phrases its interest as "racial integration," but integration certainly does not require the sort of racial proportionality reflected in its plan. Even in the context of mandatory desegregation, we have stressed that racial proportionality is not required, see Milliken, 433 U.S., at 280, n.14 ("[A desegregation] order contemplating the substantive constitutional right [to a] particular degree of racial balance or mixing is . . . infirm as a matter of law" (internal quotation marks omitted)); Swann v. Charlotte-Mecklenburg Bd. of Ed., 402 U.S. 1, 24 (1971) ("The constitutional command to desegregate schools does not mean that every school in every community must always reflect the racial composition of the school system as a whole"), and here Jefferson County has already been found to have eliminated the vestiges of its prior segregated school system.

The en banc Ninth Circuit declared that "when a racially diverse school system is the goal (or racial concentration or isolation is the problem), there is no more effective means than a consideration of race to achieve the solution." For the foregoing reasons, this conclusory argument cannot sustain the plans. However closely related race-based assignments may be to achieving racial balance, that itself cannot be the goal, whether labeled "racial diversity" or anything else. To the extent the objective is sufficient diversity so that students see fellow students as individuals rather than solely as members of a racial group, using means that treat students solely as members of a racial group is fundamentally at cross-purposes with that end.

C (Maj)

The districts assert, as they must, that the way in which they have employed individual racial classifications is necessary to achieve their stated ends. The minimal effect these classifications have on student assignments, however, suggests that other means would be effective. Seattle's racial tiebreaker results, in the end, only in shifting a small number of students between schools. . . . Similarly, Jefferson County's use of racial classifications has only a minimal effect on the assignment of students. . . . While we do not suggest that *greater* use of race would be preferable, the minimal impact of the districts' racial classifications on school enrollment casts doubt on the necessity of using racial classifications. . . .

The districts have also failed to show that they considered methods other than explicit racial classifications to achieve their stated goals. Narrow tailoring requires "serious, good faith consideration of workable race-neutral alternatives," *Grutter*, and yet in Seattle several alternative assignment plans—many of which would not have used express racial classifications—were rejected with little or no consideration. Jefferson County has failed to present any evidence that it considered alternatives, even though the district already claims that its goals are achieved primarily through means other than the racial classifications.

IV. (no K)

. . . Justice Breyer seeks to justify the plans at issue under our precedents recognizing the compelling interest in remedying past intentional discrimination. . . . The distinction between segregation by state action and racial imbalance caused by other factors has been central to our jurisprudence in this area for generations. The dissent elides this distinction between *de jure* and *de facto* segregation, casually intimates that Seattle's school attendance patterns reflect illegal segregation, and fails to credit the judicial determination—under the most rigorous standard—that Jefferson County had eliminated the vestiges of prior segregation. The dissent thus alters in fundamental ways not only the facts presented here but the established law. . . . The present cases are before us, however, because the Seattle school district was never segregated by law, and the Jefferson County district has been found to be unitary, having eliminated the vestiges of its prior dual status. . . . The dissent's persistent refusal to accept this distinction—its insistence on viewing the racial classifications here as . . . "devised to overcome a history of segregated public schools," explains its inability to understand why the remedial justification for racial classifications cannot decide these cases.

Justice Breyer's dissent next relies heavily on dicta from Swann v. Charlotte Mecklenburg Bd. of Ed. [W]hen *Swann* was decided, this Court had not yet confirmed that strict scrutiny applies to racial classifications like those before us. [Moreover,] *Swann* addresses only a possible state objective; it says nothing of the permissible *means*—race conscious or otherwise—that a school district might employ to achieve that objective. The reason for this omission is clear enough, since the case did not involve any voluntary means adopted by a school district. The dissent's characterization of *Swann* as recognizing that "the Equal Protection Clause permits local school boards to use race-conscious criteria to achieve positive race-related goals" is—at best—a dubious inference. . . .

Justice Breyer's dissent also . . . overreads *Grutter* . . . in suggesting that it renders pure racial balancing a constitutionally compelling interest; *Grutter* itself recognized that using race simply to achieve racial balance would be "patently unconstitutional." . . . We simply do not understand how Justice Breyer can maintain that classifying every schoolchild as black or white, and using that classification as a determinative factor in assigning children to achieve pure racial balance, can be regarded as "less burdensome, and hence more narrowly tailored" than the consideration of race in *Grutter*, when the Court in *Grutter* stated that "[t]he importance of . . . individualized consideration" in the program was "paramount," and consideration of race was one factor in a "highly individualized, holistic review." . . .

   . . . Justice Breyer's dissent candidly dismisses the significance of this Court's repeated *holdings* that all racial classifications must be reviewed under strict scrutiny, arguing that a different standard of review should be applied because the districts use race for beneficent rather than malicious purposes. . . . Justice Breyer . . . relies on the good intentions and motives of the school districts, stating that he has found "no case that . . . repudiated this constitutional asymmetry between that which seeks to *exclude* and that which seeks to *include* members of minority races." We have found many. Our cases clearly reject the argument that motives affect the strict scrutiny analysis. See *Johnson* [v. California]; *Adarand*; *Croson*.

This argument that different rules should govern racial classifications designed to include rather than exclude is not new; it has been repeatedly pressed in the past, and has been repeatedly rejected.

   . . .

Justice Breyer also suggests that other means for achieving greater racial diversity in schools are necessarily unconstitutional if the racial classifications at issue in these cases cannot survive strict scrutiny. These other means—e.g., where to construct new schools, how to allocate resources among schools, and which academic offerings to provide to attract students to certain schools—implicate different considerations than the explicit racial classifications at issue in these cases, and we express no opinion on their validity—not even in dicta. Rather, we employ the familiar and well-established analytic approach of strict scrutiny to evaluate the plans at issue today, an approach that in no way warrants the dissent's cataclysmic concerns. Under that approach, the school districts have not carried their burden of showing that the ends they seek justify the particular extreme means they have chosen—classifying individual students on the basis of their race and discriminating among them on that basis.

. . .

If the need for the racial classifications embraced by the school districts is unclear, even on the districts' own terms, the costs are undeniable. "[D]istinctions between citizens solely because of their ancestry are by their very nature odious to a free people whose institutions are founded upon the doctrine of equality." *Adarand.* Government action dividing us by race is inherently suspect because such classifications promote "notions of racial inferiority and lead to a politics of racial hostility," *Croson,* "reinforce the belief, held by too many for too much of our history, that individuals should be judged by the color of their skin," Shaw v. Reno, 509 U.S. 630, 657 (1993), and "endorse race-based reasoning and the conception of a Nation divided into racial blocs, thus contributing to an escalation of racial hostility and conflict." As the Court explained in Rice v. Cayetano, 528 U.S. 495, 517 (2000), "[o]ne of the principal reasons race is treated as a forbidden classification is that it demeans the dignity and worth of a person to be judged by ancestry instead of by his or her own merit and essential qualities."

All this is true enough in the contexts in which these statements were made—government contracting, voting districts, allocation of broadcast licenses, and electing state officers—but when it comes to using race to assign children to schools, history will be heard. In Brown v. Board of Education, 347 U.S. 483 (1954) (*Brown I*), we held that segregation deprived black children of equal educational opportunities regardless of whether school facilities and other tangible factors were equal, because government classification and separation on grounds of race themselves denoted inferiority. It was not the inequality of the facilities but the fact of legally separating children on the basis of race on which the Court relied to find a constitutional violation in 1954. See *id.,* at 494 ("'The impact [of segregation] is greater when it has the sanction of the law'"). The next Term, we accordingly stated that "full compliance" with *Brown I* required school districts "to achieve a system of determining admission to the public schools *on a nonracial basis.*" *Brown II* (emphasis added).

The parties and their *amici* debate which side is more faithful to the heritage of *Brown,* but the position of the plaintiffs in *Brown* was spelled out in their brief and could not have been clearer: "[T]he Fourteenth Amendment prevents states from according differential treatment to American children on the basis of their color or race." What do the racial classifications at issue here do, if not accord differential treatment on the basis of race? As counsel who appeared before this Court for the plaintiffs in *Brown* put it: "We have one fundamental contention which we will seek to develop in the course of this argument, and that contention is that no State has any authority under the equal-protection clause of the Fourteenth Amendment to use race as a factor in affording educational opportunities among its citizens." There is no ambiguity in that statement. And it was that position that prevailed in this Court, which emphasized in its remedial opinion that what was "[a]t stake is the personal interest of the plaintiffs in admission to public schools as soon as practicable *on a non-discriminatory basis*," and what was required was "determining admission to the public schools *on a nonracial basis.*" *Brown II* (emphasis added). What do the racial classifications do in these cases, if not determine admission to a public school on a racial basis? Before *Brown*, schoolchildren were told where they could and could not go to school based on the color of their skin. The school districts in these cases have not carried the heavy burden of demonstrating that we should allow this once again—even for very different reasons. For schools that never segregated on the basis of race, such as Seattle, or that have removed the vestiges of past segregation, such as Jefferson County, the way "to achieve a system of determining admission to the public schools on a nonracial basis," *Brown II*, is to stop assigning students on a racial basis. The way to stop discrimination on the basis of race is to stop discriminating on the basis of race. . . .

Justice THOMAS, concurring.

Today, the Court holds that state entities may not experiment with race-based means to achieve ends they deem socially desirable. I wholly concur in The Chief Justice's opinion. I write separately to address several of the contentions in Justice Breyer's dissent. . . . Contrary to the dissent's arguments, resegregation is not occurring in Seattle or Louisville; these school boards have no present interest in remedying past segregation; and these race-based student assignment programs do not serve any compelling state interest. Accordingly, the plans are unconstitutional. Disfavoring a color-blind interpretation of the Constitution, the dissent would give school boards a free hand to make decisions on the basis of race-an approach reminiscent of that advocated by the segregationists in *Brown v. Board of Education*. This approach is just as wrong today as it was a half-century ago. The Constitution and our cases require us to be much more demanding before permitting local school boards to make decisions based on race.

I.

[R]acial imbalance is not segregation, and the mere incantation of terms like resegregation and remediation cannot make up the difference. [I]n the context of public schooling, segregation is the deliberate operation of a school system to "carry out a governmental policy to separate pupils in schools solely on the basis of race." *Swann*. . . . Racial imbalance is the failure of a school district's individual schools to match or approximate the demographic makeup of the student population at large. Racial imbalance is not segregation.[a] Although presently observed racial imbalance might result from past *de jure* segregation, racial imbalance can also result from any number of innocent private decisions, including voluntary housing choices. Because racial imbalance is not inevitably — linked to unconstitutional segregation, it is not unconstitutional in and of itself.

Although there is arguably a danger of racial imbalance in schools in Seattle and Louisville, there is no danger of resegregation. No one contends that Seattle has established or that Louisville has reestablished a dual school system that separates students on the basis of race. The statistics cited [by Justice Breyer] are not to the contrary. At most, those statistics show a national trend toward classroom racial imbalance. However, racial imbalance without intentional state action to separate the races does not amount to segregation. To raise the specter of resegregation to defend these programs is to ignore the meaning of the word and the nature of the cases before us.[b]

Just as the school districts lack an interest in preventing resegregation, they also have no present interest in remedying past segregation. The Constitution generally prohibits government race-based decisionmaking, but this Court has authorized the use of race-based measures for remedial purposes in two narrowly defined circumstances. First, in schools that were formerly segregated by law, race-based measures are sometimes constitutionally compelled to remedy prior school segregation. Second, in *Croson*, the Court appeared willing to authorize a government unit to remedy past discrimination for which it was responsible. [T]hese plans do not fall within either existing category of permissible race-based remediation.

The Constitution does not permit race-based government decisionmaking simply because a school district claims a remedial purpose and proceeds in good faith with arguably pure motives. Rather, race-based government decisionmaking is categorically prohibited unless narrowly tailored to serve a compelling interest. This exacting scrutiny "has proven automatically fatal" in most cases. And appropriately so. "The Constitution abhors classifications based on race, not only because those classifications can harm favored races or are based on illegitimate motives, but also because every time the government places citizens on racial registers and makes race relevant to the provision of

a. The dissent refers repeatedly and reverently to "'integration.'" However, outside of the context of remediation for past *de jure* segregation, "integration" is simply racial balancing. Therefore, the school districts' attempts to further "integrate" are properly thought of as little more than attempts to achieve a particular racial balance.

b. The dissent's assertion that these plans are necessary for the school districts to maintain their "hard-won gains" reveals its conflation of segregation and racial imbalance. For the dissent's purposes, the relevant hard-won gains are the present racial compositions in the individual schools in Seattle and Louisville. However, the actual hard-won gain in these cases is the elimination of the — vestiges of the system of state-enforced racial separation that once existed in Louisville. To equate the achievement of a certain statistical mix in several schools with the elimination of the system of systematic *de jure* segregation trivializes the latter accomplishment. Nothing but an interest in classroom aesthetics and a hypersensitivity to elite sensibilities justifies the school districts' racial balancing programs. But "the principle of inherent equality that underlies and infuses our Constitution" required the disestablishment of *de jure* segregation. Assessed in any objective manner, there is no comparison between the two.

burdens or benefits, it demeans us all." Therefore, as a general rule, all race based government decisionmaking—regardless of context—is unconstitutional.

This Court has carved out a narrow exception to that general rule for cases in which a school district has a "history of maintaining two sets of schools in a single school system deliberately operated to carry out a governmental policy to separate pupils in schools solely on the basis of race." In such cases, race-based remedial measures are sometimes required.[c] But without a history of state enforced racial separation, a school district has no affirmative legal obligation to take race-based remedial measures to eliminate segregation and its vestiges.

Neither of the programs before us today is compelled as a remedial measure, and no one makes such a claim. Seattle has no history of *de jure* segregation; therefore, the Constitution did not require Seattle's plan. Although Louisville once operated a segregated school system and was subject to a Federal District Court's desegregation decree, that decree was dissolved in 2000. Since then, no race-based remedial measures have been required in Louisville. Thus, the race based student-assignment plan at issue here, which was instituted the year after the dissolution of the desegregation decree, was not even arguably required by the Constitution.

Aside from constitutionally compelled remediation in schools, this Court has permitted government units to remedy prior racial discrimination only in narrow circumstances. [N]either school board asserts that its race-based actions were taken to remedy prior discrimination. Seattle provides three forward-looking— as opposed to remedial—justifications for its race-based assignment plan. Louisville asserts several similar forward-looking interests, and at oral argument, counsel for Louisville disavowed any claim that Louisville's argument "depend[ed] in any way on the prior de jure segregation,"

Furthermore, for a government unit to remedy past discrimination for which it was responsible, the Court has required it to demonstrate "a 'strong basis in evidence for its conclusion that remedial action was necessary.'" *Croson.* Establishing a "strong basis in evidence" requires proper findings regarding the extent of the government unit's past racial discrimination. The findings should "define the scope of any injury [and] the necessary remedy," and must be more than "inherently unmeasurable claims of past wrongs." Assertions of general societal discrimination are plainly insufficient. Neither school district has made any such specific findings. For Seattle, the dissent attempts to make up for this failing by adverting to allegations made in past complaints filed against the Seattle school district. However, allegations in complaints cannot

---

c. [T]he remedies this Court authorized lower courts to compel in early desegregation cases like *Green* and *Swann* were exceptional. Sustained resistance to *Brown* prompted the Court to authorize extraordinary race-conscious remedial measures (like compelled racial mixing) to turn the Constitution's dictate to desegregate into reality. Even if these measures were appropriate as remedies in the face of widespread resistance to *Brown*'s mandate, they are not forever insulated from constitutional scrutiny. Rather, "such powers should have been temporary and used only to overcome the widespread resistance to the dictates of the Constitution."

substitute for specific findings of prior discrimination—even when those allegations lead to settlements with complaining parties. As for Louisville, its slate was cleared by the District Court's 2000 dissolution decree, which effectively declared that there were no longer any effects of *de jure* discrimination in need of remediation.[d] . . .

[T]he dissent conflates the concepts of segregation and racial imbalance. [F]or at least two reasons, however, it is wrong to place the remediation of segregation on the same plane as the remediation of racial imbalance. First, as demonstrated above, the two concepts are distinct. Although racial imbalance can result from *de jure* segregation, it does not necessarily, and the further we get from the era of state-sponsored racial separation, the less likely it is that racial imbalance has a traceable connection to any prior segregation.

Second, a school cannot "remedy" racial imbalance in the same way that it ⇥ can remedy segregation. Remediation of past *de jure* segregation is a one-time process involving the redress of a discrete legal injury inflicted by an identified entity. At some point, the discrete injury will be remedied, and the school district will be declared unitary. Unlike *de jure* segregation, there is no ultimate remedy for racial imbalance. Individual schools will fall in and out of balance in the natural course, and the appropriate balance itself will shift with a school district's changing demographics. Thus, racial balancing will have to take place on an indefinite basis—a continuous process with no identifiable culpable party and no discernable end point. In part for those reasons, the Court has never permitted outright racial balancing solely for the purpose of achieving a particular racial balance.

II.

Lacking a cognizable interest in remediation, neither of these plans can survive strict scrutiny because neither plan serves a genuinely compelling state interest. The dissent avoids reaching that conclusion by unquestioningly accepting the assertions of selected social scientists while completely ignoring the fact that those assertions are the subject of fervent debate. Ultimately, the dissent's entire analysis is corrupted by the considerations that lead it initially to question whether strict scrutiny should apply at all. What emerges is a version of "strict scrutiny" that combines hollow assurances of harmlessness with reflexive

---

d. Contrary to the dissent's argument, the Louisville school district's interest in remedying its past *de jure* segregation did vanish the day the District Court found that Louisville had eliminated the vestiges of its historic *de jure* segregation. If there were further remediation to be done, the District Court could not logically have reached the conclusion that Louisville "ha[d] eliminated the vestiges associated with the former policy of segregation and its pernicious effects." Because Louisville could use race-based measures only as a remedy for past *de jure* segregation, it is not "incoherent," to say that race-based decisionmaking was allowed to Louisville one day—while it was still remedying—and forbidden to it the next—when remediation was finished. That seemingly odd turnaround is merely a result of the fact that the remediation of *de jure* segregation is a jealously guarded exception to the Equal Protection Clause's general rule against government race-based decisionmaking.

acceptance of conventional wisdom. When it comes to government race-based decisionmaking, the Constitution demands more.

A

[W]e have made it unusually clear that strict scrutiny applies to *every* racial classification. *Adarand*; *Grutter*; Johnson v. California. There are good reasons not to apply a lesser standard to these cases. The constitutional problems with government race-based decisionmaking are not diminished in the slightest by the presence or absence of an intent to oppress any race or by the real or asserted well-meaning motives for the race-based decisionmaking. *Adarand.* Purportedly benign race-based decisionmaking suffers the same constitutional infirmity as invidious race-based decisionmaking. *Id.,* at 240 (Thomas, J., concurring in part and concurring in judgment) ("As far as the Constitution is concerned, it is irrelevant whether a government's racial classifications are drawn by those who wish to oppress a race or by those who have a sincere desire to help those thought to be disadvantaged").

Even supposing it mattered to the constitutional analysis, the race-based student assignment programs before us are not as benign as the dissent believes. As these programs demonstrate, every time the government uses racial criteria to "bring the races together," someone gets excluded, and the person excluded suffers an injury solely because of his or her race. The petitioner in the Louisville case received a letter from the school board informing her that her *kindergartener* would not be allowed to attend the school of petitioner's choosing because of the child's race. Doubtless, hundreds of letters like this went out from both school boards every year these race-based assignment plans were in operation. This type of exclusion, solely on the basis of race, is precisely the sort of government action that pits the races against one another, exacerbates racial tension, and "provoke[s] resentment among those who believe that they have been wronged by the government's use of race." . . .

B

[A]ccording to the dissent, integration involves "an interest in setting right the consequences of prior conditions of segregation." For the reasons explained above, the records in these cases do not demonstrate that either school board's plan is supported by an interest in remedying past discrimination.

Moreover, the school boards have no interest in remedying the sundry consequences of prior segregation unrelated to schooling, such as "housing patterns, employment practices, economic conditions, and social attitudes." General claims that past school segregation affected such varied societal trends are "too amorphous a basis for imposing a racially classified remedy," because "[i]t is sheer speculation" how decades-past segregation in the school system might have affected these trends. Consequently, school boards seeking to remedy those societal problems with race-based measures in schools today would have no way to gauge the proper scope of the remedy. Indeed, remedial measures geared toward such broad and unrelated societal ills have " 'no logical stopping point,' " and threaten to become "ageless in their reach into the past, and timeless in their ability to affect the future," *Wygant*. . . .

Next, the dissent argues that the interest in integration has an educational element. The dissent asserts that racially balanced schools improve educational outcomes for black children. In support, the dissent unquestioningly cites certain social science research to support propositions that are hotly disputed among social scientists. In reality, it is far from apparent that coerced racial — mixing has any educational benefits, much less that integration is necessary to black achievement.

Scholars have differing opinions as to whether educational benefits arise from racial balancing. Some have concluded that black students receive genuine educational benefits. Others have been more circumspect. And some have concluded that there are no demonstrable educational benefits. The *amicus* briefs in the cases before us mirror this divergence of opinion.

[A]dd to the inconclusive social science the fact of black achievement in "racially isolated" environments. . . . Even after *Brown*, some schools with predominantly black enrollments have achieved outstanding educational results. There is also evidence that black students attending historically black colleges achieve better academic results than those attending predominantly white colleges.

The Seattle school board itself must believe that racial mixing is not necessary to black achievement. Seattle operates a K-8 "African-American Academy," which has a "nonwhite" enrollment of 99%. That school was founded in 1990 as part of the school board's effort to "increase academic achievement." According to the school's most recent annual report, "[a]cademic excellence" is its "primary goal." This racially imbalanced environment has reportedly produced test scores "higher across all grade levels in reading, writing and math." Contrary to what the dissent would have predicted, the children in Seattle's African-American Academy have shown gains when placed in a "highly segregated" environment.

Given this tenuous relationship between forced racial mixing and improved educational results for black children, the dissent cannot plausibly maintain that an educational element supports the integration interest, let alone makes it compelling. See *Jenkins*, 515 U.S., at 121-122 (Thomas, J., concurring) ("[T]here is no reason to think that black students cannot learn as well when surrounded by members of their own race as when they are in an integrated environment").

Perhaps recognizing as much, the dissent argues that the social science evidence is "strong enough to permit a democratically elected school board reasonably to determine that this interest is a compelling one." This assertion is inexplicable. It is not up to the school boards—the very government entities whose race-based practices we must strictly scrutinize—to determine what interests qualify as compelling under the Fourteenth Amendment to the United

States Constitution. Rather, this Court must assess independently the nature of the interest asserted and the evidence to support it in order to determine whether it qualifies as compelling under our precedents. In making such a determination, we have deferred to state authorities only once, see *Grutter*, and that deference was prompted by factors uniquely relevant to higher education. The dissent's proposed test—whether sufficient social science evidence supports a government unit's conclusion that the interest it asserts is compelling—calls to mind the rational-basis standard of review the dissent purports not to apply. Furthermore, it would leave our equal-protection jurisprudence at the mercy of elected government officials evaluating the evanescent views of a handful of social scientists. To adopt the dissent's deferential approach would be to abdicate our constitutional responsibilities.[e]

Finally, the dissent asserts a "democratic element" to the integration interest. It defines the "democratic element" as "an interest in producing an educational environment that reflects the 'pluralistic society' in which our children will live." Environmental reflection, though, is just another way to say racial balancing. And "[p]referring members of any one group for no reason other than race or ethnic origin is discrimination for its own sake." *Bakke* (opinion of Powell, J.). . . .

[T]he dissent argues that the racial balancing in these plans is not an end in itself but is instead intended to "teac[h] children to engage in the kind of cooperation among Americans of all races that is necessary to make a land of three hundred million people one Nation." These "generic lessons in socialization and good citizenship" are too sweeping to qualify as compelling interests. And they are not "uniquely relevant" to schools or "uniquely 'teachable' in a formal educational setting." Therefore, if governments may constitutionally use racial balancing to achieve these aspirational ends in schools, they may use racial balancing to achieve similar goals at every level—from state-sponsored 4-H clubs, to the state civil service.

Moreover, the democratic interest has no durational limit, contrary to *Grutter*'s command. In other words, it will always be important for students to learn cooperation among the races. If this interest justifies race-conscious measures today, then logically it will justify race-conscious measures forever. Thus, the

---

e. The dissent accuses me of "feel[ing] confident that, to end invidious discrimination, one must end *all* governmental use of race-conscious criteria" and chastises me for not deferring to democratically elected majorities. Regardless of what Justice Breyer's goals might be, this Court does not sit to "create a society that includes all Americans" or to solve the problems of "troubled inner-city schooling." We are not social engineers. The United States Constitution dictates that local governments cannot make decisions on the basis of race. Consequently, regardless of the perceived negative effects of racial imbalance, I will not defer to legislative majorities where the Constitution forbids it.

It should escape no one that behind Justice Breyer's veil of judicial modesty hides an inflated role for the Federal Judiciary. The dissent's approach confers on judges the power to say what sorts of discrimination are benign and which are invidious. Having made that determination (based on no objective measure that I can detect), a judge following the dissent's approach will set the level of scrutiny to achieve the desired result. Only then must the judge defer to a democratic majority. In my view, to defer to one's preferred result is not to defer at all.

democratic interest, limitless in scope and "timeless in [its] ability to affect the future," cannot justify government race-based decisionmaking.

[T]he dissent points to data that indicate that "black and white students in desegregated schools are less racially prejudiced than those in segregated schools." By the dissent's account, improvements in racial attitudes depend upon the increased contact between black and white students thought to occur in more racially balanced schools. There is no guarantee, however, that students of — different races in the same school will actually spend time with one another. Schools frequently group students by academic ability as an aid to efficient instruction, but such groupings often result in classrooms with high concentrations of one race or another. In addition to classroom separation, students of different races within the same school may separate themselves socially. Therefore, even supposing interracial contact leads directly to improvements in racial attitudes and race relations, a program that assigns students of different races to the same schools might not capture those benefits. Simply putting students together under the same roof does not necessarily mean that the students will learn together or even interact.

Furthermore, it is unclear whether increased interracial contact improves racial attitudes and relations. One researcher has stated that "the reviews of desegregation and intergroup relations were unable to come to any conclusion about what the probable effects of desegregation were . . . [;] virtually all of the reviewers determined that few, if any, firm conclusions about the impact of desegregation on intergroup relations could be drawn." Some studies have even found that a deterioration in racial attitudes seems to result from racial mixing in schools. Therefore, it is not nearly as apparent as the dissent suggests that increased interracial exposure automatically leads to improved racial attitudes or race relations. . . .

[T]he school boards cannot plausibly maintain that their plans further a compelling interest. As I explained in *Grutter*, only "those measures the State must take to provide a bulwark against anarchy . . . or to prevent violence" and "a government's effort to remedy past discrimination for which it is responsible" constitute compelling interests. Neither of the parties has argued—nor could they—that race-based student assignment is necessary to provide a bulwark against anarchy or to prevent violence. And as I explained above, the school districts have no remedial interest in pursuing these programs. Accordingly, the school boards cannot satisfy strict scrutiny. These plans are unconstitutional.

III.

Most of the dissent's criticisms of today's result can be traced to its rejection of the color-blind Constitution. The dissent attempts to marginalize the notion of a color-blind Constitution by consigning it to me and Members of today's plurality.[f] But I am quite comfortable in the company I keep. My view of the

Constitution is Justice Harlan's view in *Plessy:* "Our Constitution is color blind, and neither knows nor tolerates classes among citizens." Plessy v. Ferguson (dissenting opinion). And my view was the rallying cry for the lawyers who litigated *Brown*. See, e.g., Brief for Appellants in Brown v. Board of Education, O. T. 1953, Nos. 1, 2, and 4 p. 65 ("That the Constitution is color blind is our dedicated belief"); Brief for Appellants in Brown v. Board of Education, O. T. 1952, No. 1, p. 5 ("The Fourteenth Amendment precludes a state from imposing distinctions or classifications based upon race and color alone").

The dissent appears to pin its interpretation of the Equal Protection Clause to current societal practice and expectations, deference to local officials, likely practical consequences, and reliance on previous statements from this and other courts. Such a view was ascendant in this Court's jurisprudence for several decades. It first appeared in *Plessy,* where the Court asked whether a state law providing for segregated railway cars was "a reasonable regulation." The Court deferred to local authorities in making its determination, noting that in inquiring into reasonableness "there must necessarily be a large discretion on the part of the legislature." The Court likewise paid heed to societal practices, local expectations, and practical consequences by looking to "the established usages, customs and traditions of the people, and with a view to the promotion of their comfort, and the preservation of the public peace and good order." Guided by these principles, the Court concluded: "[W]e cannot say that a law which authorizes or even requires the separation of the two races in public conveyances is unreasonable, or more obnoxious to the Fourteenth Amendment than the acts of Congress requiring separate schools for colored children in the District of Columbia."

The segregationists in *Brown* embraced the arguments the Court endorsed in *Plessy*. Though *Brown* decisively rejected those arguments, today's dissent replicates them to a distressing extent. Thus, the dissent argues that "[e]ach plan embodies the results of local experience and community consultation." Similarly, the segregationists made repeated appeals to societal practice and expectation. The dissent argues that "weight [must be given] to a local school board's knowledge, expertise, and concerns," and with equal vigor, the segregationists argued for deference to local authorities. The dissent argues that today's decision "threatens to substitute for present calm a disruptive round of race-related litigation," and claims that today's decision "risks serious harm to the law and for the Nation." The segregationists also relied upon the likely practical consequences of ending the state-imposed system of racial separation.

---

f. [I] have no quarrel with the proposition that the Fourteenth Amendment sought to bring former slaves into American society as full members. [But] the color-blind Constitution does not bar the government from taking measures to remedy past state-sponsored discrimination-indeed, it requires that such measures be taken in certain circumstances. Race-based government measures during the 1860's and 1870's to remedy *state-enforced slavery* were therefore not inconsistent with the color-blind Constitution.

And foreshadowing today's dissent, the segregationists most heavily relied upon judicial precedent.

The similarities between the dissent's arguments and the segregationists' arguments do not stop there. Like the dissent, the segregationists repeatedly cautioned the Court to consider practicalities and not to embrace too theoretical a view of the Fourteenth Amendment. And just as the dissent argues that the need for these programs will lessen over time, the segregationists claimed that reliance on segregation was lessening and might eventually end.

What was wrong in 1954 cannot be right today.[g] Whatever else the Court's rejection of the segregationists' arguments in *Brown* might have established, it certainly made clear that state and local governments cannot take from the Constitution a right to make decisions on the basis of race by adverse possession. The fact that state and local governments had been discriminating on the basis of race for a long time was irrelevant to the *Brown* Court. The fact that racial discrimination was preferable to the relevant communities was irrelevant to the *Brown* Court. And the fact that the state and local governments had relied on statements in this Court's opinions was irrelevant to the *Brown* Court. The same principles guide today's decision. None of the considerations trumpeted by the dissent is relevant to the constitutionality of the school boards' race based plans because no contextual detail—or collection of contextual details, can "provide refuge from the principle that under our Constitution, the government may not make distinctions on the basis of race."

In place of the color-blind Constitution, the dissent would permit measures to keep the races together and proscribe measures to keep the races apart.[h] Although no such distinction is apparent in the Fourteenth Amendment, the dissent would constitutionalize today's faddish social theories that embrace that distinction. The Constitution is not that malleable. Even if current social theories favor classroom racial engineering as necessary to "solve the problems at hand," the Constitution enshrines principles independent of social theories. See *Plessy*, 163 U.S., at 559 (Harlan, J., dissenting) ("The white race deems itself to be the dominant race in this country. And so it is, in prestige, in achievements, in education, in wealth and in power. So, I doubt not, it will continue to be for all time. . . . But in view of the Constitution, in the eye of the law, there is in this country no superior, dominant, ruling class of citizens. . . .

---

g. It is no answer to say that these cases can be distinguished from *Brown* because *Brown* involved → invidious racial classifications whereas the racial classifications here are benign. How does one tell when a racial classification is invidious? The segregationists in *Brown* argued that their racial classifications were benign, not invidious. It is the height of arrogance for Members of this Court to assert blindly that their motives are better than others.

h. The dissent does not face the complicated questions attending its proposed standard. For example, where does the dissent's principle stop? Can the government force racial mixing against the will of those being mixed? Can the government force black families to relocate to white neighborhoods in the name if bringing the races together? What about historically black colleges, which have "established traditions and programs that might disproportionately appeal to one race or another"? The dissent does not and cannot answer these questions because the contours of the distinction it propounds rest entirely in the eye of the beholder.

Our Constitution is color-blind, and neither knows nor tolerates classes among citizens"). Indeed, if our history has taught us anything, it has taught us to beware of elites bearing racial theories.[i] More recently, the school district sent a delegation of high school students to a "White Privilege Conference." See Equity and Race Relations White Privilege Conference, https://www.seattle-schools.org/area/equityandrace/whiteprivilegeconference.xml. One conference participant described "white privilege" as "an invisible package of unearned assets which I can count on cashing in each day, but about which I was meant to remain oblivious. White Privilege is like an invisible weightless knapsack of special provisions, maps, passports, codebooks, visas, clothes, tools, and blank checks." See White Privilege Conference, Questions and Answers, http://www.uccs.edu/~wpc/faqs.htm; see generally Westneat, School Districts Obsessed with Race, Seattle Times, Apr. 1, 2007, p. B1 (describing racial issues in Seattle schools). See, e.g., Dred Scott v. Sandford, 19 How. 393, 407 (1857) ("[T]hey [members of the 'negro African race'] had no rights which the white man was bound to respect"). Can we really be sure that the racial theories that motivated *Dred Scott* and *Plessy* are a relic of the past or that future theories will be nothing but beneficent and progressive? That is a gamble I am unwilling to take, and it is one the Constitution does not allow.

Justice KENNEDY, concurring in part and concurring in the judgment.

[I] join Parts III-A and III-C for reasons provided below. My views do not allow me to join the balance of the opinion by The Chief Justice, which seems to me to be inconsistent in both its approach and its implications with the history, meaning, and reach of the Equal Protection Clause. Justice Breyer's dissenting opinion, on the other hand, rests on what in my respectful submission is a misuse and mistaken interpretation of our precedents. This leads it to advance propositions that, in my view, are both erroneous and in fundamental conflict with basic equal protection principles. As a consequence, this separate opinion is necessary to set forth my conclusions in the two cases before the Court.

---

i. Justice Breyer's good intentions, which I do not doubt, have the shelf life of Justice Breyer's tenure. Unlike the dissenters, I am unwilling to delegate my constitutional responsibilities to local school boards and allow them to experiment with race-based decisionmaking on the assumption that their intentions will forever remain as good as Justice Breyer's. See The Federalist No. 51, p. 349 (J. Cooke ed. 1961) ("If men were angels, no government would be necessary"). Indeed, the racial theories endorsed by the Seattle school board should cause the dissenters to question whether local school boards should be entrusted with the power to make decisions on the basis of race. The Seattle school district's Website formerly contained the following definition of "cultural racism": "Those aspects of society that overtly and covertly attribute value and normality to white people and whiteness, and devalue, stereotype, and label people of color as 'other,' different, less than, or render them invisible. Examples of these norms include defining white skin tones as nude or flesh colored, having a future time orientation, emphasizing individualism as opposed to a more collective ideology, defining one form of English as standard. . . . " After the site was removed, the district offered the comforting clarification that the site was not intended " 'to hold onto unsuccessful concepts such as melting pot or color-blind mentality.'"

I.

[T]he dissent finds that the school districts have identified a compelling interest in increasing diversity, including for the purpose of avoiding racial isolation. The plurality, by contrast, does not acknowledge that the school districts have identified a compelling interest here. For this reason, among others, I do not join Parts III-B and IV. Diversity, depending on its meaning and definition, is a compelling educational goal a school district may pursue.

[T]he inquiry into less restrictive alternatives demanded by the narrow tailoring analysis requires in many cases a thorough understanding of how a plan works. The government bears the burden of justifying its use of individual racial classifications. As part of that burden it must establish, in detail, how – decisions based on an individual student's race are made in a challenged governmental program. The Jefferson County Board of Education fails to meet this threshold mandate. . . . Jefferson County in its briefing has explained how and when it employs these classifications only in terms so broad and imprecise that they cannot withstand strict scrutiny. While it acknowledges that racial classifications are used to make certain assignment decisions, it fails to make clear, for example, who makes the decisions; what if any oversight is employed; the precise circumstances in which an assignment decision will or will not be made on the basis of race; or how it is determined which of two similarly situated children will be subjected to a given race-based decision.

[J]efferson County fails to make clear to this Court—even in the limited respects implicated by Joshua's initial assignment and transfer denial—whether in fact it relies on racial classifications in a manner narrowly tailored to the interest in question, rather than in the far-reaching, inconsistent, and ad hoc manner that a less forgiving reading of the record would suggest. When a court subjects governmental action to strict scrutiny, it cannot construe ambiguities in favor of the State.

As for the Seattle case, the school district has gone further in describing the methods and criteria used to determine assignment decisions on the basis of individual racial classifications. The district, nevertheless, has failed to make an adequate showing in at least one respect. It has failed to explain why, in a – district composed of a diversity of races, with fewer than half of the students classified as "white," it has employed the crude racial categories of "white" and "non-white" as the basis for its assignment decisions.

The district has identified its purposes as follows: "(1) to promote the educational benefits of diverse school enrollments; (2) to reduce the potentially harmful effects of racial isolation by allowing students the opportunity to opt out of racially isolated schools; and (3) to make sure that racially segregated housing patterns did not prevent non-white students from having equitable access to the most popular over-subscribed schools." Yet the school district does not explain how, in the context of its diverse student population, a blunt distinction between "white" and "non-white" furthers these goals. As the Court explains, "a school with 50 percent Asian-American students and 50 percent white students but no African-American, Native-American, or Latino students would qualify as balanced, while a school with 30 percent Asian-American, 25 percent African-American, 25 percent Latino, and 20 percent white students would not." Far from being narrowly tailored to its purposes, this system threatens to defeat its own ends, and the school district has provided no convincing explanation for its design. Other problems are evident in Seattle's system, but there is no need to address them now. As the district fails to account for the classification system it has chosen, despite what appears to be its ill fit, Seattle has not shown its plan to be narrowly tailored to achieve its own ends; and thus it fails to pass strict scrutiny.

II.

[P]arts of the opinion by The Chief Justice imply an all-too-unyielding insistence that race cannot be a factor in instances when, in my view, it may be taken into account. The plurality opinion is too dismissive of the legitimate interest government has in ensuring all people have equal opportunity regardless of their race. The plurality's postulate that "[t]he way to stop discrimination on the basis of race is to stop discriminating on the basis of race," is not sufficient to decide these cases. Fifty years of experience since Brown v. Board of Education, should teach us that the problem before us defies so easy a solution. School districts can seek to reach *Brown*'s objective of equal educational opportunity. The plurality opinion is at least open to the interpretation that the Constitution requires school districts to ignore the problem of *de facto* resegregation in schooling. I cannot endorse that conclusion. To the extent the plurality opinion suggests the Constitution mandates that state and local school authorities must accept the status quo of racial isolation in schools, it is, in my view, profoundly mistaken.

The statement by Justice Harlan that "[o]ur Constitution is color-blind" was most certainly justified in the context of his dissent in Plessy v. Ferguson, 163 U.S. 537, 559 (1896). [A]s an aspiration, Justice Harlan's axiom must command our assent. In the real world, it is regrettable to say, it cannot be a universal constitutional principle.

In the administration of public schools by the state and local authorities it is permissible to consider the racial makeup of schools and to adopt general policies to encourage a diverse student body, one aspect of which is its racial composition. If school authorities are concerned that the student-body compositions of certain schools interfere with the objective of offering an equal educational opportunity to all of their students, they are free to devise race conscious measures to address the problem in a general way and without treating each student in different fashion solely on the basis of a systematic, individual typing by race.

School boards may pursue the goal of bringing together students of diverse backgrounds and races through other means, including strategic site selection of new schools; drawing attendance zones with general recognition of the demographics of neighborhoods; allocating resources for special programs; recruiting students and faculty in a targeted fashion; and tracking enrollments, performance, and other statistics by race. These mechanisms are race conscious but do not lead — to different treatment based on a classification that tells each student he or she is to be defined by race, so it is unlikely any of them would demand strict scrutiny to be found permissible. Executive and legislative branches, which for generations now have considered these types of policies and procedures, should be permitted to employ them with candor and with confidence that a constitutional violation does not occur whenever a decisionmaker considers the impact a given approach might have on students of different races. Assigning to each student a — personal designation according to a crude system of individual racial classifications is quite a different matter; and the legal analysis changes accordingly.

Each respondent has asserted that its assignment of individual students by race is permissible because there is no other way to avoid racial isolation in the school districts. Yet, as explained, each has failed to provide the support necessary for that proposition. And individual racial classifications employed in this manner may be considered legitimate only if they are a last resort to achieve a compelling interest.

In the cases before us it is noteworthy that the number of students whose assignment depends on express racial classifications is limited. I join Part III-C of the Court's opinion because I agree that in the context of these plans, the small number of assignments affected suggests that the schools could have achieved their stated ends through different means. These include the facially race-neutral means set forth above or, if necessary, a more nuanced, individual evaluation of school needs and student characteristics that might include race as a component. The latter approach would be informed by *Grutter*, though of course the criteria relevant to student placement would differ based on the age of the students, the needs of the parents, and the role of the schools.

III.

The dissent rests on the assumptions that these sweeping race-based classifications of persons are permitted by existing precedents; that its confident endorsement of race categories for each child in a large segment of the community presents no danger to individual freedom in other, prospective realms of governmental regulation; and that the racial classifications used here cause no hurt or anger of the type the Constitution prevents. Each of these premises is, in my respectful view, incorrect. [I]n his critique of that analysis, I am in many respects in agreement with The Chief Justice. The conclusions he has set forth — in Part III-A of the Court's opinion are correct, in my view, because the compelling interests implicated in the cases before us are distinct from the interests the Court has recognized in remedying the effects of past intentional discrimination and in increasing diversity in higher education. As the Court notes, we recognized the compelling nature of the interest in remedying past intentional discrimination in Freeman v. Pitts, 503 U.S. 467, 494 (1992), and of the interest in diversity in higher education in *Grutter*. At the same time, these compelling interests, in my view, do help inform the present inquiry. And to the extent the plurality opinion can be interpreted to foreclose consideration of these interests, I disagree with that reasoning.

[T]he general conclusions upon which [the dissent] relies have no principled limit and would result in the broad acceptance of governmental racial classifi-cations in areas far afield from schooling. The dissent's permissive strict scrutiny (which bears more than a passing resemblance to rational-basis review) could invite widespread governmental deployment of racial classifications. There is every reason to think that, if the dissent's rationale were accepted, Congress, assuming an otherwise proper exercise of its spending authority or commerce power, could mandate either the Seattle or the Jefferson County plans nationwide. There seems to be no principled rule, moreover, to limit the dissent's rationale to the context of public schools. The dissent emphasizes local control, the unique history of school desegregation, and the fact that these plans make less use of race than prior plans, but these factors seem more rhetorical than integral to the analytical structure of the opinion.

[T]o say, [as the dissent does], that we must ratify the racial classifications here at issue based on the majority opinions in *Gratz* and *Grutter* is, with all respect, simply baffling.

Gratz involved a system where race was not the entire classification. The procedures in *Gratz* placed much less reliance on race than do the plans at issue here. The issue in *Gratz* arose, moreover, in the context of college admissions where students had other choices and precedent supported the proposition that First Amendment interests give universities particular latitude in defining diversity. Even so the race factor was found to be invalid.

[In] *Grutter* . . . the Court sustained a system that, it found, was flexible enough to take into account "all pertinent elements of diversity," and consid-ered race as only one factor among many, *id.*, at 340. Seattle's plan, by contrast, relies upon a mechanical formula that has denied hundreds of students their preferred schools on the basis of three rigid criteria: placement of siblings, distance from schools, and race. If those students were considered for a whole range of their talents and school needs with race as just one consideration, *Grutter* would have some application. That, though, is not the case. . . .

B

To uphold these programs the Court is asked to brush aside two concepts of central importance for determining the validity of laws and decrees designed to alleviate the hurt and adverse consequences resulting from race discrimination. The first is the difference between *de jure* and *de facto* segregation; the second, the presumptive invalidity of a State's use of racial classifications to differenti-ate its treatment of individuals.

[T]o remedy the wrong [of segregation], school districts that had been segregated by law had no choice, whether under court supervision or pursuant to voluntary desegregation efforts, but to resort to extraordinary measures including individual student and teacher assignment to schools based on race. . . . Our cases recognized a fundamental difference between those school districts that had engaged in *de jure* segregation and those whose segregation was the result of other factors. School districts that had engaged in *de jure* segregation had an affirmative constitutional duty to desegregate; those that were *de facto* segregated did not. The distinctions between *de jure* and *de facto* segregation extended to the remedies available to governmental units in addition to the courts. For example, in Wygant v. Jackson Bd. of Ed., 476 U.S. 267, 274 (1986), the plurality noted: "This Court never has held that societal discrimination alone is sufficient to justify a racial classification. Rather, the Court has insisted upon some showing of prior discrimination by the governmental unit involved before allowing limited use of racial classifications in order to remedy such discrimination." The Court's decision in *Croson* reinforced the difference between the remedies available to redress *de facto* and *de jure* discrimination [by rejecting the] "claim that past societal discrimination alone can serve as the basis for rigid racial preferences." . . .

From the standpoint of the victim, it is true, an injury stemming from racial prejudice can hurt as much when the demeaning treatment based on race identity stems from bias masked deep within the social order as when it is imposed by law. The distinction between government and private action, furthermore, can be amorphous both as a historical matter and as a matter of present-day finding of fact. Laws arise from a culture and vice versa. Neither can assign to the other all responsibility for persisting injustices.

Yet, like so many other legal categories that can overlap in some instances, the constitutional distinction between *de jure* and *de facto* segregation has been thought to be an important one. It must be conceded its primary function in school cases was to delimit the powers of the Judiciary in the fashioning of remedies. See, e.g., *Milliken*. The distinction ought not to be altogether disregarded, however, when we come to that most sensitive of all racial issues, an attempt by the government to treat whole classes of persons differently based on the government's systematic classification of each individual by race. There, too, the distinction serves as a limit on the exercise of a power that reaches to the very verge of constitutional authority. Reduction of an individual to an assigned racial identity for differential treatment is among the most pernicious actions our government can undertake. The allocation of governmental burdens and benefits, contentious under any circumstances, is even more divisive when allocations are made on the basis of individual racial classifications. See, e.g., *Bakke*; *Adarand*.

Notwithstanding these concerns, allocation of benefits and burdens through individual racial classifications was found sometimes permissible in the context of remedies for *de jure* wrong. Where there has been *de jure* segregation, there is a cognizable legal wrong, and the courts and legislatures have broad power to remedy it. The remedy, though, was limited in time and limited to the wrong. The Court has allowed school districts to remedy their prior *de jure* segregation by classifying individual students based on their race. The limitation of this power to instances where there has been *de jure* segregation serves to confine the nature, extent, and duration of governmental reliance on individual racial classifications.

The cases here were argued upon the assumption, and come to us on the premise, that the discrimination in question did not result from *de jure* actions. And when *de facto* discrimination is at issue our tradition has been that the remedial rules are different. The State must seek alternatives to the classification and differential treatment of individuals by race, at least absent some extraordinary showing not present here.

C

[One might object:] If it is legitimate for school authorities to work to avoid racial isolation in their schools, must they do so only by indirection and general policies? Does the Constitution mandate this inefficient result? Why may the authorities not recognize the problem in candid fashion and solve it altogether through resort to direct assignments based on student racial classifications? . . .

The argument ignores the dangers presented by individual classifications, dangers that are not as pressing when the same ends are achieved by more indirect means. When the government classifies an individual by race, it must first define what it means to be of a race. Who exactly is white and who is nonwhite? To be forced to live under a state-mandated racial label is inconsistent with the dignity of individuals in our society. And it is a label that an individual is powerless to change. Governmental classifications that command people to march in different directions based on racial typologies can cause a new divisiveness. The practice can lead to corrosive discourse, where race serves not as an element of our diverse heritage but instead as a bargaining chip in the political process. On the other hand race-conscious measures that do not rely on differential treatment based on individual classifications present these problems to a lesser degree.

The idea that if race is the problem, race is the instrument with which to solve it cannot be accepted as an analytical leap forward. And if this is a frustrating duality of the Equal Protection Clause it simply reflects the duality of our history and our attempts to promote freedom in a world that sometimes seems set against it. Under our Constitution the individual, child or adult, can find his own identity, can define her own persona, without state intervention that classifies on the basis of his race or the color of her skin.

. . .

This Nation has a moral and ethical obligation to fulfill its historic commitment to creating an integrated society that ensures equal opportunity for all of its children. A compelling interest exists in avoiding racial isolation, an interest that a school district, in its discretion and expertise, may choose to pursue. Likewise, a district may consider it a compelling interest to achieve a diverse student population. Race may be one component of that diversity, but other demographic factors, plus special talents and needs, should also be considered.

What the government is not permitted to do, absent a showing of necessity not made here, is to classify every student on the basis of race and to assign each of them to schools based on that classification. Crude measures of this sort threaten to reduce children to racial chits valued and traded according to one school's supply and another's demand.

[A] sense of stigma may already become the fate of those separated out by circumstances beyond their immediate control. But ... [e]ven so, measures other than differential treatment based on racial typing of individuals first must be exhausted.

The decision today should not prevent school districts from continuing the important work of bringing together students of different racial, ethnic, and economic backgrounds. Due to a variety of factors—some influenced by government, some not—neighborhoods in our communities do not reflect the diversity of our Nation as a whole. Those entrusted with directing our public schools can bring to bear the creativity of experts, parents, administrators, and other concerned citizens to find a way to achieve the compelling interests they face without resorting to widespread governmental allocation of benefits and burdens on the basis of racial classifications.

With this explanation I concur in the judgment of the Court.

Justice STEVENS, dissenting.

. . . There is a cruel irony in The Chief Justice's reliance on our decision in Brown v. Board of Education. The first sentence in the concluding paragraph of his opinion states: "Before *Brown,* schoolchildren were told where they could and could not go to school based on the color of their skin." . . . The Chief Justice fails to note that it was only black schoolchildren who were so ordered; indeed, the history books do not tell stories of white children struggling to attend black schools. In this and other ways, The Chief Justice rewrites the history of one of this Court's most important decisions.

. . .

The Court's misuse of the three-tiered approach to Equal Protection analysis merely reconfirms my own view that there is only one such Clause in the Constitution. If we look at cases decided during the interim between *Brown* and *Adarand,* we can see how a rigid adherence to tiers of scrutiny obscures *Brown*'s clear message. Perhaps the best example is provided by our approval of the decision of the Supreme Judicial Court of Massachusetts in 1967 upholding a state statute mandating racial integration in that State's school system. See School Comm. of Boston v. Board of Education, 352 Mass. 693, 227 N. E. 2d 729. Rejecting arguments comparable to those that the plurality accepts today, that court noted: "It would be the height of irony if the racial imbalance act, enacted as it was with the laudable purpose of achieving equal educational opportunities, should, by prescribing school pupil allocations based on race, founder on unsuspected shoals in the Fourteenth Amendment." . . . Our ruling on the merits [on appeal] simply stated that the appeal was "dismissed for want of a substantial federal question." School Comm. of Boston v. Board of

Education, 389 U.S. 572 (1968) (per curiam). That decision not only expressed our appraisal of the merits of the appeal, but it constitutes a precedent that the Court overrules today. The subsequent statements by the unanimous Court in Swann v. Charlotte-Mecklenburg Bd. of Ed., 402 U.S. 1, 16 (1971), by then Justice Rehnquist in chambers in Bustop, Inc. v. Los Angeles Bd. of Ed., 439 U.S. 1380, 1383 (1978), and by the host of state court decisions cited by Justice Breyer, were fully consistent with that disposition. Unlike today's decision, they were also entirely loyal to *Brown.*

The Court has changed significantly since it decided *School Comm. of Boston* in 1968. It was then more faithful to *Brown* and more respectful of our precedent than it is today. It is my firm conviction that no Member of the Court that I joined in 1975 would have agreed with today's decision.

Justice BREYER, with whom Justice STEVENS, Justice SOUTER, and Justice GINSBURG join, dissenting.

[I]n dozens of . . . cases [following *Brown*], this Court told school districts previously segregated by law what they must do at a minimum to comply with *Brown*'s constitutional holding. The measures required by those cases often included race-conscious practices, such as mandatory busing and race based restrictions on voluntary transfers.

Beyond those minimum requirements, the Court left much of the determination of how to achieve integration to the judgment of local communities. . . . As a result, different districts—some acting under court decree, some acting in order to avoid threatened lawsuits, some seeking to comply with federal administrative orders, some acting purely voluntarily, some acting after federal courts had dissolved earlier orders—adopted, modified, and experimented with hosts of different kinds of plans, including race-conscious plans, all with a similar objective: greater racial integration of public schools. The techniques that different districts have employed range "from voluntary transfer programs to mandatory reassignment." . . .

Overall these efforts brought about considerable racial integration. More recently, however, progress has stalled. Between 1968 and 1980, the number of black children attending a school where minority children constituted more than half of the school fell from 77% to 63% in the Nation (from 81% to 57% in the South) but then reversed direction by the year 2000, rising from 63% to 72% in the Nation (from 57% to 69% in the South). Similarly, between 1968 and 1980, the number of black children attending schools that were more than 90% minority fell from 64% to 33% in the Nation (from 78% to 23% in the South), but that too reversed direction, rising by the year 2000 from 33% to 37% in the Nation (from 23% to 31% in the South). As of 2002, almost 2.4 million students, or over 5% of all public school enrollment, attended schools with a white population of less than 1%. Of these, 2.3 million were black and Latino students, and only 72,000 were white. Today, more than one in six black children attend a school that is 99-100% minority. In light of the evident risk of a return to school systems that are in fact (though not in law) resegregated, many school districts have felt a need to maintain or to extend their integration efforts.

The upshot is that myriad school districts operating in myriad circumstances have devised myriad plans, often with race-conscious elements, all for the sake of eradicating earlier school segregation, bringing about integration, or preventing retrogression. Seattle and Louisville are two such districts, and the histories of their present plans set forth typical school integration stories.

[T]he distinction between *de jure* segregation (caused by school systems) and *de facto* segregation (caused, e.g., by housing patterns or generalized societal discrimination) is meaningless in the present context, thereby dooming the plurality's endeavor to find support for its views in that distinction. [R]eal-world efforts to substitute racially diverse for racially segregated schools (however caused) are complex, to the point where the Constitution cannot plausibly be interpreted to rule out categorically all local efforts to use means that are "conscious" of the race of individuals.

In both Seattle and Louisville, the local school districts began with schools that were highly segregated in fact. In both cities plaintiffs filed lawsuits claiming unconstitutional segregation. In Louisville, a federal district court found that school segregation reflected pre-*Brown* state laws separating the races. In Seattle, the plaintiffs alleged that school segregation unconstitutionally reflected not only generalized societal discrimination and residential housing patterns, but also *school board policies and actions* that had helped to create, maintain, and aggravate racial segregation. In Louisville, a federal court entered a remedial decree. In Seattle, the parties settled after the school district pledged to undertake a desegregation plan. In both cities, the school boards adopted plans designed to achieve integration by bringing about more racially diverse schools. In each city the school board modified its plan several times in light of, for example, hostility to busing, the threat of resegregation, and the desirability of introducing greater student choice. And in each city, the school boards' plans have evolved over time in ways that progressively *diminish* the plans' use of explicit race-conscious criteria.

[Justice Breyer offers a detailed history of desegregation efforts in both cities. He points out that complaints about Seattle's segregated schools began as early as 1956, pointing to segregative housing practices and school board policies that exacerbated racial segregation. The NAACP filed its first lawsuit against the Seattle School Board in 1969, leading to a plan that required race-based transfers and mandatory busing. The NAACP filed a complaint with the Office of Civil Rights (OCR) of the Department of Health, Education and Welfare in 1977, which led to a formal settlement agreement, the "Seattle Plan," which also used busing to prevent racial imbalance in the schools. To prevent the plan from taking effect, Washington State voters passed an initiative that required students to be assigned to the schools closest to their homes. The U.S. Supreme Court struck the referendum down in Washington v. Seattle School Dist. No. 1 458 U.S. 457 (1982). By 1988, many white families had left the district, and many Asian families had moved in. Seattle moved to a school-choice plan with race-based constraints. In

1996, the school board adopted the present plan, which deemphasized racial criteria and increased the likelihood that a student would receive an assignment to his first or second choice high school.

In 1956, Louisville created a geography-based student assignment policy in response to *Brown*, but by 1972 the school district remained heavily segregated. Civil rights groups brought suit in 1972, leading to a federal court order requiring desegregation, redrawing school attendance zones, closing 12 schools, and busing groups of students. The district court removed the case from its active docket in 1978; by 1984, several schools had fallen out of compliance with the order's target racial percentages due to changing demographics. The school board created a new plan. By 1991, the board tried a new strategy that emphasized student choice, devised in consultation with parents and the local community. In 1996, the board further revised its plan after further consultations with the community. The district court dissolved the 1975 order in 2000; and the board continued its 1996 plan.]

Both [Louisville and Seattle] faced problems that reflected initial periods of severe racial segregation, followed by such remedial efforts as busing, followed by evidence of resegregation, followed by a need to end busing and encourage the return of, e.g., suburban students through increased student choice. When formulating the plans under review, both districts drew upon their considerable experience with earlier plans, having revised their policies periodically in light of that experience. Both districts rethought their methods over time and explored a wide range of other means, including nonrace-conscious policies. Both districts also considered elaborate studies and consulted widely within their communities.

Both districts sought greater racial integration for educational and democratic, as well as for remedial, reasons. Both sought to achieve these objectives while preserving their commitment to other educational goals, e.g., districtwide commitment to high-quality public schools, increased pupil assignment to neighborhood schools, diminished use of busing, greater student choice, reduced risk of white flight, and so forth. Consequently, the present plans expand student choice; they limit the burdens (including busing) that earlier plans had imposed upon students and their families; and they use race-conscious criteria in limited and gradually diminishing ways. In particular, they use race-conscious criteria only to mark the outer bounds of broad population-related ranges.

The histories also make clear the futility of looking simply to whether earlier school segregation was *de jure* or *de facto* in order to draw firm lines separating the constitutionally permissible from the constitutionally forbidden use of "race-conscious" criteria. . . .

No one here disputes that Louisville's segregation was *de jure*. But what about Seattle's? Was it *de facto? De jure?* A mixture? Opinions differed. Or is it that a prior federal court had not adjudicated the matter? Does that make a difference? Is Seattle free on remand to say that its schools were *de jure* segregated, just as in 1956 a memo for the School Board admitted? . . .

A court finding of *de jure* segregation cannot be the crucial variable. After all, a number of school districts in the South that the Government or private plaintiffs challenged as segregated *by law* voluntarily desegregated their schools *without a court order*—just as Seattle did. . . . Moreover, Louisville's history makes clear that a community under a court order to desegregate might submit a race-conscious remedial plan *before* the court dissolved the order, but with every intention of following that plan even *after* dissolution. How could such a plan be lawful the day before dissolution but then become unlawful the very next day? On what legal ground can the majority rest its contrary view?

Are courts really to treat as merely *de facto* segregated those school districts that avoided a federal order by voluntarily complying with *Brown*'s requirements? This Court has previously done just the opposite, permitting a race conscious remedy without any kind of court decree. Because the Constitution emphatically does not forbid the use of race-conscious measures by districts in the South that voluntarily desegregated their schools, on what basis does the plurality claim that the law forbids Seattle to do the same?

The histories also indicate the complexity of the tasks and the practical difficulties that local school boards face when they seek to achieve greater racial integration. The boards work in communities where demographic patterns change, where they must meet traditional learning goals, where they must attract and retain effective teachers, where they should (and will) take account of parents' views and maintain *their* commitment to public school education, where they must adapt to court intervention, where they must encourage voluntary student and parent action—where they will find that their own good faith, their knowledge, and their understanding of local circumstances are always necessary but often insufficient to solve the problems at hand. . . .

II.

. . .

A longstanding and unbroken line of legal authority tells us that the Equal Protection Clause permits local school boards to use race-conscious criteria to achieve positive race-related goals, even when the Constitution does not compel it [In] *Swann* [v. Charlotte-Mecklenburg Bd. of Ed., 402 U.S. 1, 16 (1971)] Chief Justice Burger, on behalf of a unanimous Court in a case of exceptional importance, wrote:

> School authorities are traditionally charged with broad power to formulate and implement educational policy and might well conclude, for example, that in order to prepare students to live in a pluralistic society each school should have a prescribed ratio of Negro to white students reflecting the proportion for the district as a whole. To do this as an educational policy is within the broad discretionary powers of school authorities.

[I]n North Carolina Bd. of Ed. v. Swann, 402 U.S. 43, 45 (1971), this Court, citing *Swann,* restated the point. "[S]chool authorities," the Court said, "have wide discretion in formulating school policy, and . . . as a matter of educational policy school authorities may well conclude that some kind of racial balance in the schools is desirable quite apart from any constitutional requirements." Then-Justice Rehnquist echoed this view in Bustop, Inc. v. Los Angeles Bd. of Ed., 439 U.S. 1380, 1383 (1978) (opinion in chambers), making clear that he too believed that *Swann*'s statement reflected settled law: "While I have the gravest doubts that [a state supreme court] was *required* by the United States Constitution to take the [desegregation] action that it has taken in this case, I have very little doubt that it was *permitted* by that Constitution to take such action." (Emphasis in original.)

These statements nowhere suggest that this freedom is limited to school districts where court-ordered desegregation measures are also in effect. Indeed, in McDaniel v. Barresi, 402 U.S. 39 (1971), a case decided the same day as *Swann*, a group of parents challenged a race-conscious student assignment plan that the Clarke County School Board had *voluntarily* adopted as a remedy without a court order (though under federal agency pressure—pressure Seattle also encountered). . . . This Court upheld the plan, rejecting the parents' argument that "a person may not be *included* or *excluded* solely because he is a Negro or because he is white."

Federal authorities had claimed—as the NAACP and the OCR did in Seattle—that Clarke County schools were segregated in law, not just in fact. The plurality's claim that Seattle was "never segregated by law" is simply not accurate. The plurality could validly claim that *no court* ever found that Seattle schools were segregated in law. But that is also true of the Clarke County schools in *McDaniel*. Unless we believe that the Constitution enforces one legal standard for the South and another for the North, this Court should grant Seattle the permission it granted Clarke County, Georgia.

This Court has also held that school districts may be required by federal statute to undertake race-conscious desegregation efforts even when there is no likelihood that *de jure* segregation can be shown. In Board of Ed. of City School Dist. of New York v. Harris, 444 U.S. 130, 148-149 (1979), the Court concluded that a federal statute required school districts receiving certain federal funds to remedy faculty segregation, even though in this Court's view the racial disparities in the affected schools were purely *de facto* and would not have been actionable under the Equal Protection Clause. Not even the dissenters thought the race-conscious remedial program posed a *constitutional* problem.

Lower state and federal courts had considered the matter settled and uncontroversial even before this Court decided *Swann*. . . . *Swann* was not a sharp or unexpected departure from prior rulings; it reflected a consensus that had already emerged among state and lower federal courts. . . . Numerous state and federal courts explicitly relied upon *Swann*'s guidance for decades to follow. . . . [The] principle [in *Swann*] has been accepted by every branch of government and is rooted in the history of the Equal Protection Clause itself. Thus, Congress has enacted numerous race-conscious statutes that illustrate that principle or rely upon its validity. See, e.g., 20 U.S.C. §6311(b)(2)(C)(v) (No Child Left Behind Act); §1067 *et seq.* (authorizing aid to minority institutions).

In fact, without being exhaustive, I have counted 51 federal statutes that use racial classifications. I have counted well over 100 state statutes that similarly employ racial classifications. Presidential administrations for the past half-century have used and supported various race-conscious measures. And during the same time, hundreds of local school districts have adopted student assignment plans that use race-conscious criteria.

That *Swann*'s legal statement should find such broad acceptance is not surprising. For *Swann* is predicated upon a well-established legal view of the Fourteenth Amendment. That view understands the basic objective of those who wrote the Equal Protection Clause as forbidding practices that lead to racial exclusion. The Amendment sought to bring into American society as full members those whom the Nation had previously held in slavery.

There is reason to believe that those who drafted an Amendment with this basic purpose in mind would have understood the legal and practical difference between the use of race-conscious criteria in defiance of that purpose, namely to keep the races apart, and the use of race-conscious criteria to further that purpose, namely to bring the races together. Although the Constitution almost always forbids the former, it is significantly more lenient in respect to the latter.

Sometimes Members of this Court have disagreed about the degree of leniency that the Clause affords to programs designed to include. But I can find no case in which this Court has followed Justice Thomas' "colorblind" approach. And I have found no case that otherwise repudiated this constitutional asymmetry between that which seeks to *exclude* and that which seeks to *include* members of minority races.

[T]he constitutional principle enunciated in *Swann,* reiterated in subsequent cases, and relied upon over many years, provides, and has widely been thought to provide, authoritative legal guidance. And if the plurality now chooses to reject that principle, it cannot adequately justify its retreat simply by affixing the label "dicta" to reasoning with which it disagrees. Rather, it must explain to the courts and to the Nation *why* it would abandon guidance set forth many years before, guidance that countless others have built upon over time, and which the law has continuously embodied.

[N]o case—not *Adarand, Gratz, Grutter*, or any other—has ever held that the test of "strict scrutiny" means that all racial classifications—no matter whether they seek to include or exclude—must in practice be treated the same. . . . [In] *Adarand*, [t]he Court made clear that "[s]trict scrutiny does not trea[t] dissimilar race-based decisions as though they were equally objectionable." It added that the fact that a law "treats [a person] unequally because of his or her race . . . says nothing about the ultimate validity of any particular law." And the Court, . . . sought to *"dispel the notion* that strict scrutiny" is as likely to condemn *inclusive* uses of "race-conscious" criteria as it is to invalidate *exclusionary* uses. That is, it is *not* in all circumstances " 'strict in theory, but fatal in fact.' " . . . The Court's holding in *Grutter* demonstrates that the Court meant what it said, for the Court upheld an elite law school's race conscious admissions program.

The upshot is that the cases to which the plurality refers, though all applying strict scrutiny, do not treat exclusive and inclusive uses the same. Rather, they apply the strict scrutiny test in a manner that is "fatal in fact" only to racial classifications that harmfully *exclude*; they apply the test in a manner that is *not* fatal in fact to racial classifications that seek to *include*. . . .

Governmental use of race-based criteria can arise in the context of, for example, census forms, research expenditures for diseases, assignments of police officers patrolling predominantly minority-race neighborhoods, efforts to desegregate racially segregated schools, policies that favor minorities when distributing goods or services in short supply, actions that create majority minority electoral districts, peremptory strikes that remove potential jurors on the basis of race, and others. Given the significant differences among these contexts, it would be surprising if the law required an identically strict legal test for evaluating the constitutionality of race-based criteria as to each of them.

Here, the context is one in which school districts seek to advance or to maintain racial integration in primary and secondary schools. It is a context, as *Swann* makes clear, where history has required special administrative remedies. And it is a context in which the school boards' plans simply set race-conscious limits at the outer boundaries of a broad range.

This context is *not* a context that involves the use of race to decide who will receive goods or services that are normally distributed on the basis of merit and which are in short supply. It is not one in which race-conscious limits stigmatize or exclude; the limits at issue do not pit the races against each other or otherwise significantly exacerbate racial tensions. They do not impose burdens unfairly upon members of one race alone but instead seek benefits for members of all races alike. The context here is one of racial limits that seek, not to keep the races apart, but to bring them together.

[T]he districts' plans reflect efforts to overcome a history of segregation, embody the results of broad experience and community consultation, seek to expand student choice while reducing the need for mandatory busing, and use race-conscious criteria in highly limited ways that diminish the use of race compared to preceding integration efforts. They do not seek to award a scarce commodity on the basis of merit, for they are not magnet schools; rather, by design and in practice, they offer substantially equivalent academic programs and electives. Although some parents or children prefer some schools over others, school popularity has varied significantly over the years. . . .

I believe that the law requires application here of a standard of review that is not "strict" in the traditional sense of that word, . . . Nonetheless, in light of *Grutter* and other precedents, . . . I shall apply the version of strict scrutiny that those cases embody. . . .

III.

[T]he principal interest advanced in these cases [is] an interest in promoting or preserving greater racial "integration" of public schools. By this term, I mean the school districts' interest in eliminating school-by-school racial isolation and increasing the degree to which racial mixture characterizes each of the district's schools and each individual student's public school experience.

[This] interest . . . possesses three essential elements. First, there is a historical and remedial element: an interest in setting right the consequences of prior conditions of segregation. . . . It is an interest in continuing to combat the remnants of segregation caused in whole or in part by these school-related policies, which have often affected not only schools, but also housing patterns, employment practices, economic conditions, and social attitudes. It is an interest in maintaining hard-won gains. And it has its roots in preventing what gradually may become the *de facto* resegregation of America's public schools.

Second, there is an educational element: an interest in overcoming the adverse educational effects produced by and associated with highly segregated schools. Studies suggest that children taken from those schools and placed in integrated settings often show positive academic gains. Other studies reach different conclusions. But the evidence supporting an educational interest in → racially integrated schools is well established and strong enough to permit a democratically elected school board reasonably to determine that this interest is a compelling one.

Research suggests, for example, that black children from segregated educational environments significantly increase their achievement levels once they are placed in a more integrated setting. Indeed in Louisville itself the achievement gap between black and white elementary school students grew substantially smaller (by seven percentage points) after the integration plan was implemented in 1975. Conversely, to take another example, evidence from a district in Norfolk, Virginia, shows that resegregated schools led to a decline in the achievement test scores of children of all races.

One commentator, reviewing dozens of studies of the educational benefits of desegregated schooling, found that the studies have provided "remarkably consistent" results, showing that: (1) black students' educational achievement is improved in integrated schools as compared to racially isolated schools, (2) black students' educational achievement is improved in integrated classes, and (3) the earlier that black students are removed from racial isolation, the better their educational outcomes. Multiple studies also indicate that black alumni of integrated schools are more likely to move into occupations traditionally closed to African-Americans, and to earn more money in those fields.

Third, there is a democratic element: an interest in producing an educational environment that reflects the "pluralistic society" in which our children will live. It is an interest in helping our children learn to work and play together with children of different racial backgrounds. It is an interest in teaching children to engage in the kind of cooperation among Americans of all races that is necessary to make a land of three hundred million people one Nation.

Again, data support this insight. There are again studies that offer contrary conclusions. Again, however, the evidence supporting a democratic interest in racially integrated schools is firmly established and sufficiently strong to permit a school board to determine, as this Court has itself often found, that this interest is compelling.

For example, one study documented that "black and white students in desegregated schools are less racially prejudiced than those in segregated schools," and that "interracial contact in desegregated schools leads to an increase in interracial sociability and friendship." Other studies have found that both black and white students who attend integrated schools are more likely to work in desegregated companies after graduation than students who attended racially isolated schools. Further research has shown that the desegregation of schools can help bring adult communities together by reducing segregated housing. Cities that have implemented successful school desegregation plans have witnessed increased interracial contact and neighborhoods that tend to become less racially segregated. These effects not only reinforce the prior gains of integrated primary and secondary education; they also foresee a time when there is less need to use race-conscious criteria.

. . . In light of this Court's conclusions in *Grutter,* the "compelling" nature of these interests in the context of primary and secondary public education follows here *a fortiori.* . . . Hence, I am not surprised that Justice Kennedy finds that, "a district may consider it a compelling interest to achieve a diverse student population," including a *racially* diverse population.

The compelling interest at issue here, then, includes an effort to eradicate the remnants, not of general "societal discrimination," but of primary and secondary school segregation; it includes an effort to create school environments that provide better educational opportunities for all children; it includes an effort to help create citizens better prepared to know, to understand, and to work with people of all races and backgrounds, thereby furthering the kind of democratic government our Constitution foresees. If an educational interest that combines these three elements is not "compelling," what is?

[H]ow do the educational and civic interests differ in kind from those that underlie and justify the racial "diversity" that the law school sought in *Grutter,* where this Court found a compelling interest? The plurality tries to draw a distinction by reference to the well-established conceptual difference between *de jure* segregation ("segregation by state action") and *de facto* segregation ("racial imbalance caused by other factors"). But that distinction concerns what the Constitution *requires* school boards to do, not what it *permits* them to do.

The opinions cited by the plurality to justify its reliance upon the *de jure/de facto* distinction only address what remedial measures a school district may be constitutionally *required* to undertake. As to what is *permitted,* nothing in our equal protection law suggests that a State may right only those wrongs that it committed. No case of this Court has ever relied upon the *de jure/de facto* distinction in order to limit what a school district is voluntarily allowed to do. . . .

Nor does any precedent indicate, as the plurality suggests with respect to Louisville, that remedial interests vanish the day after a federal court declares that a district is "unitary." Of course, Louisville adopted those portions of the plan at issue here *before* a court declared Louisville "unitary." Moreover, in *Freeman*, this Court pointed out that in "one sense of the term, vestiges of past segregation by state decree do remain in our society and in our schools. Past wrongs to the black race, wrongs committed by the State and in its name, are a stubborn fact of history. And stubborn facts of history linger and persist." I do not understand why this Court's cases, which rest the significance of a "unitary" finding in part upon the wisdom and desirability of returning schools to local control, should deprive those local officials of legal *permission* to use means they once found necessary to combat persisting injustices.

For his part, Justice Thomas faults my citation of various studies supporting the view that school districts can find compelling educational and civic interests in integrating their public schools. He is entitled of course to his own opinion as to which studies he finds convincing . . . [But] [i]f we are to insist upon unanimity in the social science literature before finding a compelling interest, we might never find one. I believe only that the Constitution allows democratically elected school boards to make up their own minds as to how best to include people of all races in one America.

. . .

I next ask whether the plans before us are "narrowly tailored" to achieve these "compelling" objectives. . . . Several factors, taken together, . . . lead me to conclude that the boards' use of race-conscious criteria in these plans passes even the strictest "tailoring" test.

First, the race-conscious criteria at issue only help set the outer bounds of *broad* ranges. They constitute but one part of plans that depend primarily upon other, nonracial elements. To use race in this way is not to set a forbidden "quota."

In fact, the defining feature of both plans is greater emphasis upon student choice. In Seattle, for example, in more than 80% of all cases, that choice alone determines which high schools Seattle's ninth graders will attend. After ninth grade, students can decide voluntarily to transfer to a preferred district high school (without any consideration of race-conscious criteria). *Choice*, therefore, is the "predominant factor" in these plans. *Race* is not.

Indeed, the race-conscious ranges at issue in these cases often have no effect, either because the particular school is not oversubscribed in the year in question, or because the racial makeup of the school falls within the broad range, or because the student is a transfer applicant or has a sibling at the school. In these respects, the broad ranges are less like a quota and more like the kinds of "useful starting points" that this Court has consistently found permissible, even when they set boundaries upon voluntary transfers, and even when they are based upon a community's general population.

Second, broad-range limits on voluntary school choice plans are less burdensome, and hence more narrowly tailored, than other race-conscious restrictions this Court has previously approved. See, e.g., *Swann*. Indeed, the plans before us are *more narrowly tailored* than the race-conscious admission plans that this Court approved in *Grutter*. Here, race becomes a factor only in a fraction of students' non-merit-based assignments—not in large numbers of students' merit-based applications. Moreover, the effect of applying race conscious criteria here affects potentially disadvantaged students *less severely,* not more severely, than the criteria at issue in *Grutter.* Disappointed students are not rejected from a State's flagship graduate program; they simply attend a different one of the district's many public schools, which in aspiration and in fact are substantially equal. And, in Seattle, the disadvantaged student loses at most one year at the high school of his choice. . . .

Third, the manner in which the school boards developed these plans itself reflects "narrow tailoring." Each plan was devised to overcome a history of segregated public schools. Each plan embodies the results of local experience and community consultation. Each plan is the product of a process that has sought to enhance student choice, while diminishing the need for mandatory busing. And each plan's use of race-conscious elements is *diminished* compared to the use of race in preceding integration plans.

The school boards' widespread consultation, their experimentation with numerous other plans, indeed, the 40-year history [of their attempts at deseg-regation], make clear that plans that are less explicitly race-based are unlikely to achieve the board's "compelling" objectives. The history of each school system reveals highly segregated schools, followed by remedial plans that involved forced busing, followed by efforts to attract or retain students through the use of plans that abandoned busing and replaced it with greater student choice. Both cities once tried to achieve more integrated schools by relying solely upon measures such as redrawn district boundaries, new school building construction, and unrestricted voluntary transfers. In neither city did these prior attempts prove sufficient to achieve the city's integration goals.

Moreover, giving some degree of weight to a local school board's knowl-edge, expertise, and concerns in these particular matters is not inconsistent with rigorous judicial scrutiny. It simply recognizes that judges are not well suited to act as school administrators. Indeed, in the context of school desegregation, this Court has repeatedly stressed the importance of acknowledging that local school boards better understand their own communities and have a better knowledge of what in practice will best meet the educational needs of their pupils. . . .

Having looked at dozens of *amicus* briefs, public reports, news stories, and the records in many of this Court's prior cases, which together span 50 years of desegregation history in school districts across the Nation, I have discovered many examples of districts that sought integration through explicitly race conscious methods, including mandatory busing. Yet, I have found *no* example or model that would permit this Court to say to Seattle and to Louisville: "Here is an instance of a desegregation plan that is likely to achieve your objectives and also makes less use of race-conscious criteria than your plans." And, if the plurality cannot suggest such a model—and it cannot—then it seeks to impose a "narrow tailoring" requirement that in practice would never be met.

[T]he plurality also points to the school districts' use of numerical goals based upon the racial breakdown of the general school population, and it faults the districts for failing to prove that *no other set of numbers will work.* The plurality refers to no case in support of its demand. Nor is it likely to find such a case. After all, this Court has in many cases explicitly permitted districts to use target ratios based upon the district's underlying population. See, e.g., *Swann*; *North Carolina Bd. of Ed; Montgomery County Bd. of Ed..* The reason is obvious: In Seattle, where the overall student population is 41% white, permitting 85% white enrollment at a single school would make it much more likely that other schools would have very few white students, whereas in Jefferson County, with a 60% white enrollment, one school with 85% white students would be less likely to skew enrollments elsewhere.

Moreover, there is research-based evidence supporting, for example, that a ratio no greater than 50% minority—which is Louisville's starting point, and as close as feasible to Seattle's starting point—is helpful in limiting the risk of "white flight." . . . What other numbers are the boards to use as a "starting point"?

[N]or could the school districts have accomplished their desired aims (e.g., avoiding forced busing, countering white flight, maintaining racial diversity) by other means. Nothing in the extensive history of desegregation efforts over the past 50 years gives the districts, or this Court, any reason to believe that another method is possible to accomplish these goals.

[Justice Kennedy asks:] Why does Seattle's plan group Asian-Americans, Hispanic-Americans, Native-Americans, and African-Americans together, treating all as similar minorities? The majority suggests that Seattle's classification system could permit a school to be labeled "diverse" with a 50% Asian American and 50% white student body, and no African-American students, Hispanic students, or students of other ethnicity.

The 50/50 hypothetical has no support in the record here; it is conjured from the imagination. In fact, Seattle apparently began to treat these different minority groups alike in response to the federal Emergency School Aid Act's requirement that it do so. Moreover, maintaining this federally mandated system of classification makes sense insofar as Seattle's experience indicates that the relevant circumstances in respect to each of these different minority groups are roughly similar, e.g., in terms of residential patterns, and call for roughly similar responses. This is confirmed by the fact that Seattle has been able to achieve a desirable degree of diversity without the *greater* emphasis on race that drawing fine lines among minority groups would require. . . . [T]he plurality cannot object that the constitutional defect is the individualized use of race and simultaneously object that not enough account of individuals' race has been taken.

[T]he Court seeks to distinguish *Grutter* from these cases by claiming that *Grutter* arose in " 'the context of higher education.' " But . . . I do not believe the Constitution could possibly find "compelling" the provision of a racially diverse education for a 23-year-old law student but not for a 13-year-old high school pupil. [Nor is it relevant] that these school districts did not examine the merits of applications "individual[ly]." The context here does not involve admission by merit; a child's academic, artistic, and athletic "merits" are not at all relevant to the child's placement. These are not affirmative action plans, and hence "individualized scrutiny" is simply beside the point. . . .

IV.

. . .

No one claims that (the relevant portion of) Louisville's plan was unlawful in 1996 when Louisville adopted it. To the contrary, there is every reason to believe that it represented part of an effort to implement the 1978 desegregation order. But if the plan was lawful when it was first adopted and if it was lawful the day before the District Court dissolved its order, how can the plurality now suggest that it became *unlawful* the following day? Is it conceivable that the Constitution, implemented through a court desegregation order, could permit (perhaps *require*) the district to make use of a race-conscious plan the day before the order was dissolved and then *forbid* the district to use the identical plan the day after? The Equal Protection Clause is not incoherent. And federal courts would rightly hesitate to find unitary status if the consequences of the ruling were so dramatically disruptive.

[T]he original Seattle Plan [was] a *more heavily race-conscious predecessor* of the very plan now before us. In *Seattle School Dist. No. 1*, this Court struck down a state referendum that effectively barred implementation of Seattle's desegregation plan and "burden[ed] all future attempts to integrate Washington schools in districts throughout the State." Because the referendum would have prohibited the adoption of a school-integration plan that involved mandatory busing, and because it would have imposed a special burden on school integration plans (plans that sought to integrate previously segregated schools), the Court found it unconstitutional. . . . It is difficult to believe that the Court that held unconstitutional a referendum that would have interfered with the implementation of this plan thought that the integration plan it sought to preserve was itself an *unconstitutional* plan. And if *Seattle School Dist. No. 1* is premised upon the constitutionality of the original Seattle Plan, it is equally premised upon the constitutionality of the present plan, for the present plan *is* the Seattle Plan, modified only insofar as it places even *less* emphasis on race-conscious elements than its predecessors.

It is even more difficult to accept the plurality's contrary view, namely that the underlying plan was unconstitutional. If that is so, then *all* of Seattle's earlier (even more race-conscious) plans must also have been unconstitutional. That necessary implication of the plurality's position strikes the 13th chime of the clock. How could the plurality adopt a constitutional standard that would hold unconstitutional large numbers of race-conscious integration plans adopted by numerous school boards over the past 50 years while remaining true to this Court's desegregation precedent?

V.

[C]onsider the effect of the plurality's views on the parties before us and on similar school districts throughout the Nation. Will Louisville and all similar school districts have to return to systems like Louisville's initial 1956 plan, which did not consider race at all? That initial 1956 plan proved ineffective. . . . The districts' past and current plans are not unique. They resemble other plans, promulgated by hundreds of local school boards, which have attempted a variety of desegregation methods that have evolved over time in light of experience. . . . A majority of these desegregation techniques explicitly considered a student's race. Transfer plans, for example, allowed students to shift from a school in which they were in the racial majority to a school in which they would be in a racial minority. Some districts, such as Richmond, California, and Buffalo, New York, permitted only "one-way" transfers, in which only black students attending predominantly black schools were permitted to transfer to designated receiver schools.

[A]t a minimum, the plurality's views would threaten a surge of race-based litigation. Hundreds of state and federal statutes and regulations use racial classifications for educational or other purposes. In many such instances, the contentious force of legal challenges to these classifications, meritorious or not, would displace earlier calm.

[D]e facto resegregation is on the rise. It is reasonable to conclude that such resegregation can create serious educational, social, and civic problems. Given the conditions in which school boards work to set policy, they may need all of the means presently at their disposal to combat those problems. Yet the plurality would deprive them of at least one tool that some districts now consider vital— the limited use of broad race-conscious student population ranges.

I use the words "may need" here deliberately. The plurality, or at least those who follow Justice Thomas' " 'color-blind' " approach, may feel confident that, to end invidious discrimination, one must end *all* governmental use of race conscious criteria including those with inclusive objectives. By way of contrast, I do not claim to know how best to stop harmful discrimination; how best to create a society that includes all Americans; how best to overcome our serious problems of increasing *de facto* segregation, troubled inner city schooling, and poverty correlated with race. But, as a judge, I do know that the Constitution does not authorize judges to dictate solutions to these problems. Rather, the Constitution creates a democratic political system through which the people themselves must together find answers. And it is for them to debate how best to educate the Nation's children and how best to administer America's schools to achieve that aim. The Court should leave them to their work. And it is for them to decide, to quote the plurality's slogan, whether the best "way to stop discrimination on the basis of race is to stop discriminating on the basis of race." That is why the Equal Protection Clause outlaws invidious discrimination, but does not similarly forbid all use of race-conscious criteria. . . .

VI.

[T]he plurality cites in support those who argued in *Brown* against segregation, and Justice Thomas likens the approach that I have taken to that of segregation's defenders. But segregation policies did not simply tell schoolchildren "where they could and could not go to school based on the color of their skin"; they perpetuated a caste system rooted in the institutions of slavery and 80 years of legalized subordination. The lesson of history is not that efforts to continue racial segregation are constitutionally indistinguishable from efforts to achieve racial integration. Indeed, it is a cruel distortion of history to compare Topeka, Kansas, in the 1950's to Louisville and Seattle in the modern day—to equate the plight of Linda Brown (who was ordered to attend a Jim Crow school) to the circumstances of Joshua McDonald (whose request to transfer to a school closer to home was initially declined). This is not to deny that there is a cost in applying "a state-mandated racial label." But that cost does not approach, in degree or in kind, the terrible harms of slavery, the resulting caste system, and 80 years of legal racial segregation.

[N]ot everyone welcomed this Court's decision in *Brown*. Three years after that decision was handed down, the Governor of Arkansas ordered state militia to block the doors of a white schoolhouse so that black children could not enter. The President of the United States dispatched the 101st Airborne Division to Little Rock, Arkansas, and federal troops were needed to enforce a desegregation decree. See Cooper v. Aaron, 358 U.S. 1 (1958). Today, almost 50 years later, attitudes toward race in this Nation have changed dramatically. Many parents, white and black alike, want their children to attend schools with children of different races. Indeed, the very school districts that once spurned integration now strive for it. The long history of their efforts reveals the complexities and difficulties they have faced. And in light of those challenges, they have asked us not to take from their hands the instruments they have used to rid their schools of racial segregation, instruments that they believe are needed to overcome the problems of cities divided by race and poverty. The plurality would decline their modest request.

The plurality is wrong to do so. The last half-century has witnessed great strides toward racial equality, but we have not yet realized the promise of *Brown*. To invalidate the plans under review is to threaten the promise of *Brown*. The plurality's position, I fear, would break that promise. This is a decision that the Court and the Nation will come to regret.

Discussion

1. *Fighting over the legacy of* Brown. All the Justices claim to be faithful to the memory and the principles of *Brown v. Board of Education*. But they have very different ideas of what *Brown* meant. The plurality argues that *Brown* stood for color blindness in student assignment policies and strict scrutiny for racial classifications by the state. The dissent argues that *Brown* stood for the principles of racial integration and antisubordination.

Justice Thomas tries to show that the arguments of the dissenters are the same as those of the defenders of segregation and massive resistance. On the other hand, Justice Thomas's own arguments have much in common with segregationist critics of *Brown*. Thomas is deeply skeptical of elite and social science arguments that integration is good for children—or that racial isolation is bad. He finds little advantage to racial mixing, assumes that different races will self segregate socially, and suggests that predominantly black schools may be better for blacks.

During the 1960s and 1970s proponents of racial integration often looked to federal courts to enforce *Brown* against recalcitrant state school boards; their opponents sought to promote states' rights, localism, and deference to the expertise of local school boards. In *Parents Involved*, the plurality wants federal courts to carefully supervise school districts so that they do not violate the Equal Protection Clause in their quest for racial integration, which the plurality refers to as "racial balancing." Conversely, the dissent, which supports the school boards' attempts at integration, wants to defer to their expertise and knowledge of local conditions. During the 1960s and 1970s, opponents of student assignment policies accused federal courts of judicial activism, elitism, and "social engineering" when they second-guessed local school boards in the name of the Constitution. In *Parents Involved*, Justice Thomas accuses the Seattle and Louisville school boards of elitism and social engineering in pursuing racial integration and insists that federal courts must stop them in the name of the Constitution.

2. De jure *and* de facto. Behind the wrangling over the meaning of *Swann* and over the *de facto/de jure* distinction is the political context of early attempts at desegregation. After *Brown*, federal courts faced the task of desegregating the nation's schools, and often encountered a hostile reception from local school boards. Federal courts could not enjoin every school board in the country, and they could not long succeed against school boards determined to resist them. Any realistic attempt at integration required substantial compliance and cooperation by local school boards. As a result, courts encouraged voluntary plans for integration, as *Swann* itself suggests. This meant that the *de jure/de facto* distinction became relevant only if a school district actually went to court and contested its duty to integrate.

The political context of the 1960s and 1970s meant that courts would look favorably on school boards that chose to integrate without a court order as well as school boards that worked with courts to produce integration plans and maintained them over time without court supervision. Similarly, courts might want to declare districts unitary and turn over the task of desegregation to school districts that they believed had acted in good faith and were willing to take the political heat for integration. Thus, declaring a district unitary did not necessarily mean that desegregation plans were no longer needed; rather it assumed that they would continue under the supervision and adjustment of the local school board as opposed to a federal court. Moreover, in the 1990s, in cases like Board of Education of Oklahoma City v. Dowell and Freeman v. Pitts, (see casebook at pp. 943-944), a more conservative Supreme Court strongly signaled to the lower courts that they should end federal court supervision and declare districts unitary as soon as possible. In Freeman v. Pitts, the Court held that federal courts could declare districts unitary even before full compliance had occurred, as long as school districts had made "a good faith commitment to the entirety of a desegregation plan."

The plurality opinion does not focus on this history. It regards school districts that voluntarily desegregated without court order as never having any constitutional obligation to desegregate. And it regards school districts that federal courts declared unitary as being legally pristine—in the same position as districts that were never segregated. As a result, it treats race-conscious plans by districts in Seattle and Louisville not as attempts to continue and adjust remedial plans but as illegal attempts at racial balancing.

3. *Desegregation, not integration.* Following *Brown*, critics who wanted to limit the force of the opinion argued that it required only desegregation, not integration. Section III-B of the plurality opinion (which Justice Kennedy does not join) suggests that "racial balancing" is not a compelling interest. Is racial integration a legitimate interest for the plurality? How does the plurality explain the difference between racial balancing and racial integration? One theory would be that a school is racially integrated if it has been declared unitary, as in the case of Louisville, or, as in the case of Seattle, has never been found to engage in unlawful segregation. If so, would this mean that any attempts to change the racial demographics of schools that are not required by court order are illegitimate racial balancing?

4. *Justice Kennedy's Concurrence.* Because his vote is necessary to make a majority, Justice Kennedy's limiting concurrence will no doubt be the focus of much future litigation. Like Justice Powell's *Bakke* opinion, it may determine what *Parents Involved* actually means in practice.

Two points about Kennedy's approach are worth noting at the outset. First, contrary to the plurality, Justice Kennedy argues that increasing diversity and avoiding racial isolation can be compelling state interests. Second, Kennedy argues that school districts may take race-conscious measures to combat *de facto* resegregation and bring students of different backgrounds together.

Kennedy primarily objects to student assignment policies that use the race of an individual student as the controlling factor in determining where that individual student goes to school. Thus, Kennedy distinguishes between two kinds of race-conscious policies. The first considers the race of an individual student in deciding where the student goes to school. Any such policy, Kennedy argues, is subject to strict scrutiny.

To survive strict scrutiny, the school district must show that other policies that do not assign individual students to schools based on their race will not be as effective. Kennedy believes that the minimal effects of race-based assignment policies in this case show that they were unnecessary and therefore not narrowly tailored. Does this mean that if race-based assignment policies produced far more significant effects than the alternatives that they would be narrowly tailored? Kennedy also objects to the use of a binary white/nonwhite divide in racial assignment policies. Does this mean that if school districts used more racial categories their plans would be narrowly tailored?

Kennedy also suggests that student assignment policies that use the race of individual students to determine where the student will be placed must involve, at a minimum, multifactor individualized considerations roughly akin to the sort approved in *Grutter*. We might call this the *Grutter*-ization of school assignment policies.

Requiring multifactor individualized considerations of individual students would convert student assignment policies into something more like individual applications to colleges. Individualized considerations would be costly and thus far less likely to be employed by large school districts. Note that Kennedy also objected to the Louisville plan because the criteria it used were not sufficiently transparent. Ironically, *Grutter* is premised on the notion that decisions using multifactor individualized considerations will be less transparent and therefore less overtly based on race.

A second type of race-conscious policy does not assign individual students to schools on the basis of their race. Rather, it uses facially race-neutral criteria for race-conscious reasons. Examples would be decisions about where to place new schools, where to draw attendance zones, and student assignment criteria based on poverty and socioeconomic status. Kennedy suggests that "it is unlikely that any of [these policies] would demand strict scrutiny to be found permissible." Does that mean that narrow tailoring requirements would not apply? Would rational basis apply?

Note that Chief Justice Roberts's plurality opinion specifically avoids stating its views about the constitutionality of such race-conscious policies. However, if the avowed purpose of these policies is to assign percentages of students to different schools because of their race, why aren't these policies subject to strict scrutiny under Washington v. Davis? Kennedy's approach seems to view benign race-conscious *purpose* that uses race-neutral *means* as outside of strict scrutiny. Given the plurality's views about motive in Part IV, can the Justices in the plurality adopt the same approach?

Insert the following on p. 1035 after discussion note 4:

RICCI v. DESTEFANO, 129 S. Ct. 2658 (2009), 2009 WL 1835138: Title VII of the 1964 Civil Rights Act makes it unlawful for an employer "to discriminate against any individual with respect to his compensation, terms, conditions, or privileges of employment, because of such individual's race, color, religion, sex, or national origin." 42 U.S.C. §2000e-2(a)(1). It prohibits both disparate treatment discrimination and disparate impact discrimination.

Disparate treatment discrimination occurs when an employer has treated a particular person less favorably than others because of a protected trait. A disparate-treatment plaintiff must establish that the defendant had a discriminatory intent or motive for taking a job-related action. Disparate impact discrimination occurs when an employer uses a particular employment practice that causes a disparate impact on the basis of race, color, religion, sex, or national origin. 42 U.S.C. §2000e-2(k)(1)(A)(i). The employer may defend by demonstrating that the practice is job related for the position in question and consistent with business necessity. If the employer meets that burden, a plaintiff may still succeed by showing that the employer refuses to adopt an available alternative employment practice that has less disparate impact and serves the employer's legitimate needs. §§2000e-2(k)(1)(A)(ii) and (C).

The City of New Haven, Connecticut used a combination of written and oral tests to identify firefighters for promotion to vacant lieutenant and captain positions. Under these tests, white candidates significantly outperformed minority candidates. Under the rules for filling vacancies, only white candidates would be immediately promoted to lieutenant; of the nine candidates who would be immediately promoted to captain, seven where white and two were Hispanic. No African-American candidates would be immediately promoted to either position. A rancorous public debate ensued, with different groups arguing about whether the tests were fair or biased. Those claiming bias argued that the tests had a discriminatory impact on racial minorities and threatened a disparate impact lawsuit if the City made promotions based on the tests. Those claiming the tests were fair and neutral threatened a disparate treatment lawsuit if the City, relying on the statistical racial disparity, ignored the test results and denied promotions to the candidates who had performed well.

The City ultimately threw out the examination results. Seventeen white firefighters and one Hispanic firefighter who passed the exams sued the City on a disparate treatment theory, arguing that throwing out the test results treated them less favorably than other employees because of race. They also alleged a violation of the Equal Protection Clause. The City argued in defense that if it had certified the test results, it could have faced Title VII liability for adopting a practice that had a disparate impact on minority firefighters. The District Court granted summary judgment for the defendants, and the Second Circuit affirmed.

The Supreme Court reversed, in an opinion by Justice Kennedy. "The City's actions would violate the disparate-treatment prohibition of Title VII absent some valid defense. All the evidence demonstrates that the City chose not to certify the examination results because of the statistical disparity based on race—i.e., how minority candidates had performed when compared to white candidates. . . . Whatever the City's ultimate aim—however well intentioned or benevolent it might have seemed—the City made its employment decision because of race. The City rejected the test results solely because the higher scoring candidates were white."

The Court then considered when "the purpose to avoid disparate-impact liability excuses what otherwise would be prohibited disparate-treatment discrimination." The Court rejected the petitioner's argument "that an employer in fact must be in violation of the disparate-impact provision before it can use compliance as a defense in a disparate-treatment suit." Justice Kennedy argued that Congress intended to encourage voluntary compliance with desegregation of workplaces. "Forbidding employers to act unless they know, with certainty, that a practice violates the disparate-impact provision would bring compliance efforts to a near standstill. Even in the limited situations when this restricted standard could be met, employers likely would hesitate before taking voluntary action for fear of later being proven wrong in the course of litigation and then held to account for disparate treatment." Justice Kennedy also rejected the respondents' argument "that an employer's good-faith belief that its actions are necessary to comply with Title VII's disparate-impact provision should be enough" to avoid liability for disparate treatment. Such a test "would encourage race-based action at the slightest hint of disparate impact" and "would amount to a de facto quota system, in which a focus on statistics . . . could put undue pressure on employers to adopt inappropriate prophylactic measures. Even worse, an employer could discard test results (or other employment practices) with the intent of obtaining the employer's preferred racial balance."

Borrowing from the Court's affirmative action cases construing the Equal Protection Clause, Justice Kennedy argued that in Title VII cases, before an employer can engage in intentional discrimination to avoid or remedy an unintentional disparate impact, the employer must "demonstrate a strong basis in evidence that, had it not taken the action, it would have been liable under the disparate-impact statute." The Court held that the City of New Haven could not meet that standard, and therefore violated Title VII. It therefore did not reach the question whether New Haven's actions also violated the Equal Protection Clause, or "whether a legitimate fear of disparate impact is ever sufficient to justify discriminatory treatment under the Constitution."

Justice Ginsberg, joined by Justices Stevens, Souter, and Breyer, dissented. She disagreed with the majority's assumption that "[w]hen an employer changes an employment practice in an effort to comply with Title VII's disparate-impact provision . . . it acts 'because of race.'" Justice Ginsburg argued that "Title VII's disparate-treatment and disparate-impact proscriptions must be read as complementary" rather than in conflict, as the majority did, because Title VII's purpose is to encourage voluntary compliance to desegregate workplaces. "[E]mployers who reject . . . criteria [that operate to the disadvantage of minorities] due to reasonable doubts about their reliability can hardly be held to have engaged in discrimination 'because of' race. . . . I would therefore hold that an employer who jettisons a selection device when its disproportionate racial impact becomes apparent does not violate Title VII's disparate-treatment bar automatically or at all, subject to this key condition: The employer must have good cause to believe the device would not withstand examination for business necessity."

Justice Ginsburg pointed to New Haven's choice of a 60/40 ratio for written and oral parts of the examination as particularly vulnerable to criticism. The weighting toward written questions was not necessary to effective job performance, because "the oral component, more so than the written component, addressed the sort of 'real-life scenarios' fire officers encounter on the job." In addition, many municipalities prefer assessment tests that simulate actual work conditions.

Even so, the majority's new "strong basis in evidence" standard, she argued, would make efforts at voluntary compliance more difficult, would encourage "costly disparate treatment litigation," and was tantamount to a demand that the employer establish that it has violated the law.

Justice Alito, concurring, agreed with the majority's "strong basis in evidence" test and also agreed that New Haven could not meet that standard. He argued that no matter which test was used, summary judgment for the city was inappropriate if "professed concern about disparate-impact litigation was simply a pretext" for intentional racial discrimination. Justice Alito argued that there was evidence that "the City's real reason was illegitimate, namely, the desire to placate a politically important racial constituency," in this case African-Americans, who were essential to the mayor's political viability.

Justice Ginsburg responded: "The real issue . . . is not whether the mayor and his staff were politically motivated; it is whether their attempt to score political points was legitimate (i.e., nondiscriminatory). Were they seeking to exclude white firefighters from promotion (unlikely, as a fair test would undoubtedly result in the addition of white firefighters to the officer ranks), or did they realize, at least belatedly, that their tests could be toppled in a disparate-impact suit? In the latter case, there is no disparate-treatment violation. Justice Alito, I recognize, would disagree."

Justice Scalia, concurring, argued that the case raised the larger issue of whether disparate impact liability was constitutional in the first place. The present case asked "[w]hether . . . Title VII's disparate-treatment provisions forbid 'remedial' race-based actions when a disparate-impact violation would *not* otherwise result." But the real problem, Justice Scalia explained, is that Title VII "not only permits but affirmatively *requires* [race based] actions when a disparate-impact violation *would* otherwise result."

"But if the Federal Government is prohibited from discriminating on the basis of race, then surely it is also prohibited from enacting laws mandating that third parties—e.g., employers, whether private, State, or municipal-discriminate on the basis of race. As the facts of these cases illustrate, Title VII's disparate-impact provisions place a racial thumb on the scales, often requiring employers to evaluate the racial outcomes of their policies, and to make decisions based on (because of) those racial outcomes. That type of racial decisionmaking is, as the Court explains, discriminatory. See Personnel Administrator of Mass. v. Feeney, 442 U.S. 256 (1979)."

"To be sure, the disparate-impact laws do not mandate imposition of quotas, but it is not clear why that should provide a safe harbor. Would a private employer not be guilty of unlawful discrimination if he refrained from establishing a racial hiring quota but intentionally designed his hiring practices to achieve the same end? Surely he would. Intentional discrimination is still occurring, just one step up the chain. Government compulsion of such design would therefore seemingly violate equal protection principles. Nor would it matter that Title VII requires consideration of race on a wholesale, rather than retail, level. . . . And of course the purportedly benign motive for the disparate-impact provisions cannot save the statute. See Adarand Constructors, Inc. v. Pena, 515 U.S. 200 (1995)."

"It might be possible to defend the law by framing it as simply an evidentiary tool used to identify genuine, intentional discrimination—to "smoke out," as it were, disparate treatment. . . . But arguably the disparate-impact provisions sweep too broadly to be fairly characterized in such a fashion—since they fail to provide an affirmative defense for good-faith (i.e., nonracially motivated) conduct, or perhaps even for good faith plus hiring standards that are entirely reasonable. . . . It is one thing to free plaintiffs from proving an employer's illicit intent, but quite another to preclude the employer from proving that its motives were pure and its actions reasonable."

"The Court's resolution of these cases makes it unnecessary to resolve these matters today. But the war between disparate impact and equal protection will be waged sooner or later, and it behooves us to begin thinking about how—and on what terms—to make peace between them."

Discussion

Although *Ricci* is specifically decided on non-constitutional grounds, the Justices clearly have constitutional issues in mind. These concern what is a racial classification and what is an improper discriminatory purpose.

1. *When is a decision "because of" or "based on" race?*: Allied to the debate over intention is the question of what we mean by a decision "based on" race. The majority in *Ricci* assumes that New Haven's decision to change the employment test was "based on" race because the City was concerned that using the test might result in its hiring no African-American officers. At other points in its opinion, however, the majority suggests that the City violated the law, not because it was concerned with the potential exclusionary impact of the test, but because it publicly adopted the test and then publicly invalidated the test for race-related reasons, changing course in ways that invited reliance and stimulated racial resentments.

If government decisionmakers recognize that one of several possible methods of meeting the government needs will have a foreseeable adverse impact on minorities and, consequently, decide to meet the government's needs in some other way, is that change of course an unlawful decision "because of" race? Consider Justice Kennedy's concurring opinion in *Parents Involved*:

> School boards may pursue the goal of bringing together students of diverse backgrounds and races through other means, including strategic site selection of new schools; drawing attendance zones with general recognition of the demographics of neighborhoods; allocating resources for special programs; recruiting students and faculty in a targeted fashion; and tracking enrollments, performance, and

other statistics by race. These mechanisms are race conscious but do not lead to different treatment based on a classification that tells each student he or she is to be defined by race, so it is unlikely any of them would demand strict scrutiny to be found permissible. See Bush v. Vera, 517 U.S. 952, 958 (1996) (plurality opinion) ("Strict scrutiny does not apply merely because redistricting is performed with consciousness of race. . . . Electoral district lines are 'facially race neutral' so a more searching inquiry is necessary before strict scrutiny can be found applicable in redistricting cases than in cases of 'classifications based explicitly on race'" (quoting *Adarand*)). Executive and legislative branches, which for generations now have considered these types of policies and procedures, should be permitted to employ them with candor and with confidence that a constitutional violation does not occur whenever a decisionmaker considers the impact a given approach might have on students of different races. Assigning to each student a personal designation according to a crude system of individual racial classifications is quite a different matter; and the legal analysis changes accordingly.

Parents Involved, 127 S. Ct. at 2792 (Kennedy, J., concurring).

Is the choice or invalidation of the employment test in *Ricci* more like the strategic site selection of a new school—or instead more like the consideration of the race of individual applicants for school admission that the Court rejected in *Parents Involved*? If the City may consider how changing the site of a school will affect its likely racial composition, why may it not consider how changing an employment test will affect the likely racial composition of the pool from which it may select officers for its fire department? (Suppose, for example, that the City learns from various experts that a test that emphasizes oral presentations and assessments of on-the-job-skills will likely result in improved achievement by minority applicants.) May it consider this information before selecting an employment test? If it may, why not after? Is the problem then that the City should have thought of this before it administered the test, and now it looks bad for it to change the rules after the test has been given? Put another way, is the motive or mental state of the decisionmaker crucial, or is the crucial factor the perceptions—and likely resentment—of the public? Is there any principled basis on which appearance could or should matter in deciding whether a policy decision is impermissibly race-based?

2. *What is discriminatory purpose?*: In the 1970s and 1980s, in cases such as *Washington v. Davis*, the Court developed doctrines that allowed government policies with a disparate racial impact on racial minorities—even if entirely known or foreseeable—unless plaintiffs could show intentional discrimination. To prove intentional discrimination, plaintiffs would have to show government animus toward the group suffering disparate impact. As the Court put it in *Personnel Administrator v. Feeney*, "the decisionmaker [must have] selected or reaffirmed a particular course of action at least in part 'because of,' not merely 'in spite of,' its adverse effects upon an identifiable group."

In *Ricci*, however, and in disparate impact situations more generally, an employer's decision to take steps to prevent disparate impact on minorities primarily burdens whites. Justice Scalia assumes that deliberately choosing employment practices to prevent disparate impact on minorities would violate *Feeney*. Is this correct? Why isn't the employer's decision "in spite of" the effects on whites? Perhaps more to the point, since the state action in this case is the federal government's, why isn't the federal government's purpose the integration of workforces rather than a desire to harm members of the white majority?

Suppose one applied Scalia's interpretation of *Washington v. Davis* and *Feeney* to previous constitutional challenges of legislation that had disparate impacts on African-Americans Latinos and women. Would the cases come out differently?

Perhaps Scalia's argument is that disparate impact is constitutionally troublesome because it requires employers to consider the racial effects of their actions. If so, why wouldn't this concern make unconstitutional any federal policies that encourage voluntary compliance with workplace integration? Note that Scalia's argument in *Ricci* recapitulates in the employment context the debate between the Justices in *Parents Involved* about whether voluntary attempts to integrate schools are a forbidden form of racial balancing.

Note also the issue of symmetry between deliberate integration and segregation implicit in Scalia's argument: Scalia assumes that federal attempts to get employers to integrate workforces (through threats of disparate impact liability) are just as constitutionally objectionable as federal efforts to encourage the maintenance of segregated workforces because both "requir[e] employers to evaluate the racial outcomes of their policies, and to make decisions based on (because of) those racial outcomes." Should the Constitution treat these two purposes differently?

Justice Alito's concurrence focuses on the statutory question of forbidden purpose in Title VII. He assumes that scrapping the firefighter's test to please a powerful African-American constituency is an illegitimate form of racial discrimination. But if so, does this mean that making political decisions with predictable disparate impacts on minorities in order to please white voters also makes a decision illegitimate?

Suppose that a state decides to offer admission to any person who graduates in the top ten percent of their high school class to the state university, regardless of their test scores or cumulative grade point average, with the purpose of increasing minority enrollments. Suppose also that the state adopts this policy in order to please minority voters while simultaneously avoiding political opposition by white parents who are opposed to race-based affirmative action. Assuming that the state has limited slots available, the foreseeable effect is that fewer whites will be admitted to the university. Is this a racially motivated decision under *Feeney*?

Chapter 8

Implied Fundamental Rights: The Constitution, the Family, and the Body

Insert the following after discussion note 5 on p. 1465:

GONZALES v. CARHART [CARHART II]
550 U.S. 124 (2007)

[Following the decision in *Stenberg v. Carhart*, Congress passed the Partial-Birth Abortion Act of 2003. The act bans a method of performing abortions, called "intact dilation and extraction" (intact D & E) or "dilation and extraction" (D & X), usually performed in the second and third trimesters of pregnancy. In the usual second-trimester procedure, "dilation and evacuation" (D & E), the doctor dilates the cervix and then inserts surgical instruments into the uterus and maneuvers them to grab the fetus and pull it back through the cervix and vagina. The fetus is usually ripped apart as it is removed, and the doctor may take 10 to 15 passes to remove it in its entirety. The federal act bans a variation of the standard D & E, intact D & E. To perform an intact D & E abortion, a doctor extracts the fetus intact or largely intact with only a few passes, pulling out its entire body instead of ripping it apart. In order to allow the head to pass through the cervix, the doctor typically pierces or crushes the skull.

The federal Partial Birth Abortion Act defines "partial-birth abortion," in §1531(b)(1), as a procedure in which the doctor: "(A) deliberately and intentionally vaginally delivers a living fetus until, in the case of a head-first presentation, the entire fetal head is outside the [mother's] body . . . , or, in the case of breech presentation, any part of the fetal trunk past the navel is outside the [mother's] body . . . , for the purpose of performing an overt act that the person knows will kill the partially delivered living fetus"; and "(B) performs the overt act, other than completion of delivery, that kills the fetus."

Congress found that, despite the district court's findings in *Stenberg* (accepted by the Supreme Court in that case), there was a moral, medical, and ethical consensus that partial-birth abortion is a gruesome and inhumane procedure that is never medically necessary and should be prohibited. The act contains an exception for situations where the mother's life is endangered: Section 1531(a) of the act prohibits "knowingly perform[ing] a partial-birth abortion . . . that is [not] necessary to save the life of a mother." It contains no exception for cases in which the mother's health would be endangered by using another method of abortion. Physicians challenged the act on the ground that it imposed an undue burden on a woman's right to choose a second-trimester abortion, that the crime defined by the statute was unduly vague, and that it contained no health exception.]

Justice KENNEDY delivered the opinion of the Court.

. . .

II.

The principles set forth in the joint opinion in Planned Parenthood of Southeastern Pa. v. Casey, did not find support from all those who join the instant opinion. Whatever one's views concerning the *Casey* joint opinion, it is evident a premise central to its conclusion—that the government has a legitimate and substantial interest in preserving and promoting fetal life—would be repudiated were the Court now to affirm the judgments of the Courts of Appeals. . . . [W]e must determine whether the Act furthers the legitimate interest of the Government in protecting the life of the fetus that may become a child.

We assume the following principles for the purposes of this opinion. Before viability, a State "may not prohibit any woman from making the ultimate decision to terminate her pregnancy." It also may not impose upon this right an undue burden, which exists if a regulation's "purpose or effect is to place a substantial obstacle in the path of a woman seeking an abortion before the fetus attains viability." On the other hand, "[r]egulations which do no more than create a structural mechanism by which the State, or the parent or guardian of a minor, may express profound respect for the life of the unborn are permitted, if they are not a substantial obstacle to the woman's exercise of the right to choose."

III.

A

The Act does not restrict an abortion procedure involving the delivery of an expired fetus. The Act, furthermore, is inapplicable to abortions that do not involve vaginal delivery (for instance, hysterotomy or hysterectomy). The Act does apply both previability and postviability because, by common understanding and scientific terminology, a fetus is a living organism while within the womb, whether or not it is viable outside the womb. . . .

Second, the Act's definition of partial-birth abortion requires the fetus to be delivered "until, in the case of a head-first presentation, the entire fetal head is outside the body of the mother, or, in the case of breech presentation, any part of the fetal trunk past the navel is outside the body of the mother." §1531(b)(1)(A). The Attorney General concedes, and we agree, that if an abortion procedure does not involve the delivery of a living fetus to one of these "anatomical 'landmarks' "—where, depending on the presentation, either the fetal head or the fetal trunk past the navel is outside the body of the mother—the prohibitions of the Act do not apply.

Third, to fall within the Act, a doctor must perform an "overt act, other than completion of delivery, that kills the partially delivered living fetus." §1531(b)(1)(B). For purposes of criminal liability, the overt act causing the fetus' death must be separate from delivery. And the overt act must occur after the delivery to an anatomical landmark. This is because the Act proscribes killing "the partially delivered" fetus, which, when read in context, refers to a fetus that has been delivered to an anatomical landmark.

Fourth, the Act contains scienter requirements concerning all the actions involved in the prohibited abortion. To begin with, the physician must have "deliberately and intentionally" delivered the fetus to one of the Act's anatomical landmarks. §1531(b)(1)(A). If a living fetus is delivered past the critical point by accident or inadvertence, the Act is inapplicable. In addition, the fetus must have been delivered "for the purpose of performing an overt act that the [doctor] knows will kill [it]." *Ibid.* If either intent is absent, no crime has occurred. This follows from the general principle that where scienter is required no crime is committed absent the requisite state of mind.

B

[The Partial Birth Abortion Act is not vague.] Unlike the statutory language in *Stenberg* that prohibited the delivery of a " 'substantial portion' " of the fetus . . . [d]octors performing D & E will know that if they do not deliver a living fetus to an anatomical landmark they will not face criminal liability. . . . [Moreover] [b]ecause a doctor performing a D & E will not face criminal liability if he or she delivers a fetus beyond the prohibited point by mistake, the Act cannot be described as "a trap for those who act in good faith." [Nor should] the Act . . . be invalidated on its face because it encourages arbitrary or discriminatory enforcement. Just as the Act's anatomical landmarks provide doctors with objective standards, they also "establish minimal guidelines to govern law enforcement." The scienter requirements narrow the scope of the Act's prohibition and limit prosecutorial discretion. . . .

C

We next determine whether the Act imposes an undue burden, as a facial matter, because its restrictions on second-trimester abortions are too broad. . . . The Act excludes most D & Es in which the fetus is removed in pieces, not intact. If the doctor intends to remove the fetus in parts from the outset, the doctor will not have the requisite intent to incur criminal liability. A doctor performing a standard D & E procedure can often "tak[e] about 10-15 'passes' through the uterus to remove the entire fetus." Removing the fetus in this manner does not violate the Act because the doctor will not have delivered the living fetus to one of the anatomical landmarks or committed an additional overt act that kills the fetus after partial delivery.

The [Nebraska] statute in *Stenberg* prohibited "'deliberately and intention-ally delivering into the vagina a living unborn child, or a substantial portion thereof, for the purpose of performing a procedure that the person performing such procedure knows will kill the unborn child and does kill the unborn child.'" The Court concluded that this statute encompassed D & E because "D & E will often involve a physician pulling a 'substantial portion' of a still living fetus, say, an arm or leg, into the vagina prior to the death of the fetus. The Court also rejected the limiting interpretation urged by Nebraska's Attorney General that the statute's reference to a "procedure" that "'kill[s] the unborn child'" was to a distinct procedure, not to the abortion procedure as a whole.

Congress, it is apparent, responded to these concerns because the Act departs in material ways from the statute in *Stenberg*. It adopts the phrase "delivers a living fetus," instead of "'delivering . . . a living unborn child, or a substantial portion thereof.'" . . . D & E does not involve the delivery of a fetus because it requires the removal of fetal parts that are ripped from the fetus as they are pulled through the cervix. . . . The Court in *Stenberg* interpreted "'substantial portion'" of the fetus to include an arm or a leg. The Act's anatomical land-marks, by contrast, clarify that the removal of a small portion of the fetus is not prohibited. The landmarks also require the fetus to be delivered so that it is partially "outside the body of the mother." To come within the ambit of the Nebraska statute, on the other hand, a substantial portion of the fetus only had to be delivered into the vagina; no part of the fetus had to be outside the body of the mother before a doctor could face criminal sanctions. . . .

The Act makes the distinction the Nebraska statute failed to draw (but the Nebraska Attorney General advanced) by differentiating between the overall partial-birth abortion and the distinct overt act that kills the fetus. The fatal overt act must occur after delivery to an anatomical landmark, and it must be something "other than [the] completion of delivery." §1531(b)(1)(B). This distinction matters because, unlike intact D & E, standard D & E does not involve a delivery followed by a fatal act. . . .

If a doctor's intent at the outset is to perform a D & E in which the fetus would not be delivered to either of the Act's anatomical landmarks, but the fetus nonetheless is delivered past one of those points, the requisite and prohibited scienter is not present. When a doctor in that situation completes an abortion by performing an intact D & E, the doctor does not violate the Act. It is true that intent to cause a result may sometimes be inferred if a person "knows that that result is practically certain to follow from his conduct." Yet abortion doctors intending at the outset to perform a standard D & E procedure will not know that a prohibited abortion "is practically certain to follow from" their conduct. A fetus is only delivered largely intact in a small fraction of the overall number of D & E abortions.

The evidence also supports a legislative determination that an intact delivery is almost always a conscious choice rather than a happenstance. Doctors, for example, may remove the fetus in a manner that will increase the chances of an intact delivery. And intact D & E is usually described as involving some manner of serial dilation. Doctors who do not seek to obtain this serial dilation perform an intact D & E on far fewer occasions. This evidence belies any claim that a standard D & E cannot be performed without intending or foreseeing an intact D & E.

Many doctors who testified on behalf of respondents, and who objected to the Act, do not perform an intact D & E by accident. On the contrary, they begin every D & E abortion with the objective of removing the fetus as intact as possible. This does not prove, as respondents suggest, that every D & E might violate the Act and that the Act therefore imposes an undue burden. It demonstrates only that those doctors who intend to perform a D & E that would involve delivery of a living fetus to one of the Act's anatomical landmarks must adjust their conduct to the law by not attempting to deliver the fetus to either of those points. Respondents have not shown that requiring doctors to intend dismemberment before delivery to an anatomical landmark will prohibit the vast majority of D & E abortions. The Act, then, cannot be held invalid on its face on these grounds.

IV.

. . . The Act does not on its face impose a substantial obstacle [to late-term, but previability, abortions.] . . . Congress stated [its purposes] as follows: "Implicitly approving such a brutal and inhumane procedure by choosing not to prohibit it will further coarsen society to the humanity of not only newborns, but all vulnerable and innocent human life, making it increasingly difficult to protect such life." The Act expresses respect for the dignity of human life.

Congress was concerned, furthermore, with the effects on the medical community and on its reputation caused by the practice of partial-birth abortion. The findings in the Act explain:

> "Partial-birth abortion . . . confuses the medical, legal, and ethical duties of physicians to preserve and promote life, as the physician acts directly against the physical life of a child, whom he or she had just delivered, all but the head, out of the womb, in order to end that life."

There can be no doubt the government "has an interest in protecting the integrity and ethics of the medical profession." Washington v. Glucksberg. Under our precedents it is clear the State has a significant role to play in regulating the medical profession.

Casey reaffirmed these governmental objectives. The government may use its voice and its regulatory authority to show its profound respect for the life within the woman. A central premise of the opinion was that the Court's precedents after *Roe* had "undervalue[d] the State's interest in potential life." The plurality opinion indicated "[t]he fact that a law which serves a valid purpose, one not designed to strike at the right itself, has the incidental effect of making it more difficult or more expensive to procure an abortion cannot be enough to invalidate it." This was not an idle assertion. . . . [*Casey*'s] third premise, that the State, from the inception of the pregnancy, maintains its own regulatory interest in protecting the life of the fetus that may become a child, cannot be set at naught by interpreting *Casey's* requirement of a health exception so it becomes tantamount to allowing a doctor to choose the abortion method he or she might prefer. Where it has a rational basis to act, and it does not impose an undue burden, the State may use its regulatory power to bar certain procedures and substitute others, all in furtherance of its legitimate interests in regulating the medical profession in order to promote respect for life, including life of the unborn.

The Act's ban on abortions that involve partial delivery of a living fetus furthers the Government's objectives. No one would dispute that, for many, D & E is a procedure itself laden with the power to devalue human life. Congress could nonetheless conclude that the type of abortion proscribed by the Act requires specific regulation because it implicates additional ethical and moral concerns that justify a special prohibition. Congress determined that the abortion methods it proscribed had a "disturbing similarity to the killing of a newborn infant," and thus it was concerned with "draw[ing] a bright line that clearly distinguishes abortion and infanticide." The Court has in the past confirmed the validity of drawing boundaries to prevent certain practices that extinguish life and are close to actions that are condemned. *Glucksberg* found reasonable the State's "fear that permitting assisted suicide will start it down the path to voluntary and perhaps even involuntary euthanasia."

Respect for human life finds an ultimate expression in the bond of love the mother has for her child. The Act recognizes this reality as well. Whether to have an abortion requires a difficult and painful moral decision. While we find no reliable data to measure the phenomenon, it seems unexceptionable to conclude some women come to regret their choice to abort the infant life they once created and sustained. See Brief for Sandra Cano et al. as *Amici Curiae* in No. 05-380, pp. 22-24. Severe depression and loss of esteem can follow.

In a decision so fraught with emotional consequence some doctors may prefer not to disclose precise details of the means that will be used, confining themselves to the required statement of risks the procedure entails. From one standpoint this ought not to be surprising. Any number of patients facing imminent surgical procedures would prefer not to hear all details, lest the usual anxiety preceding invasive medical procedures become the more intense. This is likely the case with the abortion procedures here in issue. See, e.g *., Nat. Abortion Federation* [v. Ashcroft], 330 F. Supp. 2d [436,] 466, n.22 (S.D.N.Y. 2004) ("Most of [the plaintiffs'] experts acknowledged that they do not describe to their patients what [the D & E and intact D & E] procedures entail in clear and precise terms").

It is, however, precisely this lack of information concerning the way in which the fetus will be killed that is of legitimate concern to the State. The State has an interest in ensuring so grave a choice is well informed. It is self-evident that a mother who comes to regret her choice to abort must struggle with grief more anguished and sorrow more profound when she learns, only after the event, what she once did not know: that she allowed a doctor to pierce the skull and vacuum the fast-developing brain of her unborn child, a child assuming the human form.

It is a reasonable inference that a necessary effect of the regulation and the knowledge it conveys will be to encourage some women to carry the infant to full term, thus reducing the absolute number of late-term abortions. The medical profession, furthermore, may find different and less shocking methods to abort the fetus in the second trimester, thereby accommodating legislative demand. The State's interest in respect for life is advanced by the dialogue that better informs the political and legal systems, the medical profession, expectant mothers, and society as a whole of the consequences that follow from a decision to elect a late-term abortion.

It is objected that the standard D & E is in some respects as brutal, if not more, than the intact D & E, so that the legislation accomplishes little. What we have already said, however, shows ample justification for the regulation. Partial-birth abortion, as defined by the Act, differs from a standard D & E — because the former occurs when the fetus is partially outside the mother to the point of one of the Act's anatomical landmarks. It was reasonable for Congress to think that partial-birth abortion, more than standard D & E, "undermines the public's perception of the appropriate role of a physician during the delivery process, and perverts a process during which life is brought into the world." There would be a flaw in this Court's logic, and an irony in its jurisprudence, were we first to conclude a ban on both D & E and intact D & E was overbroad and then to say it is irrational to ban only intact D & E because that does not proscribe both procedures. In sum, we reject the contention that the congressional purpose of the Act was "to place a substantial obstacle in the path of a woman seeking an abortion."

B

[T]he next question [is] whether the Act has the effect of imposing an unconstitutional burden on the abortion right because it does not allow use of the barred procedure where "'necessary, in appropriate medical judgment, for [the] preservation of the . . . health of the mother.'" The prohibition in the Act would be unconstitutional, under precedents we here assume to be controlling, if it "subject[ed] [women] to significant health risks." Ayotte v. Planned Parenthood of Northern New Eng., 546 U.S. 320, 328 (2006). In *Ayotte* the parties agreed a health exception to the challenged parental-involvement statute was necessary "to avert serious and often irreversible damage to [a pregnant minor's] health." Here, by contrast, whether the Act creates significant health risks for women has been a contested factual question. The evidence presented in the trial courts and before Congress demonstrates both sides have medical support for their position.

Respondents presented evidence that intact D & E may be the safest method of abortion, for reasons similar to those adduced in *Stenberg*. Abortion doctors testified, for example, that intact D & E decreases the risk of cervical laceration or uterine perforation because it requires fewer passes into the uterus with surgical instruments and does not require the removal of bony fragments of the dismembered fetus, fragments that may be sharp. Respondents also presented evidence that intact D & E was safer both because it reduces the risks that fetal parts will remain in the uterus and because it takes less time to complete. Respondents, in addition, proffered evidence that intact D & E was safer for women with certain medical conditions or women with fetuses that had certain anomalies.

These contentions were contradicted by other doctors who testified in the District Courts and before Congress. They concluded that the alleged health advantages were based on speculation without scientific studies to support them. They considered D & E always to be a safe alternative.

There is documented medical disagreement whether the Act's prohibition would ever impose significant health risks on women. The three District Courts that considered the Act's constitutionality appeared to be in some disagreement on this central factual question.

The question becomes whether the Act can stand when this medical uncertainty persists. The Court's precedents instruct that the Act can survive this facial attack. The Court has given state and federal legislatures wide discretion to pass legislation in areas where there is medical and scientific uncertainty.

This traditional rule is consistent with *Casey,* which confirms the State's interest in promoting respect for human life at all stages in the pregnancy. Physicians are not entitled to ignore regulations that direct them to use reasonable alternative procedures. The law need not give abortion doctors unfettered choice in the course of their medical practice, nor should it elevate their status above other physicians in the medical community. In *Casey* the controlling opinion held an informed-consent requirement in the abortion context was "no different from a requirement that a doctor give certain specific information about any medical procedure." The opinion stated "the doctor-patient relation here is entitled to the same solicitude it receives in other contexts."

Medical uncertainty does not foreclose the exercise of legislative power in the abortion context any more than it does in other contexts. The medical uncertainty over whether the Act's prohibition creates significant health risks provides a sufficient basis to conclude in this facial attack that the Act does not impose an undue burden.

The conclusion that the Act does not impose an undue burden is supported by other considerations. Alternatives are available to the prohibited procedure. As we have noted, the Act does not proscribe D & E. . . . If the intact D & E procedure is truly necessary in some circumstances, it appears likely an injection that kills the fetus is an alternative under the Act that allows the doctor to perform the procedure.

The instant cases, then, are different from Planned Parenthood of Central Mo. v. Danforth, 428 U.S. 52 (1976), in which the Court invalidated a ban on saline amniocentesis, the then-dominant second-trimester abortion method. The Court found the ban in *Danforth* to be "an unreasonable or arbitrary regulation designed to inhibit, and having the effect of inhibiting, the vast majority of abortions after the first 12 weeks." Here the Act allows, among other means, a commonly used and generally accepted method, so it does not construct a substantial obstacle to the abortion right.

In reaching the conclusion the Act does not require a health exception we reject certain arguments made by the parties on both sides of these cases. On the one hand, the Attorney General urges us to uphold the Act on the basis of the congressional findings alone. Although we review congressional factfinding under a deferential standard, we do not in the circumstances here place dispositive weight on Congress' findings. The Court retains an independent constitutional duty to review factual findings where constitutional rights are at stake.

As respondents have noted, and the District Courts recognized, some recitations in the Act are factually incorrect. Whether or not accurate at the time, some of the important findings have been superseded. Two examples suffice. Congress determined no medical schools provide instruction on the prohibited procedure. The testimony in the District Courts, however, demonstrated intact D & E is taught at medical schools. Congress also found there existed a medical consensus that the prohibited procedure is never medically necessary. The evidence presented in the District Courts contradicts that conclusion. Uncritical deference to Congress' factual findings in these cases is inappropriate.

On the other hand, relying on the Court's opinion in *Stenberg,* respondents contend that an abortion regulation must contain a health exception "if 'substantial medical authority supports the proposition that banning a particular procedure could endanger women's health.'" As illustrated by respondents' arguments and the decisions of the Courts of Appeals, *Stenberg* has been interpreted to leave no margin of error for legislatures to act in the face of medical uncertainty.

A zero tolerance policy would strike down legitimate abortion regulations, like the present one, if some part of the medical community were disinclined to follow the proscription. This is too exacting a standard to impose on the legislative power, exercised in this instance under the Commerce Clause, to regulate the medical profession. Considerations of marginal safety, including the balance of risks, are within the legislative competence when the regulation is rational and in pursuit of legitimate ends. When standard medical options are available, mere convenience does not suffice to displace them; and if some procedures have different risks than others, it does not follow that the State is altogether barred from imposing reasonable regulations. The Act is not invalid on its face where there is uncertainty over whether the barred procedure is ever necessary to preserve a woman's health, given the availability of other abortion procedures that are considered to be safe alternatives.

V.

— [T]hese facial attacks should not have been entertained in the first instance. In these circumstances the proper means to consider exceptions is by as-applied challenge. The Government has acknowledged that preenforcement, as-applied challenges to the Act can be maintained. This is the proper manner to protect the health of the woman if it can be shown that in discrete and well-defined instances a particular condition has or is likely to occur in which the procedure prohibited by the Act must be used. In an as-applied challenge the nature of the medical risk can be better quantified and balanced than in a facial attack. . . .

[R]espondents have not demonstrated that the Act would be unconstitutional in a large fraction of relevant cases. *Casey.* We note that the statute here applies to all instances in which the doctor proposes to use the prohibited procedure, not merely those in which the woman suffers from medical complications. It is neither our obligation nor within our traditional institutional role to resolve questions of constitutionality with respect to each potential situation that might develop. "[I]t would indeed be undesirable for this Court to consider every conceivable situation which might possibly arise in the application of complex and comprehensive legislation." United States v. Raines, 362 U.S. 17 (1960). For this reason, "[a]s-applied challenges are the basic building blocks of constitutional adjudication." Fallon, As-Applied and Facial Challenges and Third-Party Standing, 113 Harv. L. Rev. 1321, 1328 (2000).

The Act is open to a proper as-applied challenge in a discrete case. No as-applied challenge need be brought if the prohibition in the Act threatens a woman's life because the Act already contains a life exception. . . .

Justice THOMAS, with whom Justice SCALIA joins, concurring.

I join the Court's opinion because it accurately applies current jurisprudence . . . I write separately to reiterate my view that the Court's abortion jurisprudence, including *Casey* and Roe v. Wade, has no basis in the Constitution. I also note that whether the Act constitutes a permissible exercise of Congress' power under the Commerce Clause is not before the Court. The parties did not raise or brief that issue; it is outside the question presented; and the lower courts did not address it.

Justice GINSBURG, with whom Justice STEVENS, Justice SOUTER, and Justice BREYER join, dissenting.

. . .

Today's decision is alarming. It refuses to take *Casey* and *Stenberg* seriously. It tolerates, indeed applauds, federal intervention to ban nationwide a procedure found necessary and proper in certain cases by the American College of Obstetricians and
— Gynecologists (ACOG). It blurs the line, firmly drawn in *Casey,* between previability and postviability abortions. And, for the first time since *Roe,* the Court blesses a prohibition with no exception safeguarding a woman's health. . . .

I.

A

As *Casey* comprehended, at stake in cases challenging abortion restrictions is a woman's "control over her [own] destiny." There was a time, not so long ago," when women were "regarded as the center of home and family life, with attendant special responsibilities that precluded full and independent legal status under the Constitution." Those views, this Court made clear in *Casey,* "are no longer consistent with our understanding of the family, the individual, or the Constitution." Women, it is now acknowledged, have the talent, capacity, and right "to participate equally in the economic and social life of the Nation." Their ability to realize their full potential, the Court recognized, is intimately connected to "their ability to control their reproductive lives." Thus, legal challenges to undue restrictions on abortion procedures do not seek to vindicate some generalized notion of privacy; rather, they center on a woman's autonomy to determine her life's course, and thus to enjoy equal citizenship stature. See, e.g., Siegel, Reasoning from the Body: A Historical Perspective on Abortion Regulation and Questions of Equal Protection, 44 Stan. L. Rev. 261 (1992); Law, Rethinking Sex and the Constitution, 132 U. Pa. L. Rev. 955, 1002-1028 (1984).

[T]he Court has consistently required that laws regulating abortion, at any stage of pregnancy and in all cases, safeguard a woman's health. See, e.g., *Ayotte* ("[O]ur precedents hold ... that a State may not restrict access to abortions that are necessary, in appropriate medical judgment, for preservation of the life or health of the [woman]."; *Stenberg,* ("Since the law requires a health exception in order to validate even a postviability abortion regulation, it at a minimum requires the same in respect to previability regulation.").

We have thus ruled that a State must avoid subjecting women to health risks not only where the pregnancy itself creates danger, but also where state regulation forces women to resort to less safe methods of abortion. See *Danforth, Stenberg.* Indeed, we have applied the rule that abortion regulation must safeguard a woman's health to the particular procedure at issue here—intact dilation and evacuation (D & E).[a]

In *Stenberg,* we expressly held that a statute banning intact D & E was unconstitutional in part because it lacked a health exception. We noted that there existed a "division of medical opinion" about the relative safety of intact

---

a. Dilation and evacuation (D & E) is the most frequently used abortion procedure during the second trimester of pregnancy; intact D & E is a variant of the D & E procedure. Second-trimester abortions (i.e., midpregnancy, previability abortions) are, however, relatively uncommon. Between 85 and 90 percent of all abortions performed in the United States take place during the first three months of pregnancy.

Adolescents and indigent women, research suggests, are more likely than other women to have difficulty obtaining an abortion during the first trimester of pregnancy. Minors may be unaware they are pregnant until relatively late in pregnancy, while poor women's financial constraints are an obstacle to timely receipt of services. Severe fetal anomalies and health problems confronting the pregnant woman are also causes of second-trimester abortions; many such conditions cannot be diagnosed or do not develop until the second trimester.

D & E, but we made clear that as long as "substantial medical authority supports the proposition that banning a particular abortion procedure could endanger women's health," a health exception is required. . . . Thus, we reasoned, division in medical opinion "at most means uncertainty, a factor that signals the presence of risk, not its absence". "[A] statute that altogether forbids [intact D & E] . . . consequently must contain a health exception."

B

In 2003, a few years after our ruling in *Stenberg,* Congress passed the Partial-Birth Abortion Ban Act—without an exception for women's health. See 18 U.S.C. §1531(a) (2000 ed., Supp. IV).[b] The congressional findings on which the Partial-Birth Abortion Ban Act rests do not withstand inspection, as the lower courts have determined and this Court is obliged to concede. See National Abortion Federation v. Ashcroft, 330 F. Supp. 2d 436, 482 (S.D.N. Y.2004) ("Congress did not . . . carefully consider the evidence before arriving at its findings."), *aff'd sub nom.* National Abortion Federation v. Gonzales, 437 F.3d 278 (C.A. 2 2006). See also Planned Parenthood Federation of Am. v. Ashcroft, 320 F. Supp. 2d 957, 1019 (N.D. Cal. 2004) ("[N] one of the six physicians who testified before Congress had ever performed an intact D & E. Several did not provide abortion services at all; and one was not even an obgyn. . . . [T]he oral testimony before Congress was not only unbalanced, but intentionally polemic."), *aff'd,* 435 F.3d 1163 (C.A. 9 2006); Carhart v. Ashcroft, 331 F. Supp. 2d 805, 1011 (Neb. 2004) ("Congress arbitrarily relied upon the opinions of doctors who claimed to have no (or very little) recent and relevant experience with surgical abortions, and disregarded the views of doctors who had significant and relevant experience with those procedures."), aff'd, 413 F.3d 791 (C.A. 8 2005).

Many of the Act's recitations are incorrect. . . . Congress claimed there was a medical consensus that the banned procedure is never necessary. . . . But the evidence "very clearly demonstrate[d] the opposite." Similarly, Congress found that "[t]here is no credible medical evidence that partial-birth abortions are safe or are safer than other abortion procedures." But the congressional record includes letters from numerous individual physicians stating that pregnant women's health would be jeopardized under the Act, as well as statements from nine professional associations, including ACOG, the American Public Health Association, and the California Medical Association, attesting that intact D & E carries meaningful safety advantages over other methods. No comparable medical groups supported the ban. In fact, "all of the government's own witnesses disagreed with many of the specific congressional findings."

b. The Act's sponsors left no doubt that their intention was to nullify our ruling in *Stenberg*. See, e.g., 149 Cong. Rec. 5731 (2003) (statement of Sen. Santorum) ("Why are we here? We are here because the Supreme Court defended the indefensible. . . . We have responded to the Supreme Court."). See also 148 Cong. Rec. 14273 (2002) (statement of Rep. Linder) (rejecting proposition that Congress has "no right to legislate a ban on this horrible practice because the Supreme Court says [it] cannot").

C

In contrast to Congress, the District Courts made findings after full trials at which all parties had the opportunity to present their best evidence. The courts had the benefit of "much more extensive medical and scientific evidence . . . concerning the safety and necessity of intact D & Es."

During the District Court trials, "numerous" "extraordinarily accomplished" and "very experienced" medical experts explained that, in certain circumstances and for certain women, intact D & E is safer than alternative procedures and necessary to protect women's health.

According to the expert testimony plaintiffs introduced, the safety advantages of intact D & E are marked for women with certain medical conditions, for example, uterine scarring, bleeding disorders, heart disease, or compromised immune systems. Further, plaintiffs' experts testified that intact D & E is significantly safer for women with certain pregnancy-related conditions, such as placenta previa and accreta, and for women carrying fetuses with certain abnormalities, such as severe hydrocephalus.

Intact D & E, plaintiffs' experts explained, provides safety benefits over D & E by dismemberment for several reasons: *First,* intact D & E minimizes the number of times a physician must insert instruments through the cervix and into the uterus, and thereby reduces the risk of trauma to, and perforation of, the cervix and uterus—the most serious complication associated with nonintact D & E. *Second,* removing the fetus intact, instead of dismembering it *in utero,* decreases the likelihood that fetal tissue will be retained in the uterus, a condition that can cause infection, hemorrhage, and infertility. *Third,* intact D & E diminishes the chances of exposing the patient's tissues to sharp bony fragments sometimes resulting from dismemberment of the fetus. *Fourth,* intact D & E takes less operating time than D & E by dismemberment, and thus may reduce bleeding, the risk of infection, and complications relating to anesthesia.

Based on thoroughgoing review of the trial evidence and the congressional record, each of the District Courts to consider the issue rejected Congress' findings as unreasonable and not supported by the evidence. The trial courts concluded, in contrast to Congress' findings, that "significant medical authority supports the proposition that in some circumstances, [intact D & E] is the safest procedure."[c]

The District Courts' findings merit this Court's respect. See, e.g., Fed. Rule Civ. Proc. 52(a). Today's opinion supplies no reason to reject those findings. Nevertheless, despite the District Courts' appraisal of the weight of the evidence, and in undisguised conflict with *Stenberg,* the Court asserts that the

---

c. Even the District Court for the Southern District of New York, which was more skeptical of the health benefits of intact D & E, recognized: "[T]he Government's own experts disagreed with almost all of Congress's factual findings"; a "significant body of medical opinion" holds that intact D & E has safety advantages over nonintact D & E; "[p]rofessional medical associations have also expressed their view that [intact D & E] may be the safest procedure for some women"; and "[t]he evidence indicates that the same disagreement among experts found by the Supreme Court in *Stenberg* existed throughout the time that Congress was considering the legislation, despite Congress's findings to the contrary."

Partial-Birth Abortion Ban Act can survive "when . . . medical uncertainty persists." This assertion is bewildering. Not only does it defy the Court's longstanding precedent affirming the necessity of a health exception, with no carve-out for circumstances of medical uncertainty, it gives short shrift to the records before us, carefully canvassed by the District Courts. Those records indicate that "the majority of highly qualified experts on the subject believe intact D & E to be the safest, most appropriate procedure under certain circumstances."

The Court acknowledges some of this evidence, but insists that, because some witnesses disagreed with the ACOG and other experts' assessment of risk, the Act can stand. In this insistence, the Court brushes under the rug the District Courts' well-supported findings that the physicians who testified that intact D & E is never necessary to preserve the health of a woman had slim authority for their opinions. They had no training for, or personal experience with, the intact D & E procedure, and many performed abortions only on rare occasions. Even indulging the assumption that the Government witnesses were equally qualified to evaluate the relative risks of abortion procedures, their testimony could not erase the "significant medical authority support[ing] the proposition that in some circumstances, [intact D & E] would be the safest procedure."[d]

II.

A

The Court offers flimsy and transparent justifications for upholding a nation-wide ban on intact D & E *sans* any exception to safeguard a women's health. Today's ruling, the Court declares, advances "a premise central to [*Casey's*] conclusion"—i.e., the Government's "legitimate and substantial interest in pre-serving and promoting fetal life." But the Act scarcely furthers that interest: The law saves not a single fetus from destruction, for it targets only a *method* of performing abortion. And surely the statute was not designed to protect the lives or health of pregnant women. In short, the Court upholds a law that, while doing nothing to "preserv[e] . . . fetal life," bars a woman from choosing intact D & E although her doctor "reasonably believes [that procedure] will best protect [her]."

---

d. The majority contends that "[i]f the intact D & E procedure is truly necessary in some circum-stances, it appears likely an injection that kills the fetus is an alternative under the Act that allows the doctor to perform the procedure." But a "significant body of medical opinion believes that inducing fetal death by injection is almost always inappropriate to the preservation of the health of women undergoing abortion because it poses tangible risk and provides no benefit to the woman." In some circumstances, injections are "absolutely [medically] contraindicated." The Court also identifies medical induction of labor as an alternative. That procedure, however, requires a hospital stay, render-ing it inaccessible to patients who lack financial resources, and it too is considered less safe for many women, and impermissible for others.

As another reason for upholding the ban, the Court emphasizes that the Act does not proscribe the nonintact D & E procedure. But why not, one might ask. Nonintact D & E could equally be characterized as "brutal," involving as it does "tear[ing] [a fetus] apart" and "ripp[ing] off" its limbs. "[T]he notion that either of these two equally gruesome procedures . . . is more akin to infanticide than the other, or that the State furthers any legitimate interest by banning one but not the other, is simply irrational."

Delivery of an intact, albeit nonviable, fetus warrants special condemnation, the Court maintains, because a fetus that is not dismembered resembles an infant. But so, too, does a fetus delivered intact after it is terminated by injection a day or two before the surgical evacuation, or a fetus delivered through medical induction or cesarean. Yet, the availability of those procedures—along with D & E by dismemberment—the Court says, saves the ban on intact D & E from a declaration of unconstitutionality. Never mind that the procedures deemed acceptable might put a woman's health at greater risk.

Ultimately, the Court admits that "moral concerns" are at work, concerns that could yield prohibitions on any abortion. Notably, the concerns expressed are untethered to any ground genuinely serving the Government's interest in preserving life. By allowing such concerns to carry the day and case, overriding fundamental rights, the Court dishonors our precedent. See, e.g., *Casey*; Lawrence v. Texas.

Revealing in this regard, the Court invokes an antiabortion shibboleth for which it concededly has no reliable evidence: Women who have abortions come to regret their choices, and consequently suffer from "[s]evere depression and loss of esteem."[e] Because of women's fragile emotional state and because of the

---

e. The Court is surely correct that, for most women, abortion is a painfully difficult decision. But "neither the weight of the scientific evidence to date nor the observable reality of 33 years of legal abortion in the United States comports with the idea that having an abortion is any more dangerous to a woman's long-term mental health than delivering and parenting a child that she did not intend to have. . . ." Cohen, Abortion and Mental Health: Myths and Realities, 9 Guttmacher Policy Rev. 8 (2006); see generally Bazelon, Is There a Post-Abortion Syndrome? N.Y. Times Magazine, Jan. 21, 2007, p. 40. See also, e.g., American Psychological Association, APA Briefing Paper on the Impact of Abortion (2005) (rejecting theory of a postabortion syndrome and stating that "[a]ccess to legal abortion to terminate an unwanted pregnancy is vital to safeguard both the physical and mental health of women"); Schmiege & Russo, Depression and Unwanted First Pregnancy: Longitudinal Cohort Study, 331 British Medical J. 1303 (2005) (finding no credible evidence that choosing to terminate an unwanted first pregnancy contributes to risk of subsequent depression); Gilchrist, Hannaford, Frank, & Kay, Termination of Pregnancy and Psychiatric Morbidity, 167 British J. of Psychiatry 243, 247-248 (1995) (finding, in a cohort of more than 13,000 women, that the rate of psychiatric disorder was no higher among women who terminated pregnancy than among those who carried pregnancy to term); Stodland, The Myth of the Abortion Trauma Syndrome, 268 JAMA 2078, 2079 (1992) ("Scientific studies indicate that legal abortion results in fewer deleterious sequelae for women compared with other possible outcomes of unwanted pregnancy. There is no evidence of an abortion trauma syndrome."); American Psychological Association, Council Policy Manual: (N)(I)(3), Public Interest (1989) (declaring assertions about widespread severe negative psychological effects of abortion to be "without fact"). But see Cougle, Reardon, & Coleman, Generalized Anxiety Following Unintended Pregnancies Resolved Through Childbirth and Abortion: A Cohort Study of the 1995 National Survey of Family Growth, 19 J. Anxiety Disorders 137, 142 (2005) (advancing theory of a postabortion syndrome but acknowledging that "no causal relationship between pregnancy outcome and anxiety "bond of love the mother has for her child," the Court worries, doctors may withhold information about the nature of the intact D & E procedure.[f] The solution the Court approves, then, is *not* to require doctors to inform women, accurately and adequately, of the different procedures and their attendant risks. Instead, the Court deprives women of the right to make an autonomous choice, even at the expense of their safety.[g]

This way of thinking reflects ancient notions about women's place in the family and under the Constitution—ideas that have long since been discredited. Compare, e.g., Muller v. Oregon; Bradwell v. [Illinois] (Bradley, J., concurring) ("Man is, or should be, woman's protector and defender. The natural and proper timidity and delicacy which belongs to the female sex evidently unfits it for many of the occupations of civil life. . . . The paramount destiny and mission of woman are to fulfil[l] the noble and benign offices of wife and mother."), with United States v. Virginia; Califano v. Goldfarb, 430 U.S. 199 (1977) (gender-based Social Security classification rejected because it rested on "archaic and overbroad generalizations" "such as assumptions as to [women's] dependency" (internal quotation marks omitted)).

Though today's majority may regard women's feelings on the matter as "self-evident," this Court has repeatedly confirmed that "[t]he destiny of the woman must be shaped . . . on her own conception of her spiritual imperatives and her place in society." *Casey.*

---

could be determined" from study); Reardon et al., Psychiatric Admissions of Low-Income Women following Abortion and Childbirth, 168 Canadian Medical Assn. J. 1253, 1255-1256 (May 13, 2003) (concluding that psychiatric admission rates were higher for women who had an abortion compared with women who delivered); cf. Major, Psychological Implications of Abortion—Highly Charged and Rife with Misleading Research, 168 Canadian Medical Assn. J. 1257, 1258 (May 13, 2003) (critiquing Reardon study for failing to control for a host of differences between women in the delivery and abortion samples).

f. Notwithstanding the "bond of love" women often have with their children, not all pregnancies, this Court has recognized, are wanted, or even the product of consensual activity. See *Casey*, 505 U.S., at 891, 112 S. Ct. 2791 ("[O]n an average day in the United States, nearly 11,000 women are severely assaulted by their male partners. Many of these incidents involve sexual assault.") See also Glander, Moore, Michielutte, & Parsons, The Prevalence of Domestic Violence Among Women Seeking Abortion, 91 Obstetrics & Gynecology 1002 (1998); Holmes, Resnick, Kilpatrick, & Best, Rape-Related Pregnancy; Estimates and Descriptive Characteristics from a National Sample of Women, 175 Am. J. Obstetrics & Gynecology 320 (Aug. 1996).

g. Eliminating or reducing women's reproductive choices is manifestly not a means of protecting them. When safe abortion procedures cease to be an option, many women seek other means to end unwanted or coerced pregnancies. See, e.g., World Health Organization, Unsafe Abortion: Global and Regional Estimates of the Incidence of Unsafe Abortion and Associated Mortality in 2000, pp. 3, 16 (4th ed. 2004) ("Restrictive legislation is associated with a high incidence of unsafe abortion" worldwide; unsafe abortion represents 13% of all "maternal" deaths); Henshaw, Unintended Pregnancy and Abortion: A Public Health Perspective, in A Clinician's Guide to Medical and Surgical Abortion 11, 19 (M. Paul, E. Lichtenberg, L. Borgatta, D. Grimes, & P. Stubblefield eds. 1999) ("Before legalization, large numbers of women in the United States died from unsafe abortions."); H. Boonstra, R. Gold, C. Richards, & L. Finer, Abortion in Women's Lives 13, and fig. 2.2 (2006) ("as late as 1965, illegal abortion still accounted for an estimated . . . 17% of all officially reported pregnancy-related deaths"; "[d]eaths from abortion declined dramatically after legalization").

B

In cases on a "woman's liberty to determine whether to [continue] her pregnancy," this Court has identified viability as a critical consideration. . . . Today, the Court blurs that line, maintaining that "[t]he Act [legitimately] appl[ies] both previability and postviability because . . . a fetus is a living organism while within the womb, whether or not it is viable outside the womb." Instead of drawing the line at viability, the Court refers to Congress' purpose to differentiate "abortion and infanticide" based not on whether a fetus can survive outside the womb, but on where a fetus is anatomically located when a particular medical procedure is performed.

One wonders how long a line that saves no fetus from destruction will hold in face of the Court's "moral concerns." The Court's hostility to the right *Roe* and *Casey* secured is not concealed. Throughout, the opinion refers to obstetrician-gynecologists and surgeons who perform abortions not by the titles of their medical specialties, but by the pejorative label "abortion doctor." A fetus is described as an "unborn child," and as a "baby;" second-trimester, previability abortions are referred to as "late-term;" and the reasoned medical judgments of highly trained doctors are dismissed as "preferences" motivated by "mere convenience." Instead of the heightened scrutiny we have previously applied, the Court determines that a "rational" ground is enough to uphold the Act. And, most troubling, *Casey's* principles, confirming the continuing vitality of "the essential holding of *Roe,*" are merely "assume[d]" for the moment, rather than "retained" or "reaffirmed," *Casey.*

III.

A

The Court further confuses our jurisprudence when it declares that "facial attacks" are not permissible in "these circumstances," i.e., where medical uncertainty exists. This holding is perplexing given that, in materially identical circumstances we held that a statute lacking a health exception was unconstitutional on its face. *Stenberg.*

Without attempting to distinguish *Stenberg* and earlier decisions, the majority asserts that the Act survives review because respondents have not shown that the ban on intact D & E would be unconstitutional "in a large fraction of relevant cases." But *Casey* makes clear that, in determining whether any restriction poses an undue burden on a "large fraction" of women, the relevant class is *not* "all women," nor "all pregnant women," nor even all women "seeking abortions." Rather, a provision restricting access to abortion, "must be judged by reference to those [women] for whom it is an actual rather than an irrelevant restriction," Thus the absence of a health exception burdens *all* women for whom it is relevant—women who, in the judgment of their doctors, require an intact D & E because other procedures would place their health at risk.[h] It makes no sense to conclude that this facial challenge fails because respondents have not shown that a health exception is necessary for a large fraction of second-trimester abortions, including those for which a health exception is unnecessary: The very purpose of a health *exception* is to protect women in *exceptional* cases.

B

If there is anything at all redemptive to be said of today's opinion, it is that the Court is not willing to foreclose entirely a constitutional challenge to the Act. "The Act is open," the Court states, "to a proper as-applied challenge in a discrete case." But the Court offers no clue on what a "proper" lawsuit might look like. Nor does the Court explain why the injunctions ordered by the District Courts should not remain in place, trimmed only to exclude instances in which another procedure would safeguard a woman's health at least equally well. Surely the Court cannot mean that no suit may be brought until a woman's health is immediately jeopardized by the ban on intact D & E. A woman "suffer[ing] from medical complications," needs access to the medical procedure at once and cannot wait for the judicial process to unfold.

The Court appears, then, to contemplate another lawsuit by the initiators of the instant actions. In such a second round, the Court suggests, the challengers could succeed upon demonstrating that "in discrete and well-defined instances a particular condition has or is likely to occur in which the procedure prohibited by the Act must be used." One may anticipate that such a preenforcement challenge will be mounted swiftly, to ward off serious, sometimes irremediable harm, to women whose health would be endangered by the intact D & E prohibition.

The Court envisions that in an as-applied challenge, "the nature of the medical risk can be better quantified and balanced." But it should not escape notice that the record already includes hundreds and hundreds of pages of testimony identifying "discrete and well-defined instances" in which recourse to an intact D & E would better protect the health of women with particular conditions. Record evidence also documents that medical exigencies, unpredictable in advance, may indicate to a well-trained doctor that intact D & E is the safest procedure. In light of this evidence, our unanimous decision just one year ago in *Ayotte* counsels against reversal. See 546 U.S., at 331 (remanding for reconsideration of the remedy for the absence of a health exception, suggesting that an injunction prohibiting unconstitutional applications might suffice).

The Court's allowance only of an "as-applied challenge in a discrete case," jeopardizes women's health and places doctors in an untenable position. Even if courts were able to carve-out exceptions through piecemeal litigation for

---

h. There is, in short, no fraction because the numerator and denominator are the same: The health exception reaches only those cases where a woman's health is at risk. Perhaps for this reason, in mandating safeguards for women's health, we have never before invoked the "large fraction" test.

"discrete and well-defined instances," women whose circumstances have not been anticipated by prior litigation could well be left unprotected. In treating those women, physicians would risk criminal prosecution, conviction, and imprisonment if they exercise their best judgment as to the safest medical procedure for their patients. The Court is thus gravely mistaken to conclude that narrow as-applied challenges are "the proper manner to protect the health of the woman."

IV.

. . . Though today's opinion does not go so far as to discard *Roe* or *Casey,* the Court, differently composed than it was when we last considered a restrictive abortion regulation, is hardly faithful to our earlier invocations of "the rule of law" and the "principles of *stare decisis.*" Congress imposed a ban despite our clear prior holdings that the State cannot proscribe an abortion procedure when its use is necessary to protect a woman's health. Although Congress' findings could not withstand the crucible of trial, the Court defers to the legislative override of our Constitution-based rulings. A decision so at odds with our jurisprudence should not have staying power.

In sum, the notion that the Partial-Birth Abortion Ban Act furthers any legitimate governmental interest is, quite simply, irrational. The Court's defense of the statute provides no saving explanation. In candor, the Act, and the Court's defense of it, cannot be understood as anything other than an effort to chip away at a right declared again and again by this Court—and with increasing comprehension of its centrality to women's lives. When "a statute burdens constitutional rights and all that can be said on its behalf is that it is the vehicle that legislators have chosen for expressing their hostility to those rights, the burden is undue."

Discussion

1. *The fate of* Stenberg. Does the Court overrule Stenberg v. Carhart or merely distinguish it? If the latter, what part of *Stenberg* is still good law? If the former, does it satisfy the Court's analysis of when to overrule decisions in *Casey*?

2. *Changing justifications for the abortion right.* Note that Justice Ginsburg's dissent—joined by four Justices—no longer grounds the abortion right in "some generalized notion of privacy." Instead she bases the right on "a woman's autonomy to determine her life's course, and thus to enjoy equal citizenship stature." This is a shift to an equality-based model, foregrounded in *Casey*. (See the casebook discussion at pp. 1409-1419). Meanwhile, Justice Kennedy's majority opinion notes that the principles stated in *Casey* "did not find support from all those who join the instant opinion," and merely "assume[s] the . . . principles for the purposes of this opinion." The views of Chief Justice Roberts and Justice Alito have yet to be determined.

3. *Facial and as-applied challenges.* The Court holds that respondents cannot challenge the PBAA facially but instead must make an "as-applied" challenge.

Facial challenges claim that the language of a challenged statute is sufficient to demonstrate that it unconstitutionally burdens a constitutional right. When successful, facial challenges strike down the entire statute. As-applied challenges claim that the language of the statute has been unconstitutionally applied to the plaintiff. When successful, the law may not constitutionally be applied to a person in the plaintiff's situation.

Free speech doctrines have special rules for determining when courts will entertain facial or as-applied challenges, see Broadrick v. Oklahoma 413 U.S. 601 (1973). Outside the free speech area, the Court has stated that as-applied challenges are preferred. In United States v. Salerno, 481 U.S. 739, 745 (1987), which challenged the 1984 federal Bail Reform Act, the Court stated that facial challenges "must establish that no set of circumstances exists under which the Act would be valid," but this has not always been the Court's consistent practice because of the different substantive tests prevailing in different areas of the law. See, e.g. Bowen v. Kendrick, 487 U.S. 589, 602 (1988), which determined facial validity under the Establishment Clause by asking whether a statute had a "primary effect" of advancing religion, or required "excessive entanglement" between church and state.

In *Casey* the Court considered facial challenges to abortion regulations in the context of its "undue burden" test. It argued that Pennsylvania's spousal notification law "must be judged by reference to those for whom it is an actual, rather than an irrelevant, restriction." The class relevant for determining whether a facial challenge was appropriate was "narrower . . . than the class of women seeking abortions identified by the State: it is married women seeking abortions who do not wish to notify their husbands of their intentions and who do not qualify for one of the statutory exceptions to the notice requirement." Defining the class in that way, the Court concluded that "in a large fraction of the cases in which [the spousal notification law] is relevant, it will operate as a substantial obstacle to a woman's choice to undergo an abortion" and was therefore facially invalid.

Casey seemed to suggest that if an abortion regulation was an undue burden with respect to a specific class of women, the court could strike down the entire statute even though it did not burden a far larger class. Similarly, in *Stenberg*, the Court had invalidated Nebraska's partial-birth abortion law on its face because of the lack of a health exception. In Ayotte v. Planned Parenthood of Northern New England, 546 U.S. 320, 328 (2006), the Court suggested a different approach. New Hampshire's parental notification law prohibited doctors from performing an abortion on a pregnant minor until 48 hours after written notification to the parent or guardian. The statute made exceptions for life-threatening emergencies, but no exception for medical emergencies that threatened a minor's health. The Court, in a unanimous opinion by Justice O'Connor, noted that "New Hampshire has conceded that . . . it would be unconstitutional to apply the Act in a manner that subjects minors to significant health risks." However, in *Ayotte*, the Court remanded the case to the New Hampshire courts to determine whether they could "issue a declaratory judgment and an injunction prohibiting the statute's unconstitutional application."

In *Carhart II*, Justice Kennedy upholds the federal statute on its face because he believes that there is a factual dispute about whether a health exception is necessary, but he provides for the possibility of a subsequent as-applied challenge. Is it realistic to think that a plaintiff in an actual medical emergency could make such a challenge? If not, who would have standing to bring an as-applied challenge? If, as Justice Ginsburg suggests, a preenforcement as-applied challenge is possible, what is the difference between it and the case that was actually before the Court in *Carhart II*?

Consider whether *Carhart II* changes *Casey*'s basic approach to facial challenges. And consider the consequences of requiring as-applied challenges to abortion regulations in the future. When states pass new abortion regulations, plaintiffs will have to bring challenges to each aspect of the law they object to and prove how the statute is unconstitutional as to their situation. Will this increase the cost of litigation or make injunctions against new abortion statutes harder to obtain?

Why didn't the Court simply interpret the federal statute to include a health exception and avoid the constitutional problem? One reason is that Congress did not want a health exception, thinking it would give doctors too much leeway to perform intact D & E abortions whenever they felt it would be medically indicated.

4. W*oman-protective arguments against abortion and "post abortion syndrome."* Although upholding the federal PBAA will affect only a few hundred women a year, another aspect of *Carhart II* may prove far more important. Justice Kennedy argues that the state may prevent women from having a particular abortion procedure because they may regret it later on. Can this be described as respecting a woman's choice or is it a thinly disguised form of paternalism? Could states prohibit other abortion procedures—or indeed all abortions—on the grounds that some percentage of women will later regret their choices?

In the middle of his argument for why the state may protect women from abortions they may later regret, Justice Kennedy cites an amicus brief by Sandra Cano—the original Mary Doe in *Doe v. Bolton*—who is now a pro-life advocate. He refers obliquely to the theory of "postabortion syndrome" (PAS), in which having an abortion can later cause women "[s]evere depression and loss of self esteem." Justice Kennedy states that "[w]hile we find no reliable data to measure the phenomenon, it seems unexceptionable to conclude some women come to regret their choice to abort the infant life they once created and sustained." Justice Ginsburg's dissent, citing numerous medical studies, accuses Justice Kennedy of promoting junk science in the United States Reports.

Justice Kennedy's argument is connected to a new class of pro-life arguments for abortion regulation. Early pro-life arguments focused on the fetus and fetal development. Beginning in the 1990s pro-life advocates began to argue that abortion hurts women because of women's natural propensities for bearing children and bonding with them. As Reva Siegel explains, this new class of "[g]ender-based arguments against abortion embed claims about protecting the unborn in an elaborate set of arguments about protecting women." Reva B. Siegel, The New Politics of Abortion: An Equality Analysis of Women-Protective Abortion Restrictions, 2007 Ill. L. Rev. 991. These new woman-protective arguments against abortion seek to turn the rhetoric of "choice" against the pro-choice movement; they argue that women do not freely choose abortion. That is either because women are misled by abortion providers who do not explain to them what they are actually doing to their unborn children, or because having an abortion poses risks to their physical and mental health that they do not fully understand. Hence abortion restrictions are necessary to prevent women from making choices that are not really theirs.

Are statutes that limit access to abortion based on this reasoning vulnerable to an equal protection challenge? Consider two possible theories. The first is that statutes motivated by these concerns embody stereotypical views about women's true natures and their natural bond of affection for their unborn children: Women will naturally choose to have children whenever they become pregnant unless they are misinformed or coerced. The second is that women-protective arguments embody stereotypical views about women's reasoning capacities, and particularly about their reasoning about reproductive issues: Women do not have the independence and judgment necessary to make respon-sible decisions about abortion and hence need protection from unscrupulous abortion doctors. Are these unconstitutional purposes under the 1970s sex equality decisions? Under *Feeney*? Under *Hibbs*?

5. *Informed consent and the protection of women.* A less restrictive alter-native to prohibiting a procedure is to inform the woman about the nature of the procedure she is to undergo. *Casey* holds that states may express their prefer-ence for unborn life and attempt to persuade women not to have abortions as long as they provide women with information that is "truthful and not mislead-ing." Does *Carhart II* give states more leeway in attempting to persuade women that they should not have abortions? After *Carhart II*, can states require that all women must pay for ultrasounds and view the ultrasounds of their fetus before having an abortion?

Consider South Dakota's 2005 informed consent statute. The legislative findings accompanying the bill state that "all abortions . . . terminate the life of a whole, separate, unique, living human being," and "that there is an existing relationship between a pregnant woman and her unborn child during the entire period of gestation." "[P]rocedures terminating the life of an unborn child impose risks to the life and health of the pregnant woman . . . [A] woman seeking to terminate the life of her unborn child may be subject to pressures which can cause an emotional crisis, undue reliance on the advice of others, clouded judgment, and a willingness to violate conscience to avoid those pressures." "[P]regnant women contemplating the termination of their right to their relationship with their unborn children . . . are faced with making a pro-found decision most often under stress and pressures from circumstances and from other persons. [T]here exists a need for special protection of the rights of such pregnant women, and . . . the State of South Dakota has a compelling interest in providing such protection." S.D. Codified Laws §§34-23A-1.2 to 1.5. (2006).

The statute requires doctors to explain in detail the various risks of under-going abortions, but not the risks of carrying a pregnancy to term. According to the statute, "voluntary and informed consent" to abortion requires that "in addition to any other information that must be disclosed under the common law doctrine, the physician provides th[e] pregnant woman with . . . a statement in writing" including "the following information":

(b) That the abortion will terminate the life of a whole, separate, unique, living human being;

(c) That the pregnant woman has an existing relationship with that unborn human being and that the relationship enjoys protection under the United States Constitution and under the laws of South Dakota;

(d) That by having an abortion, her existing relationship and her existing constitutional rights with regards to that relationship will be terminated;

(e) A description of all known medical risks of the procedure and statistically significant risk factors to which the pregnant woman would be subjected, including:

(i) Depression and related psychological distress;

(ii) Increased risk of suicide ideation and suicide;

(iii) A statement setting forth an accurate rate of deaths due to abortions, including all deaths in which the abortion procedure was a substantial contributing factor;

(iv) All other known medical risks to the physical health of the woman, including the risk of infection, hemorrhage, danger to subsequent pregnancies, and infertility. . . .

S.D. Codified Laws §34-23A-10.1(b)-(e)(2006). The statute defines a "human being" "as an individual living member of the species of Homo sapiens, including the unborn human being during the entire embryonic and fetal ages from fertilization to full gestation." *Id.* at §34-23A-1. The South Dakota statute tries to combat misinformation and pressure that might lead women to choose abortions but not misinformation and pressure that might lead them to continue their pregnancies. The reason is that the state seeks to provide informed consent only where this might move women in the direction of its preferred moral choice, that women not have abortions. Moreover, section (b) suggests that state believes informed consent requires that doctors provide women with moral truths about the nature of the fetus.

Can informed-consent statutes in the abortion context avoid making some kinds of moral judgments or stating what the legislature regards as moral truths? If not, what kinds of moral judgments and statements may they properly make and not make? Is this statute consistent with women's rights under *Casey*?

6. *Informed consent requirements and postabortion syndrome: What is "medical uncertainty"?* Section (e)(i) and (e)(ii) of the South Dakota informed consent statute require, in effect, that women be informed about the dangers of the controversial phenomenon of "postabortion syndrome." Suppose that there is a consensus among the medical, psychiatric, and psychological communities that the disclosures in (e)(i) and e(ii) of the South Dakota informed statute are not in fact "statistically significant" risks of abortion, because "[t]he best studies available on psychological responses to unwanted pregnancy terminated by abortion in the United States suggest that severe negative reactions are rare, and they parallel those following other normal life stresses." N. E. Adler et al., Psychological Factors in Abortion: A Review, American Psychologist, 1194-1204, 1202 (Oct. 1992). Therefore, according to these authorities, stating that the risks are significant is false and misleading. Nevertheless, advocates of postabortion syndrome argue that these effects are quite frequent, and offer their own more recent studies to support it. Does the statute violate *Casey*? Does it violate the First Amendment rights of either doctors or their patients? See Robert Post, Informed Consent to Abortion: A First Amendment Analysis of Compelled Physician Speech, 2007 U. Ill. L. Rev. 939, 961-963.

In *Carhart II*, Justice Kennedy held that because Congress found medical experts who supported its view that intact D & E is never medically safer, the PBAA was constitutional because "state and federal legislatures [have] wide discretion to pass legislation in areas where there is medical and scientific uncertainty." After *Carhart II*, how many experts would South Dakota have to produce to establish "medical uncertainty" about the prevalence of postabortion syndrome?

Add the following after note 3 on p. 1536:

4. Dale *as a membership case.* In Rumsfeld v. FAIR, 126 S. Ct. 1297 (2006), the Forum for Academic and Institutional Rights, Inc. (FAIR), an association of law schools and law faculties, challenged the Solomon Amendment—which provides that if any portion of an educational institution denies military recruiters access equal to that provided other recruiters, the entire institution will lose federal funding. Because FAIR's members had policies opposing sexual orientation discrimination, they sought to restrict military recruiting on campuses because the military discriminates against homosexuals. They raised several First Amendment challenges to the Solomon Amendment, including a claim that, under *Dale*, the Solomon Amendment interfered with their associational freedoms. The Supreme Court, in a unanimous opinion written by Chief Justice Roberts, rejected their claims: To comply with the [Solomon Amendment], law schools must allow military recruiters on campus and assist them in whatever way the school chooses to assist other employers. Law schools therefore "associate" with military recruiters in the sense that they interact with them.

But recruiters are not part of the law school. Recruiters are, by definition, out-siders who come onto campus for the limited purpose of trying to hire students— not to become members of the school's expressive association. This distinction is critical. Unlike the public accommodations law in *Dale*, the Solomon Amend-ment does not force a law school "'to accept members it does not desire.'" . . . FAIR correctly notes that the freedom of expressive association protects more than just a group's membership decisions. For example, we have held laws unconstitutional that require disclosure of membership lists for groups seeking anonymity, Brown v. Socialist Workers '74 Campaign Comm. (Ohio), 459 U.S. 87, 101-102 (1982), or impose penalties or withhold benefits based on member-ship in a disfavored group, Healy v. James, 408 U.S. 169, 180-184 (1972). Although these laws did not directly interfere with an organization's composition, they made group membership less attractive, raising the same First Amendment concerns about affecting the group's ability to express its message.

The Solomon Amendment has no similar effect on a law school's associa-tional rights. Students and faculty are free to associate to voice their disapproval of the military's message; nothing about the statute affects the composition of the group by making group membership less desirable. The Solomon Amend-ment therefore does not violate a law school's First Amendment rights. A military recruiter's mere presence on campus does not violate a law school's right to associate, regardless of how repugnant the law school considers the recruiter's message.

Insert the following at the end of p. 1592:

DISTRICT ATTORNEY'S OFFICE FOR THE THIRD JUDICIAL DISTRICT v. OSBORNE, 129 S. Ct. 2308 (2009): Osborne was convicted of sexual assault and other crimes in Alaska. Years later, he filed suit claiming a due process right to gain access to the evidence that had been used to convict him in order to subject it to DNA testing at his own expense in order to prove his innocence. The Ninth Circuit upheld his claim, arguing that the prosecution had a duty to disclose exculpatory evidence.

The Supreme Court, in a 5-4 opinion by Chief Justice Roberts, reversed, holding that Osborne had no constitutional right to obtain postconviction access to the State's evidence for DNA testing. Chief Justice Roberts rejected Osborne's claims as a matter of constitutional criminal procedure, as a matter of procedural due process, and as a matter of substantive due process. On the last theory, he argued: "Osborne seeks access to state evidence so that he can apply new DNA-testing technology that might prove him innocent. There is no long history of such a right, and '[t]he mere novelty of such a claim is reason enough to doubt that "substantive due process" sustains it.'" *Reno v. Flores,* 507 U.S. 292 (1993). [Moreover,] [t]he elected governments of the States are actively confronting the challenges DNA technology poses to our criminal justice systems and our traditional notions of finality, as well as the opportunities it affords. To suddenly constitutionalize this area would short-circuit what looks to be a prompt and considered legislative response. The first DNA testing statutes were passed in 1994 and 1997. In the past decade, 44 States and the Federal Government have followed suit, reflecting the increased availability of DNA testing. As noted, Alaska itself is considering such legislation. 'By extending constitutional protection to an asserted right or liberty interest, we, to a great extent, place the matter outside the arena of public debate and legislative action. We must therefore exercise the utmost care whenever we are asked to break new ground in this field.' *Glucksberg*. '[J]udicial imposition of a categorical remedy . . . might pretermit other responsible solutions being considered in Congress and state legislatures.' If we extended substantive due process to this area, we would cast these statutes into constitutional doubt and be forced to take over the issue of DNA access ourselves. We are reluctant to enlist the Federal Judiciary in creating a new constitutional code of rules for handling DNA."

"Establishing a freestanding right to access DNA evidence for testing would force us to act as policymakers, and our substantive-due-process rulemaking authority would not only have to cover the right of access but a myriad of other issues. We would soon have to decide if there is a constitutional obligation to preserve forensic evidence that might later be tested. If so, for how long? Would it be different for different types of evidence? Would the State also have some obligation to gather such evidence in the first place? How much, and when? No doubt there would be a miscellany of other minor directives."

"In this case, the evidence has already been gathered and preserved, but if we extend substantive due process to this area, these questions would be before us in short order, and it is hard to imagine what tools federal courts would use to answer them. At the end of the day, there is no reason to suppose that their answers to these questions would be any better than those of state courts and legislatures, and good reason to suspect the opposite."

Justice Stevens dissented: "The State of Alaska possesses physical evidence that, if tested, will conclusively establish whether respondent William Osborne committed rape and attempted murder. If he did, justice has been served by his conviction and sentence. If not, Osborne has needlessly spent decades behind bars while the true culprit has not been brought to justice. The DNA test Osborne seeks is a simple one, its cost modest, and its results uniquely precise. Yet for reasons the State has been unable or unwilling to articulate, it refuses to allow Osborne to test the evidence at his own expense and to thereby ascertain the truth once and for all."

"The fact that nearly all the States have now recognized some postconviction right to DNA evidence makes it more, not less, appropriate to recognize a limited federal right to such evidence in cases where litigants are unfairly barred from obtaining relief in state court." . . .

"Throughout the course of state and federal litigation, the State has failed to provide any concrete reason for denying Osborne the DNA testing he seeks, and none is apparent. Because Osborne has offered to pay for the tests, cost is not a factor. And as the State now concedes, there is no reason to doubt that such testing would provide conclusive confirmation of Osborne's guilt or revelation of his innocence. In the courts below, the State refused to provide an explanation for its refusal to permit testing of the evidence, and in this Court, its explanation has been, at best, unclear. Insofar as the State has articulated any reason at all, it appears to be a generalized interest in protecting the finality of the judgment of conviction from any possible future attacks."

"[W]hile we have long recognized that States have an interest in securing the finality of their judgments, finality is not a stand-alone value that trumps a State's overriding interest in ensuring that justice is done in its courts and secured to its citizens. Indeed, when absolute proof of innocence is readily at hand, a State should not shrink from the possibility that error may have occurred. . . . DNA evidence has led to an extraordinary series of exonerations, not only in cases where the trial evidence was weak, but also in cases where the convicted parties confessed their guilt and where the trial evidence against them appeared overwhelming. The examples provided by amici of the power of DNA testing serve to convince me that the fact of conviction is not sufficient to justify a State's refusal to perform a test that will conclusively establish innocence or guilt. . . . [P]owerful state interests . . . offset the State's purported interest in finality per se. When a person is convicted for a crime he did not commit, the true culprit escapes punishment. DNA testing may lead to his identification. Crime victims, the law enforcement profession, and society at large share a strong interest in identifying and apprehending the actual perpetrators of vicious crimes, such as the rape and attempted murder that gave rise to this case."

"[W]hile it is true that recent advances in DNA technology have led to a nationwide reexamination of state and federal postconviction procedures authorizing the use of DNA testing, it is highly unlikely that [recognizing a right] would significantly affect the use of DNA testing in any of the States that have already developed statutes and procedures for dealing with DNA evidence or would require the few States that have not yet done so to postpone the enactment of appropriate legislation. Indeed, a holding by this Court that the policy judgments underlying that legislation rest on a sound constitutional foundation could only be constructive."

Justice Alito wrote a concurring opinion. Justice Souter also dissented.

Discussion

1. *Tradition and new technologies.* Chief Justice Roberts argues that there can be no right to prove innocence using DNA because the technology is so new, and hence the claim is novel. Novel claims, by definition, are inappropriate for substantive due process protection. Doesn't this depend on how one characterizes the tradition or the principle involved? The technology or the circumstances might be new but the principle involved might be quite old. (Recall the discussion in *Michael M. v. Gerald D.*). Couldn't one have said with equal force that the First Amendment doesn't protect expression on the Internet because the medium is so new? Cf. Reno v. American Civil Liberties Union,

521 U.S. 844 (1997)(holding that Internet speech deserves full free speech protection); see also Kyllo v. United States 533 U.S. 27 (2001) (opinion of Scalia, J.)(holding that use of thermal imaging technology violated Fourth Amendment ban on unreasonable searches and seizures). Note, interestingly, that Justice Stevens (who dissents in *Osborne*), wrote the opinion in *Reno*, joined by Justice Scalia; while Justice Scalia (who joins the majority in *Osborne*) wrote the opinion in *Kyllo*, with Justice Stevens dissenting.

Could Chief Justice Roberts respond that the guarantees of freedom of speech and security against unreasonable searches and seizures are textually specific, while the constitutional guarantee against denials of liberty without due process of law is not? On the other hand, isn't Osborne's claim rather closely connected to the text? After all, he is invoking a right to prove one's innocence in order to regain one's liberty.

Note that much of the power of Osborne's argument stems from the fact that DNA tests are widely believed to be a highly accurate means of demonstrating innocence. If so, Alaska seems to be unreasonably denying him a right to prove his innocence conclusively. But what if the tests are complicated and their results inherently ambiguous? And what if we discover, after many years of experience, that DNA tests are not as reliable as we first thought? Should this affect whether courts should leave the question to the political process? Might this be a stronger way to restate Chief Justice Roberts' concerns about novelty?

2. *Bringing outliers in line.* In many of the Court's decisions, like *Griswold v. Connecticut* or *Lawrence v. Texas*, the Court waits until most states have recognized a right (or decriminalized an activity) and then brings the remaining outliers into line. By contrast, in *Glucksberg* and *Vacco*, very few states had modified their laws and the Court was not prepared to get very far ahead of the potential developing social consensus—at least as measured by state recognition. Along the same lines, a familiar criticism of *Roe v. Wade* is that the Court intervened too early, when only a small number of states had begun to reform their abortion laws, and the Court actually stuck down one of the abortion reform laws (in Georgia) as insufficient. In *Osborne*, however, 46 states and the federal government had recognized a right to use DNA to prove innocence before the Court was asked to decide the question. Can one defend *Osborne* on the ground that judicial recognition was unnecessary at this point? If so, why could one not say the same of *Griswold*?